Lecture Notes in Computer Science 3087

Commenced Publication in 1973
Founding and Former Series Editors:
Gerhard Goos, Juris Hartmanis, and Jan van Leeuwen

T0218659

Davide Maltoni   Anil K. Jain (Eds.)

Biometric Authentication

ECCV 2004 International Workshop, BioAW 2004
Prague, Czech Republic, May 15th, 2004
Proceedings

 Springer

Volume Editors

Davide Maltoni
University of Bologna, Biometric Systems Laboratory
Via Sacchi 3, 47023 Cesena, Italy
E-mail: maltoni@csr.unibo.it

Anil K. Jain
Michigan State University, Department of Computer Science Engineering
3115 Engineering Building, East Lansing, MI 48824-1226, USA
E-mail: jain@cse.msu.edu

Library of Congress Control Number: 2004108951

CR Subject Classification (1998): I.5, I.4, I.2.10, I.2, K.4, K.6.5, C.3

ISSN 0302-9743
ISBN 3-540-22499-8 Springer-Verlag Berlin Heidelberg New York

Springer-Verlag is a part of Springer Science+Business Media

springeronline.com

© Springer-Verlag Berlin Heidelberg 2004
Printed in Germany

Typesetting: Camera-ready by author, data conversion by Boller Mediendesign
Printed on acid-free paper   SPIN: 11303138   06/3142   5 4 3 2 1 0

Preface

Biometric authentication is increasingly gaining popularity in a large spectrum of applications, ranging from government programs (e.g., national ID cards, visas for international travel, and the fight against terrorism) to personal applications such as logical and physical access control. Although a number of effective solutions are currently available, new approaches and techniques are necessary to overcome some of the limitations of current systems and to open up new frontiers in biometric research and development. The 30 papers presented at Biometric Authentication Workshop 2004 (BioAW 2004) provided a snapshot of current research in biometrics, and identify some new trends. This volume is composed of five sections: face recognition, fingerprint recognition, template protection and security, other biometrics, and fusion and multimodal biometrics. For classical biometrics like fingerprint and face recognition, most of the papers in Sect. 1 and 2 address robustness issues in order to make the biometric systems work in suboptimal conditions: examples include face detection and recognition under uncontrolled lighting and pose variations, and fingerprint matching in the case of severe skin distortion. Benchmarking and interoperability of sensors and liveness detection are also topics of primary interest for fingerprint-based systems. Biometrics alone is not the solution for complex security problems. Some of the papers in Sect. 3 focus on designing secure systems; this requires dealing with safe template storage, checking data integrity, and implementing solutions in a privacy-preserving fashion. The match-on-tokens approach, provided that current accuracy and cost limitations can be satisfactorily solved by using new algorithms and hardware, is certainly a promising alternative. The use of new biometric indicators like eye movement, 3D finger shape, and soft traits (e.g., height, weight and age) is investigated by some of the contributions in Sect. 4 with the aim of providing alternative choices for specific environments and applications. Improvements and new ideas are also presented for other popular biometrics like iris, palmprints and signature recognition. Multimodal biometrics has been identified as a promising area; the papers in Sect. 5 explore some insights into this topic, and they provide novel approaches for combinations at sensor, feature extraction and matching score levels.

May 2004

Davide Maltoni
Anil K. Jain

Organizing Committee

Prof. Davide Maltoni
University of Bologna
Biometric Systems Laboratory
Via Sacchi 3, 47023 Cesena (FC), Italy
e-mail: maltoni@csr.unibo.it

Prof. Anil K. Jain
Michigan State University
Department of Computer Science Engineering
3115 Engineering Building, East Lansing, Michigan 48824-1226, USA
e-mail: jain@cse.msu.edu

Program Committee Members

Josef Bigun
Halmstad University, Sweden

Raffaele Cappelli
University of Bologna, Italy

Rama Chellappa
University of Maryland, USA

Patrick Flynn
Notre Dame University, USA

Behrooz Kamgar-Parsi
Naval Research Lab, USA

Josef Kittler
University of Surrey, UK

Bhagavatula Vijay Kumar
Carnegie Mellon University, USA

Stan Li
Microsoft Research, China

Dario Maio
University of Bologna, Italy

Javier Ortega-Garcia
Universidad Politécnica de Madrid, Spain

Nalini K. Ratha
IBM Research, USA

James Reisman
Siemens Corporate Research, USA

Fabio Roli
University of Cagliari, Italy

Arun Ross
West Virginia University, USA

Table of Contents

Face Recognition

Face Recognition Based on Locally Salient ICA Information 1
J. Kim, J. Choi, J. Yi

Pose Invariant Face Recognition Under Arbitrary Unknown Lighting
Using Spherical Harmonics 10
L. Zhang, D. Samaras

Biometric Face Authentication Using Pixel-Based Weak Classifiers 24
S. Marcel, Y. Rodriguez

Null Space Approach of Fisher Discriminant Analysis for Face
Recognition 32
W. Liu, Y. Wang, S.Z. Li, T. Tan

Statistical Learning of Evaluation Function for ASM/AAM Image
Alignment 45
X. Huang, S.Z. Li, Y. Wang

Towards a Robust Face Detector 57
L. Nanni, A. Franco, R. Cappelli

Automatic Detection of the Optimal Acceptance Threshold in a Face
Verification System... 70
R. Montes Diez, C. Conde, E. Cabello

Fingerprint Recognition

Registration and Modeling of Elastic Deformations of Fingerprints 80
S. Novikov, O. Ushmaev

Benchmarking of Fingerprint Sensors 89
W.Y. Yau, T.P. Chen, P. Morguet

Detecting Liveness in Fingerprint Scanners Using Wavelets: Results of
the Test Dataset 100
S. Schuckers, A. Abhyankar

Fingerprint Distortion Measurement............................... 111
H. Lorch, P. Morguet, H. Schröder

Study of the Distinctiveness of Level 2 and Level 3 Features in
Fragmentary Fingerprint Comparison.............................. 124
K.M. Kryszczuk, P. Morier, A. Drygajlo

Biometric Sensor Interoperability: A Case Study in Fingerprints 134
A. Ross, A. Jain

Efficient Fingerprint Image Enhancement for Mobile Embedded
Systems 146
J.S. Chen, Y.S. Moon, K.F. Fong

Template Protection and Security

Capacity and Examples of Template-Protecting Biometric
Authentication Systems... 158
P. Tuyls, J. Goseling

Toward Ubiquitous Acceptance of Biometric Authentication: Template
Protection Techniques 171
M. Baltatu, R. D'Alessandro, R. D'Amico

Approximate Confidence Intervals for Estimation of Matching Error
Rates of Biometric Identification Devices........................... 184
T.J. Atkinson, M.E. Schuckers

Architectures for Biometric Match-on-Token Solutions 195
R. Sanchez-Reillo, J. Liu-Jimenez, L. Entrena

A Secure Protocol for Data Hiding in Compressed Fingerprint Images ... 205
N.K. Ratha, M.A. Figueroa-Villanueva, J.H. Connell, R.M. Bolle

Other Biometrics

Palmprint Authentication System for Civil Applications 217
D. Zhang, G. Lu, A.W.-K. Kong, M. Wong

Writer Identification Using Finger-Bend in Writing Signature........... 229
S. Hangai, T. Higuchi

3D Finger Biometrics.. 238
D.L. Woodard, P.J. Flynn

Eye Movements in Biometrics 248
P. Kasprowski, J. Ober

Integrating Faces, Fingerprints, and Soft Biometric Traits for User
Recognition 259
A.K. Jain, K. Nandakumar, X. Lu, U. Park

Robust Encoding of Local Ordinal Measures: A General Framework of
Iris Recognition 270
Z. Sun, T. Tan, Y. Wang

A Novel Digitizing Pen for the Analysis of Pen Pressure and Inclination
in Handwriting Biometrics 283
C. Hook, J. Kempf, G. Scharfenberg

An Off-line Signature Verification System Based on Fusion of Local
and Global Information 295
*J. Fierrez-Aguilar, N. Alonso-Hermira, G. Moreno-Marquez,
J. Ortega-Garcia*

Fusion and Multimodal Biometrics

Fingerprint Verification by Decision-Level Fusion of Optical and
Capacitive Sensors 307
G.L. Marcialis, F. Roli

Fusion of HMM's Likelihood and Viterbi Path for On-line Signature
Verification 318
B. Ly Van, S. Garcia-Salicetti, B. Dorizzi

A New Approach on Multimodal Biometrics Based on Combining
Neural Networks Using AdaBoost 332
K. Maghooli, M.S. Moin

Author Index 343

Face Recognition Based on Locally Salient ICA Information

Jongsun Kim, Jongmoo Choi, Juneho Yi

School of Information & Communication Engineering
Sungkyunkwan University
300, Chunchun-dong, Jangan-gu Suwon 440-746, Korea
{jskim, jmchoi, jhyi}@ece.skku.ac.kr

Abstract. ICA (Independent Component Analysis) is contrasted with PCA (Principal Component Analysis) in that ICA basis images are spatially localized, highlighting salient feature regions corresponding to eyes, eye brows, nose and lips. However, ICA basis images do not display perfectly local characteristic in the sense that pixels that do not belong to locally salient feature regions still have some weight values. These pixels in the non-salient regions contribute to the degradation of the recognition performance. We have proposed a novel method based on ICA that only employ locally salient information. The new method effectively implements the idea of "recognition by parts" for the problem of face recognition. Experimental results using AT&T, Harvard, FERET and AR databases show that the recognition performance of the proposed method outperforms that of PCA and ICA methods especially in the cases of facial images that have partial occlusions and local distortions such as changes in facial expression and at low dimensions.

1 Introduction

Over the last ten years, canonical subspace projection techniques such as PCA and ICA are widely used in the face recognition research [2-4]. These techniques employ feature vectors consisting of coefficients that are obtained by projecting facial images onto their basis images. The basis images are computed offline from a set of training images. ICA is contrasted with PCA in that ICA basis images are more spatially local than PCA basis images. Fig. 1 (a) and (b) show facial image representation using PCA and ICA basis images, respectively, that are computed from a set of images randomly selected from the AR database. PCA basis images display global properties in the sense that they assign significant weights to the same pixels. It accords with the fact that PCA basis images are just scaled versions of global Fourier filters [21]. In contrast, ICA basis images are spatially more localized, highlighting salient feature regions corresponding to eyes, eye brows, nose and lips. This local property of ICA basis images makes the performance of ICA based recognition methods better than PCA methods in terms of robustness to partial occlusions and local distortions such as changes in facial expression. Thus, ICA techniques have popularly been applied to the problem of face recognition [3-6], especially for face recognition under variations of illumination, pose and facial expression. However, ICA basis images do not display

D. Maltoni and A.K. Jain (Eds.): BioAW 2004, LNCS 3087, pp. 1-9, 2004.
© Springer-Verlag Berlin Heidelberg 2004

perfectly local characteristics in the sense that pixels that do not belong to locally salient feature regions still have some weight values. These pixels in the non-salient regions contribute to the degradation of the recognition performance.

We propose a novel method based on ICA, named LS-ICA (locally salient ICA) where the concept of "recognition by parts" [18-20] can be effectively realized for face recognition. The idea of "recognition by parts" has been a popular paradigm in object recognition research that can be successfully applied to the problem of object recognition with occlusion. Our method is characterized by two ideas: one is removal of non-salient regions in ICA basis images so that LS-ICA basis images only employ locally salient feature regions. The other is to use ICA basis images in the order of class separability so as to maximize the recognition performance. Experimental results show that LS-ICA performs better than PCA and ICA especially in the cases of partial occlusions and local distortions such as changes in facial expression. In addition, the performance improvement of LS-ICA over ICA based methods was much greater as we decrease the dimensionality (i. e. the number of basis images used).

The rest of this paper is organized as follows. Section 2 contrasts ICA with PCA in terms of locality of features. Section 3 describes the proposed LS-ICA method. Section 4 presents experimental results.

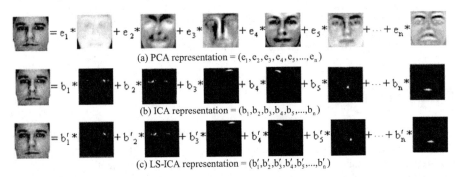

(a) PCA representation = $(e_1, e_2, e_3, e_4, e_5, ..., e_n)$

(b) ICA representation = $(b_1, b_2, b_3, b_4, b_5, ..., b_n)$

(c) LS-ICA representation = $(b'_1, b'_2, b'_3, b'_4, b'_5, ..., b'_n)$

Figure 1. Facial image representations using (a) PCA, (b) ICA and (c) LS-ICA basis images: A face is represented as a linear combination of basis images. The basis images were computed from a set of images randomly selected from the AR database. In the basis images of LS-ICA, non-salient regions of ICA basis images are removed. Using LS-ICA basis images, the concept of "recognition by parts" can be effectively implemented for face recognition.

2 ICA Versus PCA

PCA and ICA are the most widely used subspace projection techniques that project data from a high-dimensional space to a lower-dimensional space [2, 4]. PCA addresses only second-order moments of the input. It is optimal for finding a reduced representation that minimizes the reconstruction error, but it is not optimal for classification. ICA is a generalization of PCA that decorrelates the high-order statistics in addition to the second-order moments. Much of information about characteristic local structure of facial images is contained in the higher-order statistics of the images. Thus ICA, where the high-order statistics are decorrelated, may provide a more powerful representational basis for face recognition than PCA, where only the second-order statistics are correlated. Figure 2 illustrates PCA and ICA axes for the same 2D distribution. PCA finds an orthogonal set of axes pointing in the directions of maximum covariance in the data, while ICA attempts to place axes pointing in the directions of spatially localized and statistically independent basis vectors [17].

As previously described, global properties of faces may be more easily captured by PCA than ICA. As shown in Figure 1, ICA basis images are more spatially localized and never overlap unlike their PCA counterpart [1]. Since spatially localized features only influence small parts of facial images, ICA based recognition methods are less susceptible to occlusions and local distortions than are global feature based methods such as PCA. We can compute ICA basis images using various algorithms such as InfoMax [3, 10], FastICA [5, 8] and Maximum likelihood [6, 7].

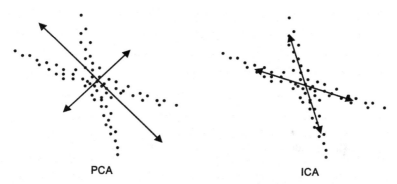

PCA   **ICA**

Figure 2. PCA and ICA axes for an identical 2D data distribution [17]

3 The LS-ICA (Locally Salient ICA) Method

The LS-ICA method features the use of new basis images made from ICA basis images that are selected in the decreasing order of class separability. Only salient feature regions are contained in the LS-ICA basis images. As in most algorithms that employ subspace projection, the LS-ICA method computes a projection matrix, off-line from a set of training images. Let W_{ls-ica} denote the projection matrix. The columns of W_{ls-ica} are LS-ICA basis images. During recognition, given an input face image $\mathbf{x}$, it is projected to $\Omega' = W_{ls-sica}^{T}\mathbf{x}$ and classified by comparison with the vectors Ω_{T}'s that were computed off-line from a set of training images.

Figure 3 shows a block diagram of the method. First, we preprocess training images by applying histogram equalization and scale normalization, where the size of images is adjusted so that they have the same distance between two eyes. Second, we com-

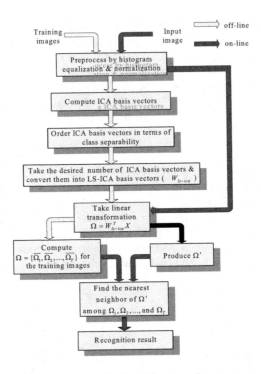

Figure 3. Algorithm overview

pute ICA basis images, using the FastICA algorithm [5, 8]. The FastICA method computes the independent components that become uncorrelated by a whitening process and then maximizes non-Gaussianity of data distribution by using kurtosis maximization [5]. We then compute a measure of class separability, r, for each ICA basis vector and sort the ICA basis vectors in the decreasing order of class separability [3]. To computer r for each ICA basis vector, the between-class variability $\sigma_{between}$ and within-class variability σ_{within} of its corresponding projection coefficients of training images are obtained as follows.

$$\sigma_{between} = \Sigma_i \left(M_i - M \right)^2 \tag{1}$$

$$\sigma_{within} = \Sigma_i \Sigma_j \left(b_{ij} - M_i \right)^2 \tag{2}$$

M and M_i are the total mean and the mean of each class, and b_{ij} is the coefficient of the jth training image in class i. The class separability, r, is then defined as the ratio

$$r = \frac{\sigma_{between}}{\sigma_{within}} . \tag{3}$$

Third, we create LS-ICA basis images from the ICA basis images selected in the decreasing order of the class separability. This way, we can achieve both dimensional reduction and good recognition performance. To create an LS-ICA basis image, we apply a series of operations to its corresponding ICA basis image as shown in Figure 4. In order to detect locally salient regions, we simply find extreme values by thresholding a histogram of pixel values (Figure 4 (b)), followed by the application of morphological operations to find a blob region (Figure 4 (d)). As a result, we get an LS-ICA basis image (Figure 4 (e)) where only pixels in the blob regions have grey values copied from the corresponding pixels in the original ICA image. The values of the rest of the pixels in the image are set to zero. These LS-ICA basis images are used to represent facial images as shown in Figure 1 (c).

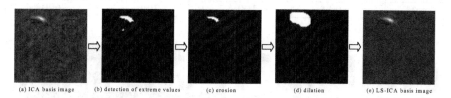

(a) ICA basis image   (b) detection of extreme values   (c) erosion   (d) dilation   (e) LS-ICA basis image

Figure 4. Illustration of creating an LS-ICA basis image

4 Experimental Results

We have used several facial image databases such as AT&T [13], Harvard [14], FERET [15] and AR [16] databases in order to compare the recognition performance of LS-ICA with that of PCA and ICA methods. For fair comparisons with PCA and ICA based methods, PCA and ICA basis images were also used in the decreasing order of class separability, r. In the case of the ICA method, the recognition performance was greater when the basis images were ordered in terms of class separability. However, the PCA method did not show any noticeable performance difference between the ordering in the class separability and the orginal ordering in terms of eigenvalues.

Table 1 lists the number of training and testing images used in each facial image databases for the experiment. Figure 5 shows example images from these databases. In the AT&T database, all the images are taken against a dark homogeneous background and the subjects are in an up-right, frontal position with tolerance for some side movement. In Harvard database, a subject held his/her head steady while being illuminated by a dominant light source. In the FERET database, we have used a subset of the images of subjects under significantly different lighting and facial expression. The AR database contains local distortions and occlusions such as changes in facial expression and sunglasses worn.

All images were converted to 256 gray-level images and background regions were removed. We have also applied histogram equalization to both training and testing images in order to minimize variations of illumination. We have experimented using thirty different sets of training and testing images for each database. We have computed recognition performances for three different distance measures (L1, L2, cosine) since we are concerned with performance variations independent of the distance measure used [1].

Table 1. Facial databases used in the experiment

Database	The number of total images	The number of persons	The number of training images	The number of testing images
AT&T	400	40	200	200
Harvard	165	5	82(83)	83(82)
FERET	605	127	127	478
AR	800	100	200	600

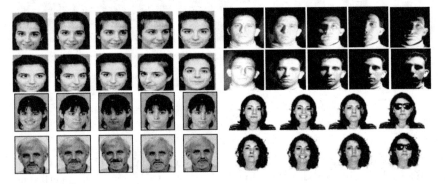

Figure 5. Example images from AT&T (top left), Harvard (top right), FERET (bottom left) and AR (bottom right) facial databases

Figure 6 shows the recognition performances of PCA, ICA and LS-ICA methods for the four facial databases. The recognition rate of the LS-ICA method was consistently better than that of PCA and ICA methods regardless of distance measures used. ICA also consistently outperformed PCA except the case where the L1 measure was used for the FERET database. What is more interesting is that LS-ICA method performed better than the other methods especially at low dimensions. This property is very important when we need to store facial feature data in a low capacity storing devices such as smart cards and barcodes. To clearly show this, we displayed in Figure 7 the performance improvement of the LS-ICA method over the ICA method. The performance improvement was the greatest in the case of the AR database, as we expected. The AR database contains local distortions and occlusions such as sunglasses worn. The LS-ICA method that only makes use of locally salient information can achieve a higher recognition rate than ordinary ICA methods that are influenced by pixels not belonging to salient regions. The experimental results show that, especially at low dimensions, LS-ICA basis images better represent facial images than ICA basis images.

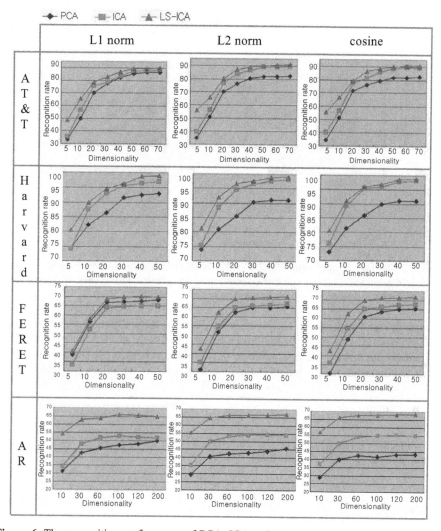

Figure 6. The recognition performance of PCA, ICA and LS-ICA methods for the four facial databases. The recognition rates represent the average performance of the experiment using thirty different sets of training and testing images.

5 Conclusion and Future Research Directions

We have proposed the LS-ICA method that only employs locally salient information in order to maximize the benefit of applying the idea of "recognition by parts" to the problem of face recognition under partial occlusion and local distortion. The performance of the LS-ICA method was consistently better than the ICA method regardless of the distance measures used. As expected, the effect was the greatest in the cases of facial images that have partial occlusions and local distortions such as

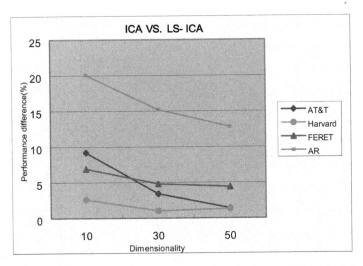

Figure 7. The performance improvement of LS-ICA method over ICA method for the four facial databases. The performance improvement was the greatest in the case of AR database that contains local distortions and occlusions such as sunglasses worn.

changes in facial expression. However, we expect that a combination of the proposed LS-ICA method with a global feature based method such as PCA will yield better recognition rates since face recognition is a holistic process [19]. Further research efforts will be made to develop an optimal method that best combines two methods.

Acknowledgements

This work was supported in part by grant No. R01-1999-000-00339-0 from the Basic Research Program KOSEF and BK21.

References

[1] K. Back, B. A. Draper, J. R. Beveridge, and K. She, "PCA vs ICA: A comparison on the FERET data set," Joint Conference on Information Sciences, Durham, N. C., 2002.

[2] M. A. Turk and A. P. Pentland, "Eigenfaces for recognition," Cognitive Neuroscience, vol.3, no.1, pp. 71-86, 1991.

[3] M. S. Bartlett, H. M. Lades, and T. J. Sejnowski, "Independent component representations for face recognition," Proceedings of the SPIE, vol. 3299: Conference on Human Vision and Electronic Imaging III, pp. 528-539, 1998.

[4] M. S. Bartlett, J. R. Movellan, and T. J. Sejnowski, "Face Recognition by Independent Component Analysis," IEEE Transaction on Neural Networks, Vol 13, pp. 1450-1464, 2002.

[5] Aapo Hyvarinen and Erki Oja, "Independent component analysis: a tutorial," http://www.cis.hut.fi/~aapo/papers/IJCNN99_tutorialweb/, 1999.

[6] J. F. Cardoso, "Infomax and Maximum Likelihood for Source Separation," IEEE Letters on Signal Processing, vol. 4, pp. 112-114, 1997.

[7] A. Hyvärinen, "The Fixed-point Algorithm and Maximum Likelihood Estimation for Independent Component Analysis," Neural Processing Letters, vol. 10, pp. 1-5, 1999.

[8] A. Hyvärinen and E. Oja, "Independent Component Analysis: Algorithms and Applications," Neural Networks, pp. 411-430, 2000.

[9] C. Liu and H. Wechsler, "Comparative Assessment of Independent Component Analysis (ICA) for Face Recognition," International Conference on Audio and Video Based Biometric Person Authentication, Washington, D.C., 1999.

[10] A. J. Bell and T. J. Sejnowski, "An information-maximization Approach to Blind Separation and Blind Deconvolution," Neural Computation, vol. 7, pp. 1129-1159, 1995.

[11] P. Belhumeur, J. Hespanha, and D. Kriegman, "Eigenfaces vs. Fisherfaces: Recognition Using Class Specific Linear Projection," Pattern Analysis and Machine Intelligence, vol. 19, no. 7, pp. 711-720, 1997.

[12] K. Fukunaga, "Introduction to statistical pattern recognition," Academic Press, second edition, 1991.

[13] http://www.uk.research.att.com/facedatabase.html.

[14] http://cvc.yale.edu/people/faculty/belhumeur.htm.

[15] P. J. Phillips, H. Moon, S. A. Rizvi, and P. J. Rauss, "The FERET Evaluation Methodology for Face Recognition Algorithms," Pattern Analysis and Machine Intelligence, vol. 22, pp. 1090-1104, 2000.

[16] A. M. Martinez and R. Benavente, "The AR face database," CVC Tech. Report #24, 1998.

[17] M. S. Bartlett, "Face Image Analysis by Unsupervised Learning," Foreword by T. J. Sejnowski, Kluwer International Series on Engineering and Computer Science, Boston: Kluwer Academic Publishers, 2001.

[18] A. P. Pentland, "Recognition by parts," IEEE Proceedings of the First International Conference on Computer Vision, pp. 612—620, 1987.

[19] W. Zhao, R. Chellappa and A. Rosenfeld, "Face Recognition: A Literature Survey," To appear in ACM Computing Surveys.

[20] D. D. Lee and H. S. Seung, "Learning the parts of objects by non-negative matrix factorization," Nature, vol. 401, pp.788-791, 1999.

[21] A. J. Bell and T. J. Sejnowski, "The independent components of natural scenes are edge filters," Advance in Neural Information Processing Systems 9, 1997.

Pose Invariant Face Recognition Under Arbitrary Unknown Lighting Using Spherical Harmonics

Lei Zhang and Dimitris Samaras

Department of Computer Science,
SUNY at Stony Brook, NY, 11790
{lzhang, samaras}@cs.sunysb.edu

Abstract. We propose a new method for face recognition under arbitrary pose and illumination conditions, which requires only one training image per subject. Furthermore, no limitation on the pose and illumination conditions for the training image is necessary. Our method combines the strengths of Morphable models to capture the variability of 3D face shape and a spherical harmonic representation for the illumination. Morphable models are successful in 3D face reconstructions from one single image. Recent research demonstrates that the set of images of a convex Lambertian object obtained under a wide variety of lighting conditions can be approximated accurately by a low-dimensional linear subspace using spherical harmonics representation. In this paper, we show that we can recover the 3D faces with texture information from one single training image under arbitrary illumination conditions and perform robust pose and illumination invariant face recognition by using the recovered 3D faces. During training, given an image under arbitrary illumination, we first compute the shape parameters from a shape error estimated by the displacements of a set of feature points. Then we estimate the illumination coefficients and texture information using the spherical harmonics illumination representation. The reconstructed 3D models serve as generative models to render sets of basis images of each subject for different poses. During testing, we recognize the face for which there exists a weighted combination of basis images that is the closest to the test face image. We provide a series of experiments on approximately 5000 images from the CMU-PIE database. We achieve high recognition rates for images under a wide range of illumination conditions, including multiple sources of illumination.

1 Introduction

Face recognition has recently received extensive attention as one of the most significant applications of image understanding. Although rapid progress has been made in this area during the last few years [29][21][16][3][35][5][19][18][8][28][24][9][20][31][33], the general task of recognition remains unsolved. In general, face appearance does not depend solely on identity. It is also influenced by illumination and viewpoint. Changes in pose and illumination will cause large changes

D. Maltoni and A.K. Jain (Eds.): BioAW 2004, LNCS 3087, pp. 10–23, 2004.

in the appearance of a face. In this paper we demonstrate a new method to recognize face images under a wide range of pose and illumination conditions using spherical harmonic images of the face and a morphable model. Our method requires only a single training image per subject. To our knowledge no other face recognition method can achieve such a high level of pose and illumination invariance when only one training image is available.

In the past few years, there have been attempts to address image variation produced by changing in illumination and pose [10][35]. Georghiades et al. [11] present a new method using the illumination cone which requires at least three images per subject to build the illumination cone. Romdhani et al. [23] recover the shape and texture parameters of a 3D Morphable Model in an analysis-by-synthesis fashion. In [23], the shape parameters are computed from a shape error estimated by optical flow and the texture parameters are obtained from a texture error. The algorithm uses linear equations to recover the shape and texture parameters irrespective of pose and lighting conditions of the face image. However, this method is bound to images taken under single directional illumination and requires the knowledge of light direction which is difficult to know in most cases.

In general, appearance-based methods like Eigenfaces [29] and SLAM [21] need a number of training images for each subject, in order to cope with pose and illumination variability. Previous research suggests that illumination variability in face images is low-dimensional e.g. [2][22][12][4][1][25][26][17]. Using spherical harmonics and signal-processing techniques, Basri et al. [2] and Ramamoorthi [22] have independently shown that the set of images of a convex Lambertian object obtained under a wide variety of lighting conditions can be approximated accurately by a 9 dimensional linear subspace. Furthermore, a simple scheme for face recognition with excellent results was described in [2]. However, to use this recognition scheme, the basis images spanning the illumination space for each face are required. These images can be rendered from a 3D scan of the face or can be estimated by applying PCA to a number of images of the same subject under different illuminations [22]. An effective approximation of this basis by 9 single light source images of a face was reported in [15] and Wang et al. [30] proposed a illumination modeling and normalization method for face recognition. The above mentioned methods need a number of training images and/or 3D scans of the subjects in the database, requiring specialized equipment and procedures for the capture of the training set, thus limiting their applicability. A promising earlier attempt by [36] used symmetric shape from shading but suffered from the drawbacks of SFS. A new approach is proposed in [34] for face recognition under arbitrary illumination conditions, for fixed pose, which requires only one training image per subject and no 3D shape information. In [34] the statistical model is based on a collection of 2D basis images, rendered from known 3D shapes. Thus 3D shape is only implicitly included in the statistical model. Here we will base our statistical model directly on 3D shapes, perform statistical analysis in 3D in order to estimate the most appropriate 3D shape and then create the 2D basis images. The ability to manipulate the 3D shape explicitly allows the generation of basis images for poses that do not exist in the training data.

In this paper we propose a method that combines a 3D morphable model and a low-dimensional illumination representation that uses spherical harmonics. Our method requires only one training image for each subject without pose and illumination limitations. Our method consists of three steps: 3D face reconstruction, basis image rendering and recognition. Initially, similar to [23], given a training image, we compute the shape parameters of a morphable model from a shape error estimated by the displacements of a set of feature points. Then we estimate the illumination coefficients and texture information using the spherical harmonics illumination representation. In the basis image rendering step, the reconstructed face models then serve as generative models that can be used to synthesize sets of basis images under novel poses and spanning the illumination field. During the recognition step, we use the recognition scheme proposed by Basri et al. [2]. We return the face from the training set for which there exists a weighted combination of basis images that is the closest to the test face image.

We use the morphable model computed from the USF 3D face database [6] and the CMU-PIE database [27] for training and testing. We provide a series of experiments that show that the method achieves high recognition accuracy although our method requires only a single training image without limitation on pose and illumination conditions. We compare the recognition rate with [23] on the images taken under single light source. We also give experiment results of recognition on the set of images under multiple light sources, and compare with [34] for known pose.

This paper is organized as follows. In the next section, we will briefly introduce the Morphable Model. In Section 3, we explain the Spherical Harmonics and how to acquire basis images from 3D face models. In Section 4, we describe the process of 3D face model reconstruction and basis image rendering. In Section 5, we describe the recognition process that uses the rendered basis images. In Section 6, we describe our experiments and their results. The final Section presents the conclusions and future work directions.

2   Morphable Model

In this section we briefly summarize the morphable model framework described in detail in [6][7]. The 3D Morphable Face Model is a 3D model of faces with separate shape and texture models that are learnt from a set of exemplar faces. Morphing between faces requires complete sets of correspondences between all of the faces. When building a 3D morphable model, we transform the shape and texture spaces into vector spaces, so that any convex combination of exemplar shapes and textures represents a realistic human face. We present the geometry of a face with a shape-vector $S = (X_1, Y_1, Z_1, X_2, ..., Y_n, Z_n)^T \in \Re^{3n}$, which contains the X, Y, Z- coordinates of its n vertices. Similarly, the texture of a face can be represented by a texture-vector $T = (R_1, G_1, B_1, R_2, ..., G_n, B_n)^T \in \Re^{3n}$ where the R, G, B texture values are sampled at the same n points. A morphable model can be constructed using a data set of m exemplar faces; exemplar i is represented by the shape-vector S_i and texture-vector T_i. New shapes s and textures t can be generated by convex combinations of the shapes and textures of the m exemplar faces: $s = \sum_{i=1}^{m} a_i S_i, t = \sum_{i=1}^{m} b_i T_i, \sum_{i=1}^{m} a_i = \sum_{i=1}^{m} b_i = 1$. To reduce the dimensionality of the shape and texture spaces, Principal Component Analysis(PCA) is applied separately on the shape and texture spaces:

$$s = \bar{s} + \sum_{i=1}^{m-1} \alpha_i \sigma_{s,i} s_i, \qquad t = \bar{t} + \sum_{i=1}^{m-1} \beta_i \sigma_{t,i} t_i \qquad (1)$$

By setting the smallest eigenvalues to zero, Eq. 1 is reformulated as:

$$s = \bar{s} + S\alpha, \qquad t = \bar{t} + T\beta \qquad (2)$$

In Eq. 2 the columns of S and T are the most significant eigenvectors s_i and t_i re-scaled by their standard deviation and the coefficients α and β constitute a pose and illumination invariant low-dimensional coding of a face [23]. PCA also provides an estimate of the probability densities of the shapes and textures, under a Gaussian assumption: $p(s) \sim e^{-\frac{1}{2}\|\alpha\|^2}$, $\qquad p(t) \sim e^{-\frac{1}{2}\|\beta\|^2}$

3   Spherical Harmonics

In this section, we will briefly explain the illumination representation by using spherical harmonics and how we render basis images from 3D models using the results of [2]. Let L denote the distant lighting distribution. By neglecting the cast shadows and near-field illumination, the irradiance E is then a function of the surface normal n only and is given by an integral over the upper hemisphere Ω_n [22]: $E(n) = \int L(\omega)(n \cdot \omega)d\omega$ We then scale E by the surface albedo λ to find the radiosity I, which corresponds to the image intensity directly:

$$I(p, n) = \lambda(p)E(n) \qquad (3)$$

Basri et al. [2] and Ramamoorthi [22] have independently shown that E can be approximated by the combination of the first nine spherical harmonics $H(x, y, z)$ for Lambertian surfaces:

$$h_{00} = \frac{1}{\sqrt{4\pi}}, \qquad h_{11}^o = \sqrt{\frac{3}{4\pi}}y, \qquad h_{21}^o = 3\sqrt{\frac{5}{12\pi}}yz$$

$$h_{10} = \sqrt{\frac{3}{4\pi}}z, \qquad h_{20} = \frac{1}{2}\sqrt{\frac{5}{4\pi}}(2z^2 - x^2 - y^2), \qquad h_{22}^e = \frac{3}{2}\sqrt{\frac{5}{12\pi}}(x^2 - y^2) \quad (4)$$

$$h_{11}^e = \sqrt{\frac{3}{4\pi}}x, \qquad h_{21}^e = 3\sqrt{\frac{5}{12\pi}}xz, \qquad h_{22}^o = 3\sqrt{\frac{5}{12\pi}}xy$$

where the superscripts e and o denote the even and the odd components of the harmonics respectively and x, y, z demote the cartesian components. Then the image intensity of a point p with surface normal $n = (n_x, n_y, n_z)$ and albedo λ can be computed according to Eq. 3 by replacing x, y, z with n_x, n_y, n_z. Fig. 1 gives an example of the mean shape and texture of the morphable model under a spherical harmonics representation.

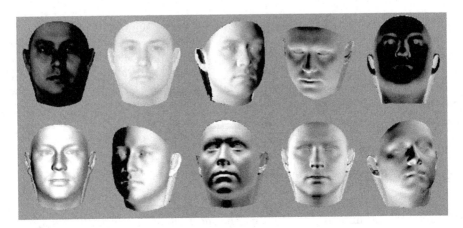

Fig. 1. The first image is the mean of the morphable model and the following nine images are the basis images under various view-points, represented by spherical harmonics. Lighter gray (0-127) represents positive values and darker gray (128-255) represents negative values.

4   Face Model Reconstruction and Basis Image Rendering

In this section, we will explain how we recover the shape and texture information of a training subject by combining a morphable model and spherical harmonics lighting representation.

4.1   Forward and Inverse Face Rendering

We can generate photo-realistic face images by using the morphable model we described in Section 2 [6]. Here we describe how we synthesize a new face image from the face shape and texture vectors s and t, thus, the inversion process of the synthesis is how we recover shape and texture information from the image.

Shape: Similar to [23], a realistic face shape can be generated by:

$$s_{2d} = fPR(\bar{s} + S\alpha + t_{3d}) + t_{2d} \tag{5}$$

where f is a scale parameter, P an orthographic projection matrix and R a rotation matrix with ϕ, γ and θ the three rotation angles for the three axes. t_{3d} and t_{2d} are translation vectors in 3D and 2D respectively. Eq. 5 relates the vector of 2D image coordinates s_{2d} and the shape parameters α. For rendering, a visibility test must still be performed by using a z-buffer method.

For a training image, inverting the rendering process, the shape parameters can be recovered from the shape error: if f, ϕ, γ and θ are kept constant, the relation between the shape s_{2d} and α is linear according to Eq. 5: $\frac{\partial s_{2d}}{\partial \alpha} = fPRS$. Thus, updating α from a shape error δs_{2d} requires only the solution of a linear system of equations. In our method, the shape error is estimated by the displacements of a set of manually picked feature points s_f [14] corresponding to image coordinates s_f^{img}. The shape reconstruction goes through the following steps:

Model Initialization: All the parameters are initialized in this step. Shape parameter α is set to 0 and pose parameters f, ϕ, γ, θ and t_{2d} are initialized manually. We do not need to know the illumination conditions of the training image, unlike [23].

Feature Correspondence: For the set of pre-picked feature points in the morphable model, we find the correspondence s_f^{img} in the training image semi-automatically. The set of feature points contains major and secondary features, see Fig. 2. After the correspondences of major features are manually set, the secondary features are updated automatically.

Rotation, Translation and Scale Parameters Update: the parameters f, ϕ, γ and θ can be recovered by using a Levenberg-Marquardt optimization to minimize the error between s_f^{img} and the model feature points [13]:

$$argmin_{f,\phi,\gamma,\theta,t_{2d}} \| s_f^{img} - (fPR(\bar{s}_f + S_f\alpha + t_{3d}) + t_{2d}) \|^2 = (\tilde{f}, \tilde{\phi}, \tilde{\gamma}, \tilde{\theta}, \tilde{t}_{2d}) \quad (6)$$

where $\bar{s}_f$ and S_f is the corresponding shape information of the feature points in the morphable model in Eq. 2.

Shape Parameter Update: The shape error of the feature points, δs_f^{2d}, is defined as the difference between s_f^{img} and the new shape information of feature points in the model that was rendered by recovered parameters $\tilde{f}, \tilde{\phi}, \tilde{\gamma}, \tilde{\theta}$ and $\tilde{t}_{2d}$. Thus, the vector of shape parameters α can be updated by solving a linear system of equations:

$$\delta s_f^{2d} = fPRS_f\delta\alpha \quad (7)$$

Texture: For texture information recovery, most of the previous methods [11][23] are applicable to images taken under single light source, which limits their applicability. Here we propose a method which performs texture fitting to a training image and has no limitation in the image illumination conditions. According to Eq. 3 and 4, the texture of a face can be generated by:

$$t = B * l, \quad B = H(n_x, n_y, n_z) \cdot \lambda \quad (8)$$

where H is the spherical harmonics representation of the reflectance function (Eq. 4) and l is the vector of illumination coefficients. Hence, if we know the illumination coefficients, the texture information is only dependent on image intensity t and surface normal n, which can be computed from the 3D shape we recovered during the shape fitting step. The texture recovery is described as following:

Basis Computation: The initial albedo λ for each vertex is set to $\bar{t}$. With the recovered shape information, we first compute the surface normal n for each vertex. Then the first nine basis images B and spherical harmonics $H(n)$ for reflectance function can be computed according to Eq. 8 and 4 respectively.

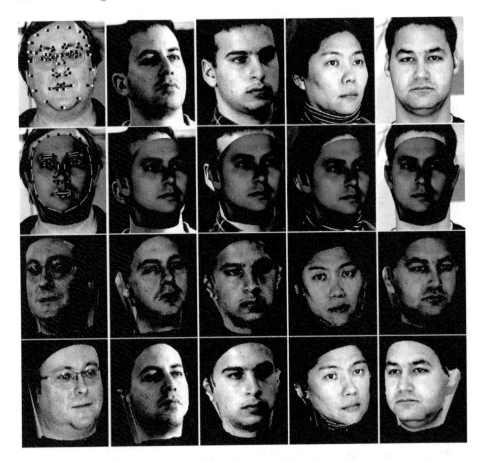

Fig. 2. Recovery Results: Images in the first row are the input training images, those in the second row are the initial fittings, the third row shows images of the recovered 3D face model and the last row gives the illuminated rotated face models. In the first column, the black points are pre-picked major features, the white points are the corresponding features and the points lying in the white line are secondary features.

Illumination Coefficients Estimation: The set of illumination coefficients l is updated by solving a linear system of equations:

$$t_{tra} = B_{cur}l \tag{9}$$

Texture Recovery: According to Eq. 8, the texture λ for each visible vertex is computed by solving: $t_{tra} = H(n_x, n_y, n_z)l \cdot \lambda$. Since texture is dependent on both current texture and illumination coefficients, the new value of λ is:

$$\lambda = (1 - \eta)\lambda_{cur} + \eta(t_{tra}/(H(n_x, n_y, n_z)l)) \tag{10}$$

We compute l and λ by solving Eq. 9 and 10 iteratively. In our experiments, weight η is first set to 0.5, then incremented by 0.1 at each step until it reaches 1. Instead of recovering texture parameters [23], we estimate the albedo value for each vertex, which will be used for basis image rendering and recognition. For occluded vertices, texture information is estimated through facial symmetry. Fig. 2 shows the results of our method.

There is human interactivity in our shape fitting part since we manually find the correspondences for major features. Automatic shape fitting of a morphable model [23] is beyond the scope of this paper which focuses on the statistics of interaction of geometry with arbitrary unknown illumination and the feature based method performed sufficiently well to demonstrate the strength of our approach.

4.2 Basis Images Rendering

For each training subject, we recover a 3D face model using the algorithm described in section 4.2. The recovered face models serve as generative models to render basis images. In this section, for each subject, a set of basis images across poses are generated, to be used during recognition. We sample the pose variance for each $5°$ in both azimuth and altitude axes. In our experiments, the range of azimuth is [-70,70] and the range of altitude is [-10,10]. Fig. 3 shows a subset of the basis images for one subject.

5 Face Recognition

In the basis image rendering step, for each subject i, a set of 145 (29*5) basis $B_j^i, j \in [1..145]$ is rendered. During testing, given a new testing image I_t, we recognize the face of subject i for which there exists a weighted combination of basis images that is the closest to the test face image [2]: $min_{i,j} \|B_j^i l - I_t\|$ where B_j^i is a set of basis images with size $d * r$, d is the number of points in the image and r the number of basis images used (9 is a natural choice, we also tried 4 in our experiments). Every column of B_j^i contains one spherical harmonic image, and the columns of B_j^i form a basis for the linear subspace. To solve the equation, we simply apply QR decomposition to B_j^i to obtain an orthonormal basis. Thus, we compute the distance from the test image, I_t, and the space spanned by B_j^i as $\|QQ^T I_t - I_t\|$.

6 Experiments and Results

In our experiments, we used the CMU-PIE database which provides images of both pose and illumination variation. The CMU-PIE database contains 68 individuals, none of which is also in the USF set used to compute the morphable model. We performed experiments on a set of 4488 images which contains 68 subjects, 3 poses for each subject and 22 different illuminations for each pose.

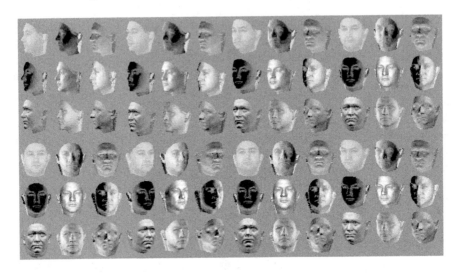

Fig. 3. A subset of the rendered basis images across poses.

6.1   Experiments of Illumination Invariance

Since our recognition method is based on the 3D face models recovered during training, it is important that the recovered face models and rendered basis images are robust. Figure 4 shows three sets of rendered basis images recovered from various face images under different illuminations for one subject. The resulting basis images rendered from images under different illumination are very close. For each subject, we calculated 10 sets of basis using 10 training images under different illumination. The per person mean variance of the 10 resulting sets of basis images was 3.32. For comparison, per person variance of the original training images was 20.25. That means the rendered basis images have much greater invariance to illumination effects than original images.

6.2   Recognition Experiments

In recognition experiments, we used the same set of 4488 images in CMU-PIE. We used only one image per subject to recover the 3D face model. We used the front and side galleries for training and all three pose galleries for testing. Notice that training images can have very different illumination conditions (unlike [23]). We performed recognition by using both all the 9 basis images and the first 4 basis images. We report our experimental results and comparison to [23] in Table 1. From the experimental results, we find that our method gives good recognition rates. When the poses of training and testing images are very different, our method is not as good as [23] because we only used a set of feature points to recover the shape information and the shape recovery is not accurate enough.

Table 1. Recognition results and comparison: The first column lists the light numbers and the following two columns list the recognition rate for each pose. The recognition rates of the LiST algorithm are taken from [23].

Light	Front Gallery Using all 9 basis			Front Gallery Using first 4 basis			Side Gallery Using all 9 basis			Side Gallery Using first 4 basis		
	Front	Side	Profile	Front	Side	Profile	Front	Side	Profile	Front	Side	Profile
1	95	89	51	89	81	49	91	92	52	79	78	52
2	89	81	34	79	73	31	80	83	34	67	67	33
3	97	88	44	89	79	42	92	96	50	83	86	48
4	98	91	52	89	83	50	94	96	62	85	88	55
5	99	89	57	89	84	52	94	97	64	87	90	59
6	100	92	55	91	86	50	100	100	64	89	89	59
7	99	95	54	88	83	51	92	96	60	86	89	58
8	99	93	62	94	89	54	94	99	70	84	85	62
9	100	96	61	90	88	55	95	100	71	83	92	64
10	100	97	60	92	87	56	98	100	69	89	88	64
11	100	98	58	88	89	50	97	95	63	90	90	63
12	98	99	61	90	88	57	94	98	72	84	86	69
13	99	93	55	89	88	50	98	99	70	87	89	63
14	100	94	53	91	86	49	95	100	62	91	92	58
15	100	93	54	91	87	49	98	99	61	89	89	52
16	99	91	53	91	82	49	95	97	60	87	89	59
17	98	92	55	91	80	50	96	99	65	89	91	61
18	95	88	52	90	78	47	92	94	62	82	87	58
19	98	90	56	89	81	51	92	95	61	82	91	55
20	99	94	58	88	80	51	93	97	63	86	88	57
21	99	96	51	90	81	50	96	96	55	84	89	54
22	99	95	62	89	81	56	94	99	65	79	90	60
mean	98.2	92.4	54.5	89.4	83.4	50.0	94.4	96.7	61.6	84.6	87.4	57.4
LiST mean	97	91	60				93	96	71			

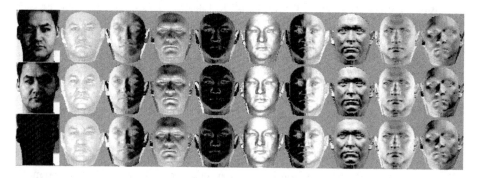

Fig. 4. Rendered basis images from training images taken under different illumination conditions. The first column shows the training images.

Table 2. Recognition results using various previous methods and our method on Yale Database B. Except for our method, the data were taken from [34]

Methods	Subset1,2	Subset3	Subset4
Eigenfaces	100	74.2	24.3
Linear Subspace	100	100	85
Cones-attached	100	100	91.4
9PL	100	100	97.2
Cones-cast	100	100	100
2D HIE	100	99.7	96.9
Our Method	100	100	97.2

We also performed experiments on the Yale Face Database B [3] and compared our recognition results with other methods for fixed frontal pose. The Yale Database contains images of 10 people with 9 poses and 64 illuminations per pose. We used 45*10 frontal face images for 10 subjects with each subject having 45 face images taken under different directional light sources. The data set is divided to 4 subsets following [15]. Table 2 compares our recognition rates with previous methods. As can be seen from Table 2, the results from our method are comparable with methods that require extensive training data per subject even though our method requires only one training image per pose. For fixed pose, the 2D HIE method in [34] performs almost as well as the our method, however the performance is very sensitive to accurate alignment of the faces.

6.3   Multiple Directional Illumination

As we mentioned, most of the previous methods are only applicable to single directional lighting. We study the performance of our method on images taken under multiple directional illumination sources to test our method under arbitrary illuminations. We synthesized images by combining face images in our data set and performed experiments on front and side galleries. For each subject, we randomly selected 2-6 images from the training data set and combined them together with random weights to simulate face images under multiple directional illumination sources(16 images per subject). We did experiments on the synthesized images both during training step and testing step. Table 3 shows the experimental results and we can see that our method also performed equally well under multiple sources of arbitrary direction.

7   Conclusions and Future Work

We have shown that by combining a morphable model and spherical harmonic lighting representation, we can recover both shape and texture information from one single image taken under arbitrary illumination conditions. Experimental results indicate that our method's recognition rates are comparable to other

Table 3. Experimental results of images under multiple directional illumination. "s" denotes images under single directional lighting and "m" denotes synthesized images under multiple illumination. "F" denotes the front gallery and "D" denotes the side gallery.

	Train:s; Test:s	Train:m; Test:s	Train:s; Test:m	Train:m; Test:m
Train:F; Test:F	98.2	98.3	97.8	98.1
Train:F; Test:D	92.4	92.0	91.5	92.2
Train:D; Test:F	94.4	93.6	94.2	94.8
Train:D; Test:D	96.7	95.9	96.3	96.1

methods for pose variant images under single illumination. Moreover our method performs as well in the case of multiple illuminants, which is not handled by most previous methods. During the training phase, we only need one image per subject without illumination and pose limitations to recover the shape and texture information. Thus, the training set can be expanded easily with new subjects, which is desirable in a Face Recognition System.

In our experiments, we tested both images under single- and multiple- directional illuminations. At this time, there exist relatively few publicly available sets of images of faces under arbitrary illumination conditions, so we plan to continue validation of our method with a database with more types of light sources, e.g. area sources. There is human interactivity in the initialization of the model and the feature correspondences. We plan to integrate head pose estimation methods [32] for model initialization and optical flow algorithms for shape error estimation. In the face recognition phase, our method needs to search the whole pose space, we expect great speed-up with a pre-filter process(again using face pose estimation algorithms) to narrow the search space.

References

[1] Y. Adini, Y. Moses, and S. Ullman. Face recognition: The problem of compensating for changes in illumination direction. *PAMI*, 19(7):721–732, July 1997.

[2] R. Basri and D.W. Jacobs. Lambertian reflectance and linear subspaces. *PAMI*, 25(2):218–233, February 2003.

[3] P.N. Belhumeur, J.P. Hespanha, and D.J. Kriegman. Eigenfaces vs. fisherfaces: Recognition using class specific linear projection. *PAMI*, 19(7):711–720, 1997.

[4] P.N. Belhumeur and D.J. Kriegman. What is the set of images of an object under all possible illumination conditions. *IJCV*, 28(3):245–260, July 1998.

[5] J. Bigun, K. Choy, and H. Olsson. Evidence on skill differences of women and men concerning face recognition. *AVBPA*, pages 44–51, 2001.

[6] V. Blanz and T. Vetter. A morphable model for the synthesis of 3d-faces. In *SIGGRAPH*, 1999.

[7] V. Blanz and T. Vetter. Face recognition based on fitting a 3d morphable model. *PAMI*, 25(9):1063–1074, Sept. 2003.

[8] R. Cappelli, D. Maio, and D. Maltoni. Subspace classification for face recognition. *Biometric Authentication*, pages 133–142, 2002.

[9] K.I. Chang, K.W. Bowyer, and P.J. Flynn. Multi-modal 2d and 3d biometrics for face recognition. *AMFG*, pages 187–194, 2003.

[10] R. Chellappa, C.L. Wilson, and S. Sirohey. Human and machine recognition of faces: A survey. *PIEEE*, 83(5):705–740, May 1995.

[11] A.S. Georghiades, P.N. Belhumeur, and D.J. Kriegman. From few to many: Illumination cone models for face recognition under variable lighting and pose. *PAMI*, 23(6):643–660, June 2001.

[12] P.W. Hallinan. A low-dimensional representation of human faces for arbitrary lighting conditions. *CVPR*, pages 995–999, 94.

[13] R. Hartley and A. Zisserman. *Multiple View Geometry in Computer Vision*. Cambridge University Press, 2000.

[14] B.W. Hwang, V. Blanz, T. Vetter, and S.W. Lee. Face reconstruction from a small number of feature points. In *ICPR*, pages Vol II: 842–845, 2000.

[15] K.C. Lee, J. Ho, and D.J. Kriegman. Nine points of light: Acquiring subspaces for face recognition under variable lighting. In *CVPR*, pages I:519–526, 2001.

[16] S.Z. Li and J.W. Lu. Face recognition using the nearest feature line method. *Neural Networks*, 10(2):439–443, 1999.

[17] S.Z. Li, J. Yan, X. Hou, Z. Li, and H. Zhang. Learning low dimensional invariant signature of 3-d object under varying view and illumination from 2-d appearances. *ICCV*, pages 635–640, 2001.

[18] C. Liu and H. Wechsler. A gabor feature classifier for face recognition. *ICCV*, pages 270–275, 2001.

[19] X.M. Liu, T. Chen, and B.V.K.V. Kumar. Face authentication for multiple subjects using eigenflow. *Pattern Recognition, Special issue on Biometric*, Nov 2001.

[20] X. Lu and A.K. Jain. Resampling for face recognition. *AVBPA03*, pages 869–877.

[21] H. Murase and S.K. Nayar. Visual learning and recognition of 3-d objects from appearance. *IJCV*, 14(1):5–24, January 1995.

[22] R. Ramamoorthi. Analytic pca construction for theoretical analysis of lighting variability in images of a lambertian object. *PAMI*, 24(10), Oct. 2002.

[23] S. Romdhani, V. Blanz, and T. Vetter. Face identification by fitting a 3d morphable model using linear shape and texture error functions. In *ECCV*, 2002.

[24] M Sadeghi, J. Kittler, A. Kostin, and K. Messer. A comparative study of automatic face verification algorithms on the banca database. *AVBPA*, pages 35–43, 2003.

[25] A. Shashua. Illumination and view position in 3d visual recognition. In *NIPS*, 1991.

[26] A. Shashua and Riklin Raviv. T. The quotient image: Class based re-rendering and recognition with varying illuminations. *PAMI*, 23(2):129–139, 2001.

[27] T. Sim, S. Baker, and M. Bsat. The cmu pose, illumination, and expression (pie) database of human faces. In *AFGR*, pages 46–51, 2002.

[28] M. Tistarelli, A. Lagorio, and E. Grosso. Understanding iconic image-based face biometrics. *Biometric Authentication*, pages 19–29, 2002.

[29] M. Turk and A.P. Pentland. Eigenfaces for recognition. *CogNeuro*, 3(1):71–96, 1991.

[30] H. Wang, S.Z. Li, Y. Wang, and W. Zhang. Illumination modeling and normalization for face recognition. In *Proc ICCV Workshop on Analysis and Modeling of Faces and Gestures*, 2003.

[31] Y. Wang, T. Tan, and A.K. Jain. Combining face and iris biometrics for identity verification. *AVBPA*, pages 805–813, 2003.

[32] Y. Wei, L. Fradet, and T. Tan. Head pose estimation using gabor eigenspace modeling. In *ICIP*, pages I: 281–284, 2002.

[33] J. Yang, D. Zhang, and A.F. Frangi. Two-dimensional pca: A new approach to appearance-based face representation and recognition. *PAMI*, 26(1):131–137, 2004.

[34] L. Zhang and D. Samaras. Face recognition under variable lighting using harmonic image exemplars. In *CVPR*, pages I: 19–25, 2003.

[35] W. Zhao, R. Chellappa, A. Rosenfeld, and P.J. Phillips. Face recognition: A literature survey. In *UMD Technical Report CAR-TR948*, 2000.

[36] W.Y. Zhao and R. Chellappa. Illumination-insensitive face recognition using symmetric shape-from-shading. In *CVPR*, pages I: 286–293, 2000.

Biometric Face Authentication Using Pixel-Based Weak Classifiers

Sébastien Marcel and Yann Rodriguez

Dalle Molle Institute for Perceptual Artificial Intelligence (IDIAP)
CP 592,
rue du Simplon 4,
1920 Martigny, Switzerland
marcel@idiap.ch
http://www.idiap.ch

Abstract. The performance of face authentication systems has steadily improved over the last few years. State-of-the-art methods use the projection of the gray-scale face image into a Linear Discriminant subspace as input of a classifier such as Support Vector Machines or Multi-layer Perceptrons. Unfortunately, these classifiers involve thousands of parameters that are difficult to store on a smart-card for instance. Recently, boosting algorithms has emerged to boost the performance of simple (weak) classifiers by combining them iteratively. The famous AdaBoost algorithm have been proposed for object detection and applied successfully to face detection. In this paper, we investigate the use of AdaBoost for face authentication to boost weak classifiers based simply on pixel values. The proposed approach is tested on a benchmark database, namely XM2VTS. Results show that boosting only hundreds of classifiers achieved near state-of-the-art results. Furthermore, the proposed approach outperforms similar work on face authentication using boosting algorithms on the same database.

1 Introduction

Identity authentication is a general task that has many real-life applications such as access control, transaction authentication (in telephone banking or remote credit card purchases for instance), voice mail, or secure teleworking.

The goal of an *automatic identity authentication system* is to either accept or reject the identity claim made by a given person. Biometric identity authentication systems are based on the characteristics of a person, such as its face, fingerprint or signature. A good introduction to identity authentication can be found in [1]. Identity authentication using face information is a challenging research area that was very active recently, mainly because of its natural and non-intrusive interaction with the authentication system.

The paper is structured as follow. In section 2 we first introduce the reader to the problem of face authentication.

D. Maltoni and A.K. Jain (Eds.): BioAW 2004, LNCS 3087, pp. 24–31, 2004.

Then, we present the proposed approach, boosting pixel-based classifiers for face authentication. We then compare our approach to state-of-the-results on the benchmark database XM2VTS. Finally, we analyze the results and conclude.

2 Face Authentication

2.1 Problem Description

An identity authentication system has to deal with two kinds of events: either the person claiming a given identity is the one who he claims to be (in which case, he is called a *client*), or he is not (in which case, he is called an *impostor*). Moreover, the system may generally take two decisions: either *accept* the *client* or *reject* him and decide he is an *impostor*.

The classical face authentication process can be decomposed into several steps, namely *image acquisition* (grab the images, from a camera or a VCR, in color or gray levels), *image processing* (apply filtering algorithms in order to enhance important features and to reduce the noise), *face detection* (detect and localize an eventual face in a given image) and finally *face authentication* itself, which consists in verifying if the given face corresponds to the claimed identity of the client.

In this paper, we assume (as it is often done in comparable studies, but nonetheless incorrectly) that the detection step has been performed perfectly and we thus concentrate on the last step, namely the face authentication step. The problem of face authentication has been addressed by different researchers and with different methods. For a complete survey and comparison of different approaches see [2].

2.2 State-of-the-Art Methods

The representation used to code input images in most state-of-the-art methods are often based on gray-scale face image [3, 4] or its projection into Principal Component subspace or Linear Discriminant subspace [5, 6]. In this section, we briefly introduce one of the best method [5].

Principal Component Analysis (PCA) identifies the subspace defined by the eigenvectors of the covariance matrix of the training data. The projection of face images into the coordinate system of eigenvectors (Eigenfaces) [7] associated with nonzero eigenvalues achieves information compression, decorrelation and dimensionality reduction to facilitate decision making. A Linear Discriminant is a simple linear projection $\hat{y} = b + \mathbf{w} \cdot \mathbf{x}$ of the input vector onto an output dimension, where the estimated output $\hat{y}$ is a function of the input vector $\mathbf{x}$, and the parameters $\{b, \mathbf{w}\}$ are chosen according to a given criterion such as the Fisher criterion [8]. A Linear Discriminant is a simple linear projection where the projection matrix is chosen according to a given criterion such as the Fisher criterion [8]. The Fisher criterion aims at maximizing the ratio of between-class scatter to within-class scatter. Finally, the Fisher Linear Discriminant subspace holds more discriminant features for classification [9] than the PCA subspace.

In [5], the projection of a face image into the system of Fisher-faces yields a representation which will emphasize the discriminatory content of the image. The main decision tool is Support Vector Machines (SVMs).

The above approach involves thousands of parameters that are difficult to store on a smart-card for instance. New approaches should be investigate to build classifiers using only hundreds of parameters. Recently, boosting algorithms has emerged to boost the performance of simple (weak) classifiers by combining them iteratively. The famous **AdaBoost** algorithm have been proposed for object detection [10] and applied successfully to face detection [11]. AdaBoost have been applied also to face authentication [12] to boost classifiers based on Haar-like features (Fig. 1) as described in [11]. Unfortunately, this boosting approach has obtained results far from the state-of-the-art.

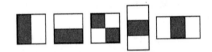

Fig. 1. Five types of Haar-like features.

3   The Proposed Approach

In face authentication, we are interested in particular objects, namely faces. The representation used to code input images in most state-of-the-art methods are often based on gray-scale face image. Thus, we propose to use AdaBoost to boost weak classifiers based simply on pixel values.

3.1   Feature Extraction

In a real application, the face bounding box will be provided by an accurate face detector [13, 14] but here the bounding box is computed using manually located eyes coordinates, assuming a perfect face detection. In this paper, the face bounding box is determined using face/head anthropometry measures [15] according to a face model (Fig. 2).

The face bounding box w/h crops the physiognomical height of the face. The width w of the face is given by zy_zy/s where s = 2·pupil_se/x_ee and x_ee is the distance between eyes in pixels. In this model, the ratio w/h is equal to the ratio 15/20. Thus, the height h of the face is given by w·20/15 and y_upper = h·(tr_gn - en_gn) / tr_gn. The constants pupil_se (pupil-facial middle distance), en_gn (lower half of the craniofacial height), tr_gn (height of the face), and zy_zy (width of the face) can be found in [15].

The extracted face is downsized to a 15x20 image. Then, we perform histogram normalization to modify the contrast of the image in order to enhance

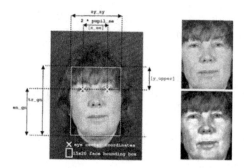

Fig. 2. Face modeling and pre-processing. On the left: the face modeling using eyes center coordinates and facial anthropometry measures. On top-right: the original face image. On the bottom-right: the pre-processed face image.

important features. Finally, we smooth the enhanced image by convolving a 3x3 Gaussian ($\sigma = 0.25$) in order to reduce the noise. After enhancement and smoothing (Fig. 2), the face image becomes a feature vector of dimension 300.

3.2   Boosting Weak Classifiers

Introduction A complete introduction to the theoretical basis of boosting and its applications can be found in [16]. The underlying idea of boosting is to linearly combine simple weak classifiers $h_i(x)$ to build a strong ensemble $f(x)$:

$$f(x) = \sum_{i=1}^{n} \alpha_i h_i(x)$$

Both coefficients α_i and hypothesis $h_i(x)$ are learned by the boosting algorithm. Each classifier $h_i(x)$ aims to minimize the training error on a particular distribution of the training examples.

At each iteration (i.e. for each weak classifier), the boosting procedure modifies the weight of each pattern in such a way that the misclassified samples get more weight in the next iteration. Boosting hence focuses on the examples that are hard to classify.

AdaBoost [17] is the most well known boosting procedure. It has been used in numerous empirical studies and have received considerable attention from the machine learning community in the last years. Freund et al. [17] showed two interesting properties of AdaBoost. First, the training error exponentially goes down to zero as the number of classifiers grows. Second, AdaBoost still learns after the training error reaches zero. Regarding the last point, Schapire et al. [18] shown that AdaBoost not only classifies samples correctly, but also compute hypothesis with large margins The margin of an example is defined as its signed distance to the hyperplane times its label. A positive margin means that the example is well classified. This observation has motivated searching for boosting procedures which maximize the margin [19, 20]. It has been shown that maximizing the margin minimizes the generalization error [18].

Boosting Pixel-Based Weak Classifiers We choose to boost weak classifiers based simply on pixel values, as described in [10] for face detection. The weak classifier h_i to boost is given by:

$$h_i(x) = \begin{cases} 1 & : \quad x_{f_i} \leq \theta_i \\ 0 & : \quad x_{f_i} > \theta_i \end{cases}$$

where x is the given input image, f_i is the index of the pixel to test in the image x and θ_i is a threshold. AdaBoost estimates iteratively the best feature $\{f_i, \theta_i\}$ for $1 \leq i \leq 300$.

4   The XM2VTS Database and Protocol

The XM2VTS database contains synchronized image and speech data recorded on 295 subjects during four sessions taken at one month intervals. The 295 subjects were divided, according to the *Lausanne Protocol* [21], into a set of 200 clients, 25 evaluation impostors, and 70 test impostors. Two different evaluation configurations were defined. They differ in the distribution of client training and client evaluation data. Both the training client and evaluation client data were drawn from the same recording sessions for Configuration I (LP1) which might lead to biased estimation on the evaluation set and hence poor performance on the test set. For Configuration II (LP2) on the other hand, the evaluation client and test client sets are drawn from different recording sessions which might lead to more realistic results. This led to the following statistics:

- Training client accesses: 3 for LP1 and 4 for LP2
- Evaluation client accesses: 600 for LP1 and 400 for LP2
- Evaluation impostor accesses: 40, 000 (25 * 8 * 200)
- Test client accesses: 400 (200 * 2)
- Test impostor accesses: 112, 000 (70 * 8 * 200)

Thus, the system may make two types of errors: *false acceptances* (FA), when the system accepts an *impostor*, and *false rejections* (FR), when the system rejects a *client*. In order to be independent on the specific dataset distribution, the performance of the system is often measured in terms of these two different errors, as follows:

$$FAR = \frac{\text{number of FAs}}{\text{number of impostor accesses}}, \tag{1}$$

$$FRR = \frac{\text{number of FRs}}{\text{number of client accesses}}. \tag{2}$$

A unique measure often used combines these two ratios into the so-called *Half Total Error Rate* (HTER) as follows:

$$\text{HTER} = \frac{\text{FAR} + \text{FRR}}{2} .$$ (3)

Most authentication systems output a score for each access. Selecting a threshold over which scores are considered genuine clients instead of impostors can greatly modify the relative performance of FAR and FRR. A typical threshold chosen is the one that reaches the *Equal Error Rate* (EER) where FAR=FRR on a separate validation set.

5   Experimental Results

In this section, we provide experimental[1] results obtained by our approach, pixel-based boosted weak classifiers, on the configuration I of the Lausanne Protocol. We compare the results obtained to the state-of-the-art and to similar work using AdaBoost.

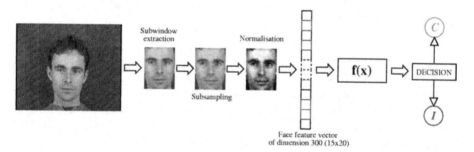

Fig. 3. Pixel-based boosted classifier for face authentication.

For each client, three shots are available. Each shot was slightly shifted, scaled and mirrored to obtain 220 examples. 2x220 patterns were used for training the client model and 1x220 patterns were used as a validation set to evaluate a threshold decision. The negative samples (pseudo-impostors) were generated by taking the three original shots of all other clients ((200-1) clients x 3 shots = 1194 patterns). A model has been trained for each client.

In table 1, we provide the results obtained by our boosting approach (*AdaPix*) using different number of classifiers (50, 100, 150, 200). We provide also results obtained by a state-of-the-art approach, namely Normalized Correlation (*NC*) [6], and results obtained using boosted classifiers based on seven Haar-like features [12] (*AdaHaar7*).

---

[1] The machine learning library used for all experiments is Torch *http://www.torch.ch.*

Table 1. Comparative results in terms of FAR/FRR and HTER for LP1

Model	FAR	FRR	HTER
NC [6]	3.46	2.75	3.1
AdaHaar7 200 [12]	6.9	8.8	7.85
AdaPix 50	3.34	4.0	3.67
AdaPix 100	3.16	3.5	3.33
AdaPix 150	3.11	3.5	3.30
AdaPix 200	2.75	3.0	**2.87**
AdaHaar3 100	2.29	5.0	3.64

From these results, it can be shown that the performance of *AdaPix* increase when increasing the number of classifiers. It can be shown also that they can be compared to the state-of-the-art (*NC*). *AdaPix* outperforms *AdaHaar7* with less classifiers. Furthermore, *AdaHaar7* obtained results far from the state-of-the-art. As a fair comparison, we used our AdaBoost algorithm to boost weak classifiers for the three first types (Fig. 1) of Haar-like features (*AdaHaar3*), and we obtained an HTER two times smaller than *AdaHaar7* with two times less classifiers.

6   Conclusion

In this paper, we proposed the use of AdaBoost for face authentication to boost weak classifiers based simply on pixel values. The proposed approach was tested on a benchmark database, namely XM2VTS, using its associate protocol. Results have shown that boosting only hundreds of classifiers achieved near state-of-the-art results. Furthermore, the proposed approach outperforms similar work on face authentication using boosting algorithms on the same database.

Boosting algorithms will certainly be used more and more often in face authentication. A new direction will be probably, to combine the efficiency of boosting algorithms with discriminant features such as LDA.

Acknowledgments

The author wants to thank the Swiss National Science Foundation for supporting this work through the National Center of Competence in Research (NCCR) on "Interactive Multimodal Information Management (IM2)".

References

[1] Verlinde, P., Chollet, G., Acheroy, M.: Multi-modal identity verification using expert fusion. Information Fusion **1** (2000) 17–33

[2] Zhang, J., Yan, Y., Lades, M.: Face recognition: Eigenfaces, Elastic Matching, and Neural Nets. In: Proceedings of IEEE. Volume 85. (1997) 1422–1435

[3] Marcel, S., Bengio, S.: Improving face verification using skin color information. In: Proceedings of the 16th ICPR, IEEE Computer Society Press (2002)

[4] Kostin, A., Sadeghi, M., Kittler, J., Messer, K.: On representation spaces for SVM based face verification. In: Proceedings of the COST275 Workshop on The Advent of Biometrics on the Internet, Rome, Italy (2002)

[5] Jonsson, K., Matas, J., Kittler, J., Li, Y.: Learning support vectors for face verification and recognition. In: 4th International Conference on Automatic Face and Gesture Recognition. (2000) 208–213

[6] Li, Y., Kittler, J., Matas, J.: On matching scores of LDA-based face verification. In Pridmore, T., Elliman, D., eds.: Proceedings of the British Machine Vision Conference BMVC2000, British Machine Vision Association (2000)

[7] Turk, M., Pentland, A.: Eigenface for recognition. Journal of Cognitive Neuroscience 3 (1991) 70–86

[8] Fisher, R.A.: The use of multiple measurements in taxonomic problems. Annals of Eugenics 7 (1936) 179–188

[9] Belhumeur, P., Hespanha, J.P., Kriegman, D.J.: Eigenfaces vs. Fisherfaces: Recognition using class specific linear projection. In: ECCV'96. (1996) 45–58 Cambridge, United Kingdom.

[10] V. Pavlovic and A. Garg: Efficient Detection of Objects and Attributes Using Boosting. In: Proceedings of the IEEE Conference on Computer Vision and Pattern Recognition. (2001)

[11] P. Viola and M. Jones: Robust Real-time Object Detection. In: IEEE ICCV Workshop on Statistical and Computational Theories of Vision. (2001)

[12] B. Fröba, S. Stecher and C. Kübleck: Boosting a Haar-Like Feature Set for Face Verification. In: Proceedings of Audio and Video based Person Authentication. (2003) 617–624

[13] Rowley, H.A., Baluja, S., Kanade, T.: Neural Network-based face detection. Transactions on Pattern Analysis and Machine Intelligence 20 (1998)

[14] Féraud, R., Bernier, O., Viallet, J.E., Collobert, M.: A fast and accurate face detector based on Neural Networks. Transactions on Pattern Analysis and Machine Intelligence 23 (2001)

[15] Farkas, L.: Anthropometry of the Head and Face. Raven Press (1994)

[16] R. Meir and G. Rätsch: An introduction to Boosting and Leveraging. (2003)

[17] Y. Freund and R. E. Schapire: Experiments with a new boosting algorithm. In: Proceedings of the IEEE International Conference on Machine Learning. (1996) 148–156

[18] Schapire, R., Freund, Y., Bartlett, P., Lee, W.: "Boosting the margin: a new explanation to the effectiveness of voting methods". Annals of statistics 26 (1998)

[19] G. Rätsch, T. Onoda and K.-R. Muller: "Soft margins for AdaBoost". Machine Learning 42 (2001) 287–320

[20] G. Rätsch and M.W. Warmuth: Efficient Margin Maximization with Boosting. In: submitted to JMLR-2002. (2002)

[21] Lüttin, J.: Evaluation protocol for the the XM2FDB database (lausanne protocol). Technical Report COM-05, IDIAP (1998)

Null Space Approach of Fisher Discriminant Analysis for Face Recognition

Wei Liu[1], Yunhong Wang[1], Stan Z. Li[2], Tieniu Tan[1]

[1] Institute of Automation, Chinese Academy of Sciences,
100080 Beijing, China
{wliu, wangyh, tnt}@nlpr.ia.ac.cn
[2] Microsoft Research Asia, Beijing Sigma Center,
100080 Beijing, China
szli@microsoft.com

Abstract. The null space of the within-class scatter matrix is found to express most discriminative information for the small sample size problem (SSSP). The null space-based LDA takes full advantage of the null space while the other methods remove the null space. It proves to be optimal in performance. From the theoretical analysis, we present the NLDA algorithm and the most suitable situation for NLDA. Our method is simpler than all other null space approaches, it saves the computational cost and maintains the performance simultaneously. Furthermore, kernel technique is incorporated into discriminant analysis in the null space. Firstly, all samples are mapped to the kernel space through a better kernel function, called Cosine kernel, which is proposed to increase the discriminating capability of the original polynomial kernel function. Secondly, a truncated NLDA is employed. The novel approach only requires one eigenvalue analysis and is also applicable to the large sample size problem. Experiments are carried out on different face data sets to demonstrate the effectiveness of the proposed methods.

1 Introduction

Linear Discriminant Analysis (LDA) has been successfully applied to face recognition. The objective of LDA is to seek a linear projection from the image space onto a low dimensional space by maximizing the between-class scatter and minimizing the within-class scatter simultaneously. Belhumeur [1] compared Fisherface with Eigenface on the *HARVARD* and *YALE* face databases, and showed that LDA was better than PCA, especially under illumination variation. LDA was also evaluated favorably under the *FERET* testing framework [2], [7].

In many practical face recognition tasks, there are not enough samples to make the within-class scatter matrix S_w nonsingular, this is called a small sample size problem. Different solutions have been proposed to deal with it in using LDA for face recognition [1]-[6].

The most widely used methods (Fisherface) [1, 2, 3] applies PCA firstly to reduce the dimension of the samples to an intermediate dimension, which must be guaranteed not more than the rank of S_w so as to obtain a full-rank within-class scatter ma-

D. Maltoni and A.K. Jain (Eds.): BioAW 2004, LNCS 3087, pp. 32–44, 2004.

trix. Then standard LDA is used to extract and represent facial features. All these methods above do not consider the importance of null space of the within-class scatter matrix, and remove the null space to make the resulting within-class scatter full-rank.

Yang et al. [4] proposed a new algorithm which incorporates the concept of null space. It first removes the null space of the between-class scatter matrix S_b and seeks a projection to minimize the within-class scatter (called Direct LDA / DLDA). Because the rank of S_b is smaller than that of S_w, removing the null space of S_b may lose part of or the entire null space of S_w, which is very likely to be full-rank after the removing operation.

Chen et al. [5] proposed a more straightforward method that makes use of the null space of S_w. The basic idea is to project all the samples onto the null space of S_w, where the resulting within-class scatter is zero, and then maximize the between-class scatter. This method involves computing eigenvalue in a very large dimension since S_w is an $n \times n$ matrix. To avoid the great computational cost, pixel grouping method is used in advance to artificially extract features and to reduce the dimension of the original samples.

Huang et al. [6] introduced a more efficient null space approach. The basic notion behind the algorithm is that the null space of S_w is particularly useful in discriminating ability, whereas, that of S_b is useless. They proved that the null space of the total scatter matrix S_t is the common null space of both S_w and S_b. Hence the algorithm firstly removes the null space of S_t and projects the samples onto the null space of S_w. Then it removes the null space of the between-class scatter in the subspace to get the optimal discriminant vectors.

Although null space-based LDA seems to be more efficient than other linear subspace analysis methods for face recognition, it is still a linear technique in nature. Hence it is inadequate to describe the complexity of real face images because of illumination, facial expression and pose variations. The kernel technique has been extensively demonstrated to be capable of efficiently representing complex nonlinear relations of the input data. Kernel Fisher Discriminant Analysis [8, 9, 10] (KFDA) is an efficient nonlinear subspace analysis method, which combines the kernel technique with LDA. After the input data are mapped into an implicit feature space, LDA is performed to yield nonlinear discriminating features of the input data.

In this paper, some elements of state-of-the-art null space techniques will be looked at in more depth and our null space approach is proposed to save the computational cost and maintain the performance simultaneously. Furthermore, we concentrate on the advantages of both the null space approach and the kernel technique. A kernel mapping based on an efficient kernel function, called Cosine kernel, is performed on all the samples firstly. In kernel space, we can find that the total scatter matrix is full-rank, so the procedure of the null space approach is greatly simplified and more stable in numerical computation.

The paper is laid out as follows. In Section 2, the related work on LDA-based algorithms will be reviewed. Next, our null space method (NLDA) will be presented. In Section 4 null space-based KFDA (NKFDA) will be proposed and some experiments will be reported in Section 5. Finally, Section 6 ends with some conclusions.

2 Previous Work

Some assumptions and definitions in mathematics are provided at first. Let n denote the dimension of the original sample space, and c is the number of classes. The between-class scatter matrix S_b and the within-class scatter S_w are defined as below:

$$S_b = \sum_{i=1}^{c} N_i (m_i - m)(m_i - m)^T = \Phi_b \Phi_b^T ,\tag{1}$$

$$S_w = \sum_{i=1}^{c} \sum_{k \in C_i} (x_k - m_i)(x_k - m_i)^T = \Phi_w \Phi_w^T ,\tag{2}$$

where N_j is the number of samples in class C_i ($i=1,2,...,c$), N is the number of all samples, m_j is the mean of the samples in the class C_i, and m is the overall mean of all samples. The total scatter matrix i.e. the covariance matrix of all the samples is defined as:

$$S_t = S_b + S_w = \sum_{i=1}^{N} (x_i - m)(x_i - m)^T = \Phi_t \Phi_t^T .\tag{3}$$

LDA tries to find an optimal projection: $W = [w_1, w_2, w_3, ..., w_{c-1}]$, which satisfies

$$J(W) = \arg \max_{W} \frac{\left| W^T S_b W \right|}{\left| W^T S_w W \right|} ,\tag{4}$$

that is just Fisher criterion function.

2.1 Standard LDA and Direct LDA

As well known, W can be constructed by the eigenvectors of $S_w^{-1} S_b$. But this method is numerically unstable because it involves the direct inversion of a likely high-dimensional matrix. The most frequently used LDA algorithm in practice is based on simultaneous diagonalization. The basic idea of the algorithm is to find a matrix W that can simultaneously diagonalize both S_w and S_b, i.e.,

$$W^T S_w W = I , W^T S_b W = \Lambda .\tag{5}$$

Most algorithms require that S_w be non-singular, because the algorithms diagonalize S_w first. The above procedure will break down when S_w becomes singular. It surely happens when the number of training samples is smaller than the dimension of the sample vector, i.e. the small sample size problem (SSSP). The singularity exists for most face recognition tasks.

An available solution to this problem is to perform PCA to project the n-dimensional image space onto a lower dimensional subspace. The PCA step essentially removes null space from both S_w and S_b. Therefore, this step potentially loses useful information.

In fact, the null space of S_w contains the most discriminative information especially when the projection of S_b is not zero in that direction. The Direct LDA (DLDA) algorithm [4] is presented to keep the null space of S_w.

DLDA removes the null space of S_b firstly by performing eigen-analysis on S_b, then a simultaneous procedure is used to seek the optimal discriminant vectors in the subspace of S_b, i.e.

$$W^T S_b W = I, W^T S_w W = D_w .$$ (6)

Because the rank of S_b is smaller than that of S_w in majority, removing the null space of S_b may lose part of or the entire null space of S_w, which is very likely to be full-rank after the removing operation. So, DLDA does not make full use of the null space.

2.2 Null Space-Based LDA

From Fisher's criterion that is objective function (4), we can find that: In standard LDA, W is seeked such that (5), so the form of the optimal solution provided by standard LDA is

$$optimum_{LDA} = \max_W |W^T S_b W| / |W^T S_w W| = |\Lambda| = opt \max / 1 .$$ (7)

In DLDA, W is seeked such that (6), so the form of the optimal solution provided by DLDA is

$$optimum_{DLDA} = \max_W |W^T S_b W| / |W^T S_w W| = 1 / |D_w| = 1 / opt \min .$$ (8)

Compared with above LDA approaches, a more reasonable method (Chen [5]), we called Null Space-based LDA, has been presented. In Chen's theory, null space-based LDA should reach below:

$$optimum_{Null} = \max_W |W^T S_b W| / |W^T S_w W| = opt \max / 0 .$$ (9)

That means the optimal projection W should satisfy

$$W^T S_w W = 0, W^T S_b W = \Lambda ,$$ (10)

i.e. the optimal discriminant vectors must exist in the null space of S_w.

In a performance benchmark, we can conclude that null space-based LDA generally outperforms LDA (Fisherface) or DLDA since

$$optimum_{Null} = \infty \geq optimum_{DLDA} \geq optimum_{LDA} .$$ (11)

Because the computational complexity of extracting the null space of S_w is very high because of the high dimension of S_w. So in [5] a pixel grouping operation is used in advance to extract geometric features and to reduce the dimension of the samples. However, the pixel grouping preprocess is irresponsible and may arouse a loss of useful facial features.

3 Our Null Space Method (NLDA)

In this section, the essence of null space-based LDA in the SSSP is revealed by theoretical justification, and the most suitable situation of null space methods is discovered. Next, we propose the NLDA algorithm, which is conceptually simple yet powerful in performance.

3.1 Most Suitable Situation

For the small sample size problem (SSSP) in which $n>N$, the dimension of null space of S_w is very large, and not all null space contributes to the discriminative power. Since both S_b and S_w are symmetric and semi-positive, we can prove, as mentioned in [6], that

$$N(S_t) = N(S_b) \bigcap N(S_w) . \tag{12}$$

From the statistical perspective, the null space of S_b is of no use in its contribution to discriminative ability. Therefore, the useful subspace of null space of S_w is

$$\hat{N}(S_w) = N(S_w) - N(S_t) = N(S_w) \bigcap \overline{N(S_t)} . \tag{13}$$

The sufficient and necessary condition so that null space methods work is

$$\hat{N}(S_w) \neq \Phi \Rightarrow N(S_w) \supset N(S_t) \Rightarrow \dim N(S_w) > \dim N(S_t) \Rightarrow$$

$$rank(S_t) > rank(S_w) . \tag{14}$$

In many cases,

$$rank(S_t) = \min\{n, N-1\}, rank(S_w) = \min\{n, N-c\} , \tag{15}$$

the dimension of discriminative null space of S_w can be evaluated from (12):

$$\dim \hat{N}(S_w) = rank(S_t) - rank(S_w) . \tag{16}$$

If $n \leq N-c$, due to $rank(S_t) = n \leq rank(S_w) = N-c$, the necessary condition (14) is not satisfied so that we can not extract any null space. That means any null space-based method does not work in the large sample size case.

If $N-c < n < N-1$, due to $rank(S_t) = n > rank(S_w) = N-c$, the dimension of effective null space can be evaluated from (16): $\dim \hat{N}(S_w) = n - N + c < c - 1$. Hence, the number of discriminant vectors would be less than c-1, and some discriminatory information maybe lost.

Only when $n \geq N-1$ (SSSP), for $rank(S_t) = N-1 > rank(S_w) = N-c$, we derive $\dim \hat{N}(S_w) = c-1$. The dimension of extracted null space is just c-1, which coincides with the number of ideal features for classification. Therefore, we can conclude that null space methods are always applicable to any small sample size problem.

Especially when n is equal to N-1, S_t is full-rank and $N(S_t)$ is null. By (13) we have $\hat{N}(S_w) = N(S_w)$, it follows all null space of S_w contributes to the discriminative power. Hence, we conclude the most suitable situation for null space-based methods:

$$n = N-1 . \tag{17}$$

3.2 NLDA

Combining (12)-(16), we develop our null space method.

algorithm I:

1. Remove the null space of S_t.

   Perform PCA to project the n-dimensional image space onto a low dimensional subspace, i.e. perform eigen-analysis on S_t., the dimension of the extracted subspace is usually N-1. The projection P, whose columns are all the eigenvectors of S_t corresponding to the nonzero eigenvalues, are calculated firstly, and then the within-class scatter and between-class scatter in the resulting subspace are obtained.

$$P^T S_t P = D_t, \quad P^T S_w P = S_w', \quad P^T S_b P = S_b'.$$

2. Extract the null space of S_w'.

   Diagonalize S_w', we have

$$V^T S_w' V = D_w,$$

   where $V^T V = I, D_w$ is diagonal matrix sorted in increasing order. Discard those with eigenvalues sufficiently far from 0, keep c-1 eigenvectors of S_w' in most cases. Let Y be the first c-1 columns of V, which is the null space of S_w', we have

$$Y^T S_w' Y = 0, \quad Y^T S_b' Y = S_b''.$$

3. Diagonalize S_b'' (usually a $(c$-1$)\times(c$-1$)$ matrix) which is full-rank.

   Perform eigen-analysis:

$$U^T S_b'' U = \Lambda,$$

   where $U^T U = I, \Lambda$ is diagonal matrix sorted in decreasing order.

   The final projection matrix is:

$$W = PYU,$$

W is usually an $n\times(c$-1$)$ matrix, which diagonalizes both the numerator and the denominator of Fisher's criterion to $(c$-1$)\times(c$-1$)$ matrices as (10) , especially leads to a denominator of 0 matrix.

It is notable that the third step of Huang [6]' algorithm is used to remove the null space of S_b''. In fact, we are able to prove that it is full-rank once through the previous two steps.

Lemmas S_b'' is full-rank, S_b'' is defined in step2 of algorithm I.

Proof:

From step1 and 2, we derive that $S_b'' = Y^T S_b' Y = Y^T S_b' Y + Y^T S_w' Y = Y^T (S_b' + S_w')Y = Y^T P^T (S_b + S_w)PY = Y^T P^T S_t PY = Y^T D_t Y$, for any vector α whose dimension is equal to that of S_b'', $\alpha^T S_b'' \alpha = \alpha^T Y^T D_t Y\alpha = (D_t^{1/2} Y\alpha)^T (D_t^{1/2} Y\alpha) \geq 0$, so S_b'' is semi-positive. Suppose there exists α such that $\alpha^T S_b'' \alpha = 0$, then $D_t^{1/2} Y\alpha = 0$. By step1, we know D_t is full-rank, thus $Y\alpha = 0$. And by step2, we derive that Y is full-rank in columns since it is the extracted null space. Hence $\alpha = 0$, iff. $\alpha^T S_b'' \alpha = 0$. Therefore S_b'' is a positive matrix which is of course full-rank.□

The third step is optional. Although it maximizes the between-class scatter in the null subspace, which appears to achieve best discriminative ability, it may incur overfitting. Because projecting all samples onto the null space of S_w is powerful enough in its clustering ability to achieve good generalization performance, step3 of algorithm I should be eliminated in order to avoid possible overfitting.

NLDA algorithm:
1. Remove the null space of S_t, i.e.
$$P^T S_t P = D_t , \quad P^T S_w P = S_w' ,$$
P is usually $n \times (N-1)$.

2. Extract the null space of S_w', i.e.
$$Y^T S_w' Y = 0 ,$$
Y is the null space, and is usually $(N-1) \times (c-1)$.

The final NLDA projection matrix is:
$$W = PY ,$$
PY is the discriminative subspace of the whole null space of S_w and is really useful for discrimination. The number of the optimal discriminant vectors is usually $c-1$, which just coincides with the number of ideal discriminant vectors [1]. Therefore, removing step3 is a feasible strategy against overfitting.

Under situation (17), S_t is full-rank and step1 of the NLDA algorithm is skipped. The NLDA projection can be extracted by performing eigen-analysis on S_w directly. The procedure of NLDA under this situation is most straightforward and only requires one eigen-analysis. We can discover that NLDA will save much computational cost under the most suitable situation it is applicable to.

4 Null Space-Based Kernel Fisher Discriminant Analysis

The key idea of Kernel Fisher Discriminant Analysis (KFDA) [8, 9, 10] is to solve the problem of LDA in an implicit feature space F, which is constructed by the kernel trick:
$$\phi : x \in R^n \rightarrow \phi(x) \in F . \tag{18}$$

The important feature of kernel techniques is that the implicit feature vector ϕ needn't be computed explicitly, while the inner product of any two vectors in F need to be computed based a kernel function.

In this section, we will present a novel method (NKFDA) in which kernel technique is incorporated into discriminant analysis in the null space.

4.1 Kernel Fisher Discriminant Analysis (KFDA)

The between-class scatter S_b and the within-class scatter S_w in F are computed as (1) and (2). But at this time, we replace x_j by $\phi(x_j)$ as samples in F. Consider performing LDA in the implicit feature space F. It caters for maximizing the Fisher criterion function (4).

Because any solution $w \in F$ must lie in the span of all the samples in F, there exist coefficients α_i, $i=1,2...N$, such that

$$w = \sum_{i=1}^{N} \alpha_i \phi_i .$$ (19)

Substitute w in (4), the solution of (4) can be obtained by solve a new Fisher problem:

$$J(\alpha) = \arg\max_{\alpha} \frac{|\alpha^T K_b \alpha|}{|\alpha^T K_w \alpha|} ,$$ (20)

where K_b and K_w (Liu [8]) are based on new samples:

$$\zeta_i = (k(x_1, x_i), k(x_2, x_i), ..., k(x_N, x_i))^T, 1 \le i \le N .$$ (21)

As for the kernel function, Liu [13] proposed a novel kernel function called Cosine kernel, which is based on the original polynomial kernel, has been demonstrated to improve the performance of KFDA. It is defined as below:

$$k(x, y) = (\phi(x) \cdot \phi(y)) = (a(x \cdot y) + b)^d ,$$ (22)

$$\tilde{k}(x, y) = \frac{k(x, y)}{\sqrt{k(x, x)k(y, y)}} .$$ (23)

In our experiments, Cosine kernel ($a=10^{-3}/sizeof$ (image), $b=0$, $d=2$) is adopted and shows good performance in face recognition. Cosine measurement should be more reliable than inner production measurement due to a better similarity representation in the implicit feature space.

4.2 NKFDA

Here we define a kernel sample set (corresponding to the kernel space in N dimensions) $\{\zeta_i\}_{1 \le i \le N}$. The optimal solution of (4) is equivalent to that of (20), so the original problem can be entirely converted to the problem of LDA on the kernel sample set.

In section 3, we know that NLDA will save much computational cost under the most suitable situation. The null space projection can be extracted from the within-class scatter directly. Our objective is just to transform the dimension of all the samples from n to N-1 through the kernel mapping, so that NLDA can work under the most suitable situation. Any method that can transform raw samples to $(N-1)$-dimensional data without adding or losing main information, can exploit the merit of NLDA.

In (19), all the training samples in F, $\{\phi_i\}_{1 \le i \le N}$, are used to represent w. Define the kernel matrix M,

$$M = (k(x_i, x_j))_{1 \le i, j \le N} = (k_{i,j})_{1 \le i, j \le N} ,$$ (24)

assume $\Phi = (\phi_1, \phi_2, ..., \phi_N)$, then $M = \Phi^T \Phi$. In mathematics,

$$rank(\Phi) = rank(M) .$$ (25)

Because $rank(M) < N$ holds, especially when the training data set is very large, it follows that $rank(M) \ll N$ [11][12], we conclude that

$$rank(\Phi) \ll N \ . \tag{26}$$

Due to (26), we may assume ϕ_N is not a basis vector of $\{\phi_i\}_{1 \le i \le N}$ without loss of generality, and consequently we can rewrite (19) as follows:

$$w = \sum_{i=1}^{N-1} \alpha_i \phi_i \ , \tag{27}$$

subsequently, K_b and K_w are recomputed, we derive :

$$\zeta_i = (k(x_1, x_i), k(x_2, x_i), ..., k(x_{N-1}, x_i))^T \ . \tag{28}$$

Now the dimension of our defined kernel space is $N-1$. My objective is just to enable NLDA work on the $(N-1)$-dimensional kernel sample set.

Input: 1) training samples $\{x_i\}_{1 \le i \le N}$ and label set $\{C_j\}_{1 \le j \le c}$

2) the kernel function and its parameters: $k(x, y)$

Algorithm:

1. For $i = 1,2,...,N$

do kernel mapping on each training sample:

$$K(x_i) = (k(x_1, x_i), k(x_2, x_i), ..., k(x_{N-1}, x_i))^T \ .$$

For a new sample x, whose corresponding point in the kernel space is

$$K(x) = (k(x_1, x), k(x_2, x), ..., k(x_{N-1}, x))^T \ .$$

2. Calculate class mean and within-class scatter:

$$m_j = \sum_{i \in C_j} K(x_i) / N_j \ ,$$

$$K_w = \sum_{j=1}^{c} \sum_{i \in C_j} (K(x_i) - m_j)(K(x_i) - m_j)^T \ .$$

3. Extract the null space Y of K_w $(N-1 \times N-1)$, such that

$Y^T K_w Y = 0$, Y is usually in $(N-1) \times (c-1)$.

Output: The resulting mapping on the raw sample set:

$$\Psi(x) = (Y^T K) \cdot (x) = Y^T \cdot K(x) \ .$$

Fig. 1. NKFDA algorithm

As shown in Fig. 1, NKFDA algorithm outputs the mapping Ψ which is a nonlinear dimensionality reduction mapping (n dimensions reduce to $c-1$). For any sample (whether it is a prototype or a query), Ψ provides a universal mapping to transform the raw sample point into a lower dimensional space. Such a technique can be applied with a reasonable implementation of generalization.

It's noticeable that our method NKFDA also cannot deal with the case that only one sample per person is available for training since KFDA can not achieve that.

For the large sample size problem ($n \ll N$), S_w is full-rank so that we can not extract any null space. That means any null space-based method does not work in the large sample size case. However, after the kernel mapping, NLDA can work on the kernel sample set. Hence the kernel mapping extends the ability of null space approaches to the large sample size problem.

5 Experiments

To demonstrate the efficiency of our method, extensive experiments are done on the ORL face database, the FERET database and the mixture database. All LDA methods were compared on the same training sets and testing sets, including Fisherface proposed in [1, 2, 3], Direct LDA proposed in [4], and our methods: NLDA and NKFDA.

5.1 ORL Database

There are 10 different images for each subject in the ORL face database composed of 40 distinct subjects. All the subjects are in up-right, frontal position. The size of each face image is 92×112. The first line of Fig. 2 shows 6 images of the same subject.

We listed the recognition rates with different number of training samples. The number of training samples per subject, k, increases from 2 to 9. In each round, k images are randomly selected from the database for training and the remaining images of the same subject for testing. For each k, 20 tests were performed and these results were averaged. Table 1 shows the average recognition rates (%). Without any pre-processing, we choose 39 (i.e. c-1) as the final dimensions. Our methods NLDA, NKFDA show an encouraging performance.

Table 1. Recognition rates on the ORL database

k	LDA	DLDA	NLDA	NKFDA
2	76.65	80.10	85.47	82.89
3	87.09	87.54	90.91	89.13
4	91.68	91.50	93.86	93.15
5	93.17	94.65	95.45	95.13
6	95.79	96.50	97.13	96.72
7	96.85	97.12	97.54	97.21
8	98.25	99.15	98.95	98.95
9	99.00	99.95	99.15	99.38

5.2 FERET Database

We have to test our method on more complex and challenging datasets such as the FERET database. We selected 70 subjects from the FERET database [7] with 6 up-right, frontal-view images of each subject. The face images involve much more variations in lighting, facial expressions and facial details. The second line of Fig. 2 shows one subject from the selected data set.

The eye locations are fixed by geometric normalization. The size of face images is normalized to 92×112, and 69 (i.e. c-1) features are extracted. Training and test process are similar to those on the *ORL* database. Similar comparisons between those methods are performed. This time k changes between 2 to 5, and the corresponding averaging recognition rates (%) are shown in table 2.

Table 2. Recognition rates on the FERET database

k	LDA	DLDA	NLDA	NKFDA
2	56.04	63.25	75.20	72.21
3	76.95	76.71	85.64	83.60
4	87.23	88.30	92.79	93.85
5	94.80	94.71	97.34	98.29

5.3 Mixture Database

To test NLDA and NKFDA on large datasets, we construct a mixture database of 125 persons and 985 images, which is a collection of three databases: (a). The *ORL* database (10×40). (b). The *YALE* database (11×15, the third line of Fig. 2 shows one subject). (c). The *FERET* database (6×70). All the images are resized to 92×112. There are facial expression, illumination and pose variations.

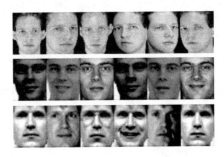

Fig. 2. Samples from the mixture database

The mixture database is divided into two non-overlapping set for training and testing. The training dataset consists of 500 images: 5 images, 6 images and 3 images per person are randomly selected from the *ORL*, the *YALE* database and the *FERET* subset respectively. The remaining 485 images are used for testing. In order to reduce the influence of some extreme illumination, histogram equalization is applied to the images as pre-processing. We compare the proposed method with Fisherface and DLDA, and the experimental results are shown in Fig. 3. It can be seen that NKFDA largely outperforms the other three when over 100 features are used, and a recognition rate of 91.65% can be achieved at the feature dimension of 124 (i.e. c-1).

5.4 Discussion

From the above three experiments, we can find that NKFDA is better than NLDA for large number of training samples (such as larger than 300), while worse than NLDA in the case of small training sample size (such as smaller than 200), and superior to DLDA in most situations. Consequently, NKFDA is more efficient in larger sample size, for the greater the sample size, the more accurately kernels can describe the nonlinear relations of samples.

As to computational cost, the most time-consuming procedure, eigen-analysis, is performed on three matrices (one of $N{\times}N$, and two of $(N\text{-}c) {\times}(N\text{-}c)$) in Fisherface method, on two matrices ($c{\times}c$ and $(c\text{-}1) {\times}(c\text{-}1)$) in DLDA, on two matrices ($N{\times}N$, $(N\text{-}1){\times}(N\text{-}1)$) in NLDA, and on one matrice ($(N\text{-}1){\times}(N\text{-}1)$) in NKFDA. Our method NKFDA only performs one eigen-analysis to achieve efficiency and good performance.

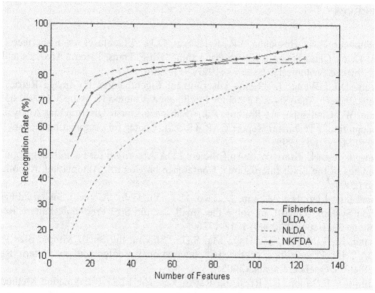

Fig. 3. Comparison of four methods

6   Conclusion

In this paper, we present two new subspace methods (NLDA, NKFDA) based on the null space approach and the kernel technique. Both of them effectively solve the small sample size problem and eliminate the possibility of losing discriminative information.

The main contributions of this paper are summarized as follows: (a) The essence of null space-based LDA in the SSSP is revealed by theoretical justification, and the most suitable situation of null space method is discovered. (b) Propose the NLDA algorithm, which is simpler than all other null space methods and saves the computational cost and maintains the performance simultaneously. (c) A more efficient Cosine kernel function is adopted to enhance the capability of the original polynomial kernel. (d) Present the NKFDA algorithm, which performs only one eigen-analysis and is more stable in numerical computation. (e) NKFDA is also applicable to the large sample size problem, and is superior to NLDA when the sample size is very large.

Acknowledgement This work is supported by research funds from the *Natural Science Foundation of China* (Grant No. 60332010). The authors thank the *Olivetti Research Laboratory* in Cambridge (UK) and the *FERET* program (USA) and the *YALE* University for their devotion of face databases, also thank Qingshan Liu and Zhouyu Fu for their constructive suggestions. Great appreciations especially to Yilin Dong for her encourage.

References

1. Belhumeur, P.N., Hespanha, J.P., Kriegman, D.J.: "Eigenfaces vs. Fisherfaces: Recognition Using Class Specific Linear Projection". IEEE Trans. Pattern Analysis and Machine Intelligence. Volume 19. Issue 7. (1997) 711-720
2. Swets, D.L., Weng, J.: "Using Discriminant Eigenfeatures for Image Retrieval". IEEE Trans. Pattern Analysis and Machine Intelligence. Volume 18. Issue 8. (1996) 831-836
3. Zhao, W., Chellappa, R., Phillips, P.J.: "Subspace Linear Discriminant Analysis for Face Recognition". Technical Report CAR-TR-914, Center for Automation Research, University of Maryland (1999)
4. Yang, J., Yu, H., Kunz, W.: "An Efficient LDA Algorithm for Face Recognition". In: Proceedings of the Sixth International Conference on Control, Automation, Robotics and Vision (2000)
5. Chen, L.F., Liao, H.Y.M., Lin, J.C., Ko, M.T., Yu, G.J.: "A New LDA-based Face Recognition System Which Can Solve the Small Sample Size Problem". Pattern Recognition. Volume 33. Issue 10. (2000) 1713-1726
6. Huang, R., Liu, Q.S., Lu, H.Q., Ma, S.D.: "Solving the Small Sample Size Problem of LDA". In: Proceedings of the 16th International Conference on Pattern Recognition (ICPR'02), Quebec, Canada (2002)
7. Phillips, P.J., Moon, H., Rizvi, S., Rauss, P.: "The FERET Evaluation Methodology for Face Recognition Algorithms". IEEE Trans. Pattern Analysis and Machine Intelligence. Volume 22. Issue 10. (2000) 1090—1104
8. Liu, Q.S., Huang, R., Lu, H.Q., Ma, S.D.: "Face Recognition Using Kernel Based Fisher Discriminant Analysis". In: Proceedings of Fifth IEEE International Conference on Automatic Face and Gesture Recognition, Washington DC, USA (2002)
9. Baudat, G., Anouar, F.: "Generalized Discriminant Analysis Using a Kernel Approach". Neural Computation. Volume 12. Issue 10. (2000) 2385-2404
10. Mika, S., Ratsch, G., Weston, J.: "Fisher Discriminant Analysis with Kernels". In: Proceedings of Neural Networks for Signal Processing Workshop, Madison, USA (1999)
11. Wu, Y., Huang T.S., Toyama, K.: "Self-Supervised Learning for Object based on Kernel Discriminant-EM Algorithm". In: Proceedings of IEEE International Conference on Computer Vision (ICCV'01), Vancouver BC, Canada (2001)
12. Baudat, G., Anouar, F.: "Kernel-based Methods and Function Approximation". In: Proceedings of International Joint Conference on Neural Networks, Washington DC, USA (2001)
13. Liu, Q.S., Lu, H.Q., Ma, S.D.: "Improving Kernel Fisher Discriminant Analysis for Face Recognition". IEEE Trans. Circuits and Systems for Video Technology. Vol. 14(1) (2004)

Statistical Learning of Evaluation Function for ASM/AAM Image Alignment

Xiangsheng Huang[1], Stan Z. Li[2], and Yangsheng Wang[1]

[1] Institute of Automation,Chinese Academy of Sciences, Beijing, China 100080
[2] Microsoft Research Asia, Beijing, China 100080

Abstract. Alignment between the input and target objects has great impact on the performance of image analysis and recognition system, such as those for medical image and face recognition. Active Shape Models (ASM)[1] and Active Appearance Models (AAM) [2, 3] provide an important framework for this task. However, an effective method for the evaluation of ASM/AAM alignment results has been lacking. Without an alignment quality evaluation mechanism, a bad alignment cannot be identified and this can drop system performance.

In this paper, we propose a statistical learning approach for constructing an evaluation function for face alignment. A *nonlinear* classification function is learned from a set of positive (good alignment) and negative (bad alignment) training examples to effectively distinguish between qualified and un-qualified alignment results. The AdaBoost learning algorithm is used, where weak classifiers are constructed based on edge features and combined into a strong classifier. Several strong classifiers is learned in stages using bootstrap samples during the training, and are then used in cascade in the test. Experimental results demonstrate that the classification function learned using the proposed approach provides semantically more meaningful scoring than the reconstruction error used in AAM for classification between qualified and un-qualified face alignment.

1 Introduction

Many image analysis and recognition application require alignment between an object in the input image and a target object. Alignment can have a great impact on the system performance. For examples, in appearance based face recognition, the alignment provide a more sensible foundation for template matching based recognition; the use of bad alignment can drop system performance significantly.

Active Shape Models (ASM) [1] and Active Appearance Models(AAM) [2, 3] have been used as alignment algorithms in medical image analysis and face recognition [4]. However, an effective method for the evaluation of ASM/AAM alignment results has been lacking: There has been no convergence criterion for ASM. As such, the ASM search can give a bad result without giving the user a warning. In the AAM, the PCA (Principal Component Analysis) reconstruction error is used as a distance measure for the evaluation of alignment quality (and for guiding the search as well). However, the reconstruction error may not be

D. Maltoni and A.K. Jain (Eds.): BioAW 2004, LNCS 3087, pp. 45–56, 2004.
© Springer-Verlag Berlin Heidelberg 2004

a good discriminant for the evaluation of alignment quality because a non-face can look like a face when projected onto the PCA face subspace.

In this paper, we propose a statistical learning approach for constructing an effective evaluation function for face alignment. A *nonlinear* classification function is learned from a training set of positive and negative training examples to effectively distinguish between qualified and un-qualified alignment results. The positive subset consists of qualified face alignment examples and the negative subset consists of obviously un-qualified and near-but-not-qualified examples.

We use AdaBoost algorithm [5, 6] for the learning. A set of candidate weak classifiers are created based on edge features extracted using Sobel-like operators. We choose to use edge features because crucial cues for alignment quality are around edges. Experimentally, we also found that the Sobel features produced significant better results than other features such as Haar wavelets. The AdaBoost learning selects or learns a sequence of best features and the corresponding weak classifiers and combines them into a strong classifier.

In the training stage several strong classifiers is learned in stages using bootstrap training samples, and in the test they are cascaded to form a stronger classifier, following an idea in boosting based face detection [7]. Such a divide-conquer strategy makes the training easier and the good-bad classification more effective. The evaluation function thus learned gives a quantitative confidence and the good-bad classification is achieved by comparing the confidence with a learned optimal threshold.

There are two important distinctions between an evaluation function thus learned and the linear evaluation function of reconstruction error used in AAM. First, the evaluation is learned in such a way to distinguish between good and bad alignment. Secondly, the scoring is nonlinear, which provides a semantically more meaningful classification between good and bad alignment. Experimental results demonstrate that the classification function learned using the proposed approach provides semantically meaningful scoring for classification between qualified and un-qualified face alignment.

The rest of the paper is organized as follows: Section 2 briefly describes the ASM method and the problem of alignment quality evaluation. AdaBoost based learning is presented in Section 3. Section 4 provides the construction of candidate weak classifiers. Section 5 proposes the learning of weak classifiers. Section 6 provides experimental results. Section 7 draws a conclusion.

2   ASM/AAM and Solution Quality Evaluation

Let us briefly describe the ASM and AAM methods before a discussion about the issue of alignment evaluation. The standard ASM consists of two statistical models: (1) global shape model, which is derived from the landmarks in the object contour; (2) local appearance models, which is derived from the profiles perpendicular to the object contour around each landmark. ASM uses local models to find the candidate shape and the global model to constrain the searched shape.

AAM makes use of the PCA techniques to model both shape variation and texture variation, and the correlations between the shape subspace and texture subspace to model the face. In searching for a solution, it assumes linear relationships between appearance variation and texture variation, and between texture variation and position variation; and learns the two linear regression models from training data. The minimizations in high dimensional space is reduced in two models facilitate. This strategy is also developed in the active blob model by Sclaroff and Isidoro [8].

While the training data for ASM consists of shape only, and that for AAM consists of both shape and texture. Denote a *shape* $S_0 = ((x_1, y_1), \ldots, (x_K, y_K)) \in \mathbb{R}^{2K}$ by a sequence of K points in the 2D image plane, and a *texture* T_0 using the patch of pixel intensities enclosed by S_0. Let $\overline{S}$ be the mean shape of all the training shapes, as illustrated in Fig. 1(a). Fig. 1(b) and (c) show two examples of shapes overlayed on the faces. In AAM, all the shapes are aligned or warping to the tangent space of the mean shape $\overline{S}$. After that, the texture T_0 is warped correspondingly to $T \in \mathbb{R}^L$, where L is the number of pixels in the mean shape $\overline{S}$. The warping may be done by pixel value interpolation, *e.g.* using a triangulation or thin plate spline method.

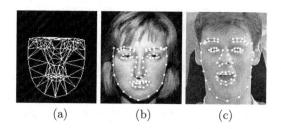

(a)   (b)   (c)

Fig. 1. (a) The mesh of the mean shape. (b) & (c): Two face instances labelled with 83 landmarks.

There has been no convergence criterion for ASM search nor quality evaluation. In ASM search, the mean shape is placed near the center of the detected image and a coarse to fine search performed. Large movements are made in the first few iterations, getting the position roughly. As the search progressing, more subtle adjustments are made. The result can gives a good match to the target image or it can fail (see Figure. 2). The failure can happen even if the starting position is near the target. When the variations of expression and illumination are large, ASM search can diverge in order to match the local image pattern.

In AAM search, the PCA reconstruction error is used to guide the search and used as the convergence and evaluation criterion. Such an error function is defined as the distance between the image patch (aimed to contain the face region only) after warping to the mean shape and the projection of the patch onto the PCA subspace of face texture. However, the reconstruction error may not be a good measure for the evaluation of alignment quality because a non-face

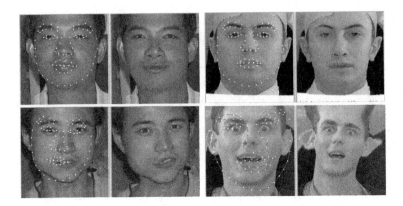

Fig. 2. Four face instances of qualified (top) and un-qualified (bottom) examples with their warped images

can look like a face when projected onto the PCA face subspace. Cootes pointed out that, of 2700 testing examples, 519 failed to converge to a satisfactory result (the mean point position error is greater than 7.5 pixels per point) [4].

In the following we present a learning based approach for learning evaluation function for ASM/AAM based alignment.

3   AdaBoost Based Learning

Our objective is to learn an evaluation function from a training set of qualified and un-qualified alignment examples. From now on, we use the terms positive and negative examples for classes of data. These examples are the face image after warping to mean shape, as shown in Fig. 2. Face alignment quality evaluation can be posed as a two class classification problem: given an alignment result x (*i.e.* warped face), the evaluation function $H(x) = +1$ if x is positive example, or -1 otherwise. we want to learn such an $H(x)$ that can provide a score in $[-1, +1]$ with a threshold around 0 for the binary classification.

For two class problems, a set of N labelled training examples is given as $(x_1, y_1), \ldots, (x_N, y_N)$, where $y_i \in \{+1, -1\}$ is the class label associated with example $x_i \in \mathbb{R}^n$. A stronger classifier is a linear combination of M weak classifiers

$$H_M(x) = \sum_{m=1}^{M} h_m(x) \tag{1}$$

In the real version of AdaBoost [5, 6], the weak classifiers can take a real value, $h_m(x) \in \mathbb{R}$, and have absorbed the coefficients needed in the discrete version ($h_m(x) \in -1, +1$ in the latter case). The class label for x is obtained as $H(x) = \text{sign}[H_M(x)]$ while the magnitude $|H_M(x)|$ indicates the confidence. Every training example is associated with a weight. During the learning process, the weights are updated dynamically in such a way that more emphasis is placed on hard examples which are erroneously classified previously. It is noted in recent studies [9, 10, 11] that the artificial operation of explicit re-weighting is unnecessary and can be incorporated into a functional optimization procedure of boosting.

---

0. (Input)
   (1) Training examples $\{(x_1, y_1), \ldots, (x_N, y_N)\}$,
       where $N = a + b$; of which a examples have $y_i = +1$
       and b examples have $y_i = -1$;
   (2) The maximum number $M_{\max}$ of weak classifiers to be combined;
1. (Initialization)
   $w_i^{(0)} = \frac{1}{2a}$ for those examples with $y_i = +1$ or
   $w_i^{(0)} = \frac{1}{2b}$ for those examples with $y_i = -1$.
   $M = 0$;
2. (Forward Inclusion)
   while $M < M_{\max}$
   (1) $M \leftarrow M + 1$;
   (2) Choose h_M according to Eq.4;
   (3) Update $w_i^{(M)} \leftarrow \exp[-y_i H_M(x_i)]$, and normalize to $\sum_i w_i^{(M)} = 1$;
3. (Output)
   $H(x) = \text{sign}[\sum_{m=1}^{M} h_m(x)]$.

Fig. 3. RealBoost Algorithm.

An error occurs when $H(x) \neq y$, or $yH_M(x) < 0$. The "margin" of an example (x, y) achieved by $h(x) \in \mathbb{R}$ on the training set examples is defined as $yh(x)$. This can be considered as a measure of the confidence of the h's prediction. The upper bound on classification error achieved by H_M can be derived as the following exponential loss function [12]

$$J(H_M) = \sum_i e^{-y_i H_M(x_i)} = \sum_i e^{-y_i \sum_{m=1}^{M} h_m(x)} \tag{2}$$

AdaBoost construct $h_m(x)$ by stagewise minimization of Eq.(2). Given the current $H_{M-1}(x) = \sum_{m=1}^{M-1} h_m(x)$, the best $h_M(x)$ for the new strong classifier $H_M(x) = H_{M-1}(x) + h_M(x)$ is the one which leads to the minimum cost

$$h_M = \arg\min_{h^\dagger} J(H_{M-1}(x) + h^\dagger(x)) \tag{3}$$

The minimizer is [5, 6]

$$h_M(x) = \frac{1}{2} \log \frac{P(y = +1|x, w^{(M-1)})}{P(y = -1|x, w^{(M-1)})} \tag{4}$$

where $w^{(M-1)}(x, y) = \exp\left(-yF_{M-1}(x)\right)$ is the weight for the labeled example (x, y) and

$$P(y = +1|x, w^{(M-1)}) = \frac{E\left(w(x, y) \cdot 1_{[y=+1]}|x\right)}{E\left(w(x, y) \mid x\right)} \tag{5}$$

where $E(\cdot)$ stands for the mathematical expectation and $1_{[C]}$ is one if C is true or zero otherwise. $P(y = -1|x, w^{(M-1)})$ is defined similarly.

The AdaBoost algorithm based on the descriptions from [5, 6] is shown in Fig. 3. There, the re-weight formula in step 2.(3) is equivalent to the multiplicative rule in the original form of AdaBoost [13, 5]. In Section 3.2, we will present a statistical model for stagewise approximation of $P(y = +1|x, w^{(M-1)})$.

4   Construction of Candidate Weak Classifiers

The optimal weak classifier at stage M is derived as Eq.(4). Using $P(y|x, w) = p(x|y, w)P(y)$, it can be expressed as

$$h_M(x) = L_M(x) - T \tag{6}$$

where

$$L_M(x) = \frac{1}{2} \log \frac{p(x|y = +1, w)}{p(x|y = -1, w)} \tag{7}$$

$$T = \frac{1}{2} \log \frac{P(y = +1)}{P(y = -1)} \tag{8}$$

The log likelihood ratio (LLR) $L_M(x)$ is learned from the training examples of the two classes. The threshold T is determined by the log ratio of prior probabilities. In practice, T can be adjusted to balance between the detection and false alarm rates (*i.e.* to choose a point on the ROC curve).

Learning optimal weak classifiers requires modelling the LLR of Eq.(7). Estimating the likelihood for high dimensional data x is a non-trivial task. In this work, we make use of the stagewise characteristics of boosting, and derive the likelihood $p(x|y, w^{(M-1)})$ based on an over-complete scalar feature set $\mathcal{Z} = \{z'_1, \ldots, z'_K\}$. More specifically, we approximate $p(x|y, w^{(M-1)})$ by $p(z_1, \ldots, z_{M-1}, z'|y, w^{(M-1)})$ where z_m $(m = 1, \ldots, M-1)$ are the features that have already been selected from $\mathcal{Z}$ by the previous stages, and z' is the feature to be selected. The following describes the candidate feature set $\mathcal{Z}$, and presents a method for constructing weak classifiers based on these features.

Because the shape is about boundaries between regions, it makes sense to use edge information (magnitude or orientation or both) extracted from a greyscale image. In this work, we use the simple Sobel filter for extracting the edge information. Two filters are used: K_w for horizontal edges and K_h for vertical edges, as follows:

$$K_w(w, h) = \begin{pmatrix} 1 & 0 & -1 \\ 2 & 0 & -2 \\ 1 & 0 & -1 \end{pmatrix} \quad and \quad K_h(w, h) = \begin{pmatrix} 1 & 2 & 1 \\ 0 & 0 & 0 \\ -1 & -2 & -1 \end{pmatrix} \tag{9}$$

The convolution of the image with the two filter masks gives two edge strength values.

$$G_w(w, h) = K_w * I(w, h) \qquad (10)$$

$$G_h(w, h) = K_h * I(w, h) \qquad (11)$$

The edge magnitude and direction are obtained as:

$$S(w, h) = \sqrt{G_w^2(w, h) + G_h^2(w, h)} \qquad (12)$$

$$\phi(w, h) = \arctan(\frac{G_h(w, h)}{G_w(w, h)}) \qquad (13)$$

The edge information based on Sobel operator is sensitive to noise. To solve this problem, we use sub-block of image to convolve with Sobel filter (see Fig. 4), which is similar to Haar-like feature calculation.

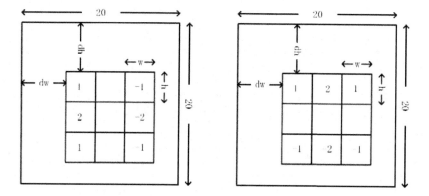

Fig. 4. The two types of simple Sobel-like filters defined on sub-windows. The rectangles are of size $w \times h$ and are at distances of (dw, dh) apart. Each feature takes a value calculated by the weighted $(\pm 1, \pm 2)$ sum of the pixels in the rectangles.

5   Statistical Learning of Weak Classifiers

A scalar feature $z_k' : x \rightarrow \mathbf{R}$ is a transform from the n-dimensional (400-D if a face example x is of size 20x20) data space to the real line. These block differences are an extension to the Sobel filters. For each face example of size 20x20, there are hundreds of thousands of different z_k' for admissible w, h, dw, dh values, so $\mathcal{Z}$ is an over-complete feature set for the intrinsically low-dimensional face pattern x. In this work, an optimal weak classifier (6) is associated with a single scalar feature; to find the best new weak classifier is to choose the best corresponding feature.

We can define the following component LLR's for the target $L_M(x)$:

$$\tilde{L}_m(x) = \frac{1}{2} \log \frac{p(z_m|y = +1, w^{(m-1)})}{p(z_m|y = -1, w^{(m-1)})} \qquad (14)$$

for the selected features, z_m's $(m = 1, \ldots, M - 1)$, and

$$L_k^{(M)}(x) = \frac{1}{2} \log \frac{p(z_k'(x)|y = +1, w^{(M-1)})}{p(z_k'(x)|y = -1, w^{(M-1)})} \qquad (15)$$

for features to be selected, $z_k' \in \mathcal{Z}$. Then, after some mathematical derivation, we can approximate the target LLR function as

$$L_M(x) = \frac{1}{2} \log \frac{p(x|y = +1, w^{(M-1)})}{p(x|y = -1, w^{(M-1)})} \approx \sum_{m=1}^{M-1} \tilde{L}_m(x) + L_k^{(M)}(x) \qquad (16)$$

Let

$$\Delta L_M(x) = L_M(x) - \sum_{m=1}^{M-1} \tilde{L}_m(x) \qquad (17)$$

The best feature is the one whose corresponding $L_k^{(M)}(x)$ best fits $\Delta L_M(x)$. It can be found as the solution to the following minimization problem

$$k^* = \arg \min_{k, \beta} \sum_{i=1}^{N} \left[\Delta L_M(x_i) - \beta L_k^{(M)}(x_i) \right]^2 \qquad (18)$$

This can be done in two steps as follows: First, find k^* for which

$$(L_k^{(M)}(x_1), L_k^{(M)}(x_2), \ldots, L_k^{(M)}(x_N)) \qquad (19)$$

is most parallel to

$$(\Delta L_M(x_1), \Delta L_M(x_2), \ldots, \Delta L_M(x_N)) \qquad (20)$$

This amounts to finding k for which $L_k^{(M)}$ is most correlated with ΔL_M over the data distribution, and set $z_M = z_{k^*}'$. Then, we compute

$$\beta^* = \frac{\sum_{i=1}^{N} \Delta L_M(x_i) L_{k^*}(x_i)}{\sum_{i=1}^{N} [L_{k^*}(x_i)]^2} \qquad (21)$$

After that, we obtain

$$\tilde{L}_M(x) = \beta^* L_{k^*}(x) \qquad (22)$$

The strong classifier is then given as

$$H_M(x) = \sum_{m=1}^{M} \left(\tilde{L}_m(x) - T \right) = \sum_{m=1}^{M} \tilde{L}_m(x) - MT \qquad (23)$$

The evaluation function $H_M(x)$ thus learned gives a quantitative confidence and the good-bad classification is achieved by comparing the confidence with the threshold value of 0 (zero).

There are two important distinctions between an evaluation functions thus learned and the linear evaluation function of reconstruction error used in AAM. First, the evaluation is learned in such a way to distinguish between good and bad alignment. Secondly, the scoring is nonlinear, which provides a semantically more meaningful classification between good and bad alignment.

6   Experimental Results

The positive and negative training examples are generated as follows: All the shapes are aligned or warping to the tangent space of the mean shape $\overline{S}$. After that, the texture T_0 is warped correspondingly to $T \in \mathbb{R}^L$, where L is the number of pixels in the mean shape $\overline{S}$.

In our work, 2536 positive examples and 3000 negative examples are used to train a strong classifier. The 2536 positive examples are derived from 1268 original positive examples plus the mirror images. The negative examples are generated by random rotating, scaling, shifting positive examples' shape points. A strong classifier is trained to reject 92% negative examples, while correctly accepting 100% of positive examples.

A cascade of classifiers is trained to obtain a computational effective model, makes training easier with divide-conquer strategy. When training a new stage, negative examples are bootstrapped based on the classifier trained in the previous stages. The details of training a cascade of 5 stages is summarized Table 1. As the result of training, we achieved 100% correct acceptance and correct rejection rates on the training set.

Table 1. Training results (WC: weak classifier)

stage	number of pos	number of neg	number of WC	False Alarm
1	2536	3000	22	0.076
2	2536	3000	237	0.069
3	2536	888	294	0.263
4	2536	235	263	0.409
5	2536	96	208	0.0

We compare the proposed Adaboost learning based method with the PCA texture reconstruction error based evaluation method, using the same data sets

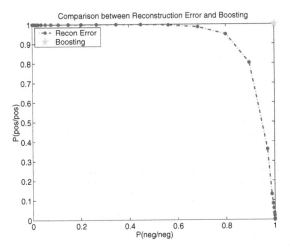

Fig. 5. Correct rate curve for the reconstruction error based alignment evaluation for the training set.

(but PCA does not need negative examples in the training). The dimensionality of the PCA subspace is chosen to retain 99% of the total variance of the data. The best threshold of reconstruction error is selected to minimize the classification error. Fig. 5 shows the ROC curve for the reconstruction error based alignment evaluation method for the training set. Note that this method cannot achieve 100% correct rates.

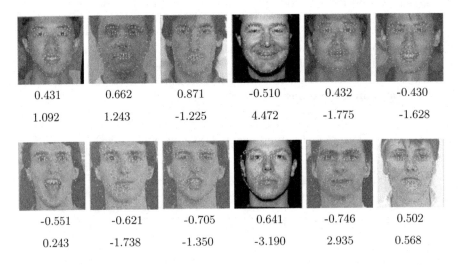

Fig. 6. Alignment quality evaluation results: qualified (top part) and un-qualified (bottom part) alignment examples

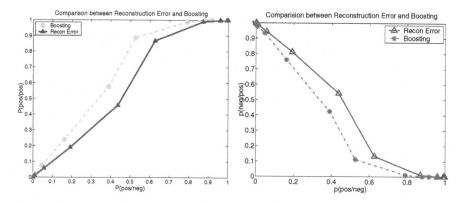

Fig. 7. Comparision between reconstruction error method and boost method

During the test, a total of 1528 aligned examples (800 qualified images and 728 un-qualified images), which are not seen during the training, are used. We evaluate each face images and give a score in terms of (a) the confidence value $H_M(x)$ for the learning based method and (b) the confidence value threshold $-$ $dist_{PCA}$ for the PCA based method. The qualified and un-qualified alignment decision is judged by comparing the score with the normalized threshold of 0. Some examples of qualified (the top part) and un-qualified (the bottom part) face alignment results are shown Fig. 6, with the corresponding scores (the first line of the numbers is for the proposed method, and the second line for the PCA based method). This qualitatively demonstrates better sensibility of the proposed method for alignment evaluation.

Fig. 7 quantitatively compares the two methods in terms of their ROC curves (first plot) and error curves (the second plot), where the axis label $P(pos/neg)$ means the false positive rate and so on. From the error curves, we can see that the equal error rate of the proposed method is about 40%, while that of recon-struction error based method is 48%. The proposed approach provides a more effective method to distinguish between qualified and un-qualified face alignment than the reconstruction error used in AAM.

Lastly, we would like to make a comment on the choice of image features for construction weak classifiers: Experimentally, we also found that the Sobel features produced significant better results than other features such as Haar wavelets. This is not elaborated here.

7   Conclusion and Future Work

In this paper, we proposed a statistical learning approach for constructing an effective evaluation function for face alignment. A set of candidate weak clas-sifiers are created based on edge features extracted using Sobel-like operators. Experimental results demonstrate that the classification function learned using the proposed approach provides semantically more meaningful scoring than the reconstruction error used in AAM for classification between qualified and un-qualified face alignment. While the number of negative examples (un-qualified alignment) is huge, so far we used only about 40,000+, and 2536 positive examples. This training set is still smaller; and so when we easily achieved 100% of training accuracy, the test performance is significantly lower. We expect a better trained nonlinear quality evaluation function when a larger training data which covers larger variation is used.

References

[1] Cootes, T.F., Taylor, C.J., Cooper, D.H., Graham, J.: "Active shape models: Their training and application". CVGIP: Image Understanding **61** (1995) 38–59
[2] Cootes, T.F., Edwards, G.J., Taylor, C.J.: Active appearance models. In: ECCV98. Volume 2. (1998) 484–498
[3] Edwards, G.J., Cootes, T.F., Taylor, C.J.: "Face recognition using active appearance models". In: Proceedings of the European Conference on Computer Vision. Volume 2. (1998) 581–695
[4] Cootes, T.F., , Taylor, C.J.: Statistical models of appearance for computer vision. Technical report, www.isbe.man.ac.uk/~bim/refs.html (2001)
[5] Schapire, R.E., Singer, Y.: "Improved boosting algorithms using confidence-rated predictions". In: Proceedings of the Eleventh Annual Conference on Computational Learning Theory. (1998) 80–91
[6] Friedman, J., Hastie, T., Tibshirani, R.: "Additive logistic regression: a statistical view of boosting". The Annals of Statistics **28** (2000) 337–374
[7] Viola, P., Jones, M.: "Robust real time object detection". In: IEEE ICCV Workshop on Statistical and Computational Theories of Vision, Vancouver, Canada (2001)
[8] Sclaroff, S., Isidoro, J.: "Active blobs". In: Proceedings of IEEE International Conference on Computer Vision, Bombay, India (1998)
[9] Friedman, J.: "Greedy function approximation: A gradient boosting machine". The Annals of Statistics **29** (2001)
[10] Mason, L., Baxter, J., Bartlett, P., Frean, M.: Functional gradient techniques for combining hypotheses. In Smola, A., Bartlett, P., Schölkopf, B., Schuurmans, D., eds.: Advances in Large Margin Classifiers. MIT Press, Cambridge, MA (1999) 221–247
[11] Zemel, R., Pitassi, T.: "A gradient-based boosting algorithm for regression problems". In: Advances in Neural Information Processing Systems. Volume 13., Cambridge, MA, MIT Press (2001)
[12] Schapire, R., Freund, Y., Bartlett, P., Lee, W.S.: "Boosting the margin: A new explanation for the effectiveness of voting methods". The Annals of Statistics **26** (1998) 1651–1686
[13] Freund, Y., Schapire, R.: "A decision-theoretic generalization of on-line learning and an application to boosting". Journal of Computer and System Sciences **55** (1997) 119–139

Towards a Robust Face Detector

Loris Nanni, Annalisa Franco, Raffaele Cappelli

DEIS, IEIIT – CNR, Università di Bologna
Viale Risorgimento 2, 40136 Bologna, Italy
{lnanni, afranco, rcappelli}@deis.unibo.it

Abstract. In this work we present the preliminary results of a face detection system based on an hybrid approach: it combines typical feature-based techniques with image-based analysis, in order to better exploit the main characteristics available in the input image. Different modules contribute to the face detection task: 1) a template-based approach initially proposed in [12], 2) an edge-extraction technique well suited to deal with illumination-changes, 3) a multiple-classifier specifically designed to discard false positives and 4) a novel method based on a featureless representation of the eye-patterns that further improves the face/non-face discrimination. The experimental results show that the system can localize faces in images with complex background, even in presence of strong illumination changes.

1. Introduction

The problem of face detection can be defined as follows: given a still image or a video, detect and localize an unknown number of faces. The solution to the problem involves segmentation, extraction, and verification of faces and facial features from an uncontrolled background.

Automatic face location is a very important task, which constitutes the first step of a large area of applications: face recognition, face retrieval by similarity, face tracking, surveillance, etc. [1], [18], [7]. In the opinion of many researchers, face location is the most critical step towards the development of practical face-based biometric systems, since its accuracy and efficiency have a direct impact on the system usability. Several factors contribute to make this task very complex, especially in the case of applications requiring to operate in real-time on gray-scale static images. The challenges associated with face detection can be attributed to the following factors:

- pose changes: face images vary for different rotations around the camera's optical axis;
- facial expressions;
- image conditions: lighting and camera characteristics could affect the appearance of a face;
- complex background.

Many face-location approaches have been proposed in the literature, depending on the type of images (gray-scale images, color images or image sequences) and on the

D. Maltoni and A.K. Jain (Eds.): BioAW 2004, LNCS 3087, pp. 57–69, 2004.
© Springer-Verlag Berlin Heidelberg 2004

constraints considered (simple or complex background, scale and rotation changes, different illuminations, etc.).

Face detection techniques can be organized in two broad categories distinguished by their different approach to exploit the face knowledge: *feature-based* and *image-based*. The techniques in the first category make explicit use of face knowledge and follow the classical detection methodology in which low level features are derived. Properties of the face such as skin color and face geometry are exploited at different system levels. These techniques have been studied since 1970s and many works in the literature refer to such approaches. The techniques in the second class address face detection as a general recognition problem. Image-based representations of faces, for example in 2D intensity arrays, are directly classified into a face group using approaches that incorporate face knowledge implicitly into the system through mapping and training schemes.

In this work a hybrid approach is presented: it adopts typical feature-based techniques (template matching) in the first step and an image-based analysis in the second step, so that all the characteristics of the image can be exploited for face detection. At present the method can deal with images containing a single upright near-frontal face; as a future work we will extend it to more complex images.

The rest of the paper is organized as follows: in section 2 an overview of the system is given, in section 3 the single system components are detailed, in section 4 the new pattern representation technique is presented, in section 5 the results of the experiments are discussed and in section 6 we draw some conclusions.

2. System Overview

The system is based on a cascade architecture: it consists of four steps (Fig. 1):

1. template matching: the first step consists in the application of the face detection algorithm presented in [12], slightly modified in some aspects, as described in subsection 0;

2. edge detection and template matching: the input image is transformed into the frequency domain (by calculating phase congruency [10]) in order to overcome problems due to illumination. The first step is then reapplied to the transformed image. The details of this procedure are reported in subsection 3.2;

3. false positives elimination: the candidate face images identified at the previous steps are analyzed and selected. A cascade of three simple classifiers is adopted to discard non-face images (subsection 3.3);

4. analysis of eyes regions: an image-based analysis is carried out in order to identify candidate eyes and, starting from them, candidate face images. A sub-image centered in the supposed eye position is extracted from the original image and classified by a pool of six classifiers, each trained to discriminate between "face" and "non-face" patterns. If the final similarity score is higher than a fixed threshold, a face is considered detected. The procedure of analysis of eye regions is described in subsection 3.4.

Not necessarily all the steps have to be performed since, as soon as a face is detected with a sufficient degree of confidence (determined on the basis of a similarity threshold), the remaining steps are not executed.

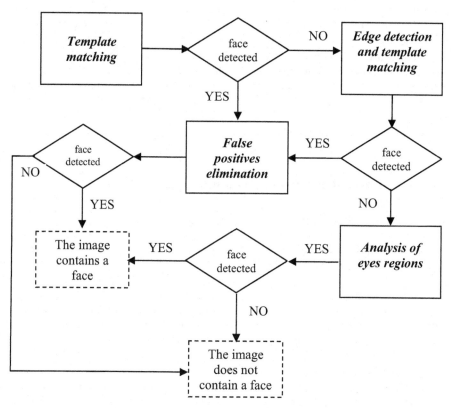

Fig. 1. Description of the steps of the proposed approach.

Each module contributes to strengthen the face detector, even in presence of challenging acquisition conditions that can cause the failure of the method presented in [12]. The development of a robust system required to modify the method in [12] retaining all the candidate face images. Obviously this approach introduces a high number of false positives that have to be filtered in a dedicated step. The step of edge detection can help to deal with limited illumination problems, since phase congruency is a measure invariant to changes in image brightness and contrast. In spite of such modifications, the template matching based approach can still fail in presence of strong illumination changes when the ellipse representing the face cannot be easily identified. For this reason, the method has been enriched with an image-base analysis based on two stages: eye detection and face detection from eye regions. In the first stage, the candidate eyes are identified. Though the eyes represent the easiest facial feature to be identified, the classification of eye images is not a simple task since they are characterized by a high variability (e.g. closed eyes, presence of glasses, etc…) and many feature extraction algorithms result ineffective in obtaining a meaningful representation. The main element of novelty of this work is the introduction of a new "featureless" representation of the patterns (eye images): each pattern is represented by its dissimilarity from the other patterns instead of by some characteristic features. The description of the new representation is quite complex and detailed separately in section 4. The adoption of such representation allows to noticeably reduce the classification error, as reported in the experimental results. The identification of candidate eyes allows to limit the search area of the face in the second stage, obtaining a lower computational complexity with respect to the methods based on sliding windows that require to scan the whole image. Finally the procedure of face detection from the eye regions employs a pool of classifiers, that have been selected among larger set of candidates on the basis of an error independence analysis carried out on a validation set. The final choice of the classifiers has been performed using the "disagreement criterion" [11].

3.   Description of the System Modules

3.1   Template Matching

The algorithm proposed in [12] starts by approximately detecting the image positions where the probability to find a face is high and then, for each of them, improves the location accuracy and verifies the presence of a real face. Assuming that, when a face is present in an image, the corresponding directional image region is characterized by vectors producing an elliptical blob, in order to identify candidate positions the authors adopt an approach based on the generalized Hough transform. Starting from these candidate positions, the face is locally searched in a small portion of the directional image by means of a mask defined in terms of directional elements, describing the global aspect of a human face.

   The algorithm, as originally proposed, lacks in some aspects, due to the limited range of face sizes it can deal with and to the sensitivity to particular illumination conditions. In the attempt to strengthen this method, slight modifications have been introduced:

- a higher number of face templates has been adopted, to account for the high size variability that characterizes the face images;
- the method [12] retains only the sub-image that gains the highest similarity score with the stored face templates. If the resulting score is higher than a prefixed threshold, a face is considered detected, otherwise no face images are supposed to be present in the image. Some experiments show that, in particular cases (and mainly in presence of challenging illumination conditions), some sub-images are erroneously discarded among those obtaining a lower similarity score. For this reason we analyze all the other candidate face images. Obviously this choice introduces a high number of false positives, making necessary the adoption of a further filtering step (described in section 3.3).

3.2 Edge Detection and Template Matching

This step helps to deal with challenging illumination conditions that could affect the detection. The algorithm adopted is based on the representation of the image in the frequency domain, which allows to mark the features present in the image since image features, such as lines and edges, correspond to points where the Fourier components are maximal in phase. Starting from this observation, the calculation of phase congruency was proposed in [13] as a technique for the extraction of image features. Phase congruency is a quantity invariant to changes in image brightness or contrast, providing an absolute measure of the significance of feature points. In this work the algorithm proposed in [10] is adopted; in [10] the authors show that phase congruency in 1D signals can be calculated from the convolution outputs of a bank of Gabor filters, and they extend the concept to 2D images. Once the image has been transformed, the first step is reapplied.

3.3 False Positives Elimination

The first two steps presented above can create a high number of false positives, particularly in images with a complex background. For this reason we introduce a step of false positives elimination where the candidate face images are analyzed and selected. A cascade of three simple classifiers is adopted to discard non-face images. Each classifier can confirm the presence of a face or reject the input image since it does not get through the related control on the basis of a similarity threshold *thr*. The first two classifiers are base on two simple features presented in [16], that allow to reduce the number of false positives with a low computational cost.

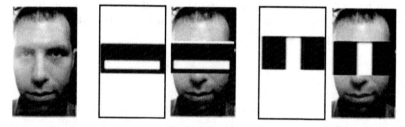

Fig. 2. The two features proposed in [16] and adopted in this work.

They simply consist in the verification of a particular distribution of grey levels in the image (see Fig. 2) that indicate the presence of a possible face. Finally, a QDC classifier [2] is adopted to classify the input image as a "face" or "non-face" pattern. Before classification, a feature vector of low dimensionality (10 in the experiments) is extracted from the gray level values of the original image by applying the KL transform [5] in order to extract the salient image features and reduce the presence of noise.

3.4 Analysis of the Eye Regions

A step of analysis of the eyes region is performed in the last stage of the proposed approach: the input image is binarized and the clusters of pixels representing potential eyes are identified; then each cluster is classified as an "eye" or "non-eye" pattern and, starting from the eye clusters, a set of candidate face images are extracted from the original image and classified by a pool of classifiers as a "face" of "non-face" pattern. In order to reduce the computational complexity of the method, the candidate eyes are not searched over the whole image, but the map of the Hough accumulator determined at the first step is considered to restrict the search area to the regions presenting values higher than a prefixed threshold.

In order to detect faces at different scales, the method requires the definition of the minimum face height (h_{face}^{min}) and width (w_{face}^{min}) expected and the number n of scales to be analyzed. The height (h_{eye}) and width (w_{eye}) of the eye are calculated as:

$$h_{eye} = 0.2 \cdot h_{face}^{min} \qquad w_{eye} = 0.25 \cdot w_{face}^{min}$$

The procedure of eye detection will be detailed in subsection 3.4.1, and in subsection 3.4.2 the approach of face detection from the eye regions is described.

3.4.1   Eye Detection

The aim of this stage is to detect the presence of eye patterns in the image. We search for a single eye instead of a couple of eyes since, in presence of particular illumination conditions, one of the eyes could not be visible.

The input for this step is the input image $\mathbf{I}$ and the grey level image $\mathbf{H}$ representing the values of the Hough accumulator determined in the first step of the method; brighter intensities represent higher values of the Hough accumulator whose values have been normalized between 0 and 256. The image $\mathbf{H}$ is binarized, setting to 1 all the pixels having a grey level value greater than a prefixed threshold th_1 and setting to 0 the others. The binarized image, is then used to filter and binarized the image I, according to the following formula:

$$\mathbf{I}(i, j) = \begin{cases} 1 & \text{if } \mathbf{H}(i, j) = 1 \text{ and } \mathbf{I}(i, j) > th_2 \\ 0 & \text{otherwise} \end{cases}$$

where th_2 is the threshold used for binarization.

The result is a new binarized image where a set of clusters (a set of connected pixels having the same value) can be identified. In Fig. 3 the input image and the images obtained at different filtering stages is shown.

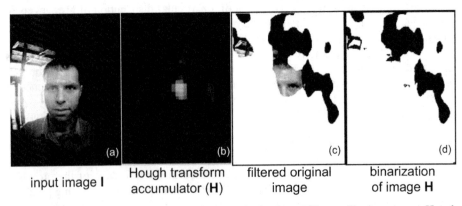

| (a) | (b) | (c) | (d) |
| input image **I** | Hough transform accumulator (**H**) | filtered original image | binarization of image **H** |

Fig. 3. The input image (a) and the images obtained at different filtering stages: Hough accumulator (b), filtered original image (c) and its binarization (c).

The candidate eye clusters are selected by applying some simple heuristic criteria:

- each cluster must contain between 10 and 400 pixels (too big and too small clusters are discarded);
- clusters having a ratio between height and width greater than 2 are discarded;
- there must be no more than 5 other clusters in a range of 25 pixels (the number of false positives due to complex backgrounds can be reduced).

A rectangle of size h_{eye} by w_{eye}, aligned with the center of each cluster, is extracted as a candidate image of an eye. A feature vector is extracted from the resulting image by applying the Karhunen-Loève transform (KL) [5], and an additional filtering step is performed by classifying the clusters as "eye" or "non-eye" patterns by means of a QDC classifier [2]. The dimensionality of the feature vector has been fixed to 4 in the experiments; the same results have been obtained with higher values.

If the similarity with respect to the class "eye" is sufficiently high, the cluster is subjected to a final selection step. Some preliminary experiments showed that the intrinsic dimensionality of the images representing single eyes is very low; moreover we experimentally verified that, in such reduced subspace, the patterns are not sufficiently scattered, making very difficult the classification task. For these reasons we introduce a space transformation, by adopting a featureless representation of the patterns. Such transformation represents the most original contribute of this work and will be detailed in section 4. The patterns in the new space are more scattered resulting in an easier classification task. The new approach to pattern representation will be detailed in the following section. The "transformed patterns" are then classified by a simple k-NN algorithm as "eye" or "non-eye" patterns.

3.4.2   Face Detection from Eye Regions

Starting from each eye candidate position, six subimages are extracted from the original image:

- n different scales are considered to detect faces also in presence of large variation of their dimensions within an input image. The initial dimension is defined by two parameters h_{face} and w_{face} (height and width of the face respectively); the other n-1 images are selected by increasing the scale factor of 1.25 each (in Fig. 4 an example of three images at different scales is reported). In the experiments the parameters have been fixed to h_{face}=95, w_{face}=58, n = 3.
- for each of the n scales, two subimages are selected supposing that the eye cluster is the left eye of the face or the right eye respectively (Fig. 5). For the extraction of the face image the same ratio between eyes and face assumed in [12] is adopted.

The six rectangles obtained represent candidate face images and are successively classified by a pool of six classifiers:

- two simple classifiers based on some of the features proposed in [16] and adopted in the step of false positives elimination (see section 3.3);
- two simple classifiers, QDC and LDC [2];
- two more complex classifiers based on Support Vector Machine [15], adopting respectively a polynomial and a Radial Basis Function kernel.

Fig. 4. Three images at different scales extracted from the same image. The analysis at different scales allows to detect faces also in presence of large variation of their dimensions within an input image.

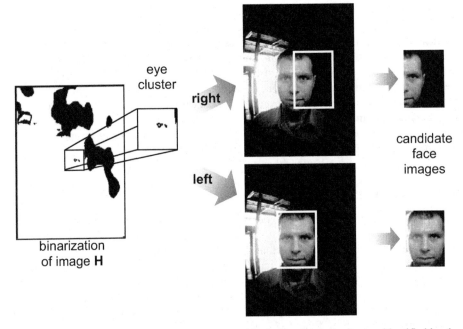

Fig. 5. Extraction of the candidate face images on the basis of the eye clusters identified by the eye detector. Two subimages for each of the three scales considered are extracted, one supposing that the eye is "right" and the other supposing that the eye is "left".

The last four classifiers analyze a feature vector obtained from the candidate face image by applying a KL transform [5]. Please note that the most complex classifiers (SVM, in the lower levels of the pool of classifiers) are applied to a very limited set of images as the first simple classifier in the cascade are able to eliminate most of the false positives.

Each classifier is trained to distinguish between "face" and "non-face" patterns. If the similarity of the pattern to the class "face" is higher than a prefixed threshold, the image is passed as input at the next classifier. If all the classifiers give a positive result, a face is considered detected by the system.

4. Featureless Representation of the Patterns

A new *featureless* representation of the patterns is proposed: each pattern is represented by its dissimilarity from the other patterns. This strategy has been considered as an appealing alternative to feature-based representation in recent works, e.g. [14] [4] [3], since it can give good results when a feasible feature-based description of objects is difficult to obtain or inefficient for learning purposes.

For each pattern, a mapping Φ is calculated from the pattern space $\Re^n$ to a new q-dimensional space. Each component Φ_i of the mapping function can be viewed as a distance function d from a pattern $\mathbf{x} \in \Re^n$ to the decision surface of the region Ψ_i

$$\Phi(\mathbf{x}) = \langle d(\mathbf{x}, \Psi_1), d(\mathbf{x}, \Psi_2), ..., d(\mathbf{x}, \Psi_q) \rangle$$

where $\Psi = \{\Psi_1, \Psi_2, ..., \Psi_q\}$ is a set of bi-dimensional regions, where the two dimensions are extracted from the original feature space. The procedure for the definition of such regions will be detailed in the following.

Our method employs fuzzy rules [9] in order to choose, among all the possible combinations, a set of bi-dimensional regions of interest. Given a set X of n-dimensional vectors, each rule R_j has the following structure:

Rule R_j: IF x_1 IS A_{j1} AND... AND x_n IS A_{jn} THEN c_j IS y with $\mathbf{x} \in X$

where:

- A_{ji}, $i = 1, .., n$ is a linguistic variable in the set $\{v_1, v_2, .., v_s\} \cup \{$"don't care"$\}$ (the value "don't care" for a variable means that the consequent class does not depend on the value of that particular variable).
- $c_j \in \{1, .., nc\}$ is the consequent class (in this work $c_j \in \{1,2\}$ where 1 is the class of "eye" and 2 represents "non-eye");
- y is the compatibility grade calculated as $\mu_j(\mathbf{x}) = \mu_{j1}(x_1) * ... * \mu_{jn}(x_n)$, where $\mu_{ji}(\cdot)$ is the membership function of the antecedent linguistic value A_{ji}, calculated as in [9].

The algorithm for the derivation of the new representation can be summarized in the following steps:

1. The complete set of fuzzy rules is created with all the possible combinations of values of the s linguistic variables ($s = 4$ in the experiments), for the n features of the patterns.
2. The rules are sorted according to their "goodness" and only the first k are retained. For each rule R_j, the patterns of the training set are ranked on the basis of their compatibility grade given by R_j. The sequence of patterns is split into two runs: the split position is given by the number of training samples belonging to the consequent class c_j. The patterns of the first run really belonging to c_j and the patterns of the second run not belonging to c_j are retained into a set S_j. The cardinality of S_j quantifies the "goodness" of the rule R_j.
3. For each rule R_j of the k retained, some two-dimensional datasets are created by projecting the elements of S_j into two selected dimensions (we use each couple (i_1, i_2) of linguistic variables in the rule with a value different from "*don't care*"). Each of these new two-dimensional datasets represents a classification problem.

We indicate with q $(q \le (k \times n \times (n-1)/2))$ the total number of classification problems.

4. For each classification problem, the two-dimensional dataset is adopted as training for a Radial Basis Function [6] classifier. The output of the classifier is a decision surface Ψ_p associated to the classification problem. These regions represent the q "candidate" axes of the new featureless space.

5. For each pattern x in the training set, calculate the mapping from the pattern space to the new q-dimensional space. We define the distance $d(x, \Psi_p)$ of a pattern x (projected into the region space) from a class region Ψ_p as the length of segment classified as belonging to the class (in Fig. 6 a graphical representation of such distance is reported). The segment is perpendicular to the i-axis and the value in the i-axis is the value of i-th feature of x.

6. Select only the best d (d is a parameter) dimensions by using a simple feature ranking technique which selects the features that maximize the distance between the centroids of the different classes of patterns.

7.

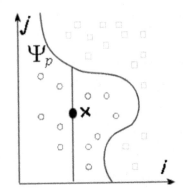

Fig. 6. A graphical representation of the distance $d(x, \Psi_p)$ of a pattern x (projected into the region space) from a class region Ψ_p.

5. Experimental Results

The experimentations have been performed on two databases:

- Yale B [17]: the database contains 5760 single light source images of 10 subjects each seen under 576 viewing conditions (9 poses x 64 illumination conditions). For every subject in a particular pose, an image with ambient (background) illumination is also captured. We selected the frontal and near-frontal images from this database (1080 images). Some example images are reported in Fig. 7.

- BioID [8]: it consists of 1521 images with human faces, recorded under natural conditions, i.e. varying illumination and complex background (Fig. 8).

Fig. 7. Some example images from the YaleB database.

Fig. 8. Some images from the BioID database.

The output of the detection system is the window containing the supposed face. The evaluation of the detection performance are calculated on the basis of:

- False Positives: percentage of hypothesized face windows that do not contain the actual face;
- Missed Faces: percentage of images where the system has been unable to find a face;
- C-Error: percentage error calculated as the Euclidean distance between the real and the supposed face center, normalized with respect to the sum of the axis of the ellipse containing face;

Table 1. Comparison of the new approach with [12] on the YaleB (frontal pose) database [17].

Algorithm	False Positive	Missed faces	C-Error
New approach	8.9%	10.3%	23%
[12]	10%	15.7%	35%

In Tab. 1 and Tab. 2 the results of both the method [12] and the new approach are reported for the YaleB and BioID database respectively. The classifiers adopted in the new approach have been trained using disjoint training and test sets. A face database internally collected has been used as training set; the same database has been used for the definition of the different thresholds required by the method.

Table 2. Comparison of the new approach with [12] on the BioID database.

Algorithm	False Positive	Missed faces	C-Error
New approach	5.99%	8.6%	10%
[12]	6.83%	13.1%	20%

The experimental results show that the new approach allows to drastically reduce the percentage of missed faces reducing at the same time the number of false positives and the error in the estimation of the face center.

The experiments show that the feature transformation approach presented in this work can drastically reduce the classification error: the eye detection subsystem achieves an error rate of 17.87%, against the 25% of the k-NN classifier in the original space.

6. Conclusions

In this paper an approach to upright frontal face detection has been presented. This approach is based on a previous work [12] that has been extended with three additional steps to improve the detection performance. The preliminary experiments carried out give encouraging results, showing that the additional steps can help in overcoming common illumination problems, allowing to obtain a noticeable performance improvement. The percentage of missed faces has been reduced from 10% to 8.9% on the Yale B database and from 6.83% to 5.99% on the BioID database (about 35% improvement on both the databases). Also the error in the estimation of the face center has been drastically reduced: from 35% to 23% on the Yale B database (35% improvement) and from 20% to 10% on the BioID database (50% improvement). Moreover the experimental results show that the new pattern representation allows to improve the classification performance of the eye detection subsystem: the error has been reduced from 25% to 17.87% (about 29% improvement).

Many aspects of the method could be further optimized. As to future research, we intend to extend the method to deal with more complex images containing several frontal and non-frontal faces.

Acknowledgement

This work was partially supported by the Italian Ministry of University and Scientific Research within the framework of the project "Distributed systems for multisensor recognition with augmented perception for ambient security and customization" (2002-2004).

7. References

[1]   R. Chellappa, S. Sirohey, C.L. Wilson, C.S. Barnes, "Human and Machine Recognition of Faces: A Survey", *Tech. Report CS-TR-3339*, Computer Visions Laboratory, University of Maryland, 1994.

[2]   R. O. Duda, P. E. Hart, D. G. Stork, *Pattern Classification,* Wiley, 2nd edition 2000.

[3]   R. P. W. Duin, "Classifiers in almost empty spaces". In *Proc. 15th International Conf. on Pattern Recognition*, Vol. 2, USA, pp. 1–7, 2000.

[4]   R. P. W. Duin, E. Pezkalska, D. de Ridder, "Relational discriminant analysis", *Pattern Recognition Letters*, vol. 20 (11–13), pp. 1175–1181, 1999.

[5]   K. Fukunaga, *Introduction on statistical Pattern Recognition*, Academic Press, 1990.

[6]   S. Haykin, *Neural Networks: A Comprehensive Foundation*, Second Edition, Macmillan, New York 1999.

[7]   E. Hjelmas, B.K. Low, "Face Detection: A Survey", *Computer Vision and Image Understanding*, 83, pp. 236-274, 2001.

[8]   http://www.humanscan.de/support/downloads/facedb.php

[9]   H. Ishibuchi, T. Nakashima, "Effect of rule weights in fuzzy rule-based classification systems", In *IEEE Transactions on Fuzzy Systems*, vol. 9, issue 4, pp. 506-515.

[10] P. Kovesi, "Image Features From Phase Congruency", *Department of Computer Science Technical Report 95/4*, June 1995.

[11] L.I. Kuncheva, C.J. Whitaker, "Ten measures of diversity in classifier ensembles: limits for two classifiers", In *Proc. Workshop on Intelligent Sensor Processing*, pp. 10/1 - 10/10, 2001.

[12] D. Maio and D. Maltoni, "Real-Time Face Location on Gray-Scale Static Images", Pattern Recognition, vol.33, no.9, pp.1525-1539, September 2000.

[13] M.C. Morrone, J.R. Ross, D.C. Burr, R.A. Owens, "Mach bans are phase dependent", *Nature*, 324(6094):250-253, November 1986.

[14] E. Pezkalska, R. P. W. Duin, "Classifiers for dissimilarity based pattern recognition", In *Proc. 15th Int. Conf. on Pattern Recognition*, vol. 2, pp. 12–16, 2000.

[15] V. Vapnik, *The nature of statistical learning theory,* Springer, New York, 1995.

[16] P. Viola and M.J. Jones, "Robust real-time object detection", In *Proc. IEEE ICCV Workshop on Statistical and Computational Theories of Vision,* Vancouver, Canada, 2001.

[17] Yale database of faces: http://cvc.yale.edu.

[18] M.H. Yang, J. Kriegman, N. Ahuja, "Detecting Faces in Images: A Survey", *IEEE Trans. on PAMI*, vol.24, no.1, 2002.

Automatic Detection of the Optimal Acceptance Threshold in a Face Verification System

Raquel Montes Diez, Cristina Conde, and Enrique Cabello

Universidad Rey Juan Carlos (ESCET),
C/Tulipán s/n,
28933 Móstoles, Spain
r.montes@escet.urjc.es
http://frav.escet.urjc.es

Abstract. We present a face verification system with an acceptance threshold automatically computed. The user is allowed to provide the rate between the costs assumed for a false acceptance and false rejection. This rate between costs can be intuitively known by the system responsible and are a starting point to fulfil user security requirements. With this user-friendly data, an algorithm based on screening techniques to compute the acceptance threshold is presented in this paper. This algorithm is applied to an original and competitive face verification system based on principal component analysis and two classifiers (neural network radial basis function and support vector machine). Experimental results with a 100 people face database are shown. This method can be also applied into other biometric applications in which this threshold should be calculated.

1 Introduction

Biometrics technology has passed in few years from research labs to commercial implementations. Media coverage has brought face recognition systems used in high profile locations such as airports, to the attention of the public. Unfortunately, the recognition of the human face is a very complex problem involving several processing steps that have not yet been completely resolved. Although technology is evolving and obtaining better results, expectations are very high and in most cases, difficult to achieve. As a consequence, several systems tested in real conditions have been rejected.

However, less attention has been paid to control access systems. In these systems, the effect of the environment is more controlled, allowing the technology to obtain better and more reliable results. Such systems could fulfil the performance criteria demanded by potential clients.

The experiment presented in this paper focused on testing the performance of a control access system based on face verification technology. In control access environments, it is possible to take advantage of a set of specific characteristics. Usually, the subject is in front of the camera, only one subject appears, the size of the face is more or less constant and the subject is usually collaborative. It is therefore possible to obtain an initial set of images and to define a personal identification

D. Maltoni and A.K. Jain (Eds.): BioAW 2004, LNCS 3087, pp. 70-79, 2004.
© Springer-Verlag Berlin Heidelberg 2004

number entered or placed in a smart card. Our system uses these advantages and proposes a control access system designed to work in such situations.

In recent years, two main approaches to face processing problem using only image information have appeared. The first approach is Principal Components Analysis (PCA) and related methods such as Fisherfaces [1] [2] [3] [4]. These methods consider only the global information of the face. Likewise, methods based on Local Feature Analysis (LFA) [5] [6], similar to PCA, consider different kernel functions which concentrate local features, such as eyes, mouth and nose. In this case, selection of facial features and kernels is an open issue. The second approach, based on Elastic Bunch Graph Matching (EBGM) [7] and similar methods, use wavelet transformation to obtain local description of the face and a graph to obtain a global face description. In the scientific literature several results with different research algorithms have been published. For example, following the success of FERET tests [8] [9] [10], a recent and extensive test of ten commercial products has been performed (FRVT 2002) [11].

A continuing problem in the design of a facial verification system is the decision of the optimum acceptance threshold. The acceptance threshold is the value that determines whether a verification is acceptance or rejection. For example, in the SVM classifier, the threshold is $w = 0$. However our experience shows that choosing a different value could result in a better performance of the system, this is, in a smaller number of false acceptance and false rejection. We understand that the acceptance threshold should then be chosen to minimize the error rate.

Furthermore, it is important to note that in a facial verification system there are two different error types; false acceptance and a false rejection, each with, possibly, different associated risk. For instance, in high security environments it is highly recommended to minimize the false acceptance rate despite the fact that the false rejection rate could be increased (subject has to key maybe twice the code). Likewise, for the access to a non-critical place, a higher false acceptance rate could be acceptable and the false rejection rate could be lowered (impostors could be accepted but to gain access, the code only has to be typed once). In order to take this into account, we propose a classification system based on costs for false acceptance and false rejection. The exact calculation of both costs (acceptance and rejection) could be difficult to found, but the rate between this costs is easier to fix. This is the input in the algorithm proposed.

In this paper we present an innovative algorithm to calculate this optimal acceptance threshold by using economic screening techniques based on different costs for different error type.

2   Experimental Set Up Description

The set up has been designed and built to test the performance of the algorithm. Figure 1 shows the image acquisition set up, consisting on two diffuse light sources placed on both sides of a video camera.

In order to minimize distortions originated by changes in the lens focal length and the camera-subject distance, it is advisable to fix both in any operation environment. These requirements are easily met in any exploitation site. In our experiments a database of 100 individuals is considered. Subjects were forced to change their pose between the acquisition of two consecutive images.

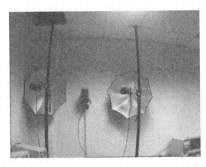

Fig. 1. Experimental set up showing diffuse lighting and the CCD camera.

Fig. 2. Examples of the Face Database

An image size is 320 x 240 pixels with face covering great part of the image (as shown in figure 2). Our face location system cropped the face to a window of 130x140 pixels. Eight images per subject were used for computing PCA matrix and training all classifiers. For tests sets, four different images per subject were considered.

3   Face Verification System

Face verification can be split into four processes: Face location, PCA computation, classifier design and automatic optimal threshold calculation. The first three parts require a training or parameter computation phase and once all parameters have been adjusted and classifiers trained, a normal operation phase. This fourth process will be detailed in chapter 4.

3.1   Face Location

In this step, the image is the input and the desired output is a window containing only the face in a standard size. The background is then eliminated to obtain a rough initial estimate of face location in the image. Subsequently, convolution with a face template is applied to obtain a more reliable and precise position of the face. Each subject in the database has their own template. The template is part of the subject's face, so convolution is more reliable where template coincides with the face in image. Initial tests suggest that one template per subject achieves better performance that one template for the whole database. When the convolution reaches the maximum over the images, a window containing the face is extracted. The final dimension was reduced to 130 x 140 pixels. In this step all images were also converted from colour to a grey scale.

3.2 Principal Components Analysis Computation

Principal Components Analysis is the *de facto* standard in face verification systems. In the training phase, the problem can be resolved computing the transformation matrix using a number of eigenvectors that retains almost 100% of the initial variance. Only one PCA matrix is computed with the training face images set. In our experiment eight images per subject are considered in order to compute the PCA matrix, in our tests 150 eigenvalues were considered.

3.3 Verification

Two classifiers have been considered: Artificial Neural Networks: Radial Basis Function (RBF) and Support Vector Machine (SVM). In all cases, training is performed with eight images per subject (the same ones used for PCA computation). Tests were carried out using four images per subject. Training and test sets did not overlap. If the output value for SVM and RBF is large this means that confidence is high. Thus positive verification has been considered when output value is greater than the acceptance threshold. This acceptance threshold has to be set to obtain the optimum value that minimizes false acceptance rate and false rejection rate, and maximizes the correct rate. The magnitude used as threshold is different for each classifier, in case of RBF, output neuron value and SVM: function decision value

RBF has been used as an artificial neural network classifier for face verification. The initial information is a subject image and personal identification number (PIN) code. The PIN code indicates which output neuron is considered. In our experiment, Gaussian functions considered are symmetric and centred in the middle of each face subject cluster.

Support Vector Machine offers excellent results in 2-class problems. This classifier could be easily used in verification problems (recognizing one subject against rest). In our experiment a linear kernel has been considered.

4   Optimal Acceptance Threshold Calculation

In order to optimize the acceptance threshold, we perform a Bayesian screening approach [12] based on two variables, namely

- A binary performance variable T, identifying whether one image has been taken ($T = 1$) or not ($T = 0$) of a given person.
- A screening variable X defining the output of a known classifier, for instance, SVM or RFB.

Since the screening variable X is not perfectly correlated with the performance variable, decisions made by using the screen are prone to error (false acceptance and false rejection).

4.1 Economic Design of the Screen

Suppose that our screening variable X is continuous and of the type *the larger the better*. That is, a large value of X tends to indicate a matching image or genuine ($T = 1$), whereas a small value of X is a sign of an impostor ($T = 0$).

Under such an assumption, a single-stage screen based on the screening variable, would naturally contain a cut-off point w, so that if X is above w, we accept the person as genuine, and if X is below w, we do not. Observe that if $X = w$ there is an arbitrary choice between accepting and rejecting the person. From now on and in order to be consistent, we shall accept items for which $X = w$, so that the screen is precisely defined as

- if $X \geq w$, the person is accepted.
- if $X < w$ the person is rejected.

4.2 Optimal Acceptance Threshold

We adopt an economic objective in which the value of the threshold w is determined in order to minimize the expected total cost of the procedure. Let c_a and c_r be the cost paid for a false acceptation and a false rejection by the system, respectively. The expected total cost of an image being classified based on the output of a classifier system such as SVM or RBF, may be expressed as a function of w, so that

$$ETC(w) = c_r P(\text{wrongly reject image}) + c_a P(\text{wrongly accept image}).$$

In formal notation,

$$ETC(w) = c_r P(T = 1, X < w) + c_a P(T = 0, X \geq w),$$

which, assuming X is continuous, becomes

$$ETC(w) = c_r \int_{-\infty}^{w} P(T = 1 \mid X = w) f(x) dx + c_a \int_{w}^{\infty} \left[1 - P(T = 1 \mid X = w) \right] f(x) dx,$$

where $f(x)$ is the marginal density function of the screening variable X.

To minimize this expected total cost for continuous X, we differentiate this expression with respect to w, and equate to zero,

$$ETC'(w) = c_r P(T = 1 \mid X = w) f(w) - c_a \left[1 - P(T = 1 \mid X = w) \right] f(w).$$

Defining

$$k = \frac{c_a}{c_a + c_r},$$

it is then straight forward to show that the equation

$$P(T = 1 | X = w) = k, \qquad (1)$$

gives the optimal value w for the acceptance threshold. Note also that, by defining the rate k, there is no need to state the value of the costs c_a and c_r. The user may just give the rate k, which should be easier that fixing the costs.

In order to identify the optimal limit for the first stage of the screen we need to solve equation (1) and, hence, to evaluate expressions of the form $P(T = 1 | X = x)$. It is necessary, therefore, to take into account the structure defining the relationship between X and T.

4.3 The Model

The structure for (X,T) is usually expressed as a parametric model with unknown parameters θ. We denote the joint probability model for (X,T) given θ by $f(x,t | \theta)$ and try to obtain the unconditional model $f(x,t)$ by using the available information about the parameters. There are two main approaches for this purpose: the estimative or classical approach and the predictive or Bayesian approach. Here we shall adopt a Bayesian approach, as it provides a natural but also rigorous theory for combining prior and experimental information as well as for making inference.

We now propose the factorisation of the joint distribution of (X,T) through the conditional model for the continuous screening variable given the value of the performance variable. We also specify the distribution of X for genuine and impostor, separately, so that

$$f(x,t | \theta) = f(x | T = 1, \mu_1, \sigma_1^2)P(T = 1 | \rho) + f(x | T = 0, \mu_0, \sigma_0^2)P(T = 0 | \rho),$$

where $\theta = (\mu_1, \sigma_1^2, \mu_0, \sigma_0^2 \rho)$ and with (μ_1, σ_1^2), (μ_0, σ_0^2) and ρ independent.

Remember that T is a binary performance variable, taking values $T = 1$ if a photograph match subject identity and $T = 0$, otherwise. Its marginal distribution may, therefore, be defined by

$$P(T = 1) = \rho,$$
$$P(T = 0) = 1 - \rho,$$

where ρ is the probability of success and hence, satisfies $0 \le \rho \le 1$.

Let us then assume that variable X follows a normal distribution with parameters (μ_1, σ_1^2) and (μ_0, σ_0^2) in each group, this is,

$$X | T = i \sim N(\mu_i, \sigma_i^2),$$

for $i = 0.1$, respectively.

Here we are interested in the conditional probability of an item with screening value $X = x$ being successful. By using Bayes theorem, this is,

$$P(T = 1 | X = x, \ data) = \frac{f(x \ | T = 1, \ data)P(T = 1 | data)}{\sum_{i=0,1} f(x \ | T = i, \ data)P(T = i | data)}. \tag{2}$$

The conditional posterior predictive densities $f(x | T = i, \ data)$ for $i = 0.1$ and the posterior predictive probability of a success $P(T = 1 | data)$ are both developed by using the Bayesian approach, both assuming non—informative prior distribution for the unknown parameters, see, for instance [12].

The predictive posteriors of $X | T = i$, are found to be *Student-t* distributions with density functions,

$$f(x | T = i, \ data) \propto \frac{1}{\sqrt{p_i}} \left\{ 1 + \frac{(x - \overline{x}_i)^2}{(n_i - 2)p_i} \right\}^{-\frac{1}{2}(n_i - 1)}$$

where $p_i = (1 + n_i^{-1})s_i^2$ and where $\overline{x}_i$, s_i and n_i are the sample mean, sample standard deviation and sample size for each one of the two different groups, $i = 0,1$, this is for genuine and impostors.

In developing the posterior probability of an image matching subject identity $P(T = 1 | data)$, it is of interest to recognize that the number of successes n_1 and the number of failures n_0 have been chosen in advance, and that no additional information about the probability of success is therefore provided by the data. Thus we set a non informative prior for the parameter p which results in equivalent posterior predictive probabilities for genuine and impostors, this is

$$P(T = 1 | data) = \frac{1}{2}.$$

Once all the elements in expression (2) have been developed, optimal values of the acceptance threshold w are easily calculated by employing numerical techniques.

5   Results and Discussion

The results are presented in two stages. Firstly we shall present the optimal acceptance threshold calculation for different acceptance and rejection costs rates, this is for different values of the constant k. Secondly, we shall show the variation of FRR and FAR in each cost case.

Exploratory analysis of the data shows that the screening variable X is continuous and of the type *the larger the better*, as required by the our screening set-up, with sufficient statistics given in Table 1.

Table 1. Sufficient statistics for genuine and impostor for the SVM and RBF classifier.

	SVM			RBF		
	$\overline{x}_i$	s_i	n_i	$\overline{x}_i$	s_i	n_i
$T = 1$	4.009	1.735	400	0.828	0.340	400
$T = 0$	0.306	0.277	39600	-1.696	0.455	39600

In order to see how the acceptance threshold w changes with the different values for c_a and c_r, we compute optimal values of w corresponding to different values of the constant k, $0 \le k \le 1$, for the two different classifiers, SVM and RBF. The results are shown in the following graphs,

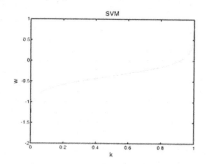

Fig. 3. SVM Optimal threshold   **Fig. 4.** RBF Optimal threshold

Recall that $k = c_a /(c_a + c_r)$, we now consider three specific values for the constant k which may be identified with three different security levels of access control or situations, in which our face verification system may be applied.

A low security level system: In our set-up, this situation might be identify by using an acceptance cost much smaller than the rejection cost. By assuming $c_a = 0.1c_r$, for instance, we obtain $k = 0.090$. In this situation the system is will not be very restrictive and the FRR is forced to be very low. This security level could be applied in a supervised parking access control, when it is important to avoid a traffic jam.

A medium security level system is represented with equivalent rejection and acceptance cost, this is the case where we assume that a false acceptance is as dangerous (or expensive) as a false rejection. Note than then $k = 2$.

A high level security system: This could be represented by using an acceptance cost much more expensive, than the cost of rejection. For instance if we assume that $c_a = 10c_r$, the value of k turns to be $k = 0.909$. In this case the FAR is nearly zero, for the RBF classifier, and null for the SVM classifier (even thought that FRR could be high). This system is highly restrictive and it could be applied to access control where we are interested in avoiding impostors to enter.

Table 2 shows the optimum acceptance threshold in three different cases: low, medium and high security level. Note that FAR decreases as security level (acceptance cost) increases.

Table 2. Optimum Acceptance Threshold variation with FAR and FRR in each case.

$c_a - c_r$ rate	k	SVM			RBF		
		w	FRR(%)	FAR(%)	w	FRR(%)	FAR(%)
$c_a = 0.1c_r$	0.091	- 0.717	1	0.17	1.081	2.00	2.45
$c_a = c_r$	0.500	- 0.366	1	0.01	1.527	7.21	0.32
$c_a = 10c_r$	0.909	0.001	3.50	0	1.888	11.72	0.31

Figure 3 shows the FRR and FAR for a wide variation of optimal acceptance thresholds. These results are presented in a conventional DET curve [13], which plots on a log-deviate scale the False Rejection Rate (FRR) as a function of the False Acceptance Rate (FAR). We present a DET curve of each classifier: SVM and RBF. The point of the DET curve corresponding to FNR = FPR is called Equal Error Rate (EER). While EER may not be useful in real world applications, it could be helpful in comparing the performance of systems or algorithms.

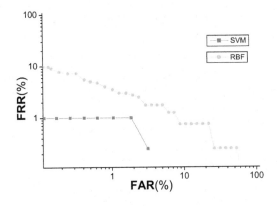

Fig. 5. DET curve

In this figure we can see how the SVM classifier is more reliable than RBF. If we consider the EER as a measure of the system performance the superiority of SVM is clear: EER(SVM)=0.99 and EER(RBF)=2.43.

6   Conclusion

In this paper we have presented a reliable face verification system with an innovate module; automatic evaluation of the optimal acceptance threshold using Bayesian screening techniques. This assure that the security level is under control while keeping a minimum error levels.

Using the algorithm proposed, the user is allow to provide the cost that is assumed to pay for false acceptance or false rejection. This allows the tailoring of our system to user security requirements. Furthermore, the user may indicate the value of the level of security required in an intuitive way, and parameter computation is hidden to the user. The system proposed can work under several security conditions that can be changed by the user.

The method proposed is valid for all face verification systems, independently of the classifier. Its integration in an existing system has been performed and results show that integration of the algorithm is not expensive.

It is of interest to note that a face verification system may be adapted to the environment and the specific conditions of the future application in order to obtain satisfactory results.

Acknowledgements

This paper has been supported by grants from Rey Juan Carlos University (PPR-2003-41, GCO-2003-15) and Comunidad de Madrid. The authors would like to thank Javier Arjona for his work.

References

1. M. Turk, A. Pentland. Eigenfaces for Recognition. Journal of Cognitive Neuroscience. V 3, N 1, P 71-86. 1991.
2. P. N. Belhumeur, J. P. Hespanha, D. J. Kriegman. Eigenfaces vs Fisherfaces: Recognition using class specific linear projection. IEEE Transactions in Pattern Analysis and Machine Intelligence, Vol 19. N 7 P 711-720. July 1997.
3. L. Wiskott, J-M Fellous, N. Krüger, C. von der Malsburg. Face Recognition by Elastic Bunch Graph Matching. IEEE Transactions on Pattern Analysis and Machine Intelligence. Vol 19, N° 7. p 775-789. Jul. 1997.
4. P. S. Penev, J. J. Atick. Local feature analysis: a general statistical theory for object representation. Network: Computation in Neural Systems. V 7, N 3, P 477-500, 1996.
5. J. J. Atick, P. A. Griffin, A. N. Redlich. Statistical approach to shape from shading: reconstruction of 3D face surfaces from single 2D images. Neural Computation. V 8. N 6. P 1321-1340. Aug. 1996.
6. R. L. Hsu. Face detection and modelling for recognition. PhD. Thesis. Michigan State University. Dpt. Computer Science and Engineering. 2002.
7. P. S. Penev, L. Sirovich. The global dimensionality of face space. Proc. Fourth IEEE International Conference on Face and Gesture Recognition. P 264-270. 2000
8. Phillips, P. J., H. Moon, S. Rizvi, and P. Rauss. 2000. "The FERET Evaluation methodology for face-recognition algorithms," IEEE Trans. Pattern Analysis and Machine Intelligence, Vol. 22, No. 10.
9. Phillips, P. J., H. Wechsler, J. Huang, and P. Rauss. 1998. "The FERET database and evaluation procedure for face-recognition algorithms," Image and Vision Computing, Vol. 16, No. 5, pp. 295-306.
10. Phillips, P. J., A. Martin, C. L. Wilson, and M. Przybocki. 2000. "An introduction to evaluating biometric systems," Computer, Vol. 33, pp. 56-63.
11. P.J. Phillips, P. Grother, R.J Micheals, D.M. Blackburn, E Tabassi, and J.M. Bone. FRVT 2002: Evaluation Report. March 2003. http://www.frvt.com
12. R. Montes Diez. Optimal Design of Two-Stage Screens: A Bayesian Approach. PhD. Thesis. University of Nottingham. Maths and Science Dpt. 2000.
13. A.Martin et al. The DET curve in assessment of detection task performance. Eurospeech 97, volume 4, pages 1895-1898, 1997.

Registration and Modeling of Elastic Deformations of Fingerprints

Sergey Novikov and Oleg Ushmaev

Biolink Technologies, Inc.
www.BioLinkUSA.com
SNovikov@BiolinkUSA.com
OUshmaev@BiolinkUSA.com

Abstract. We apply the methods of the theory of elasticity for two important problems in fingerprint based authentication: (1) registration of deformations up to the level of pixel-wise correspondence of two images; (2) parametric modeling and exact measurement of the natural deformations. The approach is based on the numerical solution of Navier linear PDE, the registration being provided even for the cases of significant losses and errors in the initial correspondences of minutiae that may be caused by various noise and distortion factors. Relatively compact and theoretically grounded model of the deformations is proposed, which allows to obtain the estimations of discrepancies in the most extreme cases.

1 Introduction

The basic distortion factors that negatively affect the performance of fingerprint verification are as follows [1,2]: small area of intersection, bad quality of the input images, and elastic deformations (ED). The first factor is rather subjective and could be avoided (by the positioning of the cuticle, for example) either by a user which is friendly to the verification system, or by an operator in the case of AFIS or civil AFIS systems [2]. Therefore, only two aspects of interest are left: noises and ED.

Once there is a distorting factor, two approaches can be involved: making the algorithm to be invariant to the factor or suppressing its influence. Since the spatial spectrum features of fingerprint minutiae are very close to the characteristics of the typical noises (smudging and loss of ridge segments) the most of the existing technologies[3-7] prefer to use suppression of distortions and recovery of the papillary lines (ridges and valleys). This choice results in the limitations on SNR, e.g. as it has been constructively shown in [8] even 50% white noise creates the areas that subjectively can be taken for minutiae. Considering separately the factor of ED, it is still not evident that ED-invariant algorithm, to say, the one which uses inter-ridge counting, provides worse performance being compared with one which uses metrical matching, but one reason in favor of ED suppression could be adduced: the associative matrices introduced by T. Kohonen[9] and modern neural networks allow to provide reliable identification with very high noise levels (up to 99%), i.e. the reducing of fingerprint matching

D. Maltoni and A.K. Jain (Eds.): BioAW 2004, LNCS 3087, pp. 80–88, 2004.

to the rigid movement (procrustean matching) is reasonable at least when both factors are present.

In spite of existence of developed theory of elastic deformations, it is rarely applied to the real-time systems due to computational complexity.

There are a number of approaches to registration of elastic deformations. One of the first approaches was introduced by D.J. Burr [10], and used the concept of rubber masks. The way suggested by A.M. Bazen and S.H. Gerez [11] is based on the thin-plate spline (TPS) models, firstly applied to biological objects by F.L. Bookstein [12]. This method requires determining correspondent points in two compared images (matching point) and it suffers from the lack of precision in case of few matching points. Modifications of TPS (approximate thin-plate splines and radial based function splines) were introduced by M. Fornefett, K. Rohr and H. Stiehl [13],[14]. They consider deformations of biological tissues. But this way also requires many matching points (more then 100) what is virtually impossible in fingerprint applications, because number of minutiae in fingerprint image rarely exceeds 50. This fact makes TPS and its variants hardly applicable to fingerprint deformations registration.

The absolutely different approach was suggested by R. Cappelli, D. Maio and D. Maltoni [15]. They developed analytical model of fingerprint deformation. But it has some shortcomings, for example, irreversibility even of small deformations. However, it was one of a few, if not the only one, work where a parametric ED model had been introduced. In [16] we have proposed an algorithm of restoration of deformations knowing correspondent points in two images, based on the numerical solution of Navier PDE by finite elements method (FEM) with the examples of its implementation and statistical analysis of the distribution of deformation energy for the existing available fingerprint databases [17,18]. Here, we consider one more approach to the problem of registration based on the convolution with pulse responses. We also propose more compact scheme for parametric description of ED, which allows to make the estimation of discrepancies in extreme cases.

2   Model of Elastic Deformation

In general the dynamics of a small elastic deformation is considered to satisfy the Navier linear elastic PDE:

$$\mathbf{L}\mathbf{u}(x, y, z, t) = -\mathbf{f}(x, y, z), \qquad (1)$$

where L is the following differential operator:

$$L = \mu\nabla^2 + (\lambda + \mu)\nabla\mathrm{div} - \rho\frac{\partial^2}{\partial t^2}, \qquad (2)$$

$\mathbf{u}$ is the vector of displacement; $\mathbf{f}$ is the external force. Coefficients λ and μ are the Lames elasticity constants. These parameters can be interpreted in the terms of Youngs modulus E and Poissons ratio ν

$$E = \frac{\mu\,(3\lambda + 2\mu)}{(\lambda + \mu)}, \tag{3}$$

$$\nu = \frac{\lambda}{2\,(\lambda + \mu)}. \tag{4}$$

In fact a fingerprint image is captured when finger is immobile, it means that the partial derivative $\rho\frac{\partial^2 \mathbf{u}}{\partial t^2} = 0$. Such solutions are called steady state and they do not depend on time t, i.e. $\mathbf{u}(x, y, z, t) = \mathbf{u}(x, y, z)$. In this case the Navier PDE has the following form:

$$\mu\nabla^2\mathbf{u} + (\lambda + \mu)\nabla\mathrm{div}\mathbf{u} + \mathbf{F} = 0. \tag{5}$$

Unlike plastic materials solution of equation (1) for elastic material depends only on current force distribution and does not depend on previous configurations (history).

Investigating properties of fingerprint deformations, it is possible to neglect 3D structure of finger and to consider 2D model for area of contact of finger and scanner surface. In fact this area carries the main information available for further processing.

Obviously in the 2D model all displacements of tissue are located in the plane of contact. Such restriction is called plain strain. The different sort of 2D elastic problem is plane stress, when the material is plane and pressure is orthogonal to this plane. The plane stress restrictions are normal for studying of dynamics of metal plates and exact solution can be found using the TPS. So the TPS is the solution of problem that is absolutely different from registration of elastic deformation of soft tissues. It is one of the possible reasons why the TPS are hardly applicable to studying of fingerprint deformations.

3   Registration by FEM

As was mentioned above, in case of elastic material, deformation depends only on current configuration, so a fingerprint deformation can be fully described by the function of displacement:

$$f : X \to \mathbb{R}^2, \tag{6}$$

Let us define the vector $(u(x, y), v(x, y))$ of displacement at the point (x, y):

$$(u, v) = f(x, y) - (x, y). \tag{7}$$

The strain tensor $\hat{\epsilon}$ is defined by the next formula:

$$\hat{\epsilon} = \begin{pmatrix} \frac{\partial u}{\partial x} + \frac{1}{2}\left(\frac{\partial u}{\partial x}\right)^2 & \frac{1}{2}\left(\frac{\partial u}{\partial y} + \frac{\partial v}{\partial x} + \frac{\partial u}{\partial y}\frac{\partial v}{\partial x}\right) \\ \frac{1}{2}\left(\frac{\partial u}{\partial y} + \frac{\partial v}{\partial x} + \frac{\partial u}{\partial y}\frac{\partial v}{\partial x}\right) & \frac{\partial v}{\partial y} + \frac{1}{2}\left(\frac{\partial v}{\partial y}\right)^2 \end{pmatrix} \tag{8}$$

The linear approximation of (8) is the following tensor:

$$\epsilon = \begin{pmatrix} \frac{\partial u}{\partial x} & \frac{1}{2}\left(\frac{\partial u}{\partial y} + \frac{\partial v}{\partial x}\right) \\ \frac{1}{2}\left(\frac{\partial u}{\partial y} + \frac{\partial v}{\partial x}\right) & \frac{\partial v}{\partial y} \end{pmatrix} \tag{9}$$

Let us assume that the material reveals linear dependence between pressure and strain (what is almost true for small deformations of biological tissues). In that case the pressure tensor σ can be calculated using the following formula:

$$\sigma = \begin{pmatrix} \frac{E(1-\nu)}{(1+\nu)(1-2\nu)}\epsilon_1^1 + \frac{E\nu}{(1+\nu)(1-2\nu)}\epsilon_1^2 & \frac{E}{2(1+\nu)}\epsilon_1^2 \\ \frac{E}{2(1+\nu)}\epsilon_2^1 & \frac{E(1-\nu)}{(1+\nu)(1-2\nu)}\epsilon_2^2 + \frac{E\nu}{(1+\nu)(1-2\nu)}\epsilon_2^1 \end{pmatrix} \tag{10}$$

Vector of involved forces is

$$\mathbf{F} = \begin{pmatrix} f_x \\ f_y \end{pmatrix} \tag{11}$$

The overall energy E_0 and energy E_d of deformation are determined by the following formula:

$$E = E_d - A = \frac{1}{2}\int_S (\epsilon_1^1\sigma_1^1 + \epsilon_2^2\sigma_2^2 + \sigma_1^2\epsilon_1^2)dS - \int_S (f_x u + f_y v)dS \tag{12}$$

In case of linear isotropic material the energy of deformation is homogeneous quadratic form that depends only on the strain tensor elements. Also it is natural to assume that the form is invariant with respect to orthogonal transformation.

$$E_d = \frac{1}{2}\int_S (c_1(\epsilon_1^1)^2 + c_2(\epsilon_2^2)^2 + c_3(\epsilon_1^2)^2 + c_4\epsilon_1^1\epsilon_1^2 + c_5\epsilon_2^2\epsilon_1^1 + c_6\epsilon_1^1\epsilon_2^2)dS \tag{13}$$

Apparently, the coefficients must satisfy the following conditions:

$$\begin{aligned} c_1 &= c_2; \\ c_4 &= c_5; \\ 4c_3 &= c_1; \\ 2c_6 &= c_1. \end{aligned} \tag{14}$$

The two independent coefficients c_1 and c_4 are determined by the internal properties of material

$$c_1 = c_2 = \frac{E(1-\nu)}{(1+\nu)(1-2\nu)}, \tag{15}$$

$$c_4 = c_5 = \frac{E\nu}{(1+\nu)(1-2\nu)}, \tag{16}$$

As is known [19] solution of Navier elastic PDE (1) minimizes the energy (12). The following method provides the solution of (1) when there is no idea how determine operating forces. One of the approaches is minimizing the function E_d of deformation energy. Without any additional constrains the function E_d is minimized by zero function of displacement. In our case additional restrictions are correspondent points of two images:

$$\mathbf{p}_i + (u(\mathbf{p}_i), v(\mathbf{p}_i)) = \mathbf{q}_i.$$

where $\{\mathbf{p}_i\}$ is the set of points in the first image and $\{\mathbf{q}_i\}$ is the correspondent set in the second image.

Let us consider the following functional that reflects deformation:

$$W(u, v) = E_d(u, v) + \Theta S(u, v), \tag{17}$$

where E_d is deformation energy and

$$S(u, v) = \sum_{i=1}^{n} |\mathbf{p}_i + (u(\mathbf{p}_i), v(\mathbf{p}_i)) - \mathbf{q}_i|^2 \tag{18}$$

reflects the measure of approximation. Coefficient Θ shows the importance of each component.

The minimum of W can be found numerically using finite elements method (FEM). The displacement is defined on rectangular lattice and interpolated to the entire image with for example bilinear splines.

4   Registration by Convolution

Let us consider the case when the distribution of forces is known up to the scale factor. We shall rewrite (5) as follows:

$$\nabla^2 \mathbf{u} + \kappa \nabla \mathrm{div} \mathbf{u} = -\mathbf{F}, \tag{19}$$

where $\kappa = \frac{\lambda + \mu}{\mu}$. Since Poisson's ratio ν for human skin is considered to vary approximately around 0.33, $\kappa \sim 2.4911$. Then one easily obtains transfer function for the reciprocal operator L^{-1}:

$$\mathbf{H}(\omega_x, \omega_y) = \begin{pmatrix} H_x \\ H_y \end{pmatrix} =$$
$$= \frac{1}{(1+\kappa)(\omega_x^2 + \omega_y^2)^2} \begin{pmatrix} \omega_x^2 + (1+\kappa)\omega_y^2 & -\kappa\omega_x\omega_y \\ -\kappa\omega_x\omega_y & (1+\kappa)\omega_x^2 + \omega_y^2 \end{pmatrix}, \tag{20}$$

and using inverse Fourier transform we have the impulse response (point spread function) $\mathbf{h}(x, y)$. Hence the solution of (19) can be obtained by convolution:

$$\mathbf{u}(x, y) = \mathbf{h}(x, y) * \mathbf{F}(x, y). \tag{21}$$

Figure 1 illustrates that the deformation caused by point force is sufficiently smooth function.

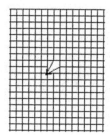 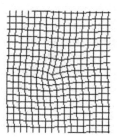

Fig. 1. The example of point force and corresponding deformation

For the ED registration by correspondent minutiae pairs after the registration of linear transform we have the solution as follows:

$$\mathbf{u}(x, y) = \gamma \sum_{i=1}^{n} (\mathbf{q}_i - \mathbf{p}_i) \, \delta \left((x, y)^T - \mathbf{p}_i \right) * \mathbf{h}(x, y), \qquad (22)$$

where coefficient γ is calculated after minimization of $S(u, v)$ from (18).

The given method allows to estimate separately the influence of each addend in (22) and exclude the wrong correspondences which give sufficient discrepancy in (17). Its disadvantage is in the integral approach, when no boundary for fingerprint is assumed, while FEM is able to yield solution inside any given region.As for the computational complexity, if we denote N as a total number of all nodes in a grid then FEM complexity is CN^2, while convolution methods complexity is CN, provided point spread functions for all directions of unit force have been calculated in advance

5   ED Modeling

First of all, the problem of ED modeling is vital for the correct statement of the recognition problem. So far in the most cases the requirements to the verification systems are formulated approximately as follows: to provide the best performance (minimum of EER, or FRR with given FAR) for a given data set. It is not clear enough why the system must operate well on the given particular data set? Inasmuch as we solve the problem by mathematical tools, it should be formulated at least to some extent exact terms. One can easily measure the overlap area, rigid movement (displacement and rotation), and even the noise level, however it is not clear how and with what tools the ED must be estimated? We have been using [16] the concept of the deformation energy W from (17) and studied its distribution on some available fingerprint databases. However, the registration is based on the mated minutiae that requires either the human intervention, or is dependent upon the particular technology of minutiae extraction and matching. That is why it is desirable to get some unbiased objective values.

Unlike [15] we regard only steady state, when fingerprint was applied to the surface, the external tangent forces being active only at the points of the region of impression, let us assume that it is an ellipse with the axes a and b. The distribution of these forces depends upon persons strain that is partially compensated by friction forces(real scheme is more complicated, but we shall take just the first approximation). Below we shall use the following definition of elliptic radius (a valuation in $\mathbb{R}^2$):

$$r(x,y) = \sqrt{\frac{x^2}{a^2} + \frac{y^2}{b^2}}. \tag{23}$$

In a of 3D ellipsoid model, assuming that pressure and hence the skin friction is distributed proportionally to the tissue deflection, we have for the maximal strain the following distribution:

$$\mathbf{F}(x,y) = \begin{cases} 0, & \text{if } r(x,y) > 1 \\ k\rho\,[\mathbf{R},\mathbf{t}]\,(x/r, y/r)^T & \text{otherwise,} \end{cases} \tag{24}$$

where $[\mathbf{R},\mathbf{t}]$ is the rigid movement [15], rotation causes the torsion and displacement is responsible for the traction (two basic ED of fingerprint), k - is an amplification factor, $\rho(x,y) = 1 - \sqrt{1 - r^2(x,y)}$.

Marginal values for local relative stretch and the distribution of discrepancies can be obtained from the force distribution (24) for the least positive k, for which the solution of PDE (19) results in one of two possible errors (stop conditions):

1) the distortion of topology (in at least one point the Jacobian becomes non-positive);

2) model inconsistency (relative stretch along one of the eigen vectors of deformation tensor [20] approaches 1 at least in one point).

We use symmetrical scheme an ellipse with $a = 0.7b$ (similar to a typical fingerprint). For the three basic ED we obtained the following marginal estimations of the average relative local stretch:

horizontal traction   -   24.46%,

vertical traction   -   12.19%,

torsion   -   37.59%.

So as to estimate the metric variability we shall use mean procrustean discrepancy (one that is left after the best rigid matching) normalized by the average diameter $(a + b)$. We have the following marginal estimations in percents with standard deviations in brackets:

horizontal traction   -   3.56 (2.95),

vertical traction   -   2.03 (1.49),

torsion   -   11.09 (5.9).

The examples of the marginal deformations are illustrated in Fig.2., the stop condition here was distortion of topology, the model inconsistency level being about 0.5. As it is seen, there is really ellipse-like quasi undeformable region inside, that was mentioned in [15], however, it is just a result of the solution of PDE (19), i.e. our approach does not require the specification of the immobile region, transitional area and empiric weight coefficients used in [15]. The whole

a   b

Fig. 2. The examples of the extreme deformations: a vertical traction; b torsion

ED model is defined only by the form of the active contour and its rigid movement - 5 independent parameters in a total, plus 3 axes of 3D ellipsoid if 3D
specification is involved, the relational variances of parameters being very slight.
About the same results have been obtained by setting the correspondences as
the vectors of rigid movement at the points of active contour and solving (1) by
FEM.

6   Conclusion

Two methods of ED registration and estimation have been introduced. The both
methods show good results [16] for the recovery of the relational deformation of
two fingerprint images from the set of mated pairs of minutiae, the convolution
approach being more fast and facilitating the estimation of contribution for each
pair, while FEM is more robust under moderate noises and can be conditioned
inside any given bounded region. We also considered the ED model based upon
the physical principles, though in a somewhat simplified approximation. The
model allowed to obtain marginal estimations of local stretch and the distribution
of discrepancies (procrustean distances) for two basic deformations (traction
and torsion). Vertical traction is the most unwanted, because under moderate
strains it results in the distortion of topology, i.e. some ridges start to overlay on
the others that causes wrong minutiae and the whole pattern, while horizontal
traction and torsion have more freedom though the final discrepancies differ
greatly. The biggest possible discrepancy is caused by the torsion, but this type
of ED is rather seldom.

In a future we shall estimate the parameters of ED model for typical distribution of deformation energy, that will allow to define typical requirements for
fingerprint based authentication systems.

Naturally, the assumptions should become more and more detailed, including
different 3D shapes, ridges structure etc. The model of 3D thin rubber plate of
finite thickness will bring definite improvement as well.

References

1. S. Pankanti, S. Prabhakar and A.K. Jain, On the Individuality of Fingerprints, IEEE Trans. PAMI, 2002, 24(8), pp. 1010-1025.
2. Wilson C.L., Watson C.I., Garris M.D., and Hicklin A., Studies of Fingerprint Matching Using the NIST Verification Test Bed (VTB) // available at ftp://sequoyah.nist.gov/pub/nist_internal_reports/ir_7020.pdf
3. Lee H.C. and Gaenssley R.E., Advances in Fingerprint Technology, Elsevier, New York, 1991.
4. Halici U., Jain L.C., Erol A., Introduction to Fingerprint Recognition, Intelligent Biometric Techniques in Fingerprint and Face Recognition, CRC Press, 1999.
5. Eleccion M., Automatic Fingerprint Identification, IEEE Spectrum, 1973, 10, pp. 36-45.
6. Jain A.K., Hong L. and Bolle R., On-Line Fingerprint Verification, IEEE Trans. On Pattern Analysis and Machine Intelligence, 1997, 19(4), pp. 302-314.
7. Jain A.K., Hong L., Pankanti S. and Bolle R., An Identity-Authentication System Using Fingerprints, Proc. of IEEE, 1997, 85(9), pp. 1365-1388.
8. Novikov S.O., Glushchenko G.N., Fingerprint ridges structure generation models, 6th Int. Workshop on Digital Image Processing and Computer Graphics. Vienna, 20-22 Oct. 1997, Proc. SPIE, vol. 3346.
9. Kohonen T. Self-Organization and Assotiative Memory, Series in Informatic Sciences, vol. 8. Springer Verlag, 1984.
10. Burr D.J., "A Dynamic Model for Image Registration" Computer Graphics and Image Processing Vol. 15 pp. 102-112, 1981
11. Bazen A.M., Gerez S.H., Thin-Plate Spline Modelling of Elastic Deformation in Fingerprints, Proceedings of 3rd IEEE Benelux Signal Processing Symposium, 2002.
12. Bookstein F.L., Principal Warps: Thin-Plate Splines and the Decomposition of Deformations, IEEE Trans. PAMI, 1989, 11(6), pp. 567-585.
13. M. Fornefett, K. Rohr and H.S. Stiehl, Elastic Medical Image Registration Using Surface Landmarks with Automatic Finding of Correspondences, In A. Horsch and T. Lehmann, editors Proc. Workshop Bildverarbeitung fur die Medizinl, Informatik actuell, Munchen, Germany, Springer-Verlag Berlin Heidelberg, 2000, pp. 48-52.
14. M. Fornefett, K. Rohr and H.S. Stiehl, Radial Basis Functions with Compact Support for Elastic Registration of Medical Images, Image and Vision Computing, 19 (1-2), 2001, pp. 87-96.
15. Raffaele Cappelli, Dario Maio, Davide Maltoni, Modelling Plastic Distortion in Fingerprint Images, ICAPR2001, pp. 369-376.
16. Ushmaev O., Novikov S., Registration of Elastic Deformations of Fingerprint Images with Automatic Finding of Correspondences, Proc. MMUA03, Santa Barbara, CA, 2003, pp. 196-201.
17. First International Competition for Fingerprint Verification Algorithms (FVC2000), bias.csr.unibo.it/fvc2000/.
18. FVC2002, the Second International Competition for Fingerprint Verification Algorithms (FVC2000), bias.csr.unibo.it/fvc2002/.
19. Shames, I.H. and Pitarresi, J.M., Introduction to Solid Mechanics, Upper Saddle River, NJ, 2000.
20. Landau L.D., Lifshits E.M., Theory of Elasticity: Course of Theoretical Physics, Butterworth-Heinemann Edition, 1995.

Benchmarking of Fingerprint Sensors

Wei Yun Yau[1], Tai Pang Chen[1], and Peter Morguet[2]

[1] Institute for Infocomm Research,
21 Heng Mui Keng Terrace, Singapore 119613
{wyyau, tpchen}@i2r.a-star.edu.sg
http://www.i2r.a-star.edu.sg
[2] Infineon Technologies AG,
St.-Martin Straße 76, D-81541 Munich, Germany
peter.morguet@infineon.com

Abstract. At present, there are many competing fingerprint sensors available. Thus, fingerprint sensor benchmarking is necessary but unfortunately no proper methodology is available. This paper attempts to address this deficiency by proposing a new methodology to benchmark the fingerprint sensors. The methodology consists of three metrics and the associated procedures to collect the data in order to compute the proposed metrics. Two small scale experiments are conducted to show the validity and efficacy of the proposed method. These include comparison of the image acquisition performance among various sensors with different skin type and under different weather condition. The effect of number of usage with acquisition performance is also analyzed. Analysis of the results shows that the proposed method does provide a basic sensor benchmarking capability.

1 Introduction

Fingerprint recognition is fast becoming a popular biometric based identity authentication technology among the consumers. Along with its increasing popularity, demand for live fingerprint capturing sensors will likewise increase. Many vendors are competing to provide the needed fingerprint sensor used to capture the live fingerprint image. Several competing sensing technology are touted, such as the traditional frustrated total internal reflection technique used in the optical sensors, measuring the difference in capacitance between the ridge and valley or the electric field variation, thermal instability, pressure, ultrasound and few others. Table 1 below shows the technology and some of the active sensor vendors using that technology (the list is non-exhaustive).

However, capturing a good fingerprint images under all conditions is extremely difficult. Not only that the environment plays a part, there is also natural variation in the skin type characterized by the amount of sweat produced by the pore. Too much sweat causes the image produced to appear smeared while too little sweat will cause the skin to become dry which is difficult to image. There are also people with thin or abraded friction ridges, producing poor fingerprint image that is difficult to have repeatable pattern. In addition, the sensor also has to withstand the many touches that result in accumulation of oil, dirty finger, dust and dirt. Thus, among the various con-

D. Maltoni and A.K. Jain (Eds.): BioAW 2004, LNCS 3087, pp. 89-99, 2004.
© Springer-Verlag Berlin Heidelberg 2004

Table 1. Technology of fingerprint sensor used and some of the respective manufacturers of the sensor

Technology	Vendor
Optical	CrossMatch, Guardware, Hunno, Secugen, DigitalPersona
Capacitance	Fujitsu, Infineon, ST Microelectronics, Veridicom
Electric Field	Authentec
Pressure	Fidelica, Hitachi
Thermal	Atmel
Ultrasound	UltraScan

ditions and with the availability of many fingerprint sensors, it is useful to have a mechanism to properly benchmark fingerprint sensors.

There are many factors that determine the quality of a fingerprint sensor. The factors can be grouped into four major categories, namely cost, acquisition performance, usability and durability. Acquisition performance will include factors such as quality of the fingerprint image produced, consistency of the fingerprint quality captured over time and the range of skin types in which acceptable fingerprint image can be obtained. Usability will include factors such as image resolution, speed of acquisition, power consumption and susceptibility to circumvention. In this paper, we will only focus on the acquisition performance aspect. We propose a set of metrics to systematically quantify the acquisition performance of a fingerprint sensor based on the analysis of the quality of the fingerprint image produced.

The effect of fingerprint quality on the performance of automated fingerprint recognition system has been studied though usually determining the fingerprint quality is done manually [1], [2], [3]. The study in [4] highlighted the need to take "classifiability", ridge definition and clarity and minutiae definition and clarity in defining the fingerprint quality metrics in order to properly analyze the effect of fingerprint quality versus the performance of automated fingerprint identification system (AFIS). However, reported works on fingerprint quality analysis are very limited. The work in [5] uses the local features to characterize the minutiae definition and global orientation to characterize the ridge definition. [6] divides the fingerprint into smaller blocks and determine weather each of the blocks is directional or in foreground. Contiguous directional foreground blocks contribute to the fingerprint quality, measured against a reference block at the core. The FBI specification for image quality concerns only fidelity of reproduction with respect to the original pattern, such as modulation transfer function and signal-to-noise ratio [7] and not to any arbitrary fingerprint image.

In order to develop a proper metrics to benchmark the fingerprint sensors, we adopted the work in [5] and extend it to provide necessary metrics to quantify the sensor acquisition performance. These metrics will be described in Section 2. In order to show the efficacy of the proposed method, a small scale attempt on sensor benchmarking is performed. This is preceded by the necessary data collection and the procedures devised are described in Section 3. Section 4 then gives the results of the benchmarking attempt while Section 5 concludes this paper.

2   Acquisition Performance Metrics

Our basic idea to systematically perform fingerprint sensor benchmarking is to compare the quality of fingerprint images acquired by various sensors from similar sources through normal usage in various conditions and with various finger types. Only the acquisition performance will be considered in the benchmarking. Since most of the current commercial off-the-shelf sensors are meant more for consumer products than for AFIS, only factors affecting fingerprint verification need to be considered in the benchmarking metrics. This implies that considering the definition and clarity of the ridge and minutiae will suffice [4]. With that, three metrics were proposed with the following definitions.

(D1)   **Image Quality Score** is defined as the degree of accuracy at which an automated fingerprint recognition system can extract unique features for subsequent recognition.

(D2)   **Usable Range** is defined as the range of the finger's skin condition over which acceptable quality fingerprints can be acquired.

(D3)   **Consistency** is defined as the rate at which the quality of fingerprint obtained varies with usage or with the duration of operation.

2.1   Image Quality Score

Ideally an Image Quality Score should be defined as the degree of similarity between the image and the actual fingerprint pattern. However, such definition is difficult to quantify as it is not easy to obtain the actual fingerprint pattern. Thus an alternative definition that is amendable to quantification is proposed as above. The advantage of the proposed definition of the Image Quality Score is that it is not based on human perceptual metrics which is also not easy to quantify. Instead it directly relates to the performance of the automatic fingerprint recognition system in which ultimately the fingerprint sensor will be used.

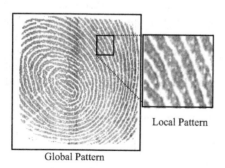

Local Pattern

Global Pattern

Fig. 1. Local and global fingerprint pattern

The fingerprint local structure constitutes the main texture-like pattern of ridges and valleys in a local region. Since a minutia is a local discontinuity, the local structure is a suitable measure for the definition and clarity of a minutia. On the other hand, valid global structure puts the ridges and valleys into a smooth flow. The flow pattern is characterized by ridges. Thus the global structure is a suitable measure for the definition and clarity of the ridges.

As per our earlier work in [5], two main measures were proposed to quantify the local structure. These are the Orientation Certainty Level (OCL) and the Ridge-Valley Structure (RVS). The former is computed using the energy ratio between the tangential and normal direction of the ridge flow which can be obtained from the ratio of the eigenvalues of the covariance matrix of the image gradient. RVS is computed by the ridge-valley fidelity measured by the ridge frequency, ridge-to-valley ratio and ridge thickness. The number of blocks (S_L) with OCL and RVS exceeding predetermined thresholds will indicate the quality. Another two main measures were also proposed to quantify the global structure. These are Orientation Continuity (S_{GO}) and Ridge-Valley Uniformity (S_{GR}). The former is given by the number of foreground blocks in the local structure with abrupt orientation change as compared to the neighbouring blocks. The latter is given by the number of foreground block in the local structure with uniform Ridge-Valley Structure. The Image Quality Score (QS) is then given by the weighted value of all these measures given in Equation (2).

$$QS = (\alpha_1 S_L + \alpha_2 S_{GO} + \alpha_3 S_{GR}) \times \frac{\min(T - T_{BL}, A_{min})}{A_{min}} \tag{2}$$

where $\alpha_1 + \alpha_2 + \alpha_3 = 1$
T = total no. of blocks.
T_{BL} = number of blank blocks.
A_{min} = predetermined minimum no of blocks for foreground.

A monotonic correlation between QS and the actual number of minutiae in fingerprint images was shown in [5].

2.2   Usable Range

The Usable Range (UR) metric measures the performance of the sensor across the various finger types due to skin condition such as wet, normal or dry. However, at present, accurate determination of the degree of wetness or dryness of a finger is difficult. Instead, all fingerprint images are classified into three main classes - normal, dry and wet. The equal weighted average percentage of number of fingerprints achieving a minimum acceptable level of QS in each class will indicate the UR. This is given as follows:

Given M classes of skin type, the Usable Range (UR) is given by Equation (3).

$$UR = \frac{\sum_{x=1}^{M} \frac{n_{ax}}{n_{tx}}}{M} \times 100 \tag{3}$$

where n_{ax} = number of fingerprints in class x with $QS \geq Ta$.
n_{tx} = total number of fingerprints in class x.
Ta = minimum QS for acceptable fingerprint quality.

2.3 Consistency

Consistency (*C*) metric measures the variation of the Image Quality Score measured over time and usage. Effectively, this metric determines the change in the image quality from its initial value after the fingerprint sensor has been used for a fixed number of time, *P* (or over a duration of time *P*). This is given by Equation (4) below.

$$C = \left(1 - \frac{QS_0 - QS_P}{QS_0}\right) \times 100 \qquad\qquad (4)$$

where QS_0 = image quality score at time 0.
              QS_P = image quality score after time *P* (or *P* number of use).

The proposed metrics as given by Equation (2) – (4) that satisfy definition D1-D3 imply that the QS metric is a useful metric to quantify the quality of a fingerprint sensor. The reliability for Consistency and Usable Range measures are dependent on the Image Quality Score. Therefore, the accuracy of QS measure is critical.

3   Procedure for Data Collection

A key element for sensor benchmarking is good data collection. Care has been taken to ensure that the fingerprint image acquired is close to what a normal system out in the field will experience and that there is as little variation as possible among the various sensors during the fingerprint acquisition.

Two main sets of data are needed. The first set is the database of fingerprint images acquired using various commercially available fingerprint sensors from people with various skin types and at various weather conditions. The second set is the database of fingerprint images of a sensor acquired over a period of time.

3.1 Acquisition with Various Sensors

The procedure employed for the data collection is as follows:
1. Classify fingerprint samples into 3 types – wet, normal & dry of equal distribution.
2. Gather sufficient number of volunteers for each group, with mixture of genders.
3. Clean all sensors to be used before the start of data collection. Use the sensors until any one of them requires cleaning. Once a sensor is cleaned, all the other sensors will be cleaned as well.
4. For each volunteer, the fingerprints of the thumb (T), index (I) and middle (M) fingers for both left (L) and right (R) hands are captured. Capture each finger following the sequence LT, LI, LM, RT, RI, RM, then repeat it again so that two sequence of data are acquired per person. Then repeat for the other sensors. There should not be any break before the entire data

acquisition process is completed (i.e the volunteer leave before all the sensors are used and return at a later time).

Table 2. Fingerprint sensors used and its specifications

Vendor	ST Micro	Veridicom	Infineon	Authentec
Product Name	TouchChip, TCS1AA	FPS110	FingerTIP v2.2	FingerLoc AF-S2
Technology	Capacitive	Capacitive	Capacitive	E-field
Sensor Array	256x360	300x300	224x288	128x128
Sensor Surface Area (mm)	18.0x12.8	15x15	11.1x14.3	13x13
Resolution (Dpi)	508	500	513	250-1000
Grey-scale	8-bit	8 bit	8bit	8 bit

Table 2 shows the fingerprint sensors used in our experiment. Three weather conditions are chosen covering the tropical weather, summer weather and winter weather. The fingerprint images for the tropical weather are collected in Singapore while both the summer and winter weather fingerprint images are collected in Munich, Germany. In each weather condition, about 40 volunteers with 12 samples per volunteer per sensor are collected. This amounted to about 480 samples per sensor per weather condition. Table 3 shows the weather condition at the time of fingerprint image acquisition.

Table 3. Recorded weather condition during data collection

Weather condition		Average Temperature (°C)	Average Relative Humidity (%)
Singapore (Tropical)		29.4	75.0
Munich (Summer) (indoor)		26.4	48.8
Munich (Winter)	indoor	26.4	26.4
	outdoor	3.8	62.2

3.2 Acquisition over Time

For this database, one of the sensors in Table 2 is selected (the name of the sensor used is purposely omitted). The sensor is continuously used over a period of about 6 months openly (anyone from the public can touch it). A total of 500,247 touches were recorded throughout the entire duration. In this 6-month period, 3 reference people are identified, each representing normal, dry and wet finger type. For each person, the procedure for data collection as described in Section 3.1 is used. At a regular time interval, the fingerprint images of these reference people are acquired. Before the fingerprint images are collected, all the sensors are cleaned to ensure that the difference in quality is not due to residue.

3.3 Preprosessing

It was observed that not all fingerprint images from all the sensors used have the same characteristic. As such, the data is preprocessed to a normalized setting as follows:

1. Resolution of 500 dpi
2. 8-bit grey scale with the histogram stretched to achieve the darkest 5% of the total number of pixels at grey level 0 and the brightest 5% of the total number of pixels at grey level 255.
3. Extract only the central region with a size of 192x192 pixels for analysis.

In all the data collection processes, the assumption made is that all the fingerprints were acquired with the optimal sensor setting. We have fixed the sequence at which the data collection is performed. This is to reduce human error as the number of sensors used is quite a lot to be manually managed. Without a proper sequence, there might be cases where a sensor is used more than once per person or not used at all. However, in doing so, we assume that the characteristic of the finger does not change much from sensor to sensor. This assumption is generally valid but may not be if a person has just washed his/her hand prior to the data collection as the finger will get dry after a while.

4   Results

4.1 Acquisition with Various Sensors

From the database of fingerprint images acquired with various sensors, the respective Image Quality Score (QS) was computed for all as described in Section 3.1. Then statistical results are derived and tabulated as the basis for sensor benchmarking. The mean value is a good measure to indicate the average acquisition performance under various conditions. The standard deviation value (std dev) gives an indication of the comparative reliability of the measurements obtained. The percentage of users satisfying the minimum score will give a good estimate of the Usable Range. Based on our experience, QS of 45% yields the minimum acceptable quality of a fingerprint image for fingerprint verification.

Table 4 shows the statistical analysis of the QS obtained from the fingerprint images collected in all the weather conditions using all the sensors selected. Table 5 shows the computed mean QS and UR for the respective sensors.

From Table 4 and Table 5 we can conclude that there are indeed differences in the performance of the fingerprint sensors. However, the influence of the weather condition to the Image Quality Score is not significant. This could be due to the somewhat similar temperature of tropical and summer weather while condition in winter may be moderated by the indoor environment. It would be interesting to study the performance of outdoor winter condition to better conclude the effect of weather.

Table 4. Statistical analysis of QS for all weather conditions using various fingerprint sensors

Analysis	ST Micro			Authentec			Veridicom			Infineon		
	Tropical	Summer	Winter	Tropical	Summer	Winter	Tropical	Summer	Winter	Tropical	Summer	Winter
Overall Analysis												
Mean	66.92	63.03	63.93	75.84	76.67	75.93	64.13	63.23	71.09	74.21	75.57	74.03
Std Dev	20.73	21.69	23.09	18.20	16.39	16.25	20.30	20.91	18.99	16.85	15.93	17.07
>=45	82.11%	78.72%	78.33%	91.46%	95.18%	95.00%	81.15%	77.41%	91.11%	92.46%	94.73%	93.55%
Data Analysis for Normal TYPE												
Mean	72.71	68.10	63.70	79.66	78.99	77.09	69.85	71.30	73.16	77.31	78.89	75.63
>=45	91.67%	85.60%	78.43%	98.33%	96.59%	97.06%	90.42%	87.88%	93.62%	98.32%	96.97%	94.09%
Data Analysis for Dry TYPE												
Mean	55.06	51.61	71.83	61.10	66.89	78.02	49.63	55.06	72.27	59.06	67.81	73.69
>=45	62.12%	63.89%	85.42%	71.96%	86.11%	97.92%	55.30%	77.78%	91.67%	77.27%	91.67%	93.75%
Data Analysis for Wet TYPE												
Mean	66.34	57.09	60.87	79.87	75.02	72.80	68.23	51.44	66.66	76.84	71.75	71.14
>=45	81.94%	70.51%	75.00%	98.48%	94.87%	89.82%	90.15%	59.61%	86.11%	97.72%	91.67%	92.45%

Table 5. Computed QS and UR metrics for the respective fingerprint sensors

	ST Micro	Authentec	Veridicom	Infineon
Mean QS	64.63	76.15	66.15	74.60
UR	79.72%	93.88%	83.22%	93.58%

Most sensors do not face difficulty with the normal fingers as the results indicated that the difference is not high. Problem occurs mainly for wet and dry fingers. It is also noted that the QS for the normal fingers is not as high as expected. This could be due to the influence by the residue left over from wet fingers during the data capture, which in turn will influence the quality of the normal fingers.

4.2 Acquisition over Time

Figure 2 shows the QS obtained (vertical axis) for a fingerprint sensor plotted against the number of touches (horizontal axis) as described in Section 3.2.

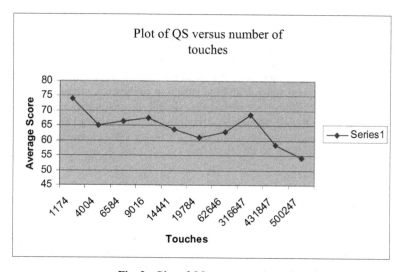

Fig. 2.   Plot of QS versus number of touches

From the results, the Consistency metric obtained is 74.15%. From Figure 2, it can be seen that there is a general trend of degradation in the QS with the number of touches although there are some local fluctuations. The local fluctuations could be due to changes in the skin condition at the time of fingerprint acquisition and to a small extent, the difference in the consistency of the sensor cleaning before use. We found that the reason for the significant drop in QS is due to minor damage of the sensor. At about 60,000 touches, two small white blobs appear in the image, which becomes gradually bigger as the number of touches increases. Figure 3 shows the fingerprint images acquired in the course of the experiment, which clearly indicate the consistent presence of two abnormal white blobs.

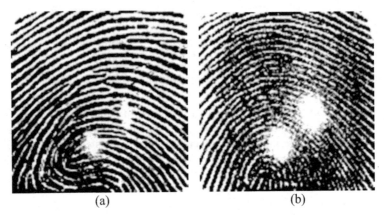

(a)   (b)

Fig. 3. Fingerprint image obtained after (a) 100,000 touches and (b) 500,247 touches

5   Conclusion

In this paper, a new methodology has been proposed to benchmark fingerprint sensors. The methodology consists of three metrics and procedures to collect the data in order to compute the proposed metrics. Two small scale experiments are conducted to show that the proposed metrics can indeed be used to benchmark the acquisition performance of fingerprint sensors and the variation in the acquisition performance of the sensors over time. The effect of weather on the acquisition performance of the sensor has also been studied. However, it is noted that the scale of the experiment is small. For a more representative benchmarking, a larger scale experiment is needed to obtain a more concrete result.

Acknowledgments

The authors would like to thank Eyung Lim of the Centre for Signal Processing, Nanyang Technological Univeristy, Singapore for his kind assistance in the image quality software. This work was supported by the R&D grant from the Agency for Science, Technology and Research, Singapore and sponsorship from Infineon Technologies AG, Germany.

References

1. Hicklin, R.A.: Comparative Fingerprint Quality and Performance, Mitretek Technology Summaries Summer 2003, pp. 13-16, (2003). http://www.biometrics.org/html/bc2002_sept_program/5_bc0145_HicklinBrief.pdf.
2. Simon-Zorita D., Ortega-Garcia J., Sanchez-Asenjo M., Ganzalez Rodiguez J.: Minutia Based Enhanced Fingerprint Verification Assessment Relaying on Image Quality Factors, Proc. IEEE Int. Conf on Image Processing, vol. 2, pp. 891-894, (2003).

3. Utah Department of Public Safety - Bureau of Criminal Identification (US), http://bci.utah.gov/AFIS/Quality.html.
4. Hicklin, A.: Comparative Fingerprint Quality and Performance: Rolls, Slaps and Flaps, Biometric Consortium Conference 2002, www.biometrics.org/html/bc2002_sept_program/ 5_bc0145_HicklinBrief.pdf (2002).
5. Lim, E.,Jiang X.D., Yau W.Y.: Fingerprint Quality and Validity Analysis, Proc. IEEE Int. Conf. on Image Processing, vol. 1, pp. 469 -472, (2002).
6. Bolle R.M., Pankanti S.U., Yao Y.S.: System and method for determining the quality of fingerprint images. US Patent No. 5963656, (1999).
7. Maltoni, D., Maio, D., Jain, A.K., Prabhakar, S.: Handbook of Fingerprint Recognition, Springer-Verlag, (2003).

Detecting Liveness in Fingerprint Scanners Using Wavelets: Results of the Test Dataset

Stephanie Schuckers[1,2] and Aditya Abhyankar[1]

[1] Department of Electrical and Computer Engineering,
Clarkson University, Potsdam, NY 13699, USA
[2] Lane Department of Computer Science and Electrical Engineering,
West Virginia University, Morgantown, West Virginia 26506, USA

Abstract. A novel method is proposed to detect "liveness" associated with fingerprint devices. The physiological phenomenon of perspiration, observed only in live people, is used as a measure to classify 'live' fingers from 'not live' fingers. Pre-processing involves filtering of the images using different image processing techniques. Wavelet analysis of the images is performed using Daubechies wavelet. Multiresolution analysis is performed to extract information from the low frequency content, while wavelet packet analysis is performed to analyze the high frequency information content. A threshold is applied to the first difference of the information in all the sub-bands. The energy content of the changing wavelet coefficients, which are directly associated with the perspiration pattern, is used as a quantified measure to differentiate live fingers from others. The proposed algorithm was applied to a data set of approximately 30 live, 30 spoof and 14 cadaver fingerprint images from three different types of scanners. The algorithm was able to completely classify 'live' fingers from 'not live' fingers providing a method for improved spoof protection.

1 Introduction

It is desired to have robust and systematic methodologies for personal identification in today's networked community. Conventional means of identification, such as signatures and photo identity cards, may fail to provide sufficient security. Biometrics could be looked upon as 'identity assurance in the information age'. Conventional means of identification are the things a person knows and carries, but biometrics are what the person is [1]. Among various biometric identifiers, fingerprints are the oldest, most widely used and most popular.

Unfortunately, with increased technological advancement, spoofing a biometric identification system has become easier. Fingerprint scanners have been found to be susceptible to different types of attacks from artificially prepared synthetic fingers, latent fingers, and, in the worst case, dismembered fingers. Among various fingerprint security issues, it is of particular interest to check whether source of input signal is a live genuine finger, in order to make the system intelligent enough to be able to differentiate it from a signal originating from a spoof or a

D. Maltoni and A.K. Jain (Eds.): BioAW 2004, LNCS 3087, pp. 100–110, 2004.
© Springer-Verlag Berlin Heidelberg 2004

cadaver. This security test added as supplement to the verification is termed as "liveness" detection [2], [3].

Improved techniques are required to make "liveness" detection more accurate. In this paper, a wavelet-based method is proposed to detect "liveness" associated with perspiration changes in a time-series of fingerprint images. This wavelet-based method uses maxima energy extraction, multiresolution analysis, and wavelet packet analysis to extract information from time series capture of images. The method is purely software-based and requires no additional hardware enhancements.

1.1 Spoofing and Liveness

Fraudulent entry of an unauthorized person into a fingerprint recognition system by using faux fingerprint sample is termed as 'spoofing' [4]. Recently different spoofing techniques have been reported, which include preparation of gummy fingers, use of latent fingerprints, fake fingers using moldable plastic, clay, play-doh, wax, and silicon [4],[5],[6],[7].

The ease with which fingerprint scanners can be spoofed is the driving force to check for "liveness" associated with fingerprint scanners. "Liveness" detection in fingerprint devices provides a possible solution to spoof attacks [2]. As the name suggests, the detection aims at making sure that the fingerprint sample introduced to the scanner has been provided by a live source.

Our laboratory has demonstrated that perspiration can be used as a measure of "liveness" detection in the case of fingerprint matching systems [8],[4]. Unlike cadaver or spoof fingers, live fingers demonstrate a distinctive spatial moisture pattern, when in physical contact with the capturing surface of the fingerprint scanner. This pattern evolves in time due to the physiological phenomenon of perspiration, and hence can be called 'perspiration pattern'. Thus this pattern of perspiration spreads along fingerprint ridges as time progresses, as shown in Figure (1). A signal processing-based method developed previously in our group has been developed which utilizes several static and dynamic features in conjunction with three classification methods: back propagation neural network, One R and discriminant analysis. This method is capable of producing classification rates in the range of 45% to 90% for several types of scanner technologies. The scope for improvement in the classification rate is the motivation for this work.

1.2 Wavelet Analysis

For this particular study, the images are captured as a time sequence. The most significant information is carried by the singularities and sharp variation points of the image. Variation points can be analyzed as locations of contours in the image, which form the most important part of feature extraction [9]. To quantify these features we first compute the wavelet transform of the images. The low frequency analysis is performed using multiresolution analysis, and high frequency content is analyzed using packet transform technique.

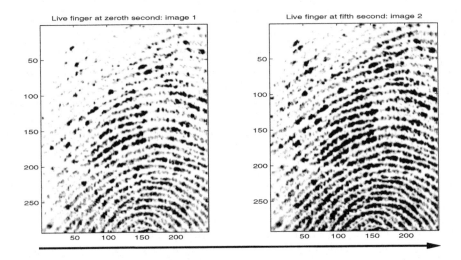

Fig. 1. Live fingerprint images captured as a time sequence. The left figure is captured at zeroth second, while the right is captured after five seconds. Perspiration is observed as time progresses.

Selection of mother wavelet is a critical issue in any wavelet based application. For this particular algorithm, Daubechies wavelet is selected as the mother wavelet. The filter was designed according to the 'cascade algorithm' given in [10]. The number of coefficients are selected to be 16. Only those roots of the periodic trigonometric polynomial are retained which lie inside the unit circle, to ensure minimum phase. By selecting maximum vanishing moments, it is possible to extract information even from the smoother parts of the images.

The main focus of the implementation is to construct compactly supported wavelets ψ [10]. The designed filters are shown in Figure (2). If the scaling function ϕ itself is chosen to have compact support, then it automatically ensures the compact support of wavelet ψ. Designed ϕ, ψ, and wavelet packet functions are shown in Figure (3). For entropy based wavelet packet expansion Coifman-Wickerhouser algorithm is used [11]. For the "liveness" algorithm the coefficients from high frequency scale 3 were used from the resultant wavelet packet transform. Multiresolution analysis (MRA) leads naturally to a hierarchial and fast scheme for the computation of the wavelet coefficients of a given function. MRA was performed using the same filters in Figure (2). For the "liveness" algorithm the coefficients from low frequency scale 2 were selected for analysis from the MRA. More details are given in section 2.2.

2   Algorithm to Detect "Liveness"

The entire procedure can be divided into three parts. The first part includes preprocessing steps so as to prepare the data for the wavelet analysis. The second

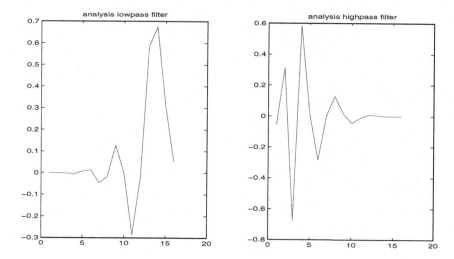

Fig. 2. Daubechies analysis filters. The left figure shows the low pass filter and the right figure shows high pass filter. The filters are designed for the number of coefficients to be 16. X axis indicates the coefficient number, while the Y axis shows the value for that coeficient number. The filter is normalized so that sum of all the filter coefficients is equal to $\sqrt{2}$.

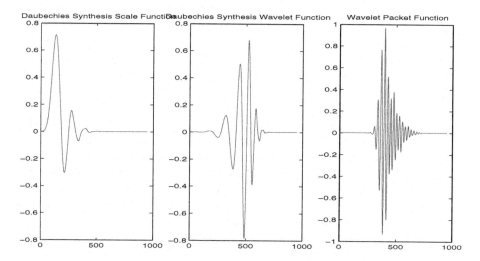

Fig. 3. Left figure indicates Daubechies scale function (ϕ), middle figure indicates Daubechies wavelet function (ψ), and right figure shows the wavelet packet function. For all figures, the number of iterations are selected to be 5.

part is the actual wavelet analysis. Post processing steps are included in the third part.

The algorithm to detect "liveness" associated with fingerprint scanners:

1. Start
   Pre-Processing Steps:
2. Sort and arrange data into training and testing data.
3. Input and convert images into a suitable format.
4. Remove noise using median filtering.
5. Equalize images using histogram equalization
   Wavelet Analysis:
6. Implement Daubechies wavelet
7. Implement wavelet transform
8. Perform maxima energy extraction
9. Perform multiresolution analysis
10. Perform wavelet packet analysis
    Post-Processing Steps:
11. Align sub-bands
12. Computer first difference and threshold
13. Analyze energy distribution
14. Select classification threshold
15. Decide whether finger is 'live' or 'not live'.
16. To analyze another finger go to step 3.
17. If not stop.

Implementation was done using MATLAB(v6.5R13).

2.1   Pre-processing Steps

Data previously collected in our laboratory is used to test the algorithm. Thirty-three live subjects were comprised of different age groups (11 people between ages 20-30 years, 9 people between 30-40, 7 people between 40-50, and 6 people greater than 50), ethnicities (Asian-Indian, Caucasian, Middle Eastern), and approximately equal numbers of men and women. Most live subjects created a fingerprint cast for development of a spoof made from Play-Doh using a method described in [8], [4]. Finally, 14 fingerprint images were collected from three cadavers. The data set consists of, in all, 69 fingerprints image sets using Precise Biometric (Capacitive DC), 73 using Ethentica (Electro-optical), and 74 using Secugen (Optical), from live, spoof, and cadaver subjects. Enrollment (up to five tries) and verification (in at least one of six trials) was the criterion for inclusion in the study resulting in different totals for each device.

Two raw images captured by a biometric scanner at zeroth second and fifth second are selected for use in the algorithm. Before doing the actual wavelet analysis it is necessary to enhance the images. The major reasons are as follows:

– Captured images may not be clean because of the dust on the fingers or due to the latent finger impressions deposited on the scanner surface.

- The images could be of varying average contrast, due to the varying pressures at the time of the capture.
- The images could be too faint or too dark depending upon whether the finger is too dry or too sweaty.

Histogram equalization and contrast stretching are performed to take into account the varying pressures at the time of captures as well as different initial moisture content of the skin. Median filter is implemented to remove sand and pepper type of noise, if any. Sharpening of the image follows this, as the median filter is a smoothing filter.

2.2   Wavelet Transform

After the images are enhanced, they are processed using Daubechies wavelet transform as described earlier.

Maxima Energy Extraction: Maxima points of the wavelet transform undergo translation, rather than modification, when the image is translated. These maxima energy points are capable of detecting sharp variation points, thus helping to characterizing patterns. Therefore, the first step performed after transforming the image is 'maxima energy extraction' for each scale. For this particular algorithm, the top 10000 coefficients are retained. This is shown in Figure (4).

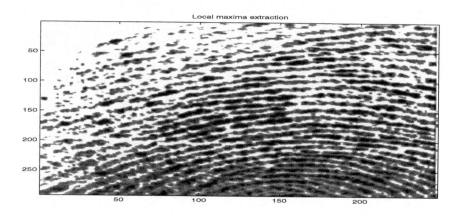

Fig. 4. Maxima energy extraction. The figure shows the inverse transform of a sample fingerprint image after retaining the most significant 10000 coefficients.

Multiresolution Analysis (MRA): MRA is used to analyze the low frequency content of the image. It simultaneously analyzes the image at different scales. For this study, the scale selected is 2. As the scale increases the image gets more and more blurred, eventually adding the low pass effect. For the varying scales, by selecting an appropriate type of analysis filters, segmentation into horizontal, vertical, and diagonal directions is possible. The combination gives the image with all the details embedded for that scale.

Wavelet Packet Analysis: Wavelet packet analysis is utilized for high pass analysis. The best basis is searched by weighing the nodes of every branch of the basis tree vector individually. For the purpose of this algorithm, the scale selected for the wavelet packet transform is 3. For this algorithm, norm values are used to calculate the weights of the node, and thus to formulate the basis vector. The wavelet packet expansion is done as per the Coifman-Wickerhouser algorithm [11]. The best basis is selected for the image captured at zeroth second, and the same basis vector is used for the image after fifth second. This is to have similar sub-band division, in order to avoid any mismatch when taking the difference. An example is shown in Figure (5).

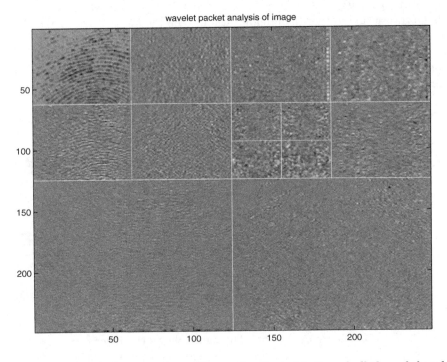

Fig. 5. Wavelet packet transform. The scale selected is 3, and all the sub-bands are shown. Only high pass scale 3 sub-bands are retained for further analysis. These are seen as the smallest four rectangles in the figure.

2.3 Post-processing

Sub-band Alignment: Although this particular step takes very little effort as far as coding and analytical mathematics is concerned, this step is extremely essential. This alignment maintains the phase of the input signal throughout the process. To equate the lengths of the input and output sub-band vectors either zero padding is implemented or alternate deletion is performed. This is performed by keeping the band energy maxima at the center.

This particular step is very important in case of Ethentica scanner, because the size of the captured images is 315×240, and the chances of mismatched sub-bands are high. The images captured by rest of the scanners are 248×292 in dimension where the chances of mismatch are comparatively less.

Threshold Selection: Both images, namely the images captured at zeroth second and after five seconds are decomposed using the MRA scheme, followed by the wavelet packet scheme, as described in section 2.2. Then, the first difference of the individual sub-bands is taken, and all of the outcomes are finally added to formulate the actual difference image. Usually, the singularities are not very obvious in image, nor are they reflected in the wavelet coefficients. So, non-significant coefficients of the discrete wavelet transform are discarded and the rest are enhanced. This process is called as "Thesholding".

A threshold value is used to decide a coefficient has experienced significant change. Each coefficient is retained if it changes more than 40% over 5 seconds, which, when transformed to the spatial domain, represents 90 on the 8-bit scale. Coefficients which do not change more than 40% are discarded.

After processing the sub-bands separately, they are added and inverse transformed to formulate the 'perspiration pattern'. These patterns for different types of fingers are shown in Figure (6). The perspiration pattern, enhanced and quantified by the algorithm described above, is observed only in 'live' fingers.

2.4 Energy Distribution Analysis

Energy Normalization: The energy content of the difference image is retained if the image captured at zeroth second correspondingly has a non-zero value associated with it. This is very essential to avoid false energy increments in case of fingerprints spreading on the edges of the image as the time progresses.

Total energy associated with the changing coefficients, described in the previous section, normalized by total energy for the 5 second image, is used as the measure to decide "liveness" associated with each pair of images.

$$e\% = (\frac{\sum \text{energy of sub bands of the difference image after applying threshold}}{\sum \text{energy of sub bands of the image captured after five seconds}}) \times 100$$

$$(1)$$

A training data set of half of the data is used to determine the threshold value for each scanners, and the threshold of the remaining half is tested with a separate data set. These results are shown in Figures (7) and (8).

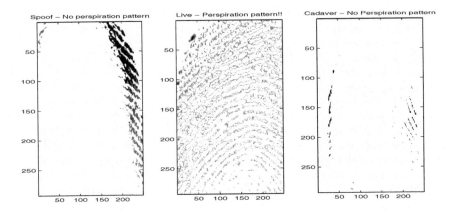

Fig. 6. Perspiration patterns. Spoof, live, and cadaver patterns are shown from left to right. The perspiration pattern is observed only in the case of 'live' finger. The perspiration pattern is the reconstruction of the wavelet coefficients obtained by the algorithm described in this paper.

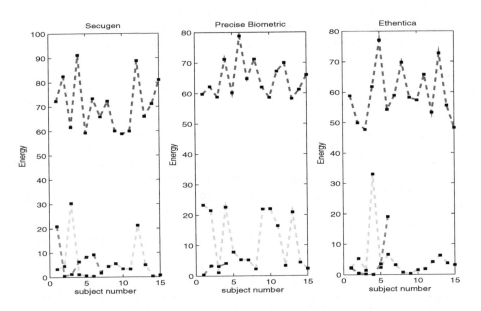

Fig. 7. Training data set results. The graphs are for optical, capacitive DC, and opto-electrical scanners, respectively, from left to right. Clear separation among energy distributions of 'live' (top line), and 'not live' (bottom lines) i s obtained.

3   Results and Discussion

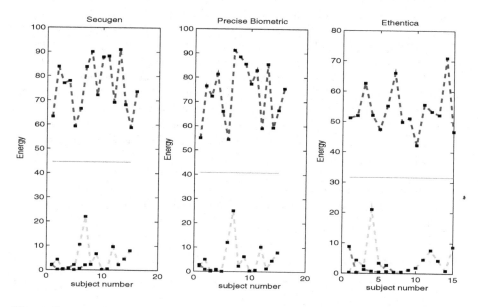

Fig. 8. Testing data set results. The graphs are for optical, capacitive DC, and opto-electrical scanners, respectively, from left to right. For the three scanners, the chosen threshold classifies the fingers, thus detecting "liveness" associated with fingerprint scanners.

Since there is no overlap between the energy content distributions of live and cadaver/spoof distribution, we can perfectly separate the two groups using a threshold that falls between the maximum of the cadaver/spoof distribution and the minimum of the live distribution. This is true for all three types of scanners. The following thresholds were chosen.

- **Threshold level of optical scanner = 44.55**
- **Threshold level of capacitive DC scanner = 40.75**
- **Threshold level of opto-electrical scanner = 31.6**

These thresholds perfectly classify 'live' and 'not-live' for all subjects in the test set.

The data collected for this particular study is at room temperature and at normal humidity conditions, from live subjects and from spoof and cadaver samples. Analyzing the perspiration changes outside of ambient conditions is beyond the scope of the work presented in this paper. In addition, it would strengthen the capability of the algorithm if tested using larger and wider data set, and for different scanner technologies.

4   Conclusion

A wavelet based approach to detect "liveness" associated with the fingerprint scanners is presented. The approach is based on detection of the perspiration pattern from two successive fingerprints captured at zeroth second and after five seconds. It can be concluded that the method presented in this paper *completely* classifies 'live' fingers from 'not live' fingers. This method is tested and found to produce desired results for three different types of scanner technologies, namely optical, opto-electrical, capacitive DC. The method is purely software based, and no hardware enhancements are required, and hence is economical.

Finally, no system is perfect or provides a complete solution. The algorithm presented in this paper is an effort to improve the robustness of the fingerprint recognition systems.

Acknowledgements:
The work was funded by NSF IUCRC Center for Identification Technology Research (CITeR).

References

[1] John D. Woodward, Nicholas M. Orlans, and Peter T. Higgins. *Biometrics.* McGraw-Hill/Osborne, 2003.

[2] Davide Maltonie, Dario Maio, Anil K. Jain, and Salil Prabhakar. *Handbook of Fingerprint Recognition.* Springer-Verlag New York, Inc., 2003.

[3] N. Ratha. Enhancing security and privacy in biometrics-based authentication systems. *IBM systems journal*, 40:614–6134, 2001.

[4] Stephanie Schuckers. Spoofing and anti-spoofing measures. In *Information Security Technical Report*, volume 7, pages 56–62, 2002.

[5] T. Matsumoto, H. Matsumoto, K. Yamada, and S. Hoshino. Impact of artificial 'gummy' fingers on fingerprint systems. In *Proceedings of SPIE*, volume 4677, Jan 2002.

[6] T. Putte and J. Keuning. Biometrical fingerprint recognition: don't get your fingers burned. In *Smart Card Research and Advanced Applications*, pages 289–303. Kluwer Academic Publisher, 2000.

[7] D. Willis and M. Lee. Biometrics under our thumb. *Network computing*, June 1998.

[8] Reza Derakshani, Stephanie Schuckers, Larry Hornak, and Lawrence Gorman. Determination of vitality from a non-invasive biomedical measurement for use in fingerprint scanners. *Pattern Recognition Journal*, 36(2), 2003.

[9] Mary Beth Ruskai, Gregory Beylkin, Ronald Coifman, Ingrid Daubechies, Stephane Mallat, Yves Meyer, and Louise Raphael. Wavelet transform maxima and multiscale edges. In *Wavelets and Their Applications*, pages 67–104, Lowell, Massachusetts, 1992.

[10] Ingrid Daubechies. *Ten Lectures on Wavelets.* Society of Industrial and Applied Mathematics, 1998.

[11] Mary Beth Ruskai, Gregory Beylkin, Ronald Coifman, Ingrid Daubechies, Stephane Mallat, Yves Meyer, and Louise Raphael. Size properties and wavelet packets. In *Wavelets and Their Applications*, pages 453–471, Lowell, Massachusetts, 1992.

Fingerprint Distortion Measurement

Henning Lorch[1], Peter Morguet[2], Hartmut Schröder[3]

[1,2] Infineon Technologies AG, Secure Mobile Solutions
St.-Martin-Str. 76, D – 81541 Munich
{Henning.Lorch, Peter.Morguet}@infineon.com
[3] Circuits and Systems Lab, University of Dortmund
Otto-Hahn-Str. 4, D – 44221 Dortmund
Hartmut.Schroeder@uni-dortmund.de

Abstract. A method for measuring deformations inside single fingerprint images is presented. State-of-the-art fingerprint recognition systems still use affine, to scale represented images. Therefore, image data from so-called sweep sensors is reconstructed to obtain conventional images. Measuring the deformation of fingerprint images facilitates other matching approaches not requiring the finger speed information, e.g. using directly concatenated slice images. Furthermore, fingerprint image compression can be realized by deleting similar content since the images can be reconstructed using deformation measurement.

1 Introduction

Semiconductor fingerprint sensors are emerging. Conventional touch sensors are easy to use and provide a complete raw image, but are very large and expensive. So-called sweep sensors (cp. [1]), with the size of a narrow stripe, are scanning the fingerprint image during a relative motion between the sensor and the finger. Sweep sensors are propagated due to their decreased silicon area and cost. Furthermore, they need less space in the case of a device, what is of great importance for miniaturized mobile applications. Even the security level is higher, because a) the finger motion prevents the remaining of latent fingerprint images on the sensor, and b) the scanned finger area is larger.

Sweep sensors put out much data at a high rate, therefore data reduction is required in miniaturized or mobile devices. New data compression approaches can lose information about the finger speed, resulting in data not directly allowing a reconstruction of the fingerprint image. Distortion measurement extends these approaches by the possibility of straightening out the data to obtain reconstructed images.

Generally, lossy fingerprint data compression by deletion of similar image content is possible since the images can be reconstructed afterwards by using distortion measurement. Furthermore, it can be utilized to evaluate fingerprints on their integrity, e.g. in forensic applications.

The paper structure is as follows: after an overview over system scenarios applying data reduction on a sweep sensor by two different types of filters (sec. 2), the usable fingerprint features and the algorithms are described, which were used for the simulations (sec. 3). The results are presented in sec. 4, and concluded in sec. 5.

D. Maltoni and A.K. Jain (Eds.): BioAW 2004, LNCS 3087, pp. 111-123, 2004.
© Springer-Verlag Berlin Heidelberg 2004

2 Scenarios

Conventionally, a sweep sensor delivers a large number of slice images whose contents overlap, respectively. A complete fingerprint image is reconstructed by determining the translations (Δx, Δy) between each two consecutive slices and merging them, commonly by applying blockmatching methods (cp. [2]).

Without knowledge of the finger speed and dimension, these sensors put out high data amounts at high speed. Presuming a certain allowed finger speed maximum, data rates up to 1 MByte/s are required. This can be handled by today's controllers, but many applications do not provide such fast internal interfaces like USB 1.1 authentication boxes, keyboards or pointing devices. Smartcards, in future to be equipped with biometric authentication, cannot provide enough memory and bandwidth to deal with this amount of data (see also [3]).

For data and bandwidth reduction, the overlap and thus redundancy must be avoided, e.g. by non-linear, data-dropping filters on the sensor. This can lead to distorted images (see section 2.1).

This distortion, as well potentially effectuated by other data compression approaches, must be determined and corrected, e.g. as proposed by distortion measurement in the single image (compare another option using image sequences in [4]).

Forensics would be another field of application. Fingerprints captured from objects in a crime scene are oftentimes heavily distorted (see [5]). Besides dirt and noise, deformations do occur. Commonly, forensic fingerprint recognition requires manual result evaluation because of poor image quality. Fingerprint deformation measurement could be applied similarly as in system B, section 2.2.

2.1 Filter Types

Data reduction on a sweep sensor is possible by different types of filters integrated into the sensor. Basically, the filter approaches can be divided into two classes:

1. **Filters gaining information about the finger movement:** finger speed detection or blockmatching based image reconstruction methods are implemented. Such filter types do need complex logic on the sensor, for example a dedicated signal processor core. The advantage is that the required computing power in the system connected to the sensor is not necessarily higher compared to a touch sensor, or is about equal to. Conventional fingerprint processing methods can be applied (compare [6], [7]). Such a sensor would be much more expensive than an ordinary sweep sensor due to either more silicon area spent for the logic parts, or the use of a newer semiconductor technology in production.

2. **Simple non-linear filters, not analyzing finger motion:** for example, this could be a filter discarding consecutive image slices of high similarity without evaluating positioning information. Such a filter could be implemented very easily and fast. But alternative fingerprint recognition methods are needed for processing and authentication, because the image data from the sensor do not form an affine representation of the fingerprint anymore.

Filters of the 2nd type are the motivation for the distortion measurement of finger-print images.

It can be assumed that these different approaches will compete in future for costs, performance and reliability.

2.2 Systems

Using the filters mentioned above on a fingerprint sweep sensor leads to essentially three system approaches. They vary in the image verification requirements (for conventional or distorted images) and the verification basics (feature or image content based).

A) Filtering Sensor with Motion Detection: a system contains a sensor, which features either a) a finger motion detection unit or b) a blockmatching unit to apply image reconstruction. A recognition system gets an ordinary fingerprint image or similar by the sensor. Commonly used, known and tested processing steps used with area touch sensors can be applied.

That way the features like minutiae can be detected and be compared to a feature template list.

B) Simple On-Sensor Data Reduction and Image Deformation Measurement: this system setup requires a sensor with only 1 pixel row, the smallest thinkable sensor. As shown in figure 1, a filter A determines the difference between the lines (e.g. by the mean square error), and only accepts lines that vary enough from the last accepted line, respectively (further described below). Figure 2 shows an example, in which a 1-line sweep sensor provides the data, and all lines with a mean square error lower than a certain limit are deleted. Then the remaining lines are concatenated.

For describing such a system it must be modeled. To be able to do so, the stochastic of the points of time when a line is deleted must be limited. This is done by a filter B, controlling the deletion rate of lines, e.g. by keeping it constant after determining a starting speed, or only allowing limited accelerations.

The rows of pixels, directly concatenated, will result in a non-affine represented fingerprint image, potentially also horizontally sheared.

Then the image deformation is determined and stored (D).

The features like minutiae are computed in a conventional way (C). The resulting feature list now contains coordinates relating to the deformed image.

The coordinates in the feature list are transformed (E) according to the determined deformation, so that the feature list corresponds to a non-deformed image. The corrected feature list finally can be compared to ordinary feature list templates.

C) Simple On-Sensor Data Reduction and Direct Data Matching. A sweep sensor contains a filter, which eliminates similar consecutive image slices. This way, the overlap and thus the redundancy are removed statistically. But in contrary to system B, the image is not reconstructed but matched on a stripe-based method, e.g. by searching the stripes in a template image (cp. [8]).

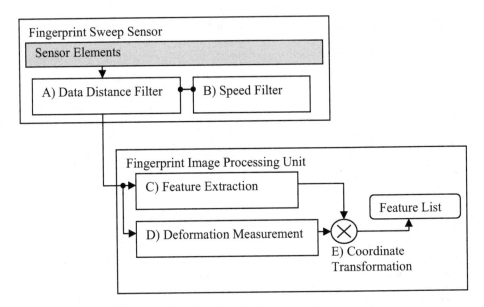

Fig. 1. Fingerprint processing system using a sweep sensor with built-in filter to eliminate similar image data. The image processing unit gets a deformed image, extracts the features, computes the deformation, and transforms back the feature list to obtain non-deformed coordinates

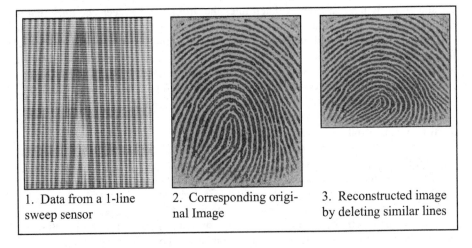

| 1. Data from a 1-line sweep sensor | 2. Corresponding original Image | 3. Reconstructed image by deleting similar lines |

Fig. 2. Example for the concatenation of lines from a sweep sensor. Here, all lines with a pairwise calculated mean square error lower than a certain limit were deleted

Verification principles of that kind do not depend on the data reduction by a filter in the sensor, they would also work with an ordinary sweep sensor. The disadvantage is that the template for verification is much larger than a feature based template (here image data compared to a minutiae list). This is significant when talking about minia-turized mobile applications like smartcards.

Comparison. The following table shows a summary of the mentioned system approaches.

Table 1. Advantages and disadvantages of the systems using on-sensor data reduction

System	A) On-sensor motion detection	B) On-sensor filter, deformation removal	C) On-sensor filter, image based matching
Pro	Less sensor data, approved algorithms	Less sensor data, smallest sensor	Less sensor data, no reconstruction required
Contra	Complex logic on sensor	New algorithms required	Very large templates

System B is the one depending on distortion measurement and thus regarded here.

3 Distortion Measurement

Deformation measurement inside single images is taking advantage of fingerprint fea-tures instead of being reliant on external information (like speed measurement). By human inspection it can be judged whether a fingerprint is heavily deformed. Our vi-sion system tells us that the proportions inside the image are not normal. This is diffi-cult to recognize for a very small image region, we need to see a larger area.

Due to variations of the underlying characteristic, proportions inside a fingerprint can only be computed statistically over a certain image region. Statistics accuracy im-proves as the amount of data increases, in this case as the image region is enlarged.

Measuring proportions means that the results are only ratios. In this case it is pre-sumed that one dimension of the fingerprint image is known. Sweep sensor images meet this requirement by being absolutely scaled in the horizontal direction of the sensor pixel array. So the results can be referred to absolute values.

3.1 Image Distortion

Assuming that one dimension in the fingerprint image is to scale, this dimension will be defined as the horizontal direction here (a system B from section 2.2 will provide an image which is to scale in the horizontal sensor orientation).

In the vertical direction the image will be stretched by a variable scaling factor $s_Y(y)$. Additionally, a skew of the finger motion will cause a shear of the image by a local angle $\delta_S(y)$ (see figure 3).

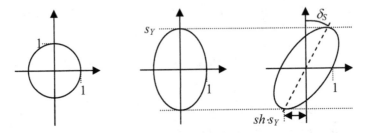

Fig. 3. Distortion by sweeping without speed information. An imaginary circle in the image with radius 1 will be deformed to an ellipse with a vertical dimension of $2 \cdot s_Y$. Skew in the finger motion will lead to shearing by δ_S, which can also be expressed by a factor sh defining horizontal skew dependently on the vertical part

3.2 Features

As features for generating a statistic about the fingerprint image deformation features can be chosen that are dependent by their orientation when the image is stretched in one dimension. These mainly are (see also figure 4):

- Pore distances: pores are sweat pores inside the skin which result in bright dots in the centre of the ridges (fingerprint lines). Pores inside the same ridge with minimal distance are named here as neighboured pores. To resolve the pores, the image quality and resolution must be high enough.
- Ridge widths.
- Ridge distances: the distances between the centres of neighboured ridges.
- 2-dimensional Fast Fourier Transformation (FFT).

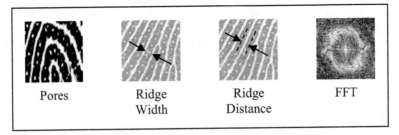

Fig. 4. The proportion features in a fingerprint are mainly the pore distances, the ridge widths, the ridge distances and the FFT geometry

3.3 Distortion Measurement

A vertical image scaling changes the vertical component of a ridge in the image, the horizontal component is sheared dependently on the vertical part. In figure 5, d_S and α_S are measured values in the distorted image, for example ridge or pore distances.

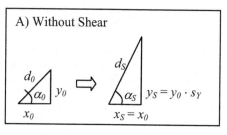 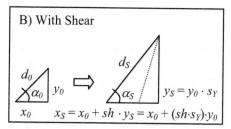

Fig. 5. Vertical deformation of a vector by a scale factor s_Y, sheared by a factor sh

Assuming that s_Y and sh are global variables inside an image region and that all others belong to one of many measurements i, the schemes in figure 5 lead to the equations (1) and (2):

$$s_Y = \frac{d_{S,i} \cdot \sin \alpha_{S,i}}{d_{0,i} \cdot \sin \alpha_{0,i}}, \text{ and } \frac{x_S}{x_0} = 1 + sh \cdot s_Y \cdot \tan \alpha_{0,i} \tag{1}$$

$$d_{S,i} = d_{0,i} \cdot \sqrt{\cos^2 \alpha_{0,i} \cdot (1 + sh \cdot s_Y \cdot \tan \alpha_{0,i})^2 + (s_Y \cdot \sin \alpha_{0,i})^2} \tag{2}$$

In a distorted image, the scaled parameters $x_{S,i}$, $y_{S,i}$, $d_{S,i}$ and $\alpha_{S,i}$ are measured. The unknown angle $\alpha_{0,i}$ is to be eliminated. For the statistic calculation, all $d_{0,i}$ are set equally to a mean d_0 (e.g., original ridge distances are assumed to be the same).

The simulations below were done without shearing the images ($sh = 0$). The equations are transformed to equation (3), containing the unknown variables s_Y and d_0:

$$d_{S,i} = d_0 \cdot \frac{1}{\sqrt{1 - \sin^2 \alpha_{S,i} \cdot (1 - s_Y^{-2})}}, \text{ for } sh = 0 \tag{3}$$

s_Y and d_0 are assumed to be constant in the regarded image region.

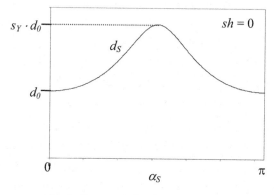

Fig. 6. Characteristic of d_S over α_S with $sh = 0$

Figure 6 shows the characteristic of d_S over α_S. This curve is approximated to all measured values of $(d_{S,i}, \alpha_{S,i})$ by s_Y and d_0.

For small shear factors, the shear angle δ_S (cp. figure 3) can be approximated by determining the difference of the maximum position of d_S and $\pi/2$ (alternatively the minimum position, if $s_Y < 1$).

3.4 Pore Neighbourhood Searching

The search for the pore locations is not new (cp. [7], [9]) and therefore not explained in detail here. The image is binarized and segmented, and the pores are detected by taking all small white areas and weighted by the area size (see figure 7 A, the pores are marked by white dots). Noise reduction is applied (all pores with a weight much smaller than the nearest neighbours' weights are deleted, cp. figure 7 B). The directions of the ridges in the image are computed (cp. also [10], [6], [11]) and stored in a fingerprint orientation array. Similarly, the local image quality is estimated and stored the same way for detecting and excluding bad image regions.

A)   B)   C)

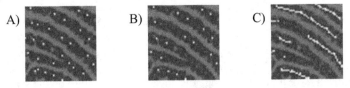

Fig. 7. Searching pores (A), deleting noise (B), determining neighbourhoods (C)

Searching the pore neighbourhoods is done as follows:

1. Generate list of pore relations (relative angle and distance)
2. Delete relations with great distance (keep only near neighbourhoods), or whose relative angle differs too much from the local orientation field (ensure that the 2 pores belong to the same ridge)
3. Then determine the neighbourhoods by the following algorithm:

```
Do until no changes occur anymore {
  For all pores do (using relation list) {
    If pore has no linked neighbour then
      Mark connection to nearest possible neighbour;
    Else if pore has exactly 1 linked neighbour then {
      Get the opposite direction of the neighbour;
      Mark connection to nearest possible neighbour in
        approximately this opposite direction;
    } // Each pore can have maximal two neighbours
  }
}
```

```
Keep matching connection marks as fixed neighbour-
    hoods by linking each 2 pores together;
   Delete all connection marks;
}
Store pore links in neighbourhood list;
```

3.5 Width Distribution

The estimation of the ridge widths is also not new (cp. [11]). After contrast enhancement, binarization and morphological noise and error removal, the ridges are thinned (also by morphological operators) to 1-pixel wide lines, as shown in figure 8 (A). Along the positions of these lines (which are marking the centres of the original ridges), image data of the grey-level image are sampled along an oriented stripe window, centred at the ridge centre, and directed orthogonal to the ridge orientation (B). In the ridge orientation, the grey values are averaged (C), and the ridge width is computed as the width of the valley in (C) at the middle of the grey level range.

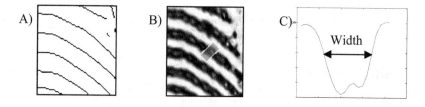

Fig. 8. Computation of the ridge widths

3.6 Distance Distribution

The ridge distances are computed analogously to the ridge widths (see figure 9), but using a larger stripe window (B). The distances are taken as the difference of the middle positions of two ridges (C).

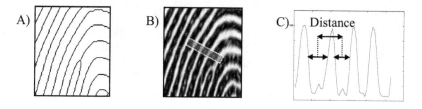

Fig. 9. Computation of the ridge distances

3.7 FFT Analysis

A 2-dimensional FFT of the globally contrast-adjusted grey image is computed and logarithmized to get reasonable values (see figure 10 A).

The range from 0 - π around the centre is resampled into polar coordinates considering the FFT size, that way the intensity array is scaled to absolute frequencies f (B).

The frequencies are transformed to period lengths d (C).

The maximums of the period intensities are detected (D) and weighted by their clearness (brightness of the dots in D).

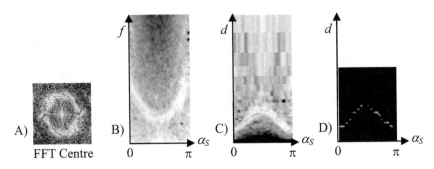

Fig. 10. Steps of the 2-dimensional FFT analysis

4 Simulation Results

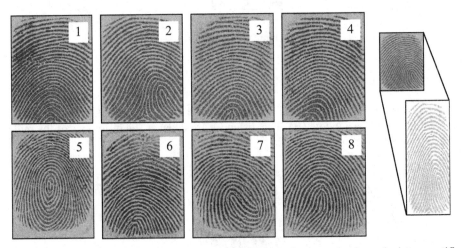

Fig. 11. 8 images are presented, for which the algorithms above are used to calculate an artificial deformation

The algorithms were tested for a series of artificially stretched images. Exemplary, 8 images and their results are presented. Figure 11 shows the original images.

All images were stretched vertically by a factor of 2 and not sheared (cp. also fig. 11). The algorithms were applied to the whole image area. The resulting values for s_Y should be 2, and the values for δ_S should be 0°.

4.1 Single Measurements

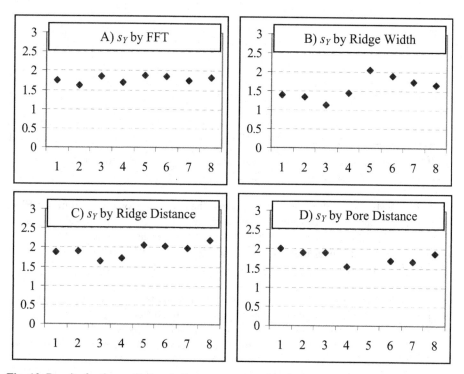

Fig. 12. Results for the vertical scale factor s_Y measured in the images 1 – 8. Image no. 5 shows too less pores for calculating a reasonable pore distance distribution

Figure 12 shows the results for s_Y for each image determined by the different methods. Apparently s_Y is scattering.

The results by the ridge width method (B) for s_Y are varying between 1 and 2, and are obviously not reasonable. The reason is easy to see: looking for instance at image no. 2 (cp. fig. 11) shows that the ridge intervals are nearly constant over the whole image. But apparently the lower half is darker than the upper one, caused by broad dark ridges and narrow spaces between them. Varying pressure while touching the sensor causes such effects. Here the pressure in the lower half of the fingerprint was higher than in the upper one. In combination with a main ridge orientation that is also different between the lower and upper half, an orientation based ridge width statistics must fail.

All other results for s_Y are mainly varying between 1.6 and 2. One value is missing, because the image no. 5 shows not enough pores in neighbourhoods for the pore distribution method to yield a reasonable statement.

4.2 Result Combinations

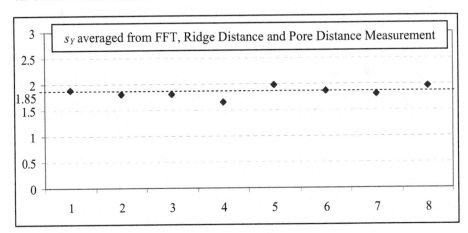

Fig. 13. The resulting values for the vertical scale factor s_Y are averaged and shown for all 8 images. They spread around a mean value of 1.85

Figure 13 shows resulting values for s_Y for the 8 images averaged from the FFT, ridge distance and pore distance distribution measurements. These values spread around a mean value of 1.85. Thus there seems to be a systematic why the values are lower than expected (lower than 2). The reason for this is still unknown.

The spread of the values is supposed to have 2 reasons:

- The algorithms are still not optimized for any image quality and properties. They were programmed to be able to extract the distribution features from most images, but not to deal with all effects (e.g. the ridge orientation and image quality estimation are sensitive to effects gained from the artificial image deformation, here the vertical scaling).
- The statistic features like pores, ridge distances and FFT cannot be perfect themselves. Furthermore the features are affected by the image quality, and a sophisticated filter for all feature values is still missing.

When including the systematic error and assuming that a resulting value of 1.85 would be correct, than the results are already lying very close to the target.

5 Conclusion

A description of a novel technique for measuring the deformation of single fingerprint images without external information has been presented.

3 of 4 examined fingerprint features proved to be suitable for computing deformations: the pore distance distribution, the ridge distance distribution and the FFT geometry allow the analysis of the proportions inside fingerprints. The results, computed with test algorithms, showed a good conformance to the target values.

A reconstruction of a distorted fingerprint image will be possible, if the distortion characteristic is known. For example, a deformed sweep sensor image can be reconstructed, if the general characteristics of the sensor and the finger motion are modeled, and if the models can be completed by deformation measurement results.

The deformation measurement on the one hand side facilitates new recognition system approaches using sweep sensors and not requiring finger speed information (e.g. for bandwidth reduction), and on the other hand side offers the opportunity to compress fingerprint images by deleting similar image content presuming afterward reconstruction using the deformation measurement.

References

1. Maltoni D., Maio D., Jain A. K., Prabhakar S.: Handbook of Fingerprint Recognition, Springer-Verlag, 2003
2. Mainguet J. F.: Fingerprint-Reading System, United States Patent No. US 6,289,114 B1, Sep. 11, 2001
3. Finger Minutiae Encoding Format and Parameters for On-Card Matching, DIN V. 66400, 2001
4. Dorai C., Ratha N., Bolle R.: Reliable Distortion Detection in Compressed Fingerprint Videos, Proc. CVPR 2000, Hilton Head SC, 2000
5. Garris M. D., McCabe R. M.: Fingerprint Minutiae from Latent and Matching Tenprint Images, NIST and FBI
6. Jain A. K., Hong L., Pankanti S., Bolle R.: An Identity Authentication System Using Fingerprints, Proceedings of the IEEE, Vol. 85, No. 9, 1997, pp. 1365 – 1388
7. Roddy A. R., Stosz J. D.: Fingerprint Features - Statistical Analysis and System Performance Estimates, Proceedings of the IEEE, vol. 85, No. 9, 1997, pp. 1390-1421
8. Wilson C. L., Watson C. I., Paek E. G.:Combined Optical and Neural Network Fingerprint Matching, Optical Pattern Recognition VIII, SPIE Proceedings, Vol. 3073, 1997, pp. 373-382
9. Levesque V., Hayward V.: Experimental Evidence of Lateral Skin Strain During Tactile Exploration, Proceedings Eurohaptics 2003
10. Watson C. I., Candela J., Grother P.: Comparison of FFT Fingerprint Filtering Methods for Neural Network Classification, Technical Report NISTIR 5493, 1994
11. Hong L., Wan Y., Jain A. K.: Fingerprint Image Enhancement Algorithm and Performance Evaluation, IEEE Transactions on Pattern Analysis and Machine Intelligence, Vol. 80, No. 8, 1998, pp. 777 – 789

Study of the Distinctiveness of Level 2 and Level 3 Features in Fragmentary Fingerprint Comparison

Krzysztof M. Kryszczuk, Patrice Morier, Andrzej Drygajlo

Signal Processing Institute
Swiss Federal Institute of Technology Lausanne (EPFL)
{krzysztof.kryszczuk, patrice.morier, andrzej.drygajlo}@epfl.ch

Abstract. In this paper we present the results of an experiment which aims to provide an insight into the problems related to the fingerprint recognition from its fragment. Level 2 and Level 3 features are considered, and their distinctive potential is estimated in respect to the considered area of a fingerprint fragment. We conclude that the use of level 3 features can offer at least a comparable recognition potential from a small area fingerprint fragment, as the level 2 features offer for fragments of larger area.

1 Introduction

The studies of distinctive fingerprint features have a long tradition. As early as 1872 a probabilistic analysis of selected level two features was performed by F. Galton [4].

Level one and level two features are related to the characteristic configuration of the ridges on the surface of the fingerprint. The characteristic ridge alignment in the center of the fingerprint is regarded as level one feature. The local discontinuities and links between ridges are considered level two features, otherwise referred to as the minutiae. The most prominent and common among the minutiae are the ridge terminations and bifurcations [7]. Level two features, are currently by far the most common feature set used for automated fingerprint recognition [4].

Level three features consist of local intra-ridge details, including the traces of the sweat pores distributed over the ridges. The pores are the termination loci of the sweat ducts that originate in the sweat glands in the dermis. An early description of the pores and their characteristics can be found in [2]. The position of the pores on the ridges is thought to be individual and distinctive for a given finger.

Level three features (the pores in particular) have only recently attracted the attention of researchers working in the area of automated fingerprint verification [10]. The reason for that can be sought in the fact that the pores are much finer features of the fingerprint than the ridges are, and they consequently require higher image resolution to detect. Due to the very same reason they are also more prone to the distortions of the image.

The main issue in biometric authentication based on any modality is the reliability of the comparison between the test and reference data, on the basis of the extracted

D. Maltoni and A.K. Jain (Eds.): BioAW 2004, LNCS 3087, pp. 124-133, 2004.
© Springer-Verlag Berlin Heidelberg 2004

features. The use of an additional feature level aims to provide additional distinctive information when verifying the identity associated with the fingerprint.

The performance of systems based on level 2 features is fairly well studied and documented [5]. Although it is possible to classify different methods of fingerprint recognition based on their performance [3], the question how distinctive and characteristic certain features of a fingerprint are, still remains relatively unanswered [8]. Even less is known of how much gain (if any) one can achieve by introducing an additional feature level.

Roddy and Stosz [7] attempted to do an extensive analysis of what verification performance can be expected from the employment of level 3 features. In their work they present a model of pore distribution which has very sound foundations in physiology. In particular, one of the underlying assumptions of their model is that the distribution of the pores follows a regular pattern, up to a specific randomness, and that is only modified by the ridge pattern (pores appearing only on the ridges, not in the valleys). The weak point of this model is that naturally a fingerprint is distributed over a 3D surface, while scanning with different methods forces the fingerprint to be a planar projection of this surface. This introduces deformations which make the assumptions about the regularity of the pore spacing rather not realistic.

It is a hard task to model the nature of the mechanical deformations of a 3D-fingerprint surface [9]. One can easily imagine a distortion large enough to make a correction of such deformations unreliable, if not impossible. Also other factors (skin conditions, inherent fingerprint features, improper fingerprint positioning on the scanner) can render parts of the fingerprint useless from the viewpoint of an automatic verification system. In such a situation, the use of the least distorted fingerprint fragment (or multiple fragments) appears as a reasonable strategy.

In order to be able to predict the reliability of a verification procedure based on a fragmentary fingerprint input it is essential to know how the robustness of the matching method changes with the size of the fingerprint used. Equipped with such knowledge, one can consciously discard the distorted parts of the input fingerprint aiming for more reliable identity verification.

In the forensic sciences comparing fragments of fingerprints is a typical task. After an extensive analysis of a fingerprint fragment it is possible to decide about the identity based on the ridge shape, even if no level 2 features are present [6] – a scenario, where a minutiae-based automated system would fail. We hypothesize that for a partially distorted fingerprint, its undistorted fragment carries at least the same amount of distinctive information as its entirety. We also expect that the use of level 3 features may boost up the recognition accuracy particularly in the case of the comparison of fragmentary fingerprints.

To verify our hypotheses we conducted a pilot study, described in [1], and two experiments, described in the following sections of this paper. First, we provide an outline of the experimental design in Section 2. Section 3 contains details on experimental procedures, results of the experiments and their discussion. Section 4 presents final conclusions and prospects for future work.

2 Verification of Fingerprints from a Fragment

In order to estimate the reliability of verification of a fingerprint from its fragment we designed two experiments based on one-to-one match. This reliability depends on how distinctive are the features used in the comparison between the test and reference fingerprint. We want to investigate how the size of the available fingerprint sample affects the distinctive potential of the features extracted from the ridge structure, the minutiae and the pores.

Figure 1: Fingerprint and its fragment with visible minutiae and pores.

Typically, for any set of features extracted from the test and reference fingerprint a measure of feature match (score) is being computed. Then, a threshold is usually being applied to decide if the test fingerprint matches the reference. The choice of the threshold depends on the desired properties of the biometric system. The threshold T can be described as a function f, such that:

$$T=f(\mu_A,\sigma_A,\mu_D,\sigma_D). \tag{1}$$

The function f takes as arguments (μ_A,σ_A) which are the mean and corresponding standard deviation of the distribution of a match score between fingerprints (or their fragments) originating from the same finger. We therefore refer to this score as the *accord score*.

Similarly, the arguments (μ_D,σ_D) describe the recognition system's response to a match between fingerprints (or their fragments) that do not originate from the same finger. We refer to this score as the *discord score*.

The estimation of the appropriate thresholding strategy is out of the scope of this paper. Hence we restrain from trying to estimate the function f. Instead, we focus on the accord and discord score measurements. From those values, having secured that the scoring mechanism is constant over the entire experiment, we intend to draw conclusions about the distinctive content that the used features carry.

3 The Scoring Procedure and the Database

The scoring algorithm was designed as follows: before comparison, the ridge, minu-tiae and pore features are extracted from the reference image. Namely, the ridge skeleton, and the coordinates of the minutiae and the coordinates of the pores are considered. The same features are also extracted from every test fingerprint fragment used in the experiment. The match score of the ridge structure is computed using normalized correlation, while the minutiae and pore features were compared based on a geometric distance criterion [4]. The details of data extraction and matching algorithms can be found in [1]. Resulting scores are from (0,1) range, where a '0' corresponds to a complete mismatch, and a '1' indicates a perfect match of extracted features.

In our experiments we used the database obtained from the IPS, UNIL[1]. The database consists of images acquired using a custom built optical scanner at the resolution of 1972×2849 pixels (ca. 2000 dpi). There are images of 6 fingers in the database, for each finger there are 10 separate fingerprints in the database. All fingerprints in the database are of comparable, high quality and were taken in same controlled conditions.

From the database we took sets of 4 fingerprints of the same finger. In total, we took such fingerprint sets of 6 different fingers. We indexed each fingerprint as X_Y, where X is the number assigned to a particular finger, and Y is the number assigned to one of the four images of X.

3.1 Accord Scores

An accord score for a given feature set (ridges, minutiae or pores) was calculated for fingerprint fragments that are known to originate from the same finger.

Fingerprint sets 1-6_1 and 1-6_2 were considered reference sets, while 1-6_3 and 1-6_4 were used as source of test images. Two separate experiments were performed: in the first experiment images from the test set 1-6_3 were compared to the reference set 1-6_1 (further called image set X_1), while in the second experiment the fingerprints from the test set 1-6_4 were compared with the reference set 1-6_2 (further called image set X_2).

For each pair of images under comparison, the reference image remained intact, while the test image was systematically fragmented and the resulting fragments compared to the reference image. In each subsequent fragmentation step the dimensions of the resulting sub-images (fragments) of the test image were:

$$[x_n, y_n] = [x_0, y_0] \cdot K^n, \qquad (2)$$

where $[x_0, y_0]$ are the dimensions of the original reference image, $[x_n, y_n]$ are the dimensions of the test fingerprint image at the nth fragmentation step, and K is the factor that controls the reduction of the fragment size between subsequent fragmentation steps. In our experiment we choose $K=0.75$ in order to arrive at a small test fragment size in reasonably few fragmentation steps. We call the value of n the *fragment size index*. An example of the original test image and its sub-images at subsequent fragmentation steps is shown in Figure 2.

---

[1] *Institut de Police Scientifique, University of Lausanne, Switzerland.*

Figure 2: Subsequent fingerprint fragmentation steps according to equation (2). From left to right: original image from the database, with automatically removed background, subsequent sub-images of fragment size index n=1,2,3,4,5.

Before scoring, the test fragment was automatically aligned with the corresponding fragment of the reference image. We used normalized correlation for the alignment procedure. We have presented the details on the choice of features used in the alignment procedure and the procedure itself in [1]. Both the tested image and the corresponding, automatically located reference fragment had to have more than 90% of their area occupied by the ridge structure (less than 10% background) in order to be scored. Every comparison returned the ridge, minutiae and pores accord score. If the algorithm failed to align the test fragment with the reference image the reported ridge matching score was set to null.

3.2   Experimental Results – Accord Scores

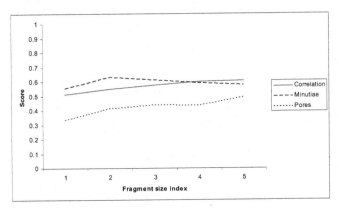

Figure 3: Average accord scores for comparison with the reference set X_1.

The accord scores show some consistent tendencies. With the decreasing size of the test fingerprint fragment the correlation scores between the test and reference fingerprint increase. This result at the first glimpse could be thought counterintuitive. It nevertheless agrees with our initial presumption that reducing the test fragment size will reduce the misalignment due to local mechanical distortions present in the 2D projection of the finger surface. It also indicates that localizing smaller fragments of a

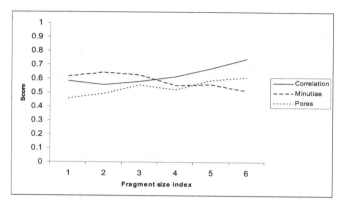

Figure 4: Average accord scores for comparison with the reference set X_2.

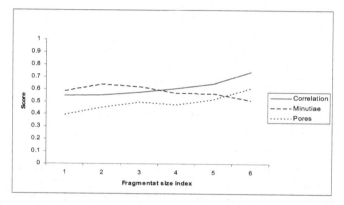

Figure 5: Combined average accord scores for reference sets X_1 and X_2.

fingerprint on the area of the reference fingerprint is likely to be more reliable than alignment of a larger fragment (or the entire fingerprint).

This conclusion holds only if we assume that the aligned fragment has been located correctly. One could suspect that with reduced area to be matched the likelihood of finding an area that is similar enough to produce high correlation value will grow. This cannot be dismissed based on the analysis of the correlation scores alone.

The minutiae-based match accord scores drop as we reduce the size of the test fingerprint fragment. This could be due to a hypothetical misalignment of the test fragment with the reference image. However, the observed drop is not large enough to be due to a misalignment, particularly, that as we go down with the fragment size the chances of finding similar minutiae configuration by sheer luck vanish. There is another plausible explanation for the diminishing minutiae match scores. Reducing area of a fingerprint fragment also decreases the number of minutiae present in this fragment (Figure 6), thus even a small mismatch between the test and the reference minutiae distribution lies heavily on the score.

The pore matching accord score displays an upward tendency as we reduce the test fragment of the fingerprint. The vast number of detected pores in a large fingerprint area makes the comparison difficult and unreliable. Even small ridge misalignments due to distortions produce large displacements of pores, relative to their sizes. For small fingerprint fragment the number of pores shrinks considerably (Figure 6), but remains large enough to make a meaningful match. The growing pore matching accord score also gives support to the presumption that the correlation-based alignment is correct. Should it be not – there would be no reason for the pore match accord scores to grow – they should in this case stay at best constant.

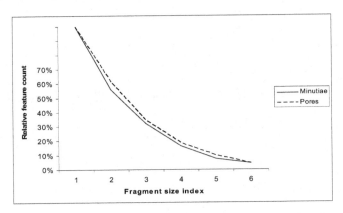

Figure 6: Relative reduction in the minutiae and pore count as a function of reduced fingerprint fragment size.

Figure 6 shows relative changes in the amount of the minutiae and pores found in a fingerprint fragment of diminishing size, averaged over all fingerprints used in the reported work. A 100% score corresponds to the feature count for the fragment size index $n = 1$, where the average number of minutiae and pores was 73.8 and 425.5, respectively (accord scores, reference set X_1), and 69.3 and 511.75 (accord scores, reference set X_2).

3.3 Discord Scores

A discord score for a given feature set (ridges, minutiae or pores) is calculated for fingerprint fragments that are known not to originate from the same finger.
Six pairs of images originating from different fingers were assembled. Following pairs of fingerprints were compared (Table 1):

Table 1: Image pairs used in the discord score calculations.

Reference set	1_1	2_1	3_1	4_1	5_1	6_1
Test set	3_2	4_2	5_2	6_2	1_2	2_2

The comparison and matching procedure was similar as in the case of the accord scores. However, since by definition the test and reference fingerprints do not match, the algorithm was not attempting to align the test fragment with the reference image.

Instead, the test fragment was scored against a randomly chosen fragment of reference fingerprint of the same size.

3.4 Experimental Results – Discord Scores

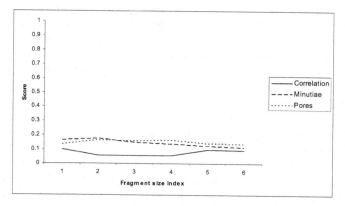

Figure 7: Average discord scores for diminishing fragment size index.

The results of the discord score measurements show the average comparison scores between non-matching fingerprint fragments of various sizes. As Figure 7 shows, the discord scores for ridge- minutiae- and pore-based comparison remain fairly constant, regardless of the size of the test fingerprint fragment. They also remain clearly separated from the accord scores (Figures 3, 4 and 5). This interesting result allows us to conclude that the considered fingerprint features are distinctive enough to be robust in the case of even small fingerprint fragments.

The constant discord scores for pore-based match provides support for the argument on the correctness of correlation-based match presented in section 3.2. If the raising correlation accord score would be associated with misalignments of the test image with the reference image, for all those cases the calculated pore-based scores would in fact be discord scores. As the experimental data presented in Figure 7 show, in such case the pore-based scores should remain at best constant, instead of having a growing tendency.

The discord scores measure the average similarity between two randomly chosen fingerprint fragments of identical size, where we are certain that they do not originate from the same fingerprint. In a real-life automatic fingerprint verification system such notion cannot exist, and the system is bound to attempt the best alignment of the test fragment with the reference image, regardless of their origin. We have addressed this scenario in [1].

4   Conclusions and Future Work

Based on the results of the presented work, we analyzed the relations between the distinctive information contained in the ridge structure, and the selected level 2 and level 3 features. The results indicate that using a fragment instead of the entire fingerprint can produce at least equally reliable recognition result, given sufficiently high fingerprint quality (level 3 features must be detectable). From our current results alone it is not possible to state that the recognition results would be better when using a fragment instead of the whole fingerprint, particularly if the entire test fingerprint is of high quality (like in the case of the database used in our experiments). It can be however speculated that if the fingerprint would be heavily locally corrupted, verification based on only undistorted fragments would produce more reliable results than a holistic approach. Also, for fingerprints that are inherently difficult to compare, a fragment-wise analysis can be expected to be more reliable.

Presented results also hint that a careful score matching techniques are needed if using level two and level three features in the recognition of fingerprint fragments of various sizes. Since the distinctiveness of the level two and level three features changes with the considered fingerprint area, the corresponding matching scores should be appropriately weighted when calculating the ultimate similarity measure in the verification process.

Our study does not claim statistical significance at any confidence level due to a scarce number of compared fingerprints (due to limited database size), we merely report consistent tendencies found in the collected data. We intend to extend this study by the analysis of the statistical distribution of the accord and discord scores, in order to test the results for statistical significance. The next step to take will be to test our findings on a larger database and apply them in a complete fingerprint recognition system.

4.1   Additional Remarks Concerning the Interpretation of the Results

Due to the limited number of pair-wise comparisons between fingerprints and the size of the available database caution must be exercised when generalizing the results of the presented experiments. In particular, two issues must be addressed.

Firstly, the factual number of comparisons between the fragments of the same fingerprint varied greatly with the considered fragment size. Namely, there were significantly more comparisons made between small than large fragments. The reason for this was that one can select only a limited number of little-overlapping, large fragments of the same fingerprint. Therefore an estimation of the distribution of both accord and discord scores was impossible – for this reason we do not present the variances – the variances of the score data for large fragments are not meaningful and not comparable to the variances for small fragments. Our future work will address this issue.

Secondly, there exists a significant difference in the mutual distinctive content between fragments of the same size index. For large fragments of the same fingerprint used in separate comparisons there exists an overlap. This makes the mean estimation of match scores reliable for the given pair of fingerprints selected for comparison. At the same time, however, it makes it impossible to compare the variance of the match scores between data collected for fragments of different area size index of the same compared fingerprints. This deficiency can be rectified by re-running the experiment on a larger volume of fingerprints, which will be included in our future work.

5 Acknowledgements

We would like to take this opportunity to send our thanks to Prof. Christophe Champod, Alexandre Anthonioz and Nicole M. Egli from the *Institut de Police Scientifique, University of Lausanne*, for their insights from the forensic perspective and for making the fingerprint database available for us to use in our study.

References

1. Kryszczuk, K.M., Drygajlo, A., Morier, P.: Extraction of Level 2 and Level 3 features for fragmentary fingerprints. In: 2nd COST275 Workshop (Biometrics on the Internet), Vigo, Spain, pp. 83-88, 2004.

2. Locard, E.: Les Pores et L'Identification des Criminels. In: Biologica, Revue Scientifique de Medecin, Vol. 22, pp. 357-362, 1912.

3. Maio, D., Maltoni, D., Capelli, R., Waylam, J.L., Jain, A.K.. FVC2000: Fingerprint Verification Competition. In: IEEE Transactions on Pattern Analysis and Machine Intelligence, Vol. 24, No. 3, 2002.

4. Maltoni, D., Maio, D., Jain, A.K., Prabhakar, S.: Handbook of Fingerprint Recognition, Springer, New York, 2003.

5. Pankanti, S., Prabhakar, S., Jain, A.K.: On the Individuality of Fingerprints. In: Proc. of the IEEE Comp. Soc. Conference on Computer Vision and Pattern Recognition, Hawaii, 2001.

6. Reneau, R. D., 2003, Unusual Latent Print Examinations: Journal of Forensic Idenfication, v. 53, pp. 531-537.

7. Roddy, A.R., Stosz J.D.: Fingerprint Features – Statistical Analysis and System Performance Estimates. In: Proceedings of the IEEE, vol. 85, no. 9, pp. 1390-1421, 1997.

8. Ross, A., Jain, A., Reisman, J.: A Hybrid Fingerprint Matcher. In: Pattern Recognition, Vol. 36, No. 7, pp. 1661-1673, 2003.

9. Senior, A., Ruud B.: Improved Fingerprint Matching by Distortion Removal. In: IEICE Trans. Inf. & Syst., Vol. E84–D, No.7, 2001.

10. Stosz, J.D., Alyea, L.A.: Automated system for fingerprint authentication using pores and ridge structure. In: Proceedings of the SPIE, Automatic Systems for the Identification and Inspection of Humans. Volume 2277, pp. 210-223, 1994.

Biometric Sensor Interoperability: A Case Study in Fingerprints

Arun Ross[1] and Anil Jain[2]

[1] West Virginia University, Morgantown, WV, USA 26506
ross@csee.wvu.edu
[2] Michigan State University, East Lansing, MI, USA 48824
jain@cse.msu.edu

Abstract. The problem of biometric sensor interoperability has received limited attention in the literature. Most biometric systems operate under the assumption that the data (viz., images) to be compared are obtained using the same sensor and, hence, are restricted in their ability to match or compare biometric data originating from different sensors. Although progress has been made in the development of common data exchange formats to facilitate the exchange of feature sets between vendors, very little effort has been invested in the actual development of algorithms and techniques to match these feature sets. In the Fingerprint Verification Competition (FVC 2002), for example, the evaluation protocol only matched images originating from the same sensor although fingerprint data from 3 different commercial sensors was available. This is an indication of the difficulty in accommodating sensor interoperability in biometric systems. In this paper we discuss this problem and present a case study involving two different fingerprint sensors.

1 Introducton

Establishing the identity of a person is becoming critical in our vastly interconnected society. Questions like "Is she really who she claims to be?", "Is this person authorized to use this facility?" or "Is he in the watchlist posted by the government?" are routinely being posed in a variety of scenarios ranging from issuing a driver's licence to gaining entry into a country. The need for reliable user authentication techniques has increased in the wake of heightened concerns about security and rapid advancements in networking, communication and mobility. Biometrics, described as the science of recognizing an individual based on her physiological or behavioral traits, is beginning to gain acceptance as a legitimate method for determining an individual's identity. Biometric systems have now been deployed in various commercial, civilian and forensic applications as a means of establishing identity. These systems rely on the evidence of fingerprints, hand geometry, iris, retina, face, hand vein, facial thermogram, signature, voice, etc. to either validate or determine an identity [1].

A generic biometric system has four important modules: (a) *sensor module* which acquires the raw biometric data of an individual; (b) *feature extraction module* which processes the acquired data to extract a feature set that represents the biometric trait; (c) *matching module* in which the extracted feature set is compared against the templates

D. Maltoni and A.K. Jain (Eds.): BioAW 2004, LNCS 3087, pp. 134–145, 2004.
© Springer-Verlag Berlin Heidelberg 2004

residing in the database through the generation of matching scores; (d) *decision-making module* in which the matching scores are used to either validate the user's claimed identity (verification) or determine her identity (identification). The *template* feature set is typically generated during enrollment when a user first interacts with the system and is refreshed or updated over a period of time in order to account for intra-class variations [2]. Ideally, the feature set extracted from the raw data is expected to be an invariant representation of a person's biometric. However, in reality, the feature set is sensitive to several factors including:

1. change in the sensor used for acquiring the raw data (e.g., optical versus solid-state sensors in a fingerprint system);
2. variations in the environment (e.g., change in lighting in a face recognition system, or dry weather resulting in faint fingerprints);
3. improper user interaction (e.g., incorrect facial pose during image acquisition, or drooping eye-lids in an iris system);
4. temporary alterations to the biometric trait itself (e.g., cuts/scars on fingerprints, or voice altered by respiratory ailments).

Raw data 'corrupted' due to improper user interaction or variations in the environment can be discarded by the application via a quality checking process [3]. Temporary alterations in the biometric trait can be accommodated by the use of a periodic template selection/update procedure [2]. However, the change in sensor scenario introduces challenges that have hitherto not been studied. The quality and nature of the raw data is significantly affected when the sensor used during enrollment and authentication are different. This directly affects the feature set extracted from the data and, subsequently, the matching score generated by the system. Consider a fingerprint matching system that acquires fingerprint images using an optical sensor during enrollment and a solid-state capacitive sensor during verification (at a later time). The raw images obtained at both these time instances will be significantly different (Figure 1) due to variations in imaging technology, resolution of the acquired image, area of the sensor, position of the sensor with respect to the user, etc. Thus, the corresponding feature sets will exhibit variability that cannot be easily handled by the matching module since very few algorithms explicitly account for the variations introduced by different sensors. This problem, known as *sensor interoperability*, has received limited attention in the literature. In this paper we briefly explore this problem and present a case study describing its impact on fingerprint systems.

2   Sensor Interoperability

Sensor interoperability refers to the ability of a biometric system to adapt to the raw data obtained from a variety of sensors. Most biometric systems are designed to compare data originating from the same sensor. In some cases the classifiers are trained on data obtained using a single sensor alone thereby restricting their ability to act on data from other sensors. This limitation prevents the use of multiple sensors with different

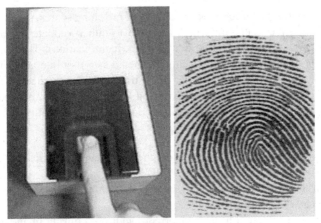

(a) An optical sensor.

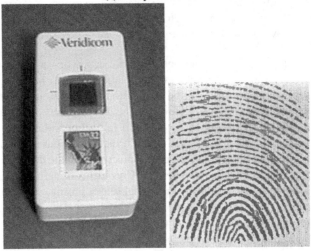

(b) A solid-state sensor.

Fig. 1. Fingerprint images of the same finger acquired using (a) Digital Biometrics' optical sensor and (b) Veridicom's solid state sensor. The number of detected minutiae points in the corresponding images are 39 and 14, respectively.

characteristics in a single biometric system. Martin et al. [4] make the following observation about the effect of the handset type (sensor) on the performance of a speaker recognition system[3]:

> "Microphone differences are one of the most serious problems facing speaker recognition, especially when dealing with the telephone, where Edison's old nonlinear carbon-button microphone still represents a significant fraction of all transducers".

_____
[3] The NIST speaker recognition evaluation.

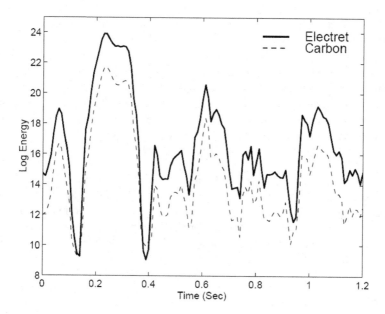

Fig. 2. The logarithmic energy of the same speech segment when passed through carbon-button and electret microphones. The energy corresponds to a specific frequency band (taken from [5]).

They report a significant dip in performance when the carbon-button microphone was used during the training phase and the electret microphone was used during the test phase (and vice-versa) in a speaker biometric system. Malayath [5] suggests the use of oriented principal component analysis (OPCA) in designing a filter to suppress the variabilities introduced by different handsets/channels.

Phillips et al. [6] state the following about the sensitivity of face verification algorithms to camera type:

"Many face verification applications make it mandatory to acquire images with the same camera. However, some applications, particularly those used in law enforcement, allow image acquisition with many camera types. This variation has the potential to affect algorithm performance as severely as changing illumination. But, unlike the effects of changing illumination, the effects on performance of using multiple camera types has not been quantified".

The International Biometric Group (IBG)[4] recently conducted a battery of tests to evaluate the performance of various sensors (including fingerprint) under different test conditions. BIO-key International, Inc., demonstrated that its fingerprint system could enroll and verify fingerprint images obtained using different sensors[5]. However, this

---

[4] http://www.biometricgroup.com/index.html
[5] http://www.biometricgroup.com/in_the_news/01_15_04.html

kind of test scenarios are extremely rare as is borne out by the following statement by IBG [7]:

> "Today, there is really very little interoperability among templates and the algorithms that the systems are using for matching. Those are proprietary technologies. So if you as an organization are considering deploying biometric technologies you should be concerned [whether] the vendor you are working with now will be around in 5 years and supporting the product. The cost to you of re-enrolling all your subjects could be significant".

This underscores the need for developing algorithms that are able to seamlessly operate on feature sets originating from different sensors. Note that the problem of sensor interoperability as defined in this paper cannot be solved by adopting a common biometric data exchange format [8]. Such a format merely aids in the *exchange* of feature sets between systems/vendors [9]. It, however, does not provide a method to *compare* feature sets obtained from different sensors.

3 Fingerprint Sensors

The advent of small-sized solid-state fingerprint sensors permit these devices to be easily embedded in various applications such as laptops, computer peripherals, cellphones, PDAs, etc. The ease of interacting with fingerprint sensors (compared to, say, iris cameras) has contributed to their increase in popularity. This has resulted in a proliferation of these devices and their subsequent inclusion in a variety of applications (Figure 3). The recently launched US-VISIT[6] program for example, obtains fingerprint (and face) information of certain travellers arriving in airports and seaports. An optical fingerprint sensor is currently being used during the enrollment phase to procure fingerprint images. However, it is not guaranteed that a similar type of sensor will be used at a later time when verifying the same individual. The cost of re-enrolling individuals every time the sensor is changed will be tremendous and will, in fact, defeat the purpose of enrolling individuals at the port of entry in the first place. In cases such as these, the need for sensor interoperability is paramount and will significantly impact the usability of the system.

A live-scan fingerprint is usually acquired using the *dab* method, in which the finger is placed on the surface of the sensor without rolling[7]. There are a number of sensing mechanisms that can be used to detect the ridges and furrows present in the fingertip. A brief description of a few of these principles is provided below:

(i) Optical Frustrated Total Internal Reflection (FTIR): This technique utilizes a glass platen, a laser light-source and a CCD (or a CMOS camera) for constructing fingerprint images. The finger is placed on the glass platen, and the laser light-source is directed toward the platen. The CCD captures the reflected light after

---

[6] United States Visitor and Immigration Status Indicator Technology.

[7] It is possible to capture a *rolled* live-scan fingerprint, although an elaborate scanner arrangement may be necessary in this case

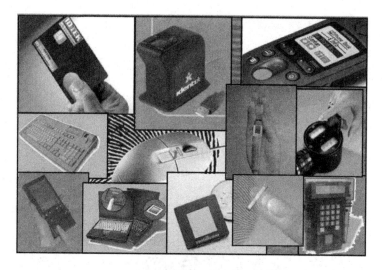

Fig. 3. A variety of fingerprint sensors with different specifications (e.g., sensing technology, image size, image resolution, image quality, etc.) are now available. These sensors have been embedded in computer peripherals and other devices to facilitate user authentication.

it has passed through a prism and a lens to facilitate image formation. The light incident on the ridges is randomly scattered (and results in a dark image), while the light incident on the valleys suffers total internal reflection (and results in a bright image). It is difficult to have this arrangement in a compact form, since the focal length of small lenses can be very large. Further, image distortions are possible when the reflected light is not focused properly.

(ii) **Ultrasound Reflection:** The ultrasonic method is based on sending acoustic signals toward the finger tip and capturing the echo signal. The echo signal is used to compute the range image of the fingerprint and, subsequently, the ridge structure itself. The sensor has two main components: the sender, that generates short acoustic pulses, and the receiver, that detects the responses obtained when these pulses bounce off the fingerprint surface [10]. This method images the sub-surface of the fingerprint and is, therefore, resilient to dirt and oil accumulations that may visually mar the fingerprint. The device is, however, expensive, and as such not suited for large-scale production.

(iii) **Piezoelectric Effect:** Pressure sensitive sensors have been designed that produce an electrical signal when a mechanical stress is applied to them. The sensor surface is made of a non-conducting dielectric material which, on encountering pressure from the finger, generates a small amount of current. (This effect is called the piezoelectric effect). The strength of the current generated depends on the pressure applied by the finger on the sensor surface. Since ridges and valleys are present at different distances from the sensor surface, they result in different amounts of current. This technique does not capture the fingerprint relief accurately because of its low sensitivity.

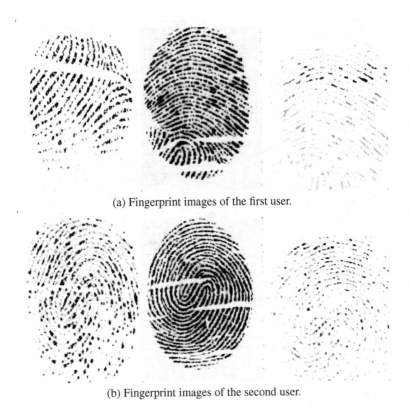

(a) Fingerprint images of the first user.

(b) Fingerprint images of the second user.

Fig. 4. The fingerprint images of 2 different users (a) and (b) obtained using Precise (left), Ethentica (middle) and Secugen (right) sensors.

(iv) Temperature Differential: Sensors operating using this mechanism are made of pyro-electric material that generate current based on temperature differentials. They rely on the temperature differential that is created when two surfaces are brought into contact. The fingerprint ridges, being in contact with the sensor surface, produce a different temperature differential than the valleys that are away from the sensor surface [11]. The sensors are typically maintained at a high temperature by electrically heating them up.

(v) Capacitance: In this arrangement, there are tens of thousands of small capacitance plates embedded in a chip. Small electrical charges are created between the surface of the finger and each of these plates when the finger is placed on the chip. The magnitude of these electrical charges depends on the distance between the fingerprint surface and the capacitance plates [12, 13]. Thus, fingerprint ridges and valleys result in different capacitance patterns across the plates. This technique is susceptible to electrostatic discharges from the tip of the finger that can drastically affect the sensor; proper grounding is necessary to avoid this problem.

While optical sensors have the longest history, the new solid-state capacitive sensors are gaining immense popularity because of their compact size and the ease of embedding them into laptops, cellular phones, smart pens, etc. Figure 4 shows the fingerprint impressions pertaining to two different users acquired using three different sensors. Visually, there are significant differences in the quality of the image corresponding to the three sensors. This clearly illustrates the difficulty in accommodating multiple sensors in a single biometric system. In the recently conducted Fingerprint Verification Competition (FVC2002[8]), only fingerprint images obtained using the same sensor were matched although images from three different types of sensors were available [14].

4   Optical Versus Solid-State Sensors: A Case Study

In this section we report experiments conducted using two different types of fingerprint sensors. The fingerprint images of 160 different non-habituated cooperative subjects were obtained using an optical sensor manufactured by Digital Biometrics (DBI) and a solid-state capacitive sensor manufactured by Veridicom (Figure 1). The optical sensor had a sensing area of approximately $1" \times 1"$. The images were acquired at a resolution of 500 dpi and were 480×508 in size. The solid-state sensor had a sensing area of approximately $0.6" \times 0.6"$. The images in this case were also obtained at a resolution of 500 dpi. However, the reduced size of the placement area resulted in 300×300 images.

The subjects mainly consisted of students at Michigan State University, and their relatives and friends. Approximately 35% of the subjects were women. Each individual was asked to provide fingerprint images of four fingers, viz., right index, right middle, left index and left middle fingers. This process was repeated to obtain a second impression of all four fingers. This resulted in a total of $1,280$ ($160 \times 4 \times 2$) fingerprint images per sensor. The subjects were asked to provide their fingerprint images again after a period of 6 weeks. During this time, another $1,280$ ($160 \times 4 \times 2$) fingerprint images per sensor were obtained. Thus, a total of $2,560$ fingerprint images per sensor pertaining to 640 different fingers were made available. The databases corresponding to the optical and solid-state sensors were labelled as MSU_DBI and MSU_VERIDICOM, respectively [15].

We used the minutiae-based fingerprint matcher developed by Hong et al. [16] in order to compare fingerprint images. The matcher uses an adaptive elastic string matching technique to establish correspondences between the minutiae pattern of two images. In this technique, the minutiae points in an image are first represented as a "string" in the polar coordinate system. Two such "strings" are then compared via a dynamic programming algorithm. The similarity between two minutiae patterns is indicated by a score that represents the percentage of matching minutiae pairs. If this score is greater than a threshold then the two minutiae patterns are said to originate from the same fingerprint (a match).

We conducted three different types of experiments in order to study the effect of changing sensors on matching performance.

---

[8] http://bias.csr.unibo.it/fvc2002/

1. Matching images within the MSU_DBI database.
2. Matching images within the MSU_VERIDICOM database.
3. Matching images from MSU_DBI against those from MSU_VERIDICOM.

The Receiver Operating Characteristics (ROC) curves corresponding to all three cases are shown in Figure 6. Each curve depicts the Genuine Accept Rate (GAR) and the False Accept Rate (FAR) at various matching thresholds. We make the following observations:

1. The optical sensor results in a better matching performance than the solid-state sensor due to the elaborate sensing area of the former. Infact, the average number of minutiae points extracted from the images acquired using the optical sensor is substantially more than that acquired using the solid-state sensor (Figures 1 and 5).

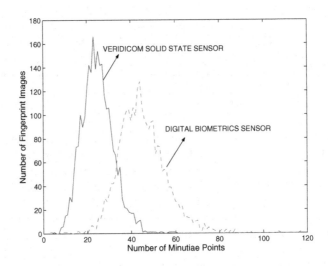

Fig. 5. Histogram of the number of minutiae points extracted from images acquired using the Veridicom and DBI sensors. A total of $2,500$ fingerprint impressions were used to compute these histograms for each sensor. The histograms suggest that substantially fewer minutiae points are available in images obtained using small-sized solid-state sensors.

2. When the images being matched originate from two different sensors then the performance of the matcher drastically decreases. The Equal Error Rate (EER) in this case is 23.13% while the EERs for the other two cases are 6.14% (MSU_DBI) and 10.39% (MSU_VERIDICOM). This illustrates the impact of changing sensors on the fingerprint matching performance. As mentioned earlier, the optical sensor results in more minutiae points than the solid-state sensor. Thus, comparing two images - one obtained from the DBI sensor and the other obtained from the Veridicom sensor - is akin to comparing a full print with a partial print, resulting in several

incorrect matches (false accepts) that increase the error rate of the system. Similar problems arise if one were to compare rolled prints with dab prints. Seldom does the methodology adopted for one type of input data work on other kinds of data.

There are several ways in which the problem of interoperability can be approached. Typically, it is the matching module that is expected to reconcile feature sets arising from the use of multiple sensors. However, reconciliation has to happen much earlier in a biometric system to mitigate the impact of changing sensors.

1. One of the obvious ways is to store the raw data in its entirety in the database (during enrollment) along with the feature set extracted from it (e.g., a fingerprint image *and* its minutiae set). During verification, the biometric system could extract feature sets from both the database and input images, and then compare them. Here, the onus is on the feature extraction module to generate a 'compatible' feature set from the database image by explicitly taking into account the *differences* between the sensors used during enrollment and verification. However, storing raw data in a central repository would raise security concerns, since compromising this information could have serious repercussions.
2. Canonical representations of the input data might be useful to offset the effect of variability in data. For example, fingerprint images may be viewed as a collection of ridge lines, with the inter-ridge spacing forced to be a constant [17]. Feature values can then be extracted from this canonical representation. Such an approach, however, presupposes the existence of a canonical form for the raw data. It also preempts the possibility of extracting a *rich* set of features from the original data.
3. In some situations a simple transformation of the template feature set might account for sensor-specific properties. Fingerprint systems could use the ridge count between minutiae pairs in an image, the location of core/delta points, etc. to 'normalize' the spatial distribution of minutiae points. In speaker recognition systems, certain normalization filters may be designed [5] to account for variability due to different handsets.

5   Summary and Future Work

The need for biometric sensor interoperability is pronounced due to the widespread deployment of biometric systems in various applications and the proliferation of vendors with proprietary algorithms that operate on a specific kind of sensor. In this paper we have illustrated the impact of changing sensors on the matching performance of a fingerprint system. Almost every biometric indicator is affected by the sensor interoperability problem. However, no systematic study has been conducted to ascertain its effect on real-world systems. Normalization at the raw data and feature set levels of a biometric system may be needed to handle this problem. There is also a definite need to develop matching algorithms that do not implicitly rely on sensor characteristics to perform matching. Biometric vendors and independent test groups (e.g., NIST, IBG) should begin incorporating interoperable scenarios in their testing protocol. This would help in understanding the effect of changing sensors on a biometric system and would

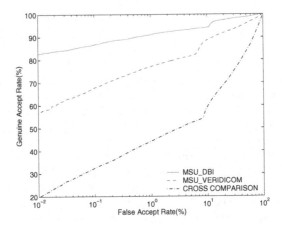

Fig. 6. ROC curves corresponding to the 3 matching experiments that were conducted. The optical sensor is seen to result in the best performance (solid line). The solid-state sensor does not exhibit good performance (dashed line) possibly due to partial prints that present limited number of minutiae points. Cross-comparing images between sensors using the same matching program results in the worst performance (dot-dash line).

encourage the development of cross-compatible feature extraction (representation) and matching algorithms.

6   Acknowledgements

Thanks to Dr. Naren Malayath for granting permission to use the graph in Figure 2.

References

[1] Jain, A.K., Ross, A., Prabhakar, S.: An introduction to biometric recognition. IEEE Trans. on Circuits and Systems for Video Technology **14** (2004) 4–20

[2] Jain, A.K., Uludag, U., Ross, A.: Biometric template selection: a case study in fingerprints. In: Proc. of 4th Int'l Conf. on Audio- and Video-based Biometric Authentication (AVBPA). Volume LNCS 2688., Guildford, UK, Springer (2003) 335–342

[3] Ratha, N.K., Bolle, R.M.: Fingerprint image quality estimation. IBM Computer Science Research Report RC21622 (1999)

[4] Martin, A., Przybocki, M., Doddington, G., Reynolds, D.: The NIST speaker recognition evaluation - overview, methodology, systems, results, perspectives. Speech Communications **31** (2000) 225–254

[5] Malayath, N.: Data-driven methods for extracting features from speech. PhD Thesis, Oregon Graduate Institute of Science and Technology (2000)

[6] Phillips, P.J., Martin, A., Wilson, C.L., Przybocki, M.: An introduction to evaluating biometric systems. IEEE Computer **33** (2000) 56–63

[7] Moore, S.: Latest tests of biometrics systems shows wide range of abilities. IEEE Spectrum Online (2004)

[8] Bolle, R.M., Ratha, N.K., Senior, A., Pankanti, S.: Minutia template exchange format. In: Proc. of IEEE Workshop on Automatic Identification Advanced Technologies, Summit, NJ (1999) 74–77

[9] Podio, F.L., Dunn, J.S., Reinert, L., Tilton, C.J., O'Gorman, L., Collier, P., Jerde, M., Wirtz, B.: Common biometric exchange file format (CBEFF). Technical Report NISTIR 6529, NIST (1999)

[10] Bicz, W., Gumienny, Z., Kosz, D., Pluta, M.: Ultrasonic setup for fingerprint patterns detection and evaluation. Acoustical Imaging 22 (1996)

[11] Edwards, D.G.: Fingerprint sensor. US Patent 4429413 (1984)

[12] Tsikos, C.: Capacitive fingerprint sensor. US Patent 4353056 (1982)

[13] Young, N.D., Harkin, G., Bunn, R.M., McCulloch, D.J., Wilks, R.W., Knapp, A.G.: Novel fingerprint scanning arrays using polysilicon TFT's on glass and polymer substrates. IEEE Electron Device Letters 18 (1997) 19–20

[14] Maio, D., Maltoni, D., Cappelli, R., Wayman, J.L., Jain, A.K.: FVC2002: Fingerprint verification competition. In: Proceedings of the International Conference on Pattern Recognition (ICPR), Quebec City, Canada (2002) 744–747

[15] Jain, A.K., Prabhakar, S., Ross, A.: Fingerprint matching: Data acquisition and performance evaluation. Technical Report MSU-TR:99-14, Michigan State University (1999)

[16] Hong, L.: Automatic personal identification using fingerprints. PhD Thesis, Michigan State University (1998)

[17] Senior, A., Bolle, R.: Improved fingerprint matching by distortion removal. IEICE Transactions on Information and Systems E84-D (2001) 825–831

Efficient Fingerprint Image Enhancement for Mobile Embedded Systems

J.S. Chen, Y.S. Moon, K.F. Fong

Department of Computer Science and Engineering, The Chinese University of Hong Kong,
Shatin, N.T. Hong Kong
{jschen, ysmoon, kffong}@cse.cuhk.edu.hk

Abstract. Fingerprint image enhancement is an important step in a fingerprint verification system. The enhancement process, however, are often not applied to mobile embedded devices in which floating-point processing units (FPU) are absent. Earlier Hong and Jain reported a fingerprint enhancement algorithm based on the Gabor Filter. This algorithm and its derivatives have been proved to be quite effective in improving the fingerprint verification reliability. In this paper, we present an efficient implementation of this algorithm in an embedded system environment. In our implementation, fixed-point arithmetic is used to replace the floating-point operations. Moreover, a special Gabor filter parameter selection constraint is also proposed to reduce the computing complexity of the kernel generation step. Experimental results show that our new approach achieves significant speed improvement and is almost as effective as the traditional floating-point based implementation.

1   Introduction

Fingerprint verification systems are now widely used for commercial and security purposes since they are convenient, cheap and relatively superior to other biometrics systems. Recent development in hardware has made it possible to incorporate fingerprint verification systems in such embedded environments as door access, PDA or even mobile phone authentication applications. In these embedded fingerprint verification systems, the important step of fingerprint image enhancement is always skipped because most embedded devices are equipped with RISC processors like the ARM and StrongARM processors without hardware floating-point processing units (FPU) while fingerprint image enhancement procedures usually require substantial quantities of floating-point operations. Such omissions can cause downgrades of the performances of most fingerprint verification systems when handling low quality fingerprint images due to predictable factors such as thin ridges, scars as well as unpredictable factors such as dry/wet fingers, moving fingers. In view of such a difficulty, creating an efficient fingerprint image enhancement implementation for the embedded environments becomes an urgent task.

Among the many proposed approaches for fingerprint image enhancement [3], [4], [5], [6], the Gabor filter based algorithm reported by Hong et al. [3] has been commonly regarded as an effective mean for improving the reliability of the fingerprint verification process [10], [12]. As the algorithm aims at the online

D. Maltoni and A.K. Jain (Eds.): BioAW 2004, LNCS 3087, pp. 146-157, 2004.

fingerprint verification system, its computational efficiency is quite suitable for the applications in which speed is critical. Therefore, our implementation is based on this algorithm. The speed optimization starts with the replacement of floating-point operations by fixed-point operations similar to work reported in [1], [8]. We then propose a simple Gabor filter parameter selection scheme that speeds up the Gabor filter kernel generation.

The rest of this paper is organized as follows. Section 2 introduces the outline of the enhancement algorithm as well as the structure of the complete system. Section 3 gives the detailed descriptions of the implementation. In section 4, we analyze the influence of the SVD on the convolution process. Experiment procedures and results are elaborated in section 5. The last section is a conclusion of our work.

2   Previous Work

2.1   Fingerprint Enhancement Algorithm

Fig. 1 shows the major steps of the fingerprint image enhancement algorithm [3]. This algorithm treats a gray-scale fingerprint image as a flow-like patter consisting of ridges and valleys. It assumes that the ridges and valleys form a sinusoidal-shaped wave with well-defined frequency and orientation varying smoothly and slowly along the flow of the ridges and valleys in a local area. After normalization in which the gray scale variations along the ridges and valleys are smoothed, the fingerprint image is divided into blocks of a suitable size. Local ridge orientation and frequency are estimated for each image block. Then, a Gabor filter kernel tuned to the estimated local orientation and frequency is applied to each image block to generate the enhanced image.

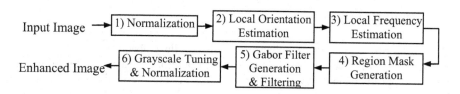

Fig. 1. The fingerprint image enhancement process

To adapt the image enhancement algorithm to our direct gray-scale based fingerprint features extraction system [7], an extra step, step 6, is inserted to tune the gray scale levels in the enhanced fingerprint images. To ensure the gray-scale consistency of the enhanced images, local normalization is applied to each image block after the gray-scale tuning.

2.2   System Structure

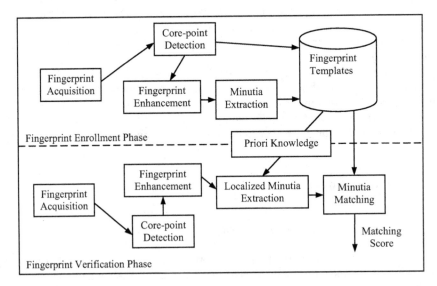

Fig. 2. The structure of the embedded fingerprint verification system with fingerprint image enhancement step

After adding the fingerprint image enhancement, the system structure [2] of the embedded fingerprint verification system is shown in Fig. 2. We can observe that fingerprint image enhancement is performed before the minutia extraction process both in the fingerprint enrollment phase and the fingerprint verification phase.

3   Implementation

To realize fingerprint image enhancement in mobile embedded systems with time efficiency, it is important that the mathematical approximations and constraints that we use to optimize the computational time do not affect the effectiveness of the image enhancement as well as the reliability of the ultimate fingerprint verification results significantly.

3.1   Fixed-Point Arithmetic

The use of fixed-point arithmetic in the embedded biometrics systems has been studied in [1], [8], [18]. In our fingerprint image enhancement implementation, we have adopted a similar approach to facilitate the whole process in the embedded environment. A commonly used representation of a fixed-point arithmetic system [9] is shown in Fig. 3.

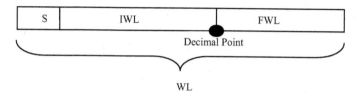

Fig. 3. Representation of the fixed-point arithmetic system: S-unsigned or two's complement (signed); WL-word length; IWL-integral word length; FWL-fractional word length

Suppose $I(i, j)$ and $N(i, j)$ are the gray-level values of the i-j pixel in the input image and the normalized image respectively. The normalization process can be defined as

$$N(i, j) = round\left(M_0 + \frac{STD_0}{STD} \times (I(i, j) - M) \right)$$ (1)

in which M and STD denote the mean and standard deviation of I, M_0 and STD_0 are the desired mean and standard deviation. Calculation of M and STD can involve large intermediate values due to the summation of the corresponding values from all the pixels. We, therefore, choose to use integer (32 bit) operation for this step. Since values of M_0, STD_0, M, STD and $I(i, j)$ are smaller than 256, selecting IWL=8 is enough for their numerical ranges. As $|I(i, j) - M|$ is always smaller than 256, if the numerical precision of STD_0/STD is smaller than 1/256, the maximum error of the final normalization result is 1 gray-level. This leads to FWL=8. Similar analyses are performed to the other enhancement steps. Table 1 shows the results of accuracy analyzing for each enhancement step in our implementation.

Table 1. Accuracy analysis results for each enhancement step

Enhancement Step	Fixed-point Arithmetic Representation	Maximum Error
Normalization	8.8	1 Gray Level
Local Orientation Estimation	8.6	0.006
Local Frequency Estimation	13.10	0.001
Region Mask Generation	--	--
Filtering	15.8	1.2%
Local Gray-scale Tuning & Local Normalization	8.8	1 Gray Level

Obviously, by using the 15.16 representation, the computational error of our implementation is not bigger than the values listed in Table 1.

3.2   Gabor Kernel Generation

Gabor filters have the properties of supporting both frequency-selection and orientation-selection [16]. It is appropriate to apply Gabor filters to the fingerprint image to remove the noises and sharpen the ridges and valleys [3], as the local area of a fingerprint is quite close to a sinusoidal shaped wave consisting of ridges and valley. As proposed in [3], [11], the even-symmetric Gabor filter used in the fingerprint image enhancement has the general form of

$$g(x, y; \phi, f) = \exp\left\{-\frac{1}{2}\left[\frac{x_\phi^2}{\delta_x^2} + \frac{y_\phi^2}{\delta_y^2}\right]\right\} \times \cos(2\pi f x_\phi) \qquad (2)$$

$$x_\phi = x\cos\phi + y\sin\phi \qquad (3)$$

$$y_\phi = -x\sin\phi + y\cos\phi \qquad (4)$$

where ϕ is the orientation of the Gabor filter, f is the frequency of the sinusoidal wave, δ_x and δ_y are the standard deviations of the Gaussian envelops along the x and y axes, respectively. If the size of the Gabor filter is $2w+1$, the values of x and y should be integers within the range of $[-w, +w]$.

Generating the Gabor kernel during fingerprint image enhancement is a time consuming process since one Gabor filter has to be generated for every image block. From (2), (3) and (4), we can see that the generation process involves add, multiple, trigonometric operations and exponential operations. To speed up the trigonometric operations, table lookup techniques have been used in the fixed-point arithmetic system as in [1]. However, the exponential operation requires special attention.

From (2), we can see that the exponential values in the Gabor filter generation are determined by ϕ, δ_x and δ_y. Fig. 4 shows the impacts of parameter selections on the Gabor filtering output.

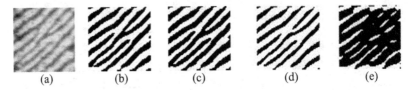

(a)   (b)   (c)   (d)   (e)

Fig. 4. Binarized Gabor filtering output under different parameter selections

Table 2. Gabor Filter parameters selection for Fig. 4

Image	δ_x	δ_y	ϕ	f
(b)	4.0	5.0	0.57	
(c)	4.0	4.0	0.57	0.14
(d)	3.5	5.0	0.57	
(e)	4.0	5.0	0.37	

Fig. 4a is the original fingerprint image block. Its local orientation and frequency are estimated to be 0.57 and 0.14, respectively. In Fig. 4b, δ_x and δ_y are carefully selected so that the filtered image best reflects the ridge structure of the original fingerprint image. Fig. 4c ~ Fig. 4e are the filtering outputs with deviations in one of the parameters as listed in Table 2. We can see that the effectiveness of Gabor filtering is very sensitive to ϕ and δ_x, but relatively less sensitive to δ_y. This is not difficult to understand. Parameter ϕ reflects the intrinsic property of ridge orientation for the fingerprint image block. Parameter δ_x influences both the noise smoothing intensity and the contrast between the ridge and valley in the filtering output while δ_y only determines the intensity of the noise smoothing along the local ridge orientation.

In our implementation, we carefully select δ_x according to the property of specific fingerprint database. Then, we let

$$\delta_y = \delta_x = \delta \tag{5}$$

In this way, equation (2) becomes

$$g(x, y; \phi, f) = \exp\left\{-\frac{1}{2\delta^2}\left[x^2 + y^2\right]\right\} \times \cos(2\pi f x_\phi) \tag{6}$$

We find that equation (6) has a very nice property that the exponential part is not affected by the choice of value for ϕ, implying that if once the value of δ and the size of the Gabor filter are determined for an image block, the exponential part will remain invariant no matter what the local orientation might be. In our implementation, a lookup table storing these exponential values is built inside our enhancement system.

3.3 Filtering

An enhanced image is obtained by performing 2D convolutions between the generated Gabor kernels and the corresponding image blocks. Suppose the size of an image I is $N \times N$ and the size of the Gabor filter matrix, G, is $2w + 1$. According to the mathematical definition of a 2D convolution, the computational complexity of a direct 2D convolution implementation is $N^2(2w + 1)^2$, a very time consuming operation. To speed up this step, we require a fast convolution algorithm. Existing fast convolution algorithms can be divided into mainly two categories: algebraic and domain transformation [17]. The domain transformation approaches always lead to extensive exponential operations that should be avoided in embedded systems. Therefore, we choose the algebraic approach.

An efficient fast 2D convolution algorithm takes advantage of the separability of G, a Gabor kernel [13]. According to [14], G can always be expressed in the form of $G = UQV^T$, where U and V are two orthogonal matrices and Q is a diagonal matrix with nonnegative diagonal entries. The number of positive diagonal entries of Q is equal to the rank of G. The process for decomposing a matrix into such a form is called Singular Value Decomposition (SVD). Suppose G has a rank of r, we can decompose G into the form

$$G = \begin{bmatrix} U_1 & U_2 & ... \end{bmatrix} \times \begin{bmatrix} \mu_1 & & & & 0 \\ & \mu_2 & & & \\ & & ... & & \\ & & & \mu_r & \\ 0 & & & & 0 \\ & & & & ... \end{bmatrix} \times \left(\begin{bmatrix} V_1 & V_2 & ... \end{bmatrix} \right)^T \tag{7}$$

where μ_i are positive numbers and U_i and V_i are column vectors. Therefore, we have

$$G = \sum_{i=1}^{r} \mu_i \times \left(U_i \times V_i^T \right) \tag{8}$$

Applying the associability of the convolution, we have

$$I * G = \sum_{i=1}^{r} \mu_i \times \left((I * U_i) * V_i^T \right) \tag{9}$$

implying that a 2D convolution can always be decomposed into combinations of 1D convolutions. The computational complexity of (9) is $2rN^2(2w+1)$. Since N is fixed, the efficiency improvement can be expressed by

$$1 - \frac{2r}{2w+1} \tag{10}$$

If r is much smaller than $2w+1$, considerable computational effort can be saved. It's easy to prove that the even symmetric Gabor Filter matrices under the mathematical constraint (5) always have a rank no bigger than 2. In our implementation, we use $w = 5$. So, according to (10), ideally we can achieve a computation complexity decrease of 64%.

A SVD algorithm using fixed-point arithmetic based on the traditional GOLUB-REINSCH algorithm [15] is used in our implementation. As the range of values represented in our fixed-point arithmetic system is more restrictive than its floating-point counterparts, overflows and underflows in the SVD process can occur more frequently. Underflows can lead to some inaccuracy in the results if we replace the underflow values by zero. On the other hand, the consequence of overflow cannot be neglected. An accuracy check step is added at the end of the decomposition. If the error of the SVD result is estimated to be bigger than a certain tolerance value, the algorithm is regarded as a failure and a direct convolution is adopted instead. We used 53454 Gabor kernel matrices of different parameters to test our SVD algorithm and found only 1552 failure cases (2.9%).

4   Complexity Analysis

Mathematical derivation shows that SVD can considerably decrease the computational complexity of the convolution process. Ideally, we can achieve computational improvement of 64% in the convolution step by using SVD. However, such an achievement has not taken into consideration of the computational complexity of the SVD algorithm itself. In our fingerprint image enhancement, one SVD has to be done for each image block. Therefore for a complete fingerprint image, the computational complexity of SVD using Golub-Reinsch algorithm is roughly equal to $(8n^3 + 6n^2)$ x B add+multiply operations, where n is the size of the Gabor filter kernel and B is the number of the image blocks. The complexity improvements under several different image sizes are shown in Table 3 in which we have assumed that the complete image is to be filtered and ignored the extra complexity which might arise due to the failure of the SVD process. The first two rows are the practical situations in which we really face in our experiments. The last row is only an imaginary situation to show the tendency. We can see that, given a fixed number of blocks, the bigger the Gabor kernel and the image, more significant performance improvements can be achieved through SVD.

Table 3. Computational complexity comparison of the convolution process with/without SVD

Image Size	Block Size	Block Number	Gabor Kernel Size	Complexity Analysis (Million add+multiply Operations)		
				No SVD	SVD	Improvement
256x256	16x16	256	11x11	7.9	6.9	13%
512x512	32x32	256	11x11	31.7	16.4	48%
1024x1024	64x64	256	17x17	303.0	83.3	72.5%

5   Experiments and Results

The purposes of our experiments are to prove that 1) considerable speed improvements 2) effectiveness of the fingerprint enhancement can be attained in our implementation.

Two fingerprint databases were used in our experiments. One is the database (FP) set up in our lab with 1149 fingerprints from 383 individuals; 3 for each: Image size is 256 x 256. The other is a subset of the NIST4 databases with 1000 fingerprints from 500 individuals; two for each: Image size is 512 x 512.

Two fingerprint image enhancement program modules were developed for comparison purpose. One adopts our fixed-point arithmetic based implementation (module A) and the other uses the traditional floating-point based implementation (module B). In both modules, the size of the Gabor kernel size is set to 11 and the block size is set to 16 for FP and 32 for the NIST4 subset. The values of δ are set to 2.0 and 4.0 for FP and the NIST4 subset respectively.

The first part of the experiments is to test the speed of our implementation. The experiments were conducted in a PDA equipped with a 206MHz StrongARM processor. 30 fingerprint images were taken from each fingerprint database.

Fingerprint image enhancement was applied to these fingerprint images using module A and module B respectively. The timings of the image enhancement process for module B and module A are listed in Table 4 and Table 5 respectively. Compared to the traditional floating-point based implementation, our fixed-point based implementation has achieved considerable improvements in processing speed. In our embedded verification system, the average computational time for enhancing one fingerprint image is near to that of the minutiae extraction [1]. Also we notice that for the NIST4 fingerprint images, the use of SVD speeds up the convolution process considerably.

Table 4. The runtime of the fingerprint image enhancement in the embedded system using floating point based implementation

Database Used	Normalization (seconds)	Orientation (seconds)	Frequency & ROI (seconds)	Local Tuning (seconds)	Filtering (seconds)	Total (seconds)
FP	1.71	0.03	0.67	0.60	70.72	73.73
NIST4	6.86	0.11	1.47	2.55	275.81	286.80

Table 5. The runtime of the fingerprint image enhancement in the embedded system using fixed point based implementation

Database Used	Normalization (seconds)	Orientation (seconds)	Frequency & ROI (seconds)	Local Tuning (seconds)	Filtering (seconds)		Total (seconds)	
					No SVD	SVD	No SVD	SVD
FP	0.03	0.03	0.09	0.08	0.60	0.67	0.83	0.90
NIST4	0.12	0.11	0.31	0.34	2.48	1.87	3.36	2.75

The second part of the experiment is to test the verification performance after the fingerprint image enhancement. Because of the storage limitation of the embedded system (32MB), this experiment was simulated in a PC Linux system.

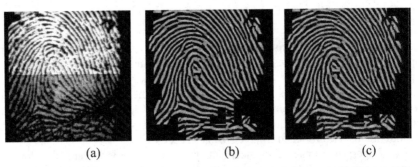

(a)   (b)   (c)

Fig. 5. Example of enhancement result: (a) Original Fingerprint Image; (b) Enhanced Image using module B; (c) Enhanced Image using module A

The experiment was performed in three steps. First the verification was performed directly on all fingerprints without any enhancement. Then, the images were enhanced using module B, and finally module A was employed for the enhancement. Samples of enhanced images using module A and module B are shown in Fig. 5.

The receiver operating curves (ROC) obtained from applying the experiments to FP and the NIST4 subset are shown in Fig. 6 and Fig. 7. Both curves show that the effectiveness of enhancement using our fixed-point arithmetic based implementation is basically similar to its floating-point arithmetic counterpart.

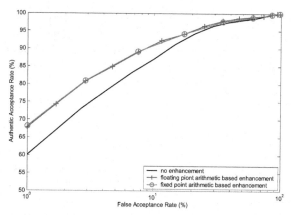

Fig. 6. Receiver Operating Curves (ROC) showing the comparison of the enhancement efficiency using module A and module B in the FP database

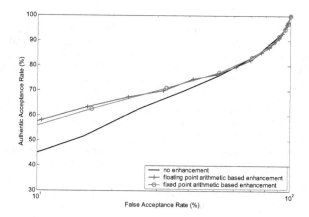

Fig. 7. Receiver Operating Curves (ROC) showing the comparison of the enhancement efficiency using module A and model B in the NIST4 subset database

6   Conclusion

We have proposed an efficient fingerprint enhancement implementation for mobile embedded systems. In our work, we set up a special constraint on the selection of the parameters for the Gabor kernel so that the complexity of the Gabor kernel generation can be significantly reduced. This parameter selection scheme also leads to the property of very low rank of the generated Gabor kernel matrices whose SVD can be easily accomplished. Experiment results show that our new implementation has achieved a considerable speed improvement, enabling fingerprint image enhancement to be accomplished in modern mobile devices.

We can observe from the experiment results that the influence on the processing speed using SVD can be negative for small fingerprint images. The main reason is that the Golub-Reinsch based SVD algorithm used in our implementation is a SVD algorithm which does not take advantage of low rank properties of the Gabor kernel matrices under the mathematical constraint stated in (5). To develop a specific SVD algorithm that makes use of such computationally efficient algebraic property will be our next task.

Acknowledgement

This work was partially supported by the Hong Kong Research Grants Council Project 2300011, "Towards Multi-Modal Human-Computer Dialog Interactions with Minimally Intrusive Biometric Security Functions".

References

1. T. Y. Tang, Y. S. Moon, K. C. Chan: Efficient Implementation of Fingerprint Verification for Mobile Embedded Systems using Fixed-point Arithmetic, Proceedings of the 2004 ACM Symposium on Applied Computing, pp. 821-825, March, 2004
2. K. C. Chan, Y. S. Moon, P. S. Cheng: Fast Fingerprint Verification Using Sub-regions of Fingerprint Images, Circuits and Systems for Video Technology, IEEE Trans., Vol. 14, Issue 1, pp. 95-101, Jan. 2004
3. H. Lin, Y. Wan, A. K. Jain, Fingerprint image enhancement: algorithm and performance evaluation, Pattern Analysis and Machine Intelligence, IEEE Trans., Vol. 20, Issue 8, pp.777, Aug. 1998
4. J. Cheng, J. Tian, H. Chen, Q. Ren, X. Yang: Fingerprint Enhancement Using Oriented Diffusion Filter, AVBPA 2003, LNCS 2688, pp.164-171
5. X. Luo, J. Tian: Knowledge Based Fingerprint Image Enhancement, Proceedings of 15th International Conference on Pattern Recognition, Vol. 4, pp.783 – 786, Sept. 2000
6. W. P. Zhang; Q. R. Wang, Tang, Y.Y.: A wavelet-based method for fingerprint image enhancement, Proceedings of International Conference on Machine Learning and Cybernetics 2002, Vol. 4, pp.1973 – 1977, Nov. 2002
7. D. Maio, D. Maltoni: Direct gray-scale minutiae detection in fingerprints, Pattern Analysis and Machine Intelligence, IEEE Trans., Vol. 19, Issue 1, pp.27 –40, Jan. 1997
8. Y. S. Moon, F. T. Luk, T. Y. Tang, K.C. Chan, C. W. Leung: Fixed-Point Arithmetic for Mobile Devices—A Fingerprint Verification Case Study, Proceedings of the SPIE 2002 Seattle, Advanced Signal Processing Algorithms, Architectures, and Implementations XII, Vol. 4791, pp. 144 -149
9. M. Willems, V. Buersgens, H. Keding, H. Meyr: FRIDGE: An Interactive Fixed-Point Code Generation Environment for HW/SW CoDesign, Proceeding of the International Conference on Acoustics, Speech, and Signal Processing '97, Apr. 1997
10. J. Yang, L. Liu, T. Jiang, Y. Fan: A modified Gabor filter design method for fingerprint image enhancement, Pattern Recognition Letters, v.24, pp.1805-1817, 2003

11. A. K. Jain, F. Farrokhnia: Unsupervised texture segmentation using Gabor filters, Proceedings of IEEE International Conference on Systems, Man and Cybernetics, pp.14–19, Nov. 1990

12. S. Greenberg, M. Aladjem, D. Kogan, I. Dimitrov: Fingerprint image enhancement using filtering techniques, Proceedings of 15th International Conference on Pattern Recognition, Vol. 3, pp.322 – 325, Sept. 2000

13. R.M. Haralick, L.G. Shapiro: Computer and Robot Vision, Vol. I, Addison-Wesley, pp.298-299, 1992

14. K. E. Atkinson: An Introduction to Numerical Analysis, John Wiley & Sons, pp. 408, 1978

15. G. H. Golub, C. Reisch: Singular value decomposition and least squares solutions, Handbook for Automatic Computation, Vol. 2 (Linear Algebra), pp.134—151, New York: Springer-Verlag, 1971

16. J. G. Daugman: Uncertainty Relation for Resolution in Space, Spatial-Frequency and Orientation Optimized by Two-Dimensional Visual Cortical Filters, J. Optical Soc. Am., Vol. 2, pp.1160-1169, 1985

17. R. Tolimieri, M. An, Chao Lu: Algorithms for discrete Fourier transform and convolution, published by New York, Springer, 1997

18. Y. S. Moon, C. C. Leung, K. H. Pun: "Fixed-point GMM-based Speaker Verification over Mobile Embedded System", Proceedings of ACM SIGMM 2003 Multimedia Biometrics Methods and Applications Workshop, pp. 53-57, Nov. 2003

Capacity and Examples of Template-Protecting Biometric Authentication Systems

Pim Tuyls and Jasper Goseling

Philips Research,
Prof. Holstlaan 4,
5656 AA Eindhoven,
The Netherlands,
pim.tuyls@philips.com, j.goseling@ieee.org

Abstract. In this paper, we formulate precisely the requirements for privacy protecting biometric authentication systems. The secrecy capacity C_s is investigated for the discrete and the continuous case. We present, furthermore, a general algorithm that meets the requirements and achieves C_s as well as C_{id} (the identification capacity). Finally, we present some practical constructions of the general algorithm and analyze their properties.

1 Introduction

The increasing demand for more reliable and convenient security systems generates a renewed interest in human identification based on biometric identifiers such as fingerprints, iris, voice and gait. Since biometrics cannot be lost or forgotten like e.g. computer passwords, biometrics have the potential to offer higher security and more convenience for the users.

A common approach to biometric authentication is to capture the biometric templates of all users during the *enrollment phase* and to store the templates in a reference database. During the *authentication phase* new measurements are matched against the database information.

The fact that biometric templates are stored in a database introduces a number of security and privacy risks. We identify the following threats:

1. Impersonation. An attacker steals templates from a database and constructs artificial biometrics that pass authentication.
2. Irrevokability. Once compromised, biometrics cannot be updated, reissued or destroyed.
3. Exposure of sensitive personal information.

The first threat was recognized by several authors [1,2,3]. When an authentication system is used on a large scale, the reference database has to be made available to many different verifiers, who, in general, cannot be trusted. Especially in a networked environment, attacks on the database pose a serious threat. It was shown explicitly by Matsumoto et al. [4] that using information stolen

D. Maltoni and A.K. Jain (Eds.): BioAW 2004, LNCS 3087, pp. 158–170, 2004.
© Springer-Verlag Berlin Heidelberg 2004

from a database, artificial biometrics can be constructed to impersonate people. Construction of artificial biometrics is possible even if only part of the template is available. Hill [5] showed that if only minutiae templates of a fingerprint are available, it is still possible to successfully construct artificial biometrics that pass authentication.

The second threat was first addressed by Schneier [6]. The problem is concisely paraphrased by: *"Theft of biometrics is theft of identity."*

The third threat is caused by the fact that biometrics contain sensitive personal information. It is shown in [7,8,9] that fingerprints contain certain genetic information. From [10] on the other hand it follows that retina scans reflect information about diseases like diabetes and strokes.

We present a general architecture that guarantees privacy protection of biometric templates. Examples of architectures that achieve protection of templates are *private biometrics* [11], *fuzzy commitment* [12], *cancelable biometrics* [13], *fuzzy vault* [14], *quantizing secret extraction* [15] and *secret extraction from significant components* [16].

All these systems are based on the use of a one-way transform to achieve protection of the biometric templates. The systems proposed in [15,16,11,12,14] are all based on the use of *helper data*. In this paper we analyze the principle behind all these systems, identify fundamental performance bounds and propose an algorithm that achieves these bounds.

This paper is organized as follows. In Section 2 we introduce our model and give definitions. In Section 3 we identify requirements to authentication systems that circumvent the threats mentioned above and we introduce the *helper data architecture*. Moreover we explain in this section the relation between protection of biometric templates and secret extraction from common randomness. In Section 4 we derive fundamental bounds for the helper data architecture. A general algorithm that implements the helper data architecture is given in Section 5. It is shown that this algorithm satisfies the requirements and that the maximum achievable performance of an identification system is not decreased by the protection of the templates. In Section 6 some concrete examples of the general algorithm are given and analyzed. These examples illustrate the relation between our work and [12,16,15]. Conclusions are given in Section 7.

2 Model and Definitions

2.1 Security Assumptions

An overview of the possible attack scenarios to a biometric authentication system is given in [1,2,3]. In this paper, we make the following security assumptions.

- Enrollment is performed at a *trusted* Certification Authority (CA). The CA enrolls all users by capturing their biometrics, performing additional processing and adding a protected form of the user data to a database.
- The database is vulnerable to attacks as well from the outside as from the inside (malicious verifier).

- During the authentication phase an attacker is able to present artificial biometrics at the sensor.
- All capturing and processing during authentication is tamper resistant, e.g. no information about biometrics can be obtained from the sensor.
- The communication channel between the sensor and the verification authority is assumed to be public, i.e. the line can be eavesdropped by an attacker.

2.2   Biometrics

Biometric templates are processed measurement data, e.g. feature vectors. We model biometric templates as realizations of a random process. Biometrics of different individuals are independent realizations of a random process that is equal for all individuals. We assume that the processing of the biometrics is such that the resulting templates are given by n independent identically distributed (i.i.d.) sequences with a known distribution. The probability that the biometric sequence X^n of a certain individual equals x^n is defined by

$$\Pr\{X^n = x^n\} = \prod_{i=1}^{n} P_X(x_i), \qquad (1)$$

where P_X is the probability distribution of each component, defined on an alphabet $\mathcal{X}$, which can be a discrete set or $\mathbb{R}$. [1]
Noisy measurements of biometrics are modeled as observations through a memoryless noisy channel. For a measurement Y^n of biometrics x^n we have

$$\Pr\{Y^n = y^n | X^n = x^n\} = \prod_{i=1}^{n} P_{Y|X}(y_i|x_i), \qquad (2)$$

where $P_{Y|X}$ characterizes the memoryless channel with input alphabet $\mathcal{X}$ and output alphabet $\mathcal{Y}$. It is assumed that the enrollment measurements of the biometric templates are noise free.

2.3   Secret Extraction Codes (SECs)

In order to deal with noisy measurements, we introduce the notion of Secret Extraction Codes (SECs). Let $\mathcal{S}$ denote the set of secrets and let $\mathcal{X}, \mathcal{Y}$ denote the input and output alphabets of the channel representing the noisy measurements.

Definition 1 (Secret Extraction Code). *Let $n, \epsilon > 0$. An $(n, |\mathcal{S}|, \epsilon)$ Secret Extraction Code $\mathcal{C}$, defined on $\mathcal{X}^n \times \mathcal{Y}^n$, is an ordered set of pairs of encoding and decoding regions*

$$\mathcal{C} = \left\{ (\mathcal{E}_i, \mathcal{D}_i) \,\middle|\, i = 1, 2, \ldots, |\mathcal{S}| \right\}, \qquad (3)$$

---

[1] For $\mathcal{X} = \mathbb{R}$ the sequence X^n is characterized by the probability density function $f_{X^n}(x^n) = \prod_i f_X(x_i)$.

where $\mathcal{E}_i \subseteq \mathcal{X}^n$ and $\mathcal{D}_i \subseteq \mathcal{Y}^n$, such that

$$\mathcal{E}_i \cap \mathcal{E}_j = \emptyset, \qquad \mathcal{D}_i \cap \mathcal{D}_j = \emptyset, \qquad \bigcup_i \mathcal{D}_i = \mathcal{Y}^n, \qquad (4)$$

for $i, j = 1, 2, \ldots, |\mathcal{S}|$, $i \neq j$ and

$$P_{Y^n|X^n}(\mathcal{D}_i|x_i^n) \geq 1 - \epsilon, \qquad (5)$$

for all $x_i^n \in \mathcal{E}_i$ and $i = 1, 2, \ldots, |\mathcal{S}|$.

Note that a SEC provides an encoding-decoding scheme of a (possibly continuous) variable into a finite alphabet $\mathcal{S} = \{1, 2, \ldots, |\mathcal{S}|\}$ by discretization. The set of all $(n, |\mathcal{S}|, \epsilon)$ SECs on $\mathcal{X}^n \times \mathcal{Y}^n$ will be denoted as $\Phi(n, |\mathcal{S}|, \epsilon)$ where the sets $\mathcal{X}^n \times \mathcal{Y}^n$ are suppressed in the notation as that should be clear from the context (otherwise they will be mentioned). We note that the condition in Eq. (4) expresses that unambiguous encoding and decoding is possible and the condition of Eq. (5) implies a low False Rejection Rate (FRR).

Note that SECs are strongly related to geometric codes [17]. Furthermore, if the sets $\mathcal{C}_i$ have cardinality one, the SECs are normal error correcting codes.

3   Protection of Templates

3.1   Requirements

The requirements for an architecture that does not suffer from the threats mentioned in the introduction are:

1. The information that is stored in the database does not give sufficient information to make successful impersonation possible.
2. The information in the database provides the least possible information about the original biometrics, in particular it reveals no sensitive information.

Note that an architecture that meets those requirements, guarantees that the biometric cannot be compromised. Therefore there is no need to focus on additional revocation mechanisms.

3.2   The Helper Data Architecture

The privacy protecting biometric authentication architecture that is proposed in [15, 16] is inspired by the protection mechanism used for computer passwords. Passwords are stored in a computer system in a cryptographically hashed form. This makes it computationally infeasible to retrieve the password from the information stored in the database. The hash function is also applied to the user input that is given in the authentication phase and matching is based on the hashed values. This approach, however, cannot be used for the protection of biometric templates in a straightforward way, because the measurements in the authentication phase are inherently noisy. Since small differences at the input of one-way functions result in completely different outputs, the hashed versions of the enrollment and the noisy authentication measurements will be different with high probability.

In order to combine biometric authentication with cryptographic techniques, we derive *helper data* during the enrollment phase. The helper data guarantees that a unique string can be derived from the biometrics of an individual as well during the authentication as during the enrollment phase. Since the helper data is stored in the database it should be considered publicly available. In order to prevent impersonation we need to derive authentication data from the biometric that is statistically independent of the helper data. In order to keep the authentication data secret for somebody having access to the database, we store the authentication data in hashed form. In this way impersonation becomes computationally infeasible.

A schematic representation of the architecture described in this section is presented in Fig. 1.

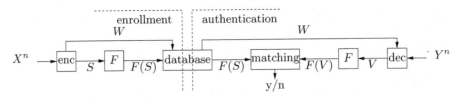

Fig. 1. The proposed authentication architecture. In the enrollment phase, the biometric template X^n is used for the derivation of a secret S and helper data W. A hashed version $F(S)$ of the secret and the helper data w are stored in a database. In the authentication phase a noisy version Y^n of the biometric template is captured. The helper data w is used to derive a secret V from Y^n. If $F(S) = F(V)$, the authentication is successful.

During the enrollment phase a secret S, belonging to an alphabet $\mathcal{S} = \{1, 2, \ldots, |\mathcal{S}|\}$, is extracted from a sequence X^n. In order to guarantee robustness to noise, the CA derives helper data W that will be used during the authentication phase to achieve noise robustness.

During the authentication phase a noisy version Y^n of the enrollment sequence X^n is obtained. Using the helper data W, which is provided to the verifier, a secret $V \in \mathcal{S}$ is derived. The scheme is designed such that V equals S with high probability. Note that in contrast to usual biometric systems, we perform an exact match on S and V.

The first requirement given in Section 3.1, is to prevent abuse of database information for impersonation. To this end the system is designed such that the mutual information between the helper data and the secret is sufficiently small and the secrets are uniformly distributed. Furthermore the set of secrets has to be sufficiently large to exclude an attack by exhaustive trial.

The helper data architecture was introduced as an architecture for verification. A single match between one set of database information and a biometric measurement is performed in order to verify an identity claim. The helper data architecture can, however, also be used in an identification setting. In that case a biometric measurement is matched against the database information of all enrolled users. In the remaining part of this paper, algorithms will be proposed in a verification setting. The extension to the identification setting is left implicit.

3.3   Relation with Secret Extraction from Common Randomness

There is a strong relation between the protection of biometric templates and *secret extraction from common randomness* [18,19]. The term common randomness is used for the situation that two parties have sequences of correlated random variables available. A well-known example of this is quantum key exchange [20]. The secret extraction problem arises if the parties want to extract a secret from the correlated data by communicating over a public channel. As the channel is public it is required that the communications over the channel do not reveal information about the secret that is derived by the parties.

Fig. 2 gives an alternative representation of the situation that was already visualized in Fig. 1. It is made explicit that the authentication sequence Y^n is a noisy observation of the enrollment sequence X^n. Furthermore it is made clear that secrets S and V are derived from the correlated variables X^n and Y^n, respectively, by means of additional communication of helper data W. Although there is no explicit public channel, we do require that W does not give any information about S or V.

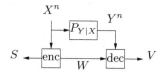

Fig. 2. The sequences X^n and Y^n are correlated random variables. The goal is to use helper data W to derive secrets S and V in such a way that W does not give much information about these secrets.

The main difference between secret extraction from biometrics and for instance quantum key exchange is that in the case of biometrics all helper data can be derived during enrollment. In quantum key exchange on the other hand, communications can only start after random variables are obtained by both parties. In general multiple rounds of communications are required.

4   Bounds: Secrecy and Identification Capacity

Secret Extraction We express the size of the secrets in the rate R_s. The maximum achievable rate is defined accordingly by the secrecy capacity C_s.

Definition 2 (Secrecy Capacity). *The secrecy capacity* C_s *is the maximal rate* R_s, *such that for all* $\epsilon > 0$, *there exist encoders and decoders that, for sufficiently large n, achieve*

$$\Pr\{V \neq S\} \leq \epsilon, \tag{6}$$

$$I(W; S) \leq \epsilon, \tag{7}$$

$$\frac{1}{n}H(S) = \frac{1}{n}\log|\mathcal{S}| \geq (R_s - \epsilon). \tag{8}$$

Eq. (6) ensures correctness of the secret, Eq. (7) ensures secrecy with respect to eavesdropping of the communication line and Eq. (8) guarantees a uniform distribution of the secrets.

According to requirement 2 from Section 3.1, $I(W; X^n)$ should be small. It was proven in [16], that in order to guarantee correctness and a large number of secrets, the helper data W should depend on the biometric template X^n. Hence $I(W; X^n)$ cannot be zero. In Section 6 we show, however, that it is possible to keep $I(W; X^n)$ small. More in particular, it will not be possible to derive from the helper data W a good (in the least squared sense) estimate of X^n. Finally, if the requirement of Eq. (7) is satisfied and the number of secrets is large, an impersonation attack based on artificial biometrics $\hat{X}^n$ (which is an estimate of X^n based on helper data W) is infeasible, hence satisfying requirement 1 of Section 3.1.

The following is a technical lemma that we state without proof.

Lemma 1. *For continuous random variables X, Y and* $\epsilon > 0$, *there exists a sequence of discretized random variables* X_d, Y_d *that converge pointwise to X, Y (when* $d \to \infty$) *such that for sufficiently large d,*

$$I(X; Y) \geq I(X_d; Y_d) \geq I(X; Y) - \epsilon. \tag{9}$$

With some modifications to the results from [18, 19], the following theorem can be proven.

Theorem 1. *The secrecy capacity of a biometric system equals*

$$C_s = I(X; Y). \tag{10}$$

Proof. We start with the achievability argument. The proof that $I(X; Y)$ can be achieved if X^n and Y^n are discrete variables, is analogous to the proof in [18]. In order to prove achievability in the continuous case, we choose $\epsilon \geq 0$, and approximate the random variables X^n, Y^n by discretized (quantized) versions, X_d^n, Y_d^n such that $I(X; Y) - I(X_d^n; Y_d^n) \leq \epsilon$. (The fact that such a quantisation exists follows from lemma 1). Then, taking the encoder that achieves the capacity for the discrete case (X_d^n, Y_d^n)s it follows that we can achieve $I(X_d^n; Y_d^n)$. Since this can be done for any $\epsilon \geq 0$ the proof follows.

The fact that $I(X; Y)$ is an upper bound for C_s for discrete random variables, follows from the Fano inequality and some entropy inequalities. For the continuous case this follows again by an approximation argument.   □

Biometric Identification In the enrollment phase of an identification setting, a database is created with data from a set of $|\mathcal{M}|$ enrolled users, each identified with an index $m \in \{1, 2, \ldots, |\mathcal{M}|\}$. In the identification phase, a measurement y^n and the information in the database are used to find the identity of an unknown (but properly enrolled) individual m. The identifier output is denoted by $\hat{m}$.

Reliability of the identification is expressed by the average error probability, assuming that the individual is chosen at random. Performance in terms of the number of users in the system is expressed by the rate R. The maximum rate at which reliable identification is possible is given by the identification capacity C_{id}.

Definition 3 (Identification Capacity). *The identification capacity C_{id} is the maximal rate R_{id}, such that for every $\epsilon > 0$, for sufficiently large n, there exists an identification strategy that achieves*

$$\text{avg } \Pr\left\{\hat{M} \neq M\right\} \leq \epsilon, \quad \text{and} \quad \frac{1}{n}\log|\mathcal{M}| \geq R_{id} - \epsilon, \tag{11}$$

where the average is over all individuals and over all random realizations of all biometrics.

It was proven in [21, 22] that all biometric identification systems, including template protecting systems, satisfy $C_{id} = I(X;Y)$.

5 Secure Biometric Authentication Algorithm (SBA)

We introduce a general algorithm that implements the architecture given in Fig. 1. The algorithm basically describes a class of encoders/decoders. It will be shown that the algorithm meets the requirements given by Equations (6), (7) and (8) at a maximum rate.

Initially we define a finite collection $\mathcal{C} \subset \Phi(n, |\mathcal{S}|, \epsilon)$ on $\mathcal{X}^n \times \mathcal{Y}^n$. The collection of SECs is made available in both the enrollment and the authentication phase. Furthermore, for $x^n \in \mathcal{C}^n$ we define $\Phi_{x^n} \subseteq \mathcal{C}$. A SEC $C = \{(\mathcal{E}_i, \mathcal{D}_i)\}_{i=1}^{|\mathcal{S}|} \in \Phi_{x^n}$ iff $x^n \in \bigcup_i \mathcal{E}_i$. The collection of SECs $\mathcal{C}$ is used as follows.

Enrollment

1. The biometrics x^n of the users are measured.
2. Choose a SEC C at random in Φ_{x^n}. Define w as the index of this SEC C. If $\Phi_{x^n} = \emptyset$, a SEC is selected at random from $\mathcal{C}$.
3. Given a $C = \{(\mathcal{E}_i, \mathcal{D}_i)\}_{i=1}^{|\mathcal{S}|}$, the secret s is defined as, $s = i$ if $x^n \in \mathcal{E}_i$. For $\Phi_{x^n} = \emptyset$, s is chosen at random.
4. The one-way function F is applied to s. The data $F(s)$ and w are stored in a database together with some metadata about the user identity.

Authentication

1. An individual makes an identity claim.
2. The database information $F(s)$ and w for the claimed user is retrieved.

3. A measurement y^n of the user's biometrics and the helper data w are given to the decoder.
4. The SEC $C(w)$ is used to derive the secret v as, $v = i$ if $y^n \in \mathcal{D}_i$.
5. If $F(v) = F(s)$, the user is positively authenticated.

Theorem 2. *For all $\epsilon > 0$ and sufficiently large n, a collection $\mathcal{C}$ of SECs for the SBA algorithm can be found such that $\frac{1}{n}\mathrm{H}(S) = \frac{1}{n}\log|\mathcal{S}| \geq \mathrm{C_s} - \epsilon = \mathrm{I}(X;Y) - \epsilon$ and the requirements of Equations (6) and (7) are satisfied.*

Proof. We start with the discrete case. Fix $\epsilon > 0$. Define a set $\mathcal{S} = \{1, 2, \ldots, |\mathcal{S}|\}$, such that $|\mathcal{S}| = \exp[n(\mathrm{C_s} - \epsilon)]$. It was proven in [18] that for sufficiently large n, one can find a size K collection $\mathcal{C}$ of $(n, |\mathcal{S}|, \frac{\epsilon}{2})$ SECs on $\mathcal{X}^n \times \mathcal{Y}^n$,

$$C^k = \left\{ \left(\{e_i^k\}, \mathcal{D}_i^k\right) \right\}_{i=1}^{|\mathcal{S}|}, \quad \text{for } k = 1, 2, \ldots, K, \tag{12}$$

such that $\mathrm{P}_{X^n}(e_i^k) = \mathrm{P}_{X^n}(e_j^k)$, $\bigcup_i\{e_i^k\} \cap \bigcup_i\{e_i^m\} = \emptyset$, for $k \neq m$ and $i, j = 1, 2, \ldots, |\mathcal{S}|$ and

$$\mathrm{P}_{X^n}\left(\bigcup_k\bigcup_i\{e_i^k\}\right) \geq 1 - \frac{\epsilon}{2}. \tag{13}$$

Using the collection $\mathcal{C}$ defined above for the SBA algorithm, it follows from Eq. (13) that $\Pr\{\Phi_{x^n} = \emptyset\} \leq \frac{\epsilon}{2}$. From the construction of the collection $\mathcal{C}$ and Eq. (5) we derive

$$\Pr\{S \neq V | \Phi_{x^n} \neq \emptyset\} \leq \frac{\epsilon}{2}, \quad \text{for } k = 1, 2, \ldots, K, \tag{14}$$

which combined with Eq. (13) leads to $\Pr\{S \neq V\} \leq \epsilon$.

Define W to be the index of the SEC in $\mathcal{C}$ that has to be used to extract the secret. Since for each code, all encoding sets have equal probability, the secrets are uniformly distributed and $\mathrm{I}(W; S) = 0$. Hence, requirements (6), (7) and (8) are fulfilled.

For the proof of the continuous case, we proceed as follows. From Lemma 1, it follows that we can construct quantized variables X_d^n, Y_d^n in such a way that

$$\mathrm{I}(X_d^n; Y_d^n) \geq \mathrm{I}(X^n; Y^n) - \frac{\epsilon}{2}, \tag{15}$$

if d is sufficiently large. The quantization of X^n, Y^n to X_d^n, Y_d^n induces a partition $\mathcal{P} = \{\mathcal{P}_1, \ldots, \mathcal{P}_d\}$ of $\mathbb{R}^n$. The random variables X_d^n and Y_d^n defined on the set $\{1, 2, \ldots, d\}$ have probability distribution $\mathrm{P}_{X_d^n}(i) = \int_{\mathcal{P}_i} f_X(x^n)dx^n$, for all $i = 1, 2, \ldots, d$. Define a size K collection $\mathcal{C}_d$ of SECs on $\{1, 2, \ldots, d\} \times \{1, 2, \ldots, d\}$ as follows,

$$C_d^k = \left\{ \left(\{e_i^k\}, \mathcal{D}_i^k\right) \right\}_{i=1}^{|\mathcal{S}|}, \quad \text{for } k = 1, 2, \ldots, K. \tag{16}$$

For each SEC C_d^k there is a corresponding SEC C^k on $\mathbb{R}^n \times \mathbb{R}^n$ given by,

$$C^k = \left\{ \left(\mathcal{P}_{e_i^k}, \bigcup_{j \in \mathcal{D}_i^k} \mathcal{P}_j \right) \right\}_{i=1}^{|\mathcal{S}|}, \tag{17}$$

resulting in a collection $\mathcal{C}$ of SECs defined on $\mathbb{R}^n \times \mathbb{R}^n$. Note that secrets derived from X^n and Y^n, by means of the collection $\mathcal{C}$, are equal to those derived from X_d^n and Y_d^n using $\mathcal{C}_d$. It was proven for the discrete case that a collection $\mathcal{C}_d$ can be found such that $\Pr\{S \neq V\} \leq \epsilon$, $I(W; S) = 0$ and

$$|\mathcal{S}| = \exp\left[n\left(I(X_d^n; Y_d^n) - \frac{\epsilon}{2} \right) \right] \geq \exp\left[n\left(C_s - \epsilon \right) \right], \tag{18}$$

where the last inequality follows from Eq. (15) and $C_s = I(X; Y)$ (Theorem 1). This concludes the proof for the continuous case. □

Theorem 3. *For all $\epsilon > 0$, there exists a collection $\mathcal{C}$ of SECs such that an identification scheme based on the SBA algorithm achieves both $\frac{1}{n}H(S) = \frac{1}{n}\log|\mathcal{S}| \geq C_s - \epsilon$ and $\frac{1}{n}\log|\mathcal{M}| \geq C_{id} - \epsilon$, while satisfying the requirements of Equations (6), (7) and (11).*

Proof. *(sketch)* Given $\epsilon > 0$, choose ϵ' such that $\epsilon > \epsilon' > 0$. Theorem 2 states that for sufficiently large n, there exists a collection $\mathcal{C}$ of SECs such that, an implementation of the SBA algorithm using $\mathcal{C}$, satisfies $|\mathcal{S}| = \exp[n(I(X; Y) - \epsilon')]$, $\Pr\{S \neq V\} \leq \frac{\epsilon}{2}$ and $I(W; S) = 0$.

Applying the SBA algorithm results in a uniform random assignment of secrets to all users. Let the number of users in the system satisfy $|\mathcal{M}| = \exp[n(I(X; Y) - \epsilon)]$. The collision probability P_{coll} that two users share the same secret is bounded as follows

$$P_{coll} = \sum_{m=2}^{|\mathcal{M}|} \frac{1}{\exp\left[n\left(I(X; Y) - \epsilon' \right) \right]} \leq \exp\left[-n(\epsilon - \epsilon') \right] \leq \frac{\epsilon}{2},$$

where the last inequality holds for sufficiently large n. The overall error probability is upper bounded by

$$\operatorname{avg} \Pr\{\hat{M} \neq M\} \leq P_{coll} + \Pr\{S \neq V\} \leq \epsilon, \tag{19}$$

which is the requirement of Eq. (11). □

6   Code Constructions for the SBA Algorithm

In this section we give two examples of such constructions and show that these constructions meet the requirements.

6.1   Secret Extraction from Significant Components

The biometrics are modeled as i.i.d sequences of Gaussian distributed random variables with zero mean, i.e. $X_i \sim \mathcal{N}(0, \sigma_X^2)$. We assume additive uncorrelated Gaussian noise, i.e. $Y^n = X^n + N^n$, $N_i \sim \mathcal{N}(0, \sigma_N^2)$. The secrecy capacity of these biometrics is $C_s = n \log(1 + \frac{\sigma_X^2}{\sigma_N^2})$.

The scheme extracts binary secrets of length k from biometric sequences of length n. The secrets are derived as the sign of k components that have "large" absolute value. We define a collection $\mathcal{C}$ of SECs for encoding and decoding. First we define some base sets,

$$E_0 = (-\infty, \infty), \quad E_{-1} = (-\infty, -\delta], \quad E_1 = [\delta, \infty), \tag{20}$$
$$D_0 = (-\infty, \infty), \quad D_{-1} = (-\infty, 0], \quad D_1 = (0, \infty), \tag{21}$$

where δ is chosen sufficiently large considering σ_X^2 and σ_N^2. The SECs in $\mathcal{C}$ are indexed by an ordered set w,

$$w = \{i_1, i_2, \ldots, i_k\} \subseteq \{1, 2, \ldots, n\}. \tag{22}$$

SEC C^w extracts a secret from the components denoted by w and is defined by

$$C^w = \left\{ \left(E_0^{w^c} \times E_{-1}^{\sigma} \times E_1^{\sigma^c} ,\ D_0^{w^c} \times D_{-1}^{\sigma} \times D_1^{\sigma^c} \right) \middle| \sigma \subseteq w \right\}, \tag{23}$$

where w^c is the complement of w relative to $\{1, 2, \ldots, n\}$ and σ^c is the complement of σ relative to w. Furthermore $E_0^{w^c} \times E_{-1}^{\sigma} \times E_1^{\sigma^c}$ is the n dimensional Cartesian product with E_0, E_{-1} and E_1 at positions w^c, σ and σ^c, respectively.

It follows from the results in [16] that $I(W; S) = 0$, $|\Phi_{x^n}|$ is sufficiently large for most $x^n \in \mathcal{X}^n$ and $I(W; X^n) < k$.

6.2   Secret Extraction on Discrete Biometrics

In this section we model the biometrics as binary uniform i.i.d. sequences $X^n \in \{0,1\}^n$. The authentication sequence Y^n is an observation of X^n through a binary symmetrical channel with cross-over probability p. It follows from Theorem 1 that this channel results in a secrecy capacity equal to $C_s = 1 - H(p)$.

Take an error correcting code $C = \{c_1^n, c_2^n, \ldots, c_{|S|}^n\}$ on $\{0,1\}^n$. The error correcting capability of C implies decoding sets (balls) $\mathcal{D}_1, \mathcal{D}_2, \ldots, \mathcal{D}_{|S|}$. A collection $\mathcal{C}$ of SECs is constructed as follows. For every $w \in \{0,1\}^n$,

$$C^w = \left\{ \left(\{c_i^n + w\}, \mathcal{D}_i + w \right) \right\}_{i=1}^{|S|}, \tag{24}$$

where $\mathcal{D}_i + w = \{x^n + w | x^n \in \mathcal{D}_i\}$. Note that $C^{x^n + c_i^n}$, $i = 1, 2, \ldots, |S|$, is a SEC containing x^n as one of the encoding regions. It follows that $|\Phi_{x^n}| = |S|$ for all $x^n \in \mathcal{X}^n$.

Proposition 1. *For all $\epsilon > 0$ and sufficiently large n, the error correcting code C used to construct $\mathcal{C}$ can be chosen such that, the scheme achieves*

$$\Pr\{S \neq V\} \leq \epsilon \tag{25}$$

$$|\mathcal{S}| = \exp[n(C_s - \epsilon)] = \exp[n(1 - H(p) - \epsilon)] \tag{26}$$

The proof follows directly from the channel coding theorem.

Proposition 2. *The scheme achieves*

$$I(W; S) = 0. \tag{27}$$

Proof. First observe that the secret extracted from x^n using the SEC $C^{x^n + c_i^n}$ is exactly i. This leads to $w = x^n + c_s^n$. Since the biometric data x^n is uniformly distributed, we have $H(W|S) = H(W|C_s^n) = n$. Furthermore, since there are 2^n different SECs, $H(W) = n$, which leads to $I(W; S) = 0$. $\qquad\square$

Finally we note that,

$$I(W; X^n) = H(X^n) - H(X^n|W) = n - \log|\mathcal{S}| \tag{28}$$

and in case of $|\mathcal{S}|$ near capacity, $I(W; X^n) \approx nH(p)$.

The construction presented here gives a rigorous formalism to *fuzzy commitment* [12] and *quantized secret extraction* [15]. We note that this construction can be generalized from binary to larger alphabets.

7   Conclusions

In this paper we formulated the template protection problem as an application of secret extraction from common randomness. We exploited the relation to secret extraction from common randomness to derive some of the performance bounds.

The SBA algorithm achieves both C_s, the secrecy capacity, and C_{id}, the identification capacity. Since C_{id} bounds the number of individuals that can be reliably identified using whatever architecture, this result implies that protecting biometric templates does not necessarily decrease identification performance.

It was illustrated by explicit code construction that the SBA algorithm is strongly related to algorithms proposed in previous work. For these algorithms there exist analogous SBA constructions.

References

[1] Putte, T.v.d., Keuning, J.: Biometrical fingerprint recognition: Don't get your fingers burned. In: IFIP TC8/WG8.8 Fourth Working Conference on Smart Card Research and Advanced Applications. Kluwer Academic Publishers (2000) 289–303

[2] Bolle, R.M., Connell, J., Pankanti, S., Ratha, N.K., Senior, A.W.: Biometrics 101. Report RC22481, IBM Research (2002)

[3] Maltoni, D., Maio, D., Jain, A.K., Prabhakar, S.: Handbook of Fingerprint Recognition. Springer-Verlag New York, Inc. (2003)

[4] Matsumoto, T., Matsumoto, H., Yamada, K., Hoshino, S.: Impact of artificial "gummy" fingers on fingerprint systems. In: Optical Sec. and Counterfeit Deterrence Techn. IV. Volume 4677 of Proc. of SPIE. (2002)

[5] Hill, C.J.: Risk of masquerade arising from the storage of biometrics. Bachelor of science thesis, Dept. of CS, Australian National University (2002)

[6] Schneier, B.: Inside risks: The uses and abuses of biometrics. Comm. of the ACM **42** (1999) 136

[7] Penrose, L.: Dermatoglyphic topology. Nature **205** (1965) 545–546

[8] Mulvhill, J.: The genesis of dermatoglyphics. The Journal of Pediatrics **75** (1969) 579–589

[9] Babler, W.: Embryologic development of epidermal ridges and their configuration. Birth Defects Original Article Series **27** (1991)

[10] Bolling, J.: A window to your health. Jacksonville Medicine **51** (2000) Special Issue: Retinal Diseases.

[11] Davida, G., Frankel, Y., Matt, B.: On enabling secure applications through off-line biometric identification. In: Proc. of the IEEE 1998 Symp. on Security and Privacy, Oakland, Ca. (1998) 148–157

[12] Juels, A., Wattenberg, M.: A fuzzy commitment scheme. In: Sixth ACM Conf. on Comp. and Comm. Security, Singapore (1999) 28–36

[13] Ratha, N., Connell, J., Bolle, R.: Enhancing security and privacy in biometrics-based authentication systems. IBM Systems Journal **40** (2001) 614–634

[14] Juels, A., Sudan, M.: A fuzzy vault scheme. In: Proc. of the 2002 IEEE Int. Symp. on Inf. Theory, Lausanne, Switzerland (2002) 408

[15] Linnartz, J.P., Tuyls, P.: New shielding functions to enhance privacy and prevent misuse of biometric templates. In: Proc. of the 4th Int. Conf. on Audio and Video Based Biometric Person Authentication, Guildford, UK (2003) 393–402

[16] Verbitskiy, E., Tuyls, P., Denteneer, D., Linnartz, J.P.: Reliable biometric authentication with privacy protection. In: Proc. of the 24th Symp. on Inf. Theory in the Benelux, Veldhoven, The Netherlands (2003) 125–132

[17] Csirmaz, L., Katona, G.: Geometrical cryptography. In: Proc. of the Int. Workshop on Coding and Cryptography, Versailles, France (2003) 101–109

[18] Ahlswede, R., Csiszar, I.: Common randomness in information theory and cryptography. I. secret sharing. **39** (1993) 1121–1132

[19] Maurer, U., Wolf, S.: Information-theoretic key agreement: From weak to strong secrecy for free. In: Advances in Cryptology — EUROCRYPT '00. Volume 1807 of LNCS., Springer-Verlag (2000) 351–368

[20] Bennett, C.: Quantum cryptography: Uncertainty in the service of privacy. Science Magazine **257** (1992) 752–753

[21] O'Sullivan, J.A., Schmid, N.A.: Large deviations performance analysis for biometrics recognition. In: Proc. of the 40th Allerton Conference. (2002)

[22] Willems, F.M.J., Kalker, T., Goseling, J., Linnartz, J.P.: On the capacity of a biometrical identification system. In: Proc. of the 2003 IEEE Int. Symp. on Inf. Theory, Yokohama, Japan (2003) 82

Toward Ubiquitous Acceptance of Biometric Authentication: Template Protection Techniques

Madalina Baltatu, Rosalia D'Alessandro, and Roberta D'Amico

Telecom Italia LAB,TILAB, Turin, Italy
{madalina.baltatu, rosalia.dalessandro, roberta.damico}@telecomitalia.it

Abstract. The present paper provides a study of theoretical and practical security issues related to the deployment of generic reliable authentication mechanisms based on the use of biometrics and personal hardware tokens, like smart cards. The analysis covers various possible authentication infrastructures, but is mainly focused on the definition of basic requirements and constraints of a particular security scheme, namely client-side authentication. The deployment of such a scheme proves to be necessary when specific application deployment constraints are encountered, particularly when there is a conspicuous need to guarantee the privacy of the users. The paper suggests several solutions to this problem, and proposes a particular template protection technique based on a secure secret sharing scheme. The fundamental goal of this technique is to secure biometric systems sensitive to privacy issues and which rely, at some extent, on authentication performed at the client end of the application.

1   Introduction

With the increasing use of the Internet for an ever wider range of applications and the advent of network technologies (wired and wireless), most of which provides different, sometimes not sufficient security features, building security inside applications has become a task of imperative importance. The heterogeneity of the network infrastructure implies different (and most of the time unreliable) degrees of network level security.

Reliable authentication of users is a *sine qua non* requirement for the majority of network applications. Common authentication schemes are based upon one of the following three principles: proof of knowledge (of some secret data), proof of possession (of an object, usually a hardware token) or proof of "being" (an authorized/enrolled person). From these three paradigms, the most reliable authentication methods are constructed either based upon the last or on combinations that include it. The authentication systems that implement this principle are known as biometric authentication systems. They use an unique, biological (physical or behavioral) characteristic of a human being for automatically recognizing or verifying his/her identity [1]. For information technology security systems, biometric authentication could represent the ultimate answer to the

D. Maltoni and A.K. Jain (Eds.): BioAW 2004, LNCS 3087, pp. 171–183, 2004.

problem of unequivocal identification of users [2]. Throughout this paper we examine different issues related to the use of biometric authentication schemes in practical application scenarios. The aspects that we take into consideration are related to system's resistance to attacks, reliability, performance, ease of use, and, very important, users' privacy.

The paper is organized as follows: it begins with a description of the generic biometric authentication scenarios together with an analysis of the security requirements of the corresponding configurations. The next section introduces the use of hardware tokens (smart cards), discusses the concept of client-side authentication, and offers a description of a basic template protection technique, which, in combination with smart cards, is meant to increase the overall biometric system security. The document ends with a conclusions and future work section.

2   Application Scenarios for Biometric Authentication

Potentially, biometric systems can be employed in all applications that need an authentication mechanism, therefore in all applications that nowadays use passwords, PINs, ID cards, one time passwords and the same. The current level reached by the technology (fingerprint, iris, retina, face and hand recognition) is quite encouraging and therefore permits application developers to propose new authentication schemes based on biometrics [3], [4]. In the optics that biometrics has reached maturity, in this work we address two security issues that were given very little consideration till now:

- provisioning of a reliable client-side security mechanism, since in many application scenarios an important amount of trust has to or could be placed at the client end of the communication[1]
- resolving privacy related problems, since for obtaining a large public acceptance, applications based on biometrics have to guarantee the privacy of their users.

The first issue represents an intrinsic problem of all client/server applications: the biometric sensor is placed at the client side and, supposedly, could be manipulated by malicious users [5], [6]. A less obvious reason for which we invoke client-side security aspects is the opportunity offered by biometric systems to provide a reliable solution to this controversial issue. The privacy aspect is a general problem of all biometric techniques[7]: individuals are generally not happy with the idea that their biometric samples are stored in unidentified and out of their control places in the Internet [8], [9]. Both these issues can be addressed by designing applications that combine the use of biometric authentication with the use of hardware tokens.

The functional scheme of biometric systems, independently of the underlying biometric technology, is tailored on the application architecture itself, and it

---

[1] This issue is also related to the current tendency of placing an increasing amount of intelligence at client-side devices.

can vary from a compact stand-alone configuration with all recognition related facilities resident, to a distributed client/server scheme, in which more systems collaborate during the authentication/authorization process. There is one fundamental difference between these two models: in the first case the biometric sample acquisition and the identity verification operations are performed by one device, meanwhile in the distributed scenario the sample acquisition is performed by the client system, while, typically, the verification is the server's task (be it a dedicated authentication server system or the application server itself).

The first model of operation is quite attractive because less complex, hence easier to administrate and render secure: only one device, quite probably not connected to a network, has to be controlled, hardened and optimized. Another feature that makes this scenario appealing is the locality of storage: the users can be guaranteed that their reference biometric samples are not traveling across the Internet, but they are confined inside the biometric device itself. The model, though, lacks of flexibility, and can be used for a limited set of applications like physical access control, computer (e.g., PC, mobile phone, PDA, etc.) and local application login.

In the field of distributed networked applications, security services are mainly required for client/server architectures. The distributed paradigm though could introduce a large amount of complexity in the application model and hence in the security model: considering only one client, there are at least two systems to be protected (which becomes three if the application and authentication server are different systems, or four if a database management server is involved). Protection, in terms of authentication, data integrity and data confidentiality is needed for all the communication channels between the systems involved. Obviously, biometrics (as it is provided today) is not enough to accomplish all these tasks, conventional security methods are still to be employed in this scenario.

One possible solution that can reduce the complexity of securing distributed applications is to place more intelligence at the client side. Depending on the amount of intelligence (i.e., functionalities, especially the security-related ones) provided at the client side, biometric authentication systems can be classified in two big categories, that we choose to call "minimal biometric client terminal" and "intelligent biometric client terminal".

The choice of one operation model or another has important consequences on the overall systems security, performance, and, eventually, on the users' perception of the application built upon it. In the next sections we examine more closely the security requirements and constraints of various client/server biometric authentication systems.

2.1   Minimal Biometric Terminal

At present, the majority of the real world network applications uses the client system as a mere biometric sample acquisition device, while the identity verification is performed by a central server. With little variations depending on the biometric technology used, the functionalities provided by the client are: biometric sample image acquisition, trait(s) localization, image normalization, image encoding, and image transmission. Typically, features extraction and template[2] creation are not client's tasks in these configurations.

Briefly, the security properties that have to be guaranteed by such a configuration, assuming that no physical surveillance of the client terminal is provided, are:

- tamper resistance of the acquisition device and related software
- client and server authentication, data integrity and data confidentiality for the transmission channel.

A lot of scientific literature exists that treats security issues of biometric systems [6], [10]. Tamper resistance of client software and hardware is a fundamental requisite for the reliability of the entire application: the biometric sample acquired when the user starts the application must be the same as the sample data sent to the server. It should not be possible for any user to insert arbitrary samples into the client application, or to change the acquisition software in any way. In the same time, it should not be possible for a malicious user to bypass the acquisition software altogether. On the other hand, the biometric data has to be protected "in transit" against the possible attacks at the communication channel (eavesdropping, data modification, connection steeling, replay attacks, client or server impersonation, etc.), hence the use of mechanisms which provide authentication of communicating parties and encryption of the transmitted data is mandatory.

Another important security related aspect is the reliability of the template storage mechanism. In order to perform user recognition, the authentication server has to maintain or have access to a repository of reference biometric templates of all authorized users. It is plausible that the authentication sever uses a local or remote database to store the reference templates. The database has to provide appropriate access control mechanisms, and very important, the users' biometric templates have to be stored encrypted. We will not insist on the importance of the comprehensive security of the server system itself, which is an essential requirement for a reliable, working configuration.

The intrinsic centralized storage mechanism used by the applications that observe this configuration model has several advantages, enumerated below:

- manageability, because the majority of the administrative and maintenance activities are performed in a single central place
- contained (and hence easier to control) complexity (complexity is the opposite of security [13])
- low cost of the client terminals
- intrinsically higher security, because one successful attack at a client terminal cannot compromise the entire system (since no templates are stored locally) and would neither compromise the use of the algorithm (since, typically, template creation is not performed by the client software).

---

[2] Alternatively, the biometric template is also known as BIR - Biometric Identification Record - in [24]

The main drawbacks of such a model are in terms of performance (can be resolved with major cost of the server system) and, possibly, in terms of user acceptance: the biometric templates are centrally stored, out of their legitimate owners' control. One would argue that only templates and no original biometric samples are stored, and that the majority of the biometric recognition algorithms declares the irreversibility of the template creation operation (i.e., the original biometric sample cannot be obtained from a given template)... Recent research, though, showed that acceptable face images can be obtained from template information if the biometric system grants access to similarity scores [11]. Similarly, in [12], Hill demonstrated that equivalent fingerprint images may be recreated from minutiae points. As a consequence, even if the irreversibility of the template creation function may be mathematically demonstrated, the skeptical public opinion has to be convinced that this feature is correctly implemented by the final application.

2.2   Intelligent Biometric Terminal

This configuration implies that client terminals are not mere biometric sensors. They can perform complex processing of users' biometric images, create biometric templates from these images and even verify the users' identity if necessary. This means that part (if not all) of the recognition algorithm resides on the clients, so major security requirements and constraints are placed at the client side of the application. Moreover, the client systems have to be granted access to biometric templates database or, alternately, they could store templates locally.

Building more functionality into the clients could mean better performance (at least one network transaction can be avoided), flexibility (we can construct applications with various degrees of distributivity), but it could also mean that applications have to rely, at some extent, on client-side authentication. Generally, this is not an acceptable condition for the application service provider, since, currently, standard, reliable client-side security mechanisms are hard to implement [13]. The classical contra-example of client-side security envisions a successful attack at one of the client terminals that would effectively compromise the entire system. Besides, with this configuration the privacy issues are still open, since the user's reference biometric template is still stored on devices that presumably (depending on the application type) are not owned by the user.

In spite of this pessimistic evaluation regarding the possibility of implementing trustworthy client-side security, the perspective to have the users reliably authenticated by the client terminals is quite attractive. The only mechanism that currently provides a good degree of client-side security based on the use of asymmetric cryptography techniques is the smart card technology [14], [15]. The challenge is how to combine biometrics and smart card technology to obtain a powerful and reliable client-side authentication mechanism. Such a solution would practically solve privacy issues as well, since the need of centralized storage is eliminated: the reference biometric template of the user is stored on the card and, possibly, will never leave the card. This last constraint can be satisfied if the client terminal plays an active role in the verification process.

As frequently succeeds in practice, a trade-off solution that would obviate the drawbacks of the above configurations stands in between the two extremes presented. In our opinion, such a solution could rely on a smart card for reference template storage, on the client terminal for the live biometric template creation, and will exhibit both client and server systems collaborating in the identity verification process.

3   Hardware Tokens and Biometric Authentication

The idea of using a portable storage support is not new to the biometric authentication field [16], [17]. There are also a plethora of commercial products that integrate the use of more or less sophisticated hardware tokens and biometric authentication technologies, especially in the field of fingerprint and hand geometry recognition and mainly for storage purposes only. On the other hand, smart cards are essential in an authentication/identification system sensitive to user privacy issues. Several of the most popular smart card-based biometric applications are identity systems that use personal ID cards (usually cheap read-only cards) containing the user's biometrics and multi-application card systems in which more applications can use the same authentication/authorization mechanism by storing specific information on the same physical support (typically a read/write card).

Since smart cards can execute complex cryptographic operations and can protect the data stored inside their processor's memory, biometric authentication systems that makes use of this technology can potentially guarantee a high level of security and privacy to its users. The common approach to biometrics and smart cards is to store the biometric template on the smart card and to request authentication for accessing it. Upon successful authentication the template can be read by the requesting application, and further used by the identity verification procedure.

Figure 1 shows the operational steps required during the enrollment and verification phases in a generic security-aware application based on the use of biometrics and smart cards. In order to ensure the subsequent deployment of a secure application, the enrollment phase will typically request two cryptographic operations: the computation of a digital signature over the biometric template and the encryption of the template or of both template and signature. We assume that known standard asymmetric cryptography methods are used (e.g, RSA [25], DSA [26], etc.). A scheme based on symmetric encryption is less expensive in terms of performance but much more vulnerable to cryptographic attacks [13]. Nevertheless, symmetric cryptography could prove to be enough for applications that do not need a high level of security or for configurations that are using additional security measures (like physical security, dedicated links or secure Virtual Private Networks, etc.).

As far as the verification phase is concerned, smart card-based biometric authentication systems can be divided in two distinct classes:

- applications in which the reference template leaves the card in the verification phase: identity verification performed by the server

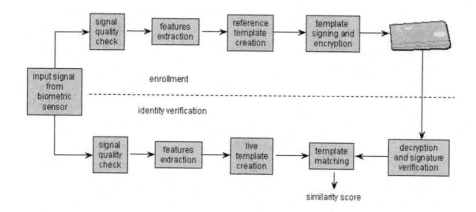

Fig. 1. Smart card and biometrics: enrollment and verification.

- applications in which the reference template does never leave the smart card: verification performed entirely by the client or by the client and server conjunctively.

Commercial smart card-based biometric authentication systems are typically of the first type. The second method of biometric verification (also known as *match-on-card*) is a relatively young technology [17], [18], even if several commercial systems exist that implement it combined mainly with fingerprint and hand geometry recognition techniques. As far as face recognition is concerned, an example of a match-on-card system is also known [22], in which only the final part of the verification process (namely the computation of the correlation between two templates) is implemented on the smart card.

3.1   Security Schemes for Smart Card-Based Biometric Systems

There are different possible security configurations for both application typologies presented in the previous section. In the followings we present some of them, underlying the security features they provide. The analysis is not based on a particular application specification, but is rather generic even if practical issues related to the deployment of the corresponding configurations are also approached.

For the sake of simplicity, the subsequent authentication schemes illustrate the simple case in which the application service provider and the authentication service provider reside on the same physical system. Depending on the real application constraints, these functions can be distributed between several servers.

Some preliminary considerations are necessary in order to understand the security characteristics of these authentication schemes. The user's reference template from the smart card is digitally signed with the private key of the entity that issued the card and provides the application service for which the

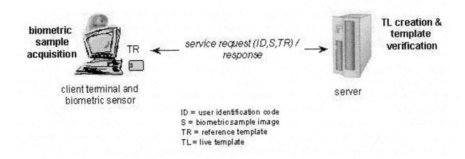

Fig. 2. First authentication scheme: server-side template verification.

biometric authentication is requested. For increased security, the template is also stored by the card in an encrypted format. The amount of data protected by the encryption depends on the application's security requirements, preferably both template and signature are encrypted. The access to this encrypted envelope is additionally protected by the smart card's access method (PIN).

We assume that asymmetric cryptography is used and the template is encrypted from the very beginning by the enrollment application itself, using the public key of the verifying entity. Of course this is not the only possible security scheme for the described application scenario, but, with this scheme the template is never passed and stored in the clear. In the same time, the user cannot read the reference template, since public-key encryption guarantees that only the entity that possesses the private key corresponding to the encryption key has access to the original unencrypted data. The successful verification of the signature attached to the template gives confidence to the verifying application that the template has not been modified since enrollment. Note that the signature is also verified by the smart card at the enrollment time, hence the smart card would not accept faked (not authenticated) reference templates. Additional proofs of authentication could be required from the smart card and from the verifying application/device before the release of the template. These are all implementation choices that depend on the application security requirements. In the identity verification phase, the smart card requires authenticated access to the encrypted template and signature are released to the biometric verification application.

The described operations produce encoded templates forms that are generally compatible or equivalent with the CBEFF template formats [19], and it is one of our main future goals to try to reach full interoperability with existing standards. Figure 2 illustrates an example configuration of the first category of applications taken into consideration, applications for which the reference template can leave the smart card. Even if not explicitly shown in Figure 2 for simplicity, there are several basic security measures that protect the information exchanges between the communicating parties. We again assume that asymmetric cryptography is used. The client request message includes the user identification code (ID) and

Fig. 3. Second authentication scheme: client-side template verification.

the biometric sample image (S) signed with the client's private key stored in the smart card. The reference template (TR) should already include the signature of the enrollment authority. The contents of the request message (or at least the ID and S fields) is encrypted with the public key of the verifying server. This message could also contain an authenticated nonce. After message decryption and signature verification, the server computes the live template from the authenticated sample S, and verifies it against the authenticated TR. The authorization response and the nonce are then sent to the client encrypted with the client's public key. For enhanced performance, the computationally intensive public key encryption can be replaced by symmetric encryption. In this case the entities have to priorly negotiate a session encryption key (e.g., they can use a known secret key establishment mechanism like authenticated Diffie-Hellman [27]).

The second category of applications is the preferred one for applications that are sensitive to users' privacy issues. In these schemes (a simple example is illustrated in Figure 3), the reference template never leaves the users' personal smart cards. There is one significant obstacle that hinders its implementation though: the increased amount of computational resources required from the smart card. In this configuration, the smart card itself performs the identity verification, hence the template verification algorithm specific to the adopted biometric recognition technique is effectively implemented on the card. While storing templates on smart cards and using strong cryptography to protect them is quite a straightforward operation, the feasibility of the template comparison algorithm porting is still under investigation for the majority of the known biometric technologies.

For the following discussion we suppose that such an algorithm exists which can be ported to a particular type of smart card. The security requirements for the application built on top of this configuration are rather different from the previous case. During enrollment the template is signed (using the issuing entity's private key) by the biometric application/device that generates it (this guarantees that the smart card has received an authentic legitimate template), but there is no need for public key encryption (further on the template is manipulated only by the card). The template is still to be stored protected by the card's PIN. More protection measures are needed for the template that enters the card during the identity verification phase. This template needs to be signed by the organization's private key and encrypted with the user's public key (its private counterpart is securely stored on the smart card). The signature guarantees the authenticity and integrity of the live template, while the encryption guarantees that only the right user's smart card can read the template and perform template similarity checking. For the reliability of the mechanism, the result computed (but not the similarity score, since brute force attacks are possible that can fabricate fake templates that could produces the scores seen on transit [20], [21]) by the smart card is signed and passed to the application server encrypted with the server's public key.

In the configuration presented in Figure 3, template verification is performed on the card, so TR is not transmitted to the server, while the live template is still computed at server-side. For identity verification, the live template (TL) is sent to the client signed by the server and encrypted with the client's public key. An authenticated nonce can also be added to these messages. The computationally intensive public key encryption operations can be substituted with symmetric encryption using secret keys re-negotiated for each new application session.

Note that it is not necessary for all the recognition logic to reside on the smart card, the server is still in charge of creating the live template, and such is actively involved in the identity verification. If the client were to create this template and also perform template verification, the authentication process would be uneven and the degree of trustworthy to be placed at the client-side could become unacceptable for some applications.

Porting more intelligence on the smart card could indeed be considered too hazardous by some application scenarios, since a successful attack of a single smart card could signify an enormous loss for the application provider. Even if successful smart card attacks are rather rare and extremely difficult to perform, since they require a trained and highly motivated attacker [23], we consider that a good level of security paranoia is acceptable when it comes to privacy issues.

An alternative mechanism can be envisioned, which does not require a large amount of computations from the smart card (identity verification is performed by the server), and in which the user's privacy is guaranteed. This mechanism is presented in the following section.

3.2   Alternative Template Protection Scheme

The main idea behind this mechanism is to increase biometric reference template protection by avoiding the storage of the entire (still encrypted) template on a single system. The mechanism is quite generic and can be applied to all authentication/authorization architectures and, very succinctly, it is based on template splitting and independent protected storage of its parts on all systems participating in the authentication scheme.

The proposed method is based on a known security paradigm [13]: secure secret splitting and secure secret share schemes. In such schemes a secret piece of data is divided between more entities, such that each part by itself is completely useless, hence an entity alone cannot reproduce the original data from the piece it possesses.

The simplest sharing scheme consists in dividing a piece of data between two systems. Given the original data, TR (e.g., the original reference template or an encoded form of it), a third party (e.g., the enrollment system) generates a random-bit string T1 by the same length as TR. The enrollment system then xors TR with T1 to generate T2. Subsequently, T1 is stored on the user's smart card and T2 on the verifying system(s). TR can be destroyed. At the identity verification time the smart card and the verifying system have to collaborate together (in an authenticated manner and using an encrypted communication channel) to obtain the reference template in order to perform template comparison. Therefore, the smart card and the verifying system work jointly to make the authorization decision, which cannot be made if one of the systems misses (i.e., was compromised in any way after an attack, or its part of the original template data is compromised/deteriorated/lost). Since both the smart card and the verifying entity participate actively in the verification process, this mechanism ensures a better overall security level for any of the underlying authentication infrastructures. Moreover the level of protection of the biometric reference templates is considerable increased, and the user privacy is guaranteed if the mechanism is implemented correctly and additional security measures are taken. These measures are mainly concerned with the destruction of the original template by the enrollment system and by any of the verifying entity (the authentication server itself or the client smart card, if the verification algorithm resides on the card).

The described technique, if properly followed, is absolutely secure. The protocol has only one drawback: if any of the template pieces gets lost the corresponding user has to re-enroll to the system. We do not consider it a high price to pay for obtaining an enhanced security authentication infrastructure.

Figure 4 illustrates such a scheme in which the identity verification is performed by the server. The same security considerations, regarding the protection of the information exchanged between the communicating parties are also valid for the present configuration (i.e., template shares, T1 and T2, are digitally signed and encrypted before transmission using the appropriate private and public keys respectively).

Template splitting and its secure storing in the described distributed manner ensure increased resistance to template directed attacks. Conventional security mechanisms (similar to the asymmetric cryptogrphy-based ones described in the previous sections) are still needed to guarantee the authenticity of the parties that take part to the secret sharing scheme and the confidentiality of the communication channels used.

4   Conclusions and Future Work

Fundamentally, our interest in biometrics arises from the need to design applications that provide a reliable client authentication mechanism and guarantee users' privacy. These properties could be offered by client-side authentication methods based on the use of a biometrics, smart cards, and secure template

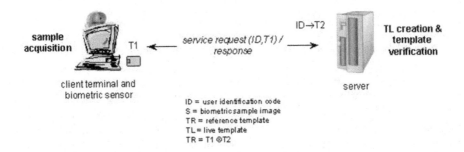

Fig. 4. Template splitting: server-side template verification and privacy guaranteed.

sharing schemes. These methods do not place any restrictions on the client terminal type or on the technology used by the recognition algorithm.

Our future activity is mainly oriented in two directions. On one hand we continue the testing and evaluation of different biometric algorithms with the main purpose of identifying algorithms ready to be ported (completely or partially) on devices that have limited computational resources, like mobile terminals and smart cards. On the other hand, we are working on a prototypal implementation of the proposed method of interaction between hardware tokens and biometric devices/applications in order to design a reliable authentication mechanism that also offers a high degree of protection to users' templates. One of our implementation's goals is to converge, where possible, to common biometric practices and standards like BioAPI [24] and CBEFF [19].

References

1. A.K. Jain, R.M. Bolle, S. Pankanti: Biometrics: The Personal Identification in Networked Society. Kluwer Academic, Norwell, MA, January 1999
2. S. Pankanti, R.M. Bolle, A.K. Jain: Biometrics: The Future of Identification. IEEE Computer, Volume 21, No.2, February, 2000
3. S. Liu, M. Silverman: A Practical Guide to Biometric Security Technology. IEEE Computer Society, IT Pro - Security, January/Fbruary 2000
4. A.K. Jain: Who's Who? Challenges in Biometric Authentication. Lecture Notes in Computer Science, Springer-Verlag Heidelberg, 2003
5. B. Schneier: Biometrics: Uses and Abuses. Inside Risks 110, Communications of the ACM, Volume 42, No. 8, August 1999
6. R.M. Bolle, J.H. Connell, N.K. Ratha: Biometric Perils and Patches. Pattern Recognition Volume 35, Issue 2, Published by Elsevier Science B.V., 2002
7. International Biometric Group (IBG) BioPrivacy Initiative: Technology Assessment. http://www.bioprivacy.org
8. W. Penny: Biometrics: A Double Edged Sword - Security and Privacy. SANS Institute, 2002
9. S. Prabhakar, S. Pankanti, A.K. Jain: Biometric Recognition: Security and Privacy Concerns, IEEE Security and Privacy Magazine, Volume 1, No. 2, March-April 2003

10. R.M. Bolle, J.H. Connell, N.K. Ratha: Biometrics breaks-in and band-aids. Pattern Recognition Letters, Volume 24, No. 13, September 2003
11. A. Adler: Sample images can be independently restored from face recognition templates, School of Information Technology and Engineering, University of Ottawa, 2003
12. C. Hill: The risk of masquerade arising from the storage of biometrics, B.S. Thesis, Australian National University, November 2001
13. Bruce Schneier: Applied Cryptography. Second Edition, John Wiley and Sons, Inc., 1996
14. Smart Card Alliance: Secure Personal Identification Systems - Policy, Process and Technology Choices foar a Privacy-Sensitive Solution. Smart Card Alliance White Paper, January, 2002
15. Smart Card Alliance: Smart Cards and Biometrics in a Privacy-Sensitive Secure Personal Identification System. Smart Card Alliance White Paper, May, 2002
16. GSAA Government Smart Card Group: Guidelines for Placing Biometrics in Smart Cards. September, 1998
17. M. Osborne, N.K. Ratha: A JC-BioAPI Compliant Smart Card with Biometrics for Secure Access Control. Lecture Notes in Computer Science, Springer-Verlag Heidelberg, January 2003
18. R. Sanchez-Reillo: Including Biometric Authentication in a Smart Card Operating System Lecture Notes in Computer Science, Springer-Verlag Heidelberg, January 2001
19. F.L. Podio, J. S. Dunn, L. Reinert, C.J. Tilton, L. O'Gorman, M.P. Collier, M. Jerde, B. Wirtz: Common Biometric Exchange File Format. NISTIR 6529, January 2001
20. B. Schneier: Security pitfalls in cryptography. Proc. of CardTech/SecureTech, Washinton D.C., April 1998
21. N.K. Ratha, J.H. Connell, R.M. Bolle: A biometrics-based secure authentication system. IBM Thomas J. Watson Research Center
22. H.K. Jee, K.H. Lee, Y.W. Chung: Integrating the Face Verification Algorithm into the Smart Card System. Electronics and Telecommunication Research Institute, Daejeon, 2001
23. P. Kocher, J. Jaffe, B. Jun: Differential power analysis: Leaking secrets. Crypto 99, pages 388-397, 1999.
24. BioAPI Consortium: http://www.bioapi.org.
25. R. L. Rivest, A. Shamir, Leonard M. Adleman: A method for obtaining digitial signatures and public-key cryptosystems. Communications of the ACM, 21,2:120, February, 1978
26. NIST: Digital Signature Standard, National Institute of Standards and Technology (NIST). FIPS Publication 186: May 1994
27. W.Diffie and M.E.Hellman: New directions in cryptography. IEEE trans, Inform. Theory, IT - 22:644-654, Nov 1976

Approximate Confidence Intervals for Estimation of Matching Error Rates of Biometric Identification Devices

Travis J. Atkinson[1] and Michael E. Schuckers[1,2]

[1] Department of Mathematics, Computer Science and Statistics
St. Lawrence University, Canton NY 13617, USA
[2] Center for Identification Technology Research (CITeR)
schuckers@stlawu.edu

Abstract. Assessing the matching error rates of a biometric identification devices is integral to understanding its performance. Here we propose and evaluate several methods for creating approximate confidence intervals for matching error rates. Testing of biometric identification devices is recognized as inducing intra-individual correlation. In order to estimate error rates associated with these devices, it is necessary to deal with these correlations. In this paper, we consider extensions of recent work on adjustments to confidence intervals for binomial proportions to correlated binary proportions. In particular we propose a Agresti-Coull type adjustment for estimation of a proportion. Here that proportion represents an error rate. We use an overdispersion model to account for intra-individual correlation. To evaluate this approach we simulate data from a Beta-binomial distribution and assess the coverage for nominally 95% confidence intervals.

1 Background

Errors often result from the matching process of a biometric identification device. Depending on the individual attempting to gain access, these errors are often classified as being either false accepts or false rejects. It is important that users of these devices have an understanding of the magnitude of these error rates. Several authors have noted the importance of this knowledge to testers of biometric devices and for users, see e.g. [1] and [2]. More recently a National Science Foundation Workshop found that "there is a need to develop statistical understanding of biometric systems sufficient to produce models useful for performance evaluation and prediction", [3]. Because of the binary nature of the outcome of the matching decision from a biometric device, it is often supposed that a binomial distribution is appropriate to analyze such data. Several authors including [1] have noted that a binomial distribution is not appropriate for biometric data under most circumstances. The problem with using the binomial distribution to describe the data is that it does not allow for intra-individual correlation in testing. [4] proposed that the Beta-binomial distribution is appropriate for describing data taken from a biometric identification device because

D. Maltoni and A.K. Jain (Eds.): BioAW 2004, LNCS 3087, pp. 184–194, 2004.
© Springer-Verlag Berlin Heidelberg 2004

it permits correlation within individuals. In that same paper, [4] proposed a methodology for making confidence intervals using this approach. An updated version is given in [5].

The purpose of this paper is to determine whether or not the methodology of interval estimation proposed by Agresti and Coull in [6] can be applied to a Beta-binomial distribution, and to establish an appropriate manner in which to do so. The approach of Agresti and Coull was to add four additional observations (two successes and two failures). They applied their approach to the binomial distribution, specifically for estimation of proportions. We are motivated in applying their methodology to Beta-binomial proportions because data taken from a biometric device often follows a Beta-binomial distribution. Again, our application is to overall error rates. To extend Agresti and Coull's approach to the Beta-binomial, we consider several methods for applying their approach and we will evaluate these by simulating data from a variety of parameter combinations. We will then compare these methods to the unaugmented approach of [5].

2 Background and Notation

We use a parametric approach for modelling the data from a biometric device. We follow the approach of [5] and use the notation found therein. Assume that we are interested in estimating an overall error rate – either the false accept rate (FAR) or false reject rate (FRR)– of π. Further, let n be the number of individuals tested and m_i be the number of times that the individual is tested, $i = 1, \ldots, n$. Agresti and Coull [6] suggested adding two "successes" and two "failures" to binomial data as a way to improve estimation. In the case of the binomial since all trials are independent, augmenting the data is straightforward. For correlated binary data any augmentation is not straightforward because of the correlated structure induced by having multiple individuals tested. We shall consider several ways to distribute these additional "observations". With these changes, some individuals will have up to four additional tests added. As will become apparent, this is not the case for Beta-binomial data. We call the occurrence of an error a "success", S; a "failure", F, would be the event that an error does not occur. Let

$$X_i = \sum_{j=1}^{m_i} \omega_{ij}.$$

And let

$$\omega_{ij} = \left\{ \begin{array}{ll} 0 & \text{if } S \\ 1 & \text{if } F \end{array} \right\} \tag{1}$$

for the jth attempt by the ith individual. Hence, X_i represents the number of errors by the ith individual and let $p_i = X_i/m_i$ represent the percentage of errors in m_i attempts made by the ith individual. In this paper we follow [4] in assuming an extravariation or overdispersion model for the data. Formally we assume that

$$E[X_i] = m_i \pi_i$$

and

$$Var[X_i] = m_i \pi_i (1 - \pi_i)(1 + (m_i + 1)\rho) \qquad (2)$$

where ρ is the intra-individual correlation of the observed data [4]. The intra-individual correlation, measures the similarity of outcomes within a single individual [7] relative to the overall variability of the X_i's. It is worth mentioning here that if $\rho = 0$ then this model simplifies to the binomial model. Using the notation described above, we can now estimate π and ρ. Estimates of parameters will be denoted with a "hat". Once these values are estimated we can derive confidence intervals for the error rate, π. To begin, suppose that we have tested a biometric identification device and have observed the X_i's. For our purposes, instead of taking data from an actual biometric identification device, we conducted simulations using the statistical software R. This allowed us to test performance of the proposed confidence intervals for a variety of different values for the parameters π and ρ. For estimation we then use,

$$\hat{\pi} = \frac{\sum X_i}{mn}$$

$$\hat{\rho} = \frac{BMS - WMS}{BMS + (m_0 - 1)WMS}$$

where

$$BMS = \frac{\sum m_i (p_i - \hat{\pi})^2}{n - 1},$$

$$WMS = \frac{\sum m_i p_i (1 - p_i)}{n(\bar{m} - 1)}$$

and

$$m_0 = \bar{m} - \frac{\sum_{i=1}^{n} (m_i - \bar{m})^2}{n\bar{m}}. \qquad (3)$$

The confidence interval for π in then

$$\hat{\pi} \pm 1.96 \left[\frac{\hat{\pi}(1 - \hat{\pi})(1 + (m_o - 1)\hat{\rho})}{\bar{m}n} \right]^{1/2}. \qquad (4)$$

The above methodology for estimating ρ is based on an ANOVA-type estimator given by [8]. In Equation (3) BMS represents between mean squares and WMS represents within mean squares.

3   Proposed Methods

The augmentation of the binomial proposed by [6] involves adding two "successes" and two "failures" to the observed successes and failures. For our purposes this is equivalent to adding two additional errors on four additional attempts. As mentioned above, we assume data is collected on n individuals each of which is tested m_i times $i = 1, \ldots, n$. Hence, we have n individuals with m_i binary observations each. The correlated structure of this data implies that adding two "successes" and two "failures" is not simple. We need to consider how to distribute these "successes" and "failures" among the n individuals. We have developed four specific approaches for doing this. We refer to these methods as A1, A2, A3, and A4. These methods will be compared to the unaugmented approach of [9] which we label A0. For all of these methods, we implicitly assume that the individuals are ordered randomly. If that is not the case then the individuals who receive additional "observations" as part of the augmentation need to be randomly chosen.

3.1   Approach 1 (A1)

The first approach involves adding two "successes" and two "failures" to a single individual, in this case the first individual. For simplicity with this and other approaches we assume $m_i = m$ for all i initially. Extensions to the more general case are straightforward. Thus,

$$m_i = \begin{cases} m + 4 & \text{for } i = 1 \\ m & \text{for } i = 2, \ldots, n \end{cases} \tag{5}$$

and

$$X_i = \begin{cases} \sum_{j=1}^{m_i} w_{ij} + 2 & \text{for } i = 1 \\ \sum_{j=1}^{m_i} w_{ij} & \text{for } i = 2, \ldots, n. \end{cases} \tag{6}$$

We then use Equation (4) to develop a confidence interval based on the updated values for the X_i's and the m_i's. Hence, the first individual tested effectively undergoes four additional tests, two of which result in a "success" and two of which result in a "failure". For example, if $n = 1000$ and each individual underwent 5 tests, then we let $m_1 = 5 + 4 = 9$ and $X_1 = \sum_{j=1}^{5} w_{ij} + 2$, while $m_i = 5$ and $X_i = \sum_{j=1}^{5} w_{ij}$ for all $i = 2, 3, \ldots, 1000$.

3.2   Approach 2 (A2)

Another approach would be to distribute the additional attempts and errors equally among two individuals. This is our second approach. Thus,

$$m_i = \begin{cases} m + 2 & \text{for } i = 1, 2 \\ m & \text{for } i = 3, \ldots, n. \end{cases} \tag{7}$$

and

$$X_i = \begin{cases} \sum_{j=1}^{m_i} w_{ij} + 1 & \text{for } i = 1, 2 \\ \sum_{j=1}^{m_i} w_{ij} & \text{for } i = 3, \ldots, n. \end{cases} \tag{8}$$

Hence, there were two additional tests added to both the first and second individuals. Each of these two individuals receives one "failure" and one "success". Again we assume that individuals are numbered randomly.

3.3   Approach 3 (A3)

The third approach adds an additional test to four separate individuals. Two of those individuals receive a "success"; the other two receive a "failure". Thus we augment the data in the following manner

$$m_i = \begin{cases} m+1 & \text{for } i = 1, 2, 3, 4 \\ m & \text{for } i = 5, \ldots, n \end{cases} \tag{9}$$

and

$$X_i = \begin{cases} \sum_{j=1}^{m_i} \omega_{ij} + 1 & \text{for } i = 1, 2 \\ \sum_{j=1}^{m_i} \omega_{ij} & \text{for } i = 3, \ldots, n. \end{cases} \tag{10}$$

By this method the four individuals effectively undergo one additional test each. For individuals 1 and 2 this test results in a "success", while for individuals 3 and 4 the additional test results in a "failure".

3.4   Approach 4 (A4)

The final augmentation approach involves adding an $n + 1^{st}$ individual who receives two "successes" and two "failures". Note that this methodology is different from the previous approaches in that we are also altering n. Thus,

$$m_i = \begin{cases} m & \text{for } i = 1, \ldots, n \\ m + 4 & \text{for } i = n + 1 \end{cases} \tag{11}$$

and

$$X_i = \begin{cases} \sum_{j=1}^{m_i} \omega_{ij} + 1 & \text{for } i = 1, \ldots, n \\ 2 & \text{for } i = n + 1. \end{cases} \tag{12}$$

4   Evaluation

Our approach to evaluating these methods is to use simulated data. We choose this approach over application to observed test data because it allows us to test many different parameter values and parameter combinations. To evaluate each of these methods, we simulate data from a variety of parameter values. To test the estimated proportion we use Equation (4) which provides a nominally 95% confidence interval. As has been stated, the goal is to test the performance of

Table 1. Coverage for A0

| | $n = 1000$ $m = 5$ | | | | $n = 1000$ $m = 10$ | | | |

π	ρ				ρ			
	0.001	0.01	0.1	0.4	0.001	0.01	0.1	0.4
0.002	0.931	0.928	0.926	0.866	0.951	0.953	0.904	0.854
0.004	0.947	0.951	0.942	0.883	0.941	0.939	0.932	0.907
0.008	0.955	0.940	0.926	0.931	0.944	0.945	0.945	0.933
0.010	0.937	0.951	0.952	0.926	0.952	0.954	0.956	0.938

| | $n = 2000$ $m = 5$ | | | | $n = 2000$ $m = 10$ | | | |

π	ρ				ρ			
	0.001	0.01	0.1	0.4	0.001	0.01	0.1	0.4
0.002	0.947	0.950	0.930	0.908	0.934	0.942	0.937	0.907
0.004	0.944	0.953	0.948	0.922	0.948	0.945	0.931	0.935
0.008	0.947	0.955	0.940	0.948	0.941	0.963	0.945	0.944
0.010	0.937	0.957	0.950	0.932	0.935	0.951	0.939	0.932

Table 2. Coverage for A1

| | $n = 1000$ $m = 5$ | | | | $n = 1000$ $m = 10$ | | | |

π	ρ				ρ			
	0.001	0.01	0.1	0.4	0.001	0.01	0.1	0.4
0.002	0.969	0.962	0.963	0.936	0.961	0.955	0.950	0.907
0.004	0.953	0.960	0.952	0.942	0.959	0.956	0.942	0.932
0.008	0.955	0.956	0.951	0.933	0.941	0.949	0.942	0.927
0.010	0.946	0.954	0.948	0.949	0.958	0.950	0.941	0.949

| | $n = 2000$ $m = 5$ | | | | $n = 2000$ $m = 10$ | | | |

π	ρ				ρ			
	0.001	0.01	0.1	0.4	0.001	0.01	0.1	0.4
0.002	0.964	0.963	0.958	0.946	0.946	0.949	0.945	0.926
0.004	0.952	0.944	0.959	0.947	0.947	0.951	0.950	0.924
0.008	0.947	0.941	0.947	0.948	0.949	0.943	0.955	0.944
0.010	0.957	0.952	0.948	0.944	0.957	0.959	0.954	0.951

the confidence interval given above. We use simulations of data given n, m, π, ρ. Running the simulations under a given set of parameters, we create a confidence interval for each data set and then compare this interval to our actual error rate. We then determine whether or not the interval contains, or "captures", π. For repeated generation of data, we expect that the percent of times that π falls in the interval created is 95%. (Recall that the definition of a 95% confidence interval is that $P(\hat{\pi}_L < \pi < \hat{\pi}_U) = 0.95$ where $\hat{\pi}_L$ and $\hat{\pi}_U$ are the lower and upper endpoints of that interval respectively.) We will refer to the proportion of times that π is within the range of the 95% confidence interval as the coverage. We will use this value to assess the overall performance of an approach. Since we use a 95% confidence interval of the estimated error rate, we expect the coverage to be 95% percent. We desire coverage that is close to 95%. The closer the coverage is to this value, the better the performance of the approach. Coverage that is too low is deficient in that it does not meet the criteria for a 95% confidence interval. Coverage that is too high is too conservative in the statistical sense that it yields intervals that are too wide.

Table 3. Coverage for A2

	$n = 1000$ $m = 5$				$n = 1000$ $m = 10$			
	ρ				ρ			
π	0.001	0.01	0.1	0.4	0.001	0.01	0.1	0.4
0.002	0.967	0.961	0.958	0.922	0.949	0.947	0.941	0.891
0.004	0.949	0.952	0.952	0.938	0.946	0.947	0.938	0.927
0.008	0.954	0.956	0.941	0.936	0.955	0.964	0.958	0.934
0.010	0.944	0.952	0.964	0.951	0.964	0.950	0.952	0.939

	$n = 2000$ $m = 5$				$n = 2000$ $m = 10$			
	ρ				ρ			
π	0.001	0.01	0.1	0.4	0.001	0.01	0.1	0.4
0.002	0.942	0.956	0.956	0.942	0.943	0.958	0.954	0.939
0.004	0.949	0.957	0.951	0.956	0.949	0.952	0.952	0.939
0.008	0.960	0.949	0.945	0.943	0.947	0.953	0.947	0.944
0.010	0.950	0.951	0.951	0.943	0.943	0.952	0.955	0.953

The parameters used in the simulation of each approach are: $n = (1000, 2000)$, $m = (5, 10)$, $\pi = (0.002, 0.004, 0.008, 0.01)$, and $\rho = (0.001, 0.01, 0.1, 0.4)$. 1000 data sets were generated under each scenario. Data were generated from a Beta-binomial distribution. The scenarios – combinations of parameters – are investigated to see how the changes in the parameters make a difference in the coverage.

The values of π were chosen to be representative of error rates produced by a BID [5]. The results of these simulations are given in Tables 1-5. Again we use simulated data because it allows us to test the performance of various parameter combinations.

Table 4. Coverage for A3

	$n = 1000$ $m = 5$				$n = 1000$ $m = 10$			
	ρ				ρ			
π	0.001	0.01	0.1	0.4	0.001	0.01	0.1	0.4
0.002	0.965	0.944	0.952	0.929	0.950	0.946	0.949	0.896
0.004	0.954	0.950	0.944	0.925	0.953	0.957	0.946	0.926
0.008	0.961	0.949	0.940	0.950	0.948	0.947	0.938	0.928
0.010	0.956	0.957	0.942	0.939	0.944	0.950	0.953	0.939

	$n = 2000$ $m = 5$				$n = 2000$ $m = 10$			
	ρ				ρ			
π	0.001	0.01	0.1	0.4	0.001	0.01	0.1	0.4
0.002	0.940	0.942	0.955	0.939	0.957	0.958	0.951	0.913
0.004	0.948	0.945	0.952	0.941	0.949	0.941	0.942	0.935
0.008	0.960	0.956	0.957	0.934	0.943	0.952	0.950	0.943
0.010	0.958	0.951	0.957	0.953	0.954	0.944	0.947	0.941

5 Results

As we examine the data in the tables, we begin with the trends that occur in all data sets regardless of the approach used. First, as π, n and m increase, the coverage increases. Coverage also increases as ρ decreases. These trends hold for all approaches. It is also apparent that as ρ increases above 0.1, the coverage decreases significantly. Again, ρ governs the degree of independence in the data. High values of this parameter imply less independent information in the data. Another way to think of this is that the effective sample size is $\frac{n\bar{m}}{1+(\bar{m}-1)\rho}$, which is equivalent to the number of independent observations in the data. From this formula, it is clear that the effective sample size decreases as ρ increases.

A phenomenon that can be seen from the data tables below is what has been called the "Hook Paradox" and occurred similarly in [5]. The paradox is that when ρ is large as the number of tests per individual, m_i increases, the coverage decreases. This is an unexpected result. It is especially apparent in the data when $\rho = 0.4$ and the error rate π is small. For example, in Table 2 when $n = 1000, m = 5, \pi = 0.002, \rho = 0.4$, the coverage is 0.936, but when m is changed to 10, the coverage decreases to 0.907. Intuitively, the coverage should increase as m_i increases since there are a larger number of tests taken. This pattern seems to occur for several confidence interval methods [9].

Turning to individual approaches, it is evident that all four approaches (A1-A4) that are modified using the Agresti and Coull adjustment (Tables 2-5) perform better than the original approach (A0) (Table 1). One method to examine coverage is to determine if it is within two standard deviations of the nominal confidence level. Here for 95% confidence intervals, the standard deviation is calculated to be $\sqrt{\frac{0.95(1-0.95)}{1000}}$. (Note that coverage probabilities should follow a binomial sampling distribution assuming the nominal coverage probability of 95% is correct.) Thus, a reasonable range of values for coverage is $0.950 \pm 2\sigma$ or $(0.936, 0.964)$. Below we report the minimum coverage, the maximum coverage and the mean coverage.

A0, proposed by [4] and seen in Table 1, had the worse coverage values of the five approaches. The coverage values for the A0 range from 0.866 to 0.963 and the mean coverage was 0.937. The data for A1-A3, seen in Tables 2-4, indicates that they all have approximately the same performance. A1 has a minimum coverage value, mean coverage value, and maximum coverage value of 0.907, 0.949, and 0.969, respectively. The same values for A2, given in the same order are 0.891, 0.948, and 0.967. These values given for A3 are 0.896, 0.946, and 0.965. The data for A4 shows that the coverage values were higher than the other four approaches. The range of values went from 0.907 for a minimum up to 0.985 for a max, which is well above the max coverage values of the other approaches. The mean of 0.957 is also high, but still better in comparison with the low mean of 0.937 that A0 generated.

Additionally, we summarize these results in Table 6. The percentages of coverage values falling below $0.95 - 2\sigma$ are given in column 2. Using this manner of evaluation, we see that A0 has the worst performance with 34.38% of coverages falling below the acceptable range. A2 and A4 performed the best each having 4.69% of values below the acceptable range. It is noteworthy that approximately 2.50% should fall below this range by chance alone.

Next, we compare the minimum coverage value, the mean coverage, and the maximum coverage value for each approach (columns 4-6 of Table 6). Looking at minimum coverage values, A0 has the lowest value with 0.866. The highest minimum coverage value belongs to A1 and A4 with 0.907. The mean coverage tells us a lot about overall performance of an estimation method. A1-A4 all perform very well, much better than the A0. They all have a mean close to 0.950. As can be seen from a max coverage of 0.985, A4 gives coverage values that are relatively high in comparison with the other approaches, but every augmented approach gives higher coverage values than the original unaugmented Beta-binomial approach.

On the whole, every augmented approach performed very well. The performances of A1-A3 were approximately the same. There are not any factors that clearly show one of these approaches performing significantly better than the oth-

Table 5. Coverage for A4

	$n = 1000$, $m = 5$				$n = 1000$, $m = 10$			
	ρ				ρ			
π	0.001	0.01	0.1	0.4	0.001	0.01	0.1	0.4
0.002	0.985	0.980	0.984	0.952	0.976	0.979	0.968	0.907
0.004	0.965	0.966	0.963	0.951	0.970	0.961	0.958	0.927
0.008	0.956	0.958	0.956	0.943	0.966	0.968	0.950	0.937
0.010	0.970	0.965	0.954	0.943	0.950	0.958	0.964	0.953

	$n = 2000$, $m = 5$				$n = 2000$, $m = 10$			
	ρ				ρ			
π	0.001	0.01	0.1	0.4	0.001	0.01	0.1	0.4
0.002	0.959	0.968	0.969	0.954	0.963	0.963	0.961	0.936
0.004	0.957	0.953	0.958	0.934	0.965	0.957	0.956	0.939
0.008	0.957	0.963	0.940	0.950	0.962	0.960	0.961	0.947
0.010	0.945	0.945	0.954	0.947	0.960	0.971	0.959	0.946

ers. A4 performed very well, but quite often had coverage values much greater than 0.950. When $\rho \leq 0.1$, this approach gives values very near to 0.950. One alternative in the future would be to construct a confidence interval approach that utilizes one of the augmented approaches A1-A3 when ρ is small and A4 when ρ is large.

Table 6. Overall summary of results

Approach	% below $0.95 - 2\sigma$	minimum coverage	mean coverage	maximum coverage
A0	34.38	0.866	0.937	0.963
A1	7.81	0.907	0.949	0.969
A2	4.69	0.891	0.948	0.967
A3	12.50	0.896	0.946	0.965
A4	4.69	0.907	0.957	0.985

Several areas for future research are suggested by this work. First a study of the property of estimators of the intra-cluster correlation to determine the reasons for the hook paradox seems warranted. Each of the four augmented approaches performed better than the original approach, so we are able to conclude that the changes proposed by [6] improve inference for the mean error rate from a Beta-binomial distribution. However, since our estimators performed poorly as ρ increased, we may want to consider adding observations as a function of ρ. One such solution might be to add $2 * (1 + (\bar{m} - 1)\rho)$ "successes" out of $4 * (1 + (\bar{m} - 1)\rho)$ attempts. Note that $1 + (\bar{m} - 1)\rho$ is known as the design effect or *deff* and reduces to 1 for the binomial.

Our evaluation of each approach shows that with any one of the augmentation methods used, proportion estimation improved significantly. Hence, headway has been made in the estimation of error rates incurred by biometric identification devices. Of the four augmented approaches, A4 had the best performance and A1-A3 performed approximately the same. Although many of the coverage values were outside the desired range for A4, most of them were above 0.950. Hence the coverage of 95% was not only reached, but often also surpassed. Though we prefer our coverage values to be nearly 0.950, we are willing to trade a slightly wider interval for increased coverage in this case. In the end A4 had the best performance in error rate estimation, but all of the methods proposed here represents an improvement over the unaugmented approach, A0.

Acknowlegements: This research was made possible by generous funding from the Ronald E. McNair Postbaccalaureate Acheivement Program at St. Lawrence University.

References

[1] James L. Wayman. *Biometrics:Personal Identification in Networked Society*, chapter 17. Kluwer Academic Publishers, Boston, 1999.

[2] Tony Mansfield and James L. Wayman. Best practices in testing and reporting performance of biometric devices. on the web at www.cesg.gov.uk/site/ast/biometrics/media/BestPractice.pdf, 2002.

[3] Edwin P. Rood and Anil K. Jain. Biometric research agenda. Report of the NSF Workshop, 2003.

[4] Michael E. Schuckers. Using the beta-binomial distribution to assess performance of a biometric identification device. *International Journal of Image and Graphics*, 3(3):523–529, 2003.

[5] Michael E. Schuckers. Estimation and sample size calculations for matching performance of biometric identification devices. Center for Identification Technology Research technical report, 2003.

[6] Alan Agresti and Brent A. Coull. Approximate is better than "exact" for interval estimation of binomial proportions. *The American Statistician*, 52(2):119–126, 1998.

[7] William G. Cochran. *Sampling Techniques*. John Wiley & Sons, New York, third edition, 1977.

[8] Kung-Jong Lui, William G. Cumberland, and Lynn Kuo. An interval estimate for the intraclass correlation in beta-binomial sampling. *Biometrika*, 52(2):412–425, 1996.

[9] Michael E. Schuckers, Anne Hawley, Katie Livingstone, Nona Mramba, and Collen Knickerbocker. A comparison of statistical methods for evaluating matching performance of a biometric identification device- a preliminary report. Center for Identification Technology Research technical report, 2004.

Architectures for Biometric Match-on-Token Solutions

Raul Sanchez-Reillo, Judith Liu-Jimenez, Luis Entrena

Carlos III University of Madrid, Microelectronics Group, Avda. Universidad 30
E-28911-Leganes (Madrid), Spain
{rsreillo, entrena, jliu}@ing.uc3m.es
http://www.uc3m.es/uc3m/dpto/IN/dpin08/dpin08d.html

Abstract. Biometric Authentication Systems face several problems related to the security and the users' potential rejection. Most of those problems comes from the high sensitivity of biometric data (whose manipulation could damage the system security or the users' privacy), and the feeling of governmental control when central databases are used. The authors have been working in providing solutions to these problems, by promoting the idea of using tokens that could perform the biometric verification internally, not allowing the template to travel through communication lines, nor the memory of an open terminal. To achieve this, a general architecture, based on a set of requirements previously defined, will be outlined. At the end, directives for the implementation of such an architecture using smartcards and USB-Tokens will be given.

1 Introduction

Many daily situations require the identification of users. To perform such identification different alternatives exist: from showing an object (token) whose data identify the person (or just the belonging of the object), to testing a knowledge (such as a password). But the belonging of an object or the knowledge of something does not identify really a human being. Unfortunately many applications need to positively verify the identity of the person trying to access the service, due to security or reliability reasons. The only way to really identify a person is by comparing a biological or behavioral aspect of that user with a previously stored information about that aspect. In that sense, using for example a passport, will allow identification via verifying the photograph attached with the face of the user. This comparison will be made by a person, such as a policeman, who will decide about the validity of that identity.

But not in all cases is possible to have a person to perform such identification. In such situations an automatic way to identify a person should be provided. Being aware that the only belonging of a token and/or knowledge of a password (e.g. a Personal Identification Number – PIN) do not really identify a person, then the use of biometric identification technology is mandatory [1-6, 8].

When implementing a biometric identification system, several approaches could be used, but regarding the way to store the users' template, they can be classified in two main groups: centralized and distributed. In a centralized system, all users' templates are stored in a central database, which is accessed to verify the current sample of a

D. Maltoni and A.K. Jain (Eds.): BioAW 2004, LNCS 3087, pp. 195-204, 2004.

user. In a distributed system, each user carries his/her own template with them, providing it as requested by the identification system. Each of the two alternatives have their advantages and inconveniences.

In a centralized system both a recognition (comparing to all users in the database) and an authentication (comparing only with the template of the claimed user) architectures could be implemented. On the positive side, all sensitive information (the biometric templates) resides in just one place, so there is only one environment to be secured. On the negative side, three main problems arise. The first one is the need of having a permanent connection with the database, so working off-line is not possible, which is a real inconvenience for many applications. The second one is the fact of having to transfer biometric information, which is really sensitive, all the time. This means that not only the communication through the cable should be secured (e.g by a PKI or other kind of solution), but also the terminals involved (avoiding any kind of undesired code, such as Trojans that could grab biometric samples, or even biometric templates, if they are transferred from the database to the terminal). The third problem is more related to privacy and user feelings, because the existence of a central database could create a 'Big Brother' effect, that could lead the users to reject the system.

On the other hand, a distributed system will only implement an authentication scheme. In this case, the roles of the above mentioned advantages and disadvantages changes. Having the templates stored in a distributed way, i.e. each user carries his/her own template, will make mandatory to highly protect all different places where the user's template is stored. Having this solved, an off-line application could be deployed and the user can forget about his/her privacy concerns. But unfortunately the security of the terminal to be used is still a major issue to be handled.

1.1 Match-on-Terminal Vs. Match-on-Token

Verifying the biometric sample of the user with his/her template determines the security constraints of the whole system. Traditionally a system is designed so that the terminal will grab a user's biometric sample and extract its feature vector. It also extracts from a token the user's template, and after that it applies the matching algorithm. Whether the terminal could be able to execute malicious code that inspects data being processed in it, major security problems arise. The first one is related to the possibility of manipulating the execution of the matching algorithm, so as to be able to change the decision taken. In that case, a non-authorized user could access the services protected, which would rise real FAR figures concerning the whole system.

The second problem is that the user's biometric sample, or even the resulting feature vector, could be copied, transferred or even manipulated. Therefore, sensitive data is exposed and could be used to trick the system injecting that sample or feature vector when a non-authorized user wants to access the service protected. This implies a minimal security requirement, which is the need of coding the user's sample or feature vector, so that it could have a validity restricted in time (i.e. not being able to be used after a certain time after the acquisition of such data).

But much more important is the third problem, which is derived from expositing the user's template. A stolen template destroys the capability of identifying the user robed, because his/her personal data has been exposed. This is a completely different issue of what could happen with a password or a PIN, because in that cases a new password or PIN could be generated, and the user could choose among different passwords, as many as the password length allows. But a user only has a restricted number of biometric patterns to be chosen (10 fingerprints, 2 irises, 1 face, etc.). Therefore, if using, for example, and iris recognition system, and the user's template is copied, then, in order to provide the system with the same level of security, that template should be eliminated and the user should use his/her other template (the other iris). If once again it is stolen, then the user could not choose any other template, so the user cannot access the system if the template is eliminated. So extreme protection of the user template must be played, not only in its storage, but also during any processing is needed with it.

These inconveniences could be mainly solved if a different strategy is followed. Instead of extracting the template from the storage token and verifying it in the terminal, a solution could be to maintain the template in the token and performing the matching also in it. With this kind of solution, only special care should be made with the biometric sample obtained in each moment from the user, meaning the rejection of replay attacks (not allowing an old sample to be presented at any moment). Additionally, when the protected information is also inside the token, it could be internally protected by the matching-on-token mechanism.

Using this approach, if what it should be protected is an information outside the token, or the access to a determine service, then the right verification of the biometric data could target the generation of a session key that, through a set of cryptographic procedures [10], could allow the access to that external information or service. If the system suffers an attack and the session key is exposed, then the attacker will only be able to use it during that session, but not the others. If the generating key (the one used for generating the session key) is what is exposed, then that key could be removed and a new one could be generated. Also, any kind of PKI (Public Key Infrastructure) could be used to increase security on the overall system, without making the user to learn passwords, PINs, and allowing a real user authentication.

In this paper, the authors define a set of architectures to provide general solutions for designing identification tokens able to be used in systems where biometric matching is to be performed inside the token, allowing personal authentication of users.

2 Token Requirements

To provide a token able to perform biometric matching, a set of requirements has to be considered, especially depending on the biometric technology used. When designing architectures for several biometric techniques, general conclusions should be obtained in order to specify the requirements needed according to storage capabilities, the security mechanisms used, data communication and processing power. In this section, each of those four issues will be treated giving an overview of the needs that could cover the different designs, leaving for following sections the limitations for each of the recommended implementations.

2.1 Storage Requirements

The initial requirement for a token to be used in a biometric system is that it should be able to store the user's template. Here the biometric technique used and the verification method play a really important role. There are some cases where the template is represented by a set of features, usually called feature vector. The length of the feature vector could vary significantly from one technique to another. For example, a feature vector in a hand geometry system [8] could be as low as 25 bytes, while in some methods for fingerprint verification, the amount of memory used could be near 1KB.

On the other hand, there are cases where the user's template is a set of parameters that define a model that characterizes the user's biometrical data (e.g. the parameters of a neural network, a GMM, or a HMM). Depending on the size of the model, the amount of data needed to specify the user's template could be much higher than in the case of the feature vectors.

One of the possibilities to implement a token is using a smartcard. Knowing that current smartcards could have up to 16KB of EEPROM to store user's data (not only the user's template, but also the rest of the data to be stored in it, such as a health record), some techniques could suffer from the impossibility to be implemented with this technology. When other implementations are chosen, such as an USB Token, where there are no constraints to the size of the semiconductor device, these problems can be overcome.

2.2 Communication Requirements

Another constraint comes with the fact that biometric data should be transferred to the biometric token. In that sense, two situations should be considered: the transmission of the template, and the communication of the current biometric sample. The first one, in a match-on-token system, is not really a constraint, because that communication will only take place once or twice in the token life (i.e. the template will only be transferred in the personalization phase, and never will go out of the token during its usage).

Sending the current biometric sample from the terminal to the token is a completely different issue. Depending on the technique and method used, it could be as simple as just transferring the feature vector (once it has been extracted from the image or signal captured) to the token. In these cases this will mean to send as many bytes as the size of the feature vector, which could be the same size as the template. The way data is transferred to the token will limit the viable length of the vector, which will also depend on the application restrictions. Usually applications need that the biometric verification could be done in less that 1 second, for not giving users the feeling of a slow identification. Considering a serial communication (which is a real restriction to reduce connection pins), there is a direct relation between the speed of the communication and the size of the vector to be transferred. As an example, considering the matching time as null (which is not at all realistic), and the lack of communication overheads (parity, ciphering, handshake, packet handling, etc.), a communication at 9600bps will restrict the size of the vector to 1200 bytes, while to be able to send 7KB, communication speed should increase to 56Kbps.

Once again some biometric algorithms could require that the amount of biometric data to be transferred to the matching algorithm makes unviable to use conventional serial communication, needing other protocols as the ones used for multimedia applications (USB 2.0 or IEEE 1394). This is the case of those situations where the matching is performed at the same time that the sample processing (for the feature extraction), because it is done by modeling solution (such as neural networks), or when the verification is made using a large set of feature vectors coming from continuous utterances of the biometric parameter of the user (as in speaker recognition systems using GMMs [6]).

2.3 Processing Capabilities

Obviously one of the major requirements for the token is the processing capabilities that should offer in order to implement the matching algorithm. Those requirements are completely different depending on the verification method used (e.g. it is completely different using a Hamming Distance [2], or an elastic matching algorithm [4] or just a Neural Network [5]). In the first case even the simplest CPUs could be used, while in the second case the CPU should provide a complex ALU (e.g. with fast multiplicators) and the precision of the data used could determine the result (it could be completely different using fixed point under 8 bits, than floating point under 32 bits).

When processing at 32 bits is mandatory, the designer can decide whether using a 32bit CPU or using a lower precision CPU and emulating the 32bit operations through software. In the first case, programming the matching algorithms is much lighter (and space needed for coding that algorithm is lower) and execution time is much lower, but the cost of the hardware needed will increase the cost of the final product. On the other hand, emulation will reduce costs, but increase the memory requirements for the coding of the algorithm, and also the time needed for the execution. So the designer must cope with those two extreme cases in order to reach the optimal solution for the constraints of the application.

2.4 Security Requirements

Last but not least, security mechanisms are mandatory to protect, at every moment, the biometric data involved in the authentication process. The minimum requirements for a token are to provide the following security mechanisms:

- Tamper proof device: tokens should be designed to avoid any inspection of the stored data by any kind of inverse engineering process. At least it should provide the mechanisms to detect any unauthorized intrusion, reacting as necessary to warranty the security of the sensitive data involved, such as auto-deleting such data or keeping it ciphered it.
- External Authentication: it should impose the external world with means for the token to determine whether the terminal trying to access is a reli-

able terminal or not. This could be done by the exchange of the ciphering of a random number with a key that both parties should know.

- Internal Authentication: Analogue to the previous mechanism, but to allow the terminal to determine whether the token being accessed is reliable or not.
- Session Keys Generation: to cipher or sign all data exchanged with the external world, so that if information is exposed, it will only be valid during that session.

3 General Architecture Design

With all the requirements stated in previous sections, the architecture of the token should be as shown in Fig. 1, where a control unit is in charge of providing the right data flow among the rest of the elements. The only interaction with the external world is via the serial communication block. As having an architecture based on a microprocessor, an Operating System should be stored in the ROM memory (non volatile). That Operating System is in charge of understanding the information received by the serial port. Considering that this information is transferred following some protocol, which encapsulates commands and data, the Operating System will decide the corresponding flow of the data involved through the blocks inside the token.

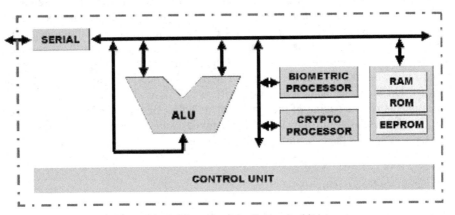

Fig. 1: Block Diagram of the Token Architecture

Different kind of commands that tokens could receive are:
1. Conventional Data Transfer: Data can be stored or read from the EEPROM memory (e.g. health record). Access to this information could be protected in reading or writing, depending on a set of access conditions controlled by the Operating System. If such access conditions are not fulfilled, then access is denied and an error is given to the external world.
2. Conventional Data Processing: In some cases the token could be able to perform some operations (arithmetic, logical or cryptographic) with the

data received. In such cases, the control unit will transfer the data to the appropriate block, such as the ALU or the Cryptographic Co-Processor. Resulting data could be stored in EEPROM or just returned to the external world. For temporal storage of results, RAM memory is needed by the Operating System.

3. Biometric Template Storage: Being one of the most sensitive commands, this must be done with all security mechanisms available and within a controlled environment (usually a personalization system in a financial institution or governmental administration). The Operating System will, therefore update that data in EEPROM or even in the Biometric Co-Processor.

4. Biometric Verification: With these commands, the Operating System should be able to verify the biometric sample transferred to the token. When this verification is correct, it will allow the access to the protected information and operations, during that session. If it is not verified, the access will be forbidden, and a counter of consecutive erroneous verifications is incremented. The Operating System should provide a certain number of consecutive incorrect verifications before blocking that access. If the security level of the application allows the unblocking, the Operating System should provide the means to unblock the biometric verification, or allow a new enrolment.

5. Biometric Security Mechanisms: As stated in the previous sections, all biometric data exchange with the external world must be highly protected. So the Operating System should provide all that security mechanisms for not allowing the insecure transfer of any biometric data.

6. Generation of External Security Mechanisms: As outlined above, when the service or information that wants to be biometrically protected is outside the token, a solution that will not risk the user's template could be using traditional security mechanisms but that have been activated after a successful biometric verification. In those cases the Cryptoprocessor will be fully activated.

4 Alternatives for the Token Implementation

When implementing a Biometric Token, different alternatives arise. The designer could start with a current secure ID-Token technology, such as the one for the smartcards [9, 12], or initiate the development of a fully new product. In both cases, the result should comply with the user expectations, which not only should present a high verification performance, but also being easy to use (for all kind of users, not only those ones that are familiar with the technology) and comfortable to wear (because it will be something to be with the user at all times).

For applications where users are familiar with the use of plastic identification cards (such as banking cards), the use of a smartcard seems to be the best choice. But as it will be illustrated below, smartcards comprise some limitations that will not allow to include some biometric verification methods, unless a full new development is decided, and standards evolve to increase the current capabilities of the smartcard (such as the communication interface).

On the other hand, there are some applications, specially those ones related to e-commerce, or any other service accessed via a computer, where hot-plug interfaces could be used. Not having other restrictions, but the communication interface, the designer can think about building a Biometric Token using other kind of interface. For example, the Token can be connected through a USB port, calling it then USB-Token. Obviously, the USB connection could be changed for an IEEE-1394, IrDA or Bluetooth, but throughout this text USB-Token will be mentioned for simplifying the reading.

This section will study both cases, showing the issues to be covered by the designer.

4.1 Smartcards – JavaCards

The most important advantages of using a smartcard is that most of the work is done. They are known by the user, are small and portable. Also they incorporate a lot of security mechanisms to be considered as a 'tamper-proof' device. And finally, it provides an Operating System that organizes the information in files within the EEPROM and implements a security architecture to provide different levels of access conditions to data and operations inside the smartcard. In theory, the only thing to do in a smartcard, is to provide the biometric validation algorithms and to improve the security architecture.

But in practice, many limitations appears when trying to insert biometric verification inside a smartcard. First of all processors used for current cards are low performance ones, and the amount of data to be saved in EEPROM is 16KB (commercially). Also the communication interface is based in an half duplex asynchronous serial port, which initial speed is 9600 bps. And what is more important, they are closed products, in the sense that modifying them to insert new capabilities usually means a new manufacturing process, which leads to high costs and large development times.

To override this last limitation, the concept of Open Operating System aroused some years ago, giving the possibility of improving the current Operating System with new capabilities, that could be inserted much after manufacturing, and being able to develop them in high level languages. In that line appeared the JavaCards [11], which are, in fact, open operating system smartcards that could be programmed in Java language, due to the incorporation inside the card of a Virtual Machine that translates the program in Java to the native code of the microprocessor of the card.

Unfortunately, integration of a Java Virtual Machine, slows down much more the CPU of the smartcard. Also JavaCards only use a subset of Java language, due to the restrictions of the hardware used (e.g.: no floating point or fixed point operations and data could be used – only integer arithmetic could be used, with a precision of 16 bits, being an option working with 32 bits). With those restrictions, the only verification algorithms that seem to be feasible of being introduced in a JavaCard are the ones based on a metric, such as a Hamming Distance or Euclidean Distance.

For other matching algorithms, two possibilities could be used. The first one will be to code the algorithms in native code, which could speed up the process, although still some algorithms could be difficult of being implemented. The other possibility is to design a Biometric Co-Processor in hardware, and connecting it to the smartcard CPU (the same way a Cryptoprocessor is included in smartcards able to support PKIs). This last approach will speed much more the biometric processes, but also the investment needed is too high for most environments.

4.2 USB-Tokens

All the inconvenience that has been noted with the smartcards, could be overcome if the identification device does not have to comply with the size and elasticity restrictions of a plastic card. In this case the device could be built using commercial components, and its improvement (adding new features) will mean reprogramming or substituting a determined component, not going into a microelectronic design. Also the components are not so limited in size, power consumption, clock rates, communication speeds. It would be possible to have a token with a floating point DSP, transferring information at 12Mbps (using USB 1.1), or even with higher capabilities. Therefore it allows the implementation of any kind of matching algorithm, obtaining results much faster than with the smartcard version.

The negative point of using an USB Token, is that usually are less comfortable for the user, in some applications it will imply to redesign current terminals to accept them (like the PoS in a shop), and there is not a mature starting point so the designer will have to work in all areas, from board design to full operating system programming. Also, as being new products from, sometimes, new companies, the security of these devices should be certified at all levels possible, to warranty that the device is not only working properly, but that it also lacks from back doors that could expose the user's template or the security of all the authentication method.

5 Conclusions

In this paper, the need of match-on-token solutions for biometric authentication systems has been illustrated. In order to achieve this kind of solutions, a set of requirements has been defined, which has led to the description of a microprocessor based architecture. This architecture can be implemented through several design lines, being the two most important, the use of smartcards, and the use of ID-Tokens connected to a conventional high-performance interface, such as an USB.

The authors, together with the other partners inside BioSec EU project are designing new devices that could allow the matching-on-token solutions to use as many biometric techniques, and methods, as possible.

Acknowledgments

Work partially funded by the European Union, through the research project IST-2002-001766 BioSec (Biometrics and Security, http://www.biosec.org), in the IST (Information Society Technologies) priority of the 6th Framework Program.

References

1. J. P. Campbell, Jr. "Speaker Recognition: A Tutorial". Proceedings of the IEEE, vol. 85, nº 9, pp. 1437-1462, Sep. 1997.
2. J. G. Daugman. "High Confidence Visual Recognition of Persons by a Test of Statistical Independence". IEEE Trans. on Pattern Analysis and Machine Intelligence, vol. 15, nº 11. Nov. 1993. pp. 1148-1161.
3. D. Maio, D. Maltoni. "Direct Gray-Scale Minutiae Detection in Fingerprints". IEEE Trans. on Pattern Analysis and Machine Intelligence, vol. 19, no. 1, January 1997.
4. A. K. Jain, L. Hong, S. Pankanti, R. Bolle. "An Identity-Authentication System Using Fingerprints". Proceedings of the IEEE, vol. 85, no. 9, September 1997.
5. A. K. Jain, R. Bolle, S. Pankanti, et al. Biometrics: Personal Identificacion in Networked Society. Kluwer Academic Publishers. 1999.
6. D. A. Reynolds, R. C. Rose. "Robust Text-Independent Speaker Identification Using Gaussian Mixture Speaker Models". IEEE Trans. on Speech and Audio Processing, vol. 3, num. 1, pp. 72-83, Jan. 1995.
7. R. Sanchez-Reillo, A. Gonzalez-Marcos. "Access Control System with Hand Geometry Verification and Smart Cards". Proc. 33rd Annual 1999 International Carnahan Conference on Security Technology. Madrid (Spain), 5-7 Oct, 1999. pp. 485-487.
8. R. Sanchez-Reillo, C. Sanchez-Avila, A. Gonzalez-Marcos. "Biometric Identification through Hand Geometry Measurements". IEEE Trans. on Pattern Analysis and Machine Intelligence, vol. 22, nº 10, Oct. 2000. pp 1168-1171.
9. R. Sanchez-Reillo. "Securing Information and Operations in a Smart Card through Biometrics". Proc. 34rd Annual 2000 International Carnahan Conference on Security Technology. Ottawa (Canada), 23-25 Oct, 2000. pp. 52-55.
10. B. Schneier. Applied Cryptography. John Wiley & Sons. 2nd Ed. 1995.
11. Sun Microsystems, Inc. http://java.sun.com/products/javacard
12. J.L. Zoreda, J.M. Oton. Smart Cards. Artech House, 1995.

A Secure Protocol for Data Hiding in Compressed Fingerprint Images

Nalini K. Ratha, Miguel A. Figueroa-Villanueva, Jonathan H. Connell, and
Ruud M. Bolle

IBM Thomas J. Watson Research Center
30 Saw Mill River Road
Hawthorne, NY 10532
{ratha, jconnell, bolle}@us.ibm.com
miguelf@msu.edu

Abstract. Data hiding techniques can be employed to enhance the security of biometrics-based authentication systems. In our previous work, we proposed a method to hide challenge responses in a WSQ-compressed fingerprint image. In this paper, we extend the work to analyze the security holes in the data hiding method and enhance the hiding technique to thwart attacks on the system. We employ several proven IT security techniques to provide a secure method of hiding responses in fingerprint images. The technique presented here can be used in hiding responses in other biometrics with minor changes to suit the domain.

1 Introduction

With rapid growth in e-commerce activities over the web, the fraud rate has also gone up significantly. A large component of the fraud can be traced to use of poor authentication methods involving traditional knowledge-based methods such as userid and password combinations. One way to alleviate this problem is to incorporate biometrics-based authentication into the system. Biometrics-based methods can provide non-repudiable authentication when properly designed and used. All automated biometrics-based person authentication systems operate by first acquiring a biometrics signal from the user, either locally or remotely. The signal is then analyzed to extract invariant features, and finally matched against a previously registered template. The authentication model can be either client-based or server-based. In client-based method, the three basic steps described earlier are carried out in the client locally. This can have several security issues while being attractive in terms of the communication needs. In contrast the server-based model deals with the whole authentication process carried out in the server after receiving the input from the client. This approach being more secure requires more communication bandwidth as the biometrics signals in general require larger bandwidth than text. In practice, one can have a combination of both client and server-based authentication where parts of the transaction are carried out locally and the rest of the steps completed in the server.

D. Maltoni and A.K. Jain (Eds.): BioAW 2004, LNCS 3087, pp. 205–216, 2004.

Fingerprint-based authentication systems are one of the most popular methods of the biometrics-based authentication. Recent developments in fingerprint sensing technology that allow a fingerprint to be acquired without using the traditional ink and paper method have enabled the use of fingerprints in many non-criminal applications. As these sensors become cheaper, fingerprints will be an obvious choice for authentication in wide ranging applications because of its mature technology and its legal standing.

However, as mentioned earlier, in both web-based or other on-line transaction processing systems, it is undesirable to send uncompressed fingerprint images to the server. A typical fingerprint image is in the order of 512×512 pixels with 256 gray levels, resulting in an image size of 256KBytes. Unfortunately, many standard image compression methods have a tendency to distort the high-frequency spatial structural ridge features of a fingerprint image. This has lead to several research proposals regarding domain-specific compression methods. As a result, a wavelet-based image compression scheme (WSQ) proposed by the FBI [6] has become the *de facto* standard in the industry because of its low distortion even at very high compression ratios. Typically, the compressed image is transmitted over a standard encrypted channel as a replacement for (or in addition to) the user's PIN or password. Yet because of the open compression standard, transmitting a WSQ compressed image over the internet is not particularly secure. If a compressed fingerprint image bit-stream can be freely intercepted (and decrypted), it can be decompressed using readily available software. This potentially allows the signal to be saved and fraudulently reused.

One way to enhance security is to use data-hiding techniques to embed additional information directly in compressed fingerprint images. For instance, assuming that the embedding algorithm remains inviolate, the service provider can look for the appropriate watermark to check that the submitted image was indeed generated by a trusted machine. Several techniques have been proposed in the literature for hiding digital watermarks in images. Bender et al. [2] and Swanson et al. [9] have presented excellent surveys of data-hiding techniques. Petitcolas et al. [11] provide a nice survey and taxonomy of information hiding techniques. Hsu and Wu [7] describe a method for hiding watermarks in JPEG compressed images. Jain and Uludag [8] implement a steganography-based biometrics authentication system. Ramkumar and Akansu [12] and Moulin and Mihcak [10] have come up with information theoretic metrics to estimate the data-hiding capacity of image sources. Most of the research, however, addresses issues involved in resolving piracy or copyright infringes, not authentication. In our earlier work [13], we presented an approach motivated by the desire to create on-line fingerprint authentication systems for commercial transactions that are secure against replay attacks in particular. To achieve this, the service provider would issue a different verification string for each transaction. The string would be mixed in with the fingerprint image before transmission. When the provider receives the image back, it can decompress and check for the presence of the correct verification string. This guards against resubmission of stored images (such as those *sniffed* of the Internet by an impostor). The method proposed here hides such messages with minimal impact on the decompressed appearance of the image. Moreover, the message is not hidden in a fixed location (which would make it more vulnerable to discovery) but is, instead, deposited in different places based on the structure of the image itself. Although this approach is presented in the framework of fingerprint image compression, it can be easily extended to other biometrics and/or compression methods such as JPEG 2000 [3].

In this paper, we describe some significant extensions to our earlier work particularly addressing the security aspects of the system. First we identify the weaknesses and then propose solution to mitigate the security threats. The following sections discuss the original WSQ compression scheme and our message embedding extensions. We describe the FBI WSQ standard fingerprint compression algorithm in section 2. Our data-hiding algorithm is presented in section 3. Section 4 gives results and statistics of our algorithm and conclusions and future work are presented in section 5.

2 WSQ Fingerprint Compression

Here we give a short review of the FBI WSQ standard fingerprint compression. More details are available in [6].

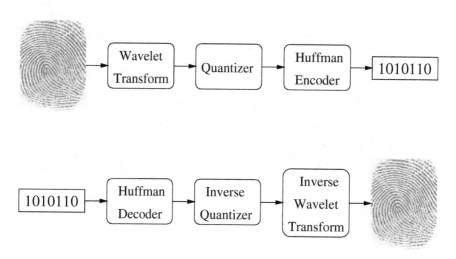

Fig. 1. FBI WSQ Standard.

The first part of Fig. 1 describes the encoding process. As a first step the fingerprint image is decomposed into 64 spatial frequency subbands using a fixed wavelet packet basis with (9,7) biorthogonal filters. These are implemented as a multirate filter bank using the pair of separable 1D biorthogonal filters. An example of the decomposition structure can be seen in Fig. 2. For example, subband

25 corresponds to the cascading path of '00,10,00,11' through the filter bank. The digits in each binary pair represent the row and column operation index, respectively. A zero specifies a low-pass filtering, while a one specifies a high-pass filtering. Boundaries are handled by symmetric extension. For more information please refer to [6, 4, 5]. The quantization and entropy coding (i.e. Huffman cod-

Fig. 2. FBI WSQ discrete wavelet packet decomposition sample.

ing) stages follow after the wavelet packet decomposition has been performed. Uniform scalar quantization is performed to convert the wavelet coefficients into integers with a small number of discrete values. Then these quantized coefficients are mapped to index values 0-255 (as given by a translation table provided by the standard) and these indices are Huffman coded. The decoder is the inverse of the steps described. First we apply the entropy decoder obtaining the quantized indices. Then we translate these back to wavelet coefficients and do the inverse quantization step. After this we apply the inverse wavelet transform and obtain the reconstructed fingerprint image.

3   Data Hiding Algorithm

Our earlier data-hiding algorithm works on the indices obtained after translation of the quantized coefficients, but before they are Huffman encoded. Note that we assume the message size is very small compared to the image size (or, equivalently, the number of wavelet coefficients). Below we briefly describe the originally proposed method followed by the modifications incorporated to enhance the security and reliability of the method.

3.1   Initially Proposed Data-Hiding Method

The application domain for which this algorithm is designed assumes that a transaction is taking place between a client and a server. This could range from a customer posting an order to an on-line business to a government agent running a fingerprint through the FBI fingerprint database. To ensure that the client is an authorized user the server will require the submission of the users fingerprint for authentication (a user id and password may also be requested by the server). To ensure that the user is not submitting a stored image (possibly obtained by spying on an earlier transaction from the authorized client) the server will send a message to the client. The client must hide this message in the fingerprint and the server will validate this message and either grant or deny access to the client.

Let m be the message length in bits, which is assumed to be very small compared to the number of pixels in the image. The data hiding algorithm during the encoding process has three stages as described below.

1. *Site selection set S:* Given the partially converted quantized integer indices, the role of this stage is to collect the indices of all possible sites where a change in the least significant bit is tolerable. In our implementation, we used the translated indices ranging from 108 to 254 but excluding 180 (an invalid code) in block 1 (i.e. subbands 7-18). These values correspond to wavelet coefficients with values of -72 to 74 excluding zero. Zeroes are run-length encoded, hence changing a particular zero coefficient could break a run-length chain and affect compression significantly. Coefficients values beyond -73 to 74 are rare and coded with escape sequences, therefore these weren't used either. We only used block 1 because it was more evenly distributed than blocks 2 and 3 (i.e. 19-51 and 52-59). The distribution for the values in blocks 2 and 3 is concentrated in two spikes at values -1 and 1 (i.e. they are composed of mostly values $\in \{-1, 0, 1\}$). Changing these values would significantly alter the distribution and make it easy to detect if there is a message hidden in the fingerprint.

2. *Random number seeding:* In this step, we select the sites from candidate set S which will be modified in a pseudo-random fashion. In order to retain predictability in coder and decoder, we decided to chose the seed for our random number generator from the subbands that do not change. For example, in the selection process we left the contents of subbands 19-59 unchanged. In

principle we can chose any statistic from these bands (e.g. the average of the indices were a -1 occurred). This seed selection ensures that both the message is embedded at varying locations (but based on the image content), and that the message can be read only if the proper seed selection algorithm is known by the decoder.

3. *Bit setting*: The message to be hidden is translated to a sequence of bits. Each bit will be stuffed into a site chosen semi-randomly from the list of suitable sites. That is, for each message bit we choose a site from the set S based on the seeded pseudo-random number generator. If the selected site has already been used, the next randomly generated site is chosen instead. We then change the low order bit of the value at the selected site to be identical to the current message bit. Half the time this results in no change at all to the coefficient value. The change is done as described by the pseudocode in Fig. 3. Note that the site selection in stage one was carefully chosen so that the outer boundaries were even and the inner ones were odd (i.e. 108 and 254 are even, 179 and 181 are odd - 180 excluded). This ensures that the algorithm in Fig. 3 is a closed function. Hence, changing a value will never result in a new value which is outside of 108-254 (excluding 180). If we change a value into one outside of this range (e.g. 108 to 107), then at decoding time we would be uncertain if the encountered value (e.g. 107) was a valid replace site from S which was changed or if it was never a member of S in the first place.

Algorithm : SETBITS($data, b$)

  let $data$ be the array of data values (quantized indices).
  let b be the m-size array of message bits.
  for $i \leftarrow 1$ **to** m
    let $data_i$ be the ith data value.
    let b_i be the ith message bit.
    $ind \leftarrow GetNextSite()$;
    if $data_{ind} < 180$
      if $isEven(data_{ind})$ **and** $b_i == 1$
        $data_{ind} \leftarrow data_{ind} + 1$
      else $isOdd(data_{ind})$ **and** $b_i == 0$
        $data_{ind} \leftarrow data_{ind} - 1$
    else if $data_{ind} > 180$
      if $isEven(data_{ind})$ **and** $b_i == 1$
        $data_{ind} \leftarrow data_{ind} - 1$
      else $isOdd(data_{ind})$ **and** $b_i == 0$
        $data_{ind} \leftarrow data_{ind} + 1$

Fig. 3. Bit setting algorithm

4. *Bit saving*: Optionally, we can save all the original low order bits and append them to the compressed bit stream as a user comment field. The appended bits are random samples in general, and hence are uncorrelated with the hidden message.

For the decoder, there are also three steps. The first two steps are the same as the first two steps described in the encoder: constructing the set S and selecting the seed for the random number generator. The third step is to run the pseudo-random number generator to select specific sites in a particular order. The least significant bits of the values at these sites are then concatenated to recover the original message.

If a restoration appendix was optionally included, the decoder can restore the original values at the sites as it goes. This allows perfect reconstruction of the image (up to the original compression) despite the embedded message. The restored decompressed image will be nearly the same as the decompressed image with the message still embedded. In practice, the error due to the embedded message is not perceptually significant, and does not affect subsequent processing and authentication of the fingerprint image. Only the right decoder can locate and extract the message from the compressed image during the decoding process. The message can either be a fixed authentication stamp, or personal ID information which must match some other part of the record (which might have been sent in the clear). Thus, if an uncoded or improperly coded bit stream is given to the special decoder, it will fail to extract the expected message and hence can reject the image.

3.2   Extensions to Proposed Data-Hiding Method

There are several security holes in the method described above. First, while the random seeding method used above is dependent on the image acquired, the underlying algorithm to seed the process is same for all the persons in the database. If the method is known to the hacker, the over all system becomes quite vulnerable. Second, a secure system should not give the impression to a hacker that the system uses a data hiding method. We call this as the *detectability* problem. The hacker may be more interested to attack when it notices use of some hiding technique. As can be seen from the description of the hiding algorithm, the number of sites can vary from image to image. A related issue to the detectability problem is what happens to the unused sites that did not participate in storing a message bit. Can they reveal any information about the data hiding algorithm? The third problem is that of *hill climbing attack*. The hacker can act as a phoney server and provide unusual messages such as gradually changing pattern to discover the sites being changed in the compressed image. In this section, we discuss secure protocol extensions to the earlier proposed data hiding algorithm to increase the applicability and reliability of our method. We propose now secure protocols to improve the overall security of the system.

To address the first problem, we propose to use a random seed composed not only of the image structure, but a combination of image structure and knowledge (i.e. password), then the impostor will not be able to correctly hide the message in the acquired image claiming it comes from it's own finger. Note that the knowledge string doesn't need to be sent to the server except at the time of enrollment. It will only be used to properly seed the random number generator.

As a second scenario, consider the possibility of an impostor posing as the server. It will send out the challenge (message) for the client to respond to. If the challenge/response interaction is naively designed, the fake server might request some carefully planned messages (i.e. one bit message, a string of zeroes) to be hidden in the image with the purpose of identifying how the message is being concealed. Note that the fake server doesn't know the real seed for the random number generator. If it manages to obtain this information it could then hide/retrieve messages in fingerprint to post unauthorized transactions.

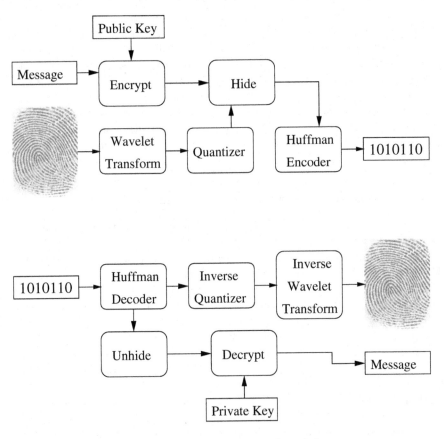

Fig. 4. Proposed Data-Hiding Scheme.

To solve this problem there are two things we can do. We can first insert the message in the image and then randomly change the bits in the remaining sites.

This will make the job of deciphering the seed and/or the order in which the bits are stored extremely difficult. The same result can be obtained by passing the message through a secure hashing function before hiding it. This will ensure that two naively constructed messages, although short or close in space, will produce very different strings to hide.

The last extension that we have applied to our data-hiding algorithm is asymmetric key encryption to the message before hiding it as shown in Fig. 4. Note that by encrypting the message we solve the previous two problems. However, it is at a cost in performance and we will need at least 1408 replace sites (i.e. size of S) to hide a message of up to 936 bits encrypted with a 1024 bit key. In section 4 we can observe that for the three databases we tested 1024 bits is a reasonable number to expect.

Using asymmetric encryption we can sign the message on the server side with a private key, which provides a higher level of assurance that the message is in fact coming from the server. The client then can decrypt the message with the public key and create the encrypted response message. The encrypted message is then hidden in the fingerprint image and sent to the server. This makes it much harder for an unauthorized user to extract the message from the image and even then he would still need to decrypt it. By using this type of encryption the client is now also enabled to send unknown data to the server. Notice that in all other scenarios the server knows the answer to its challenge and only validates it. In the case where a hash function is used we can not append data to the answer because it's an irreversible process and in the other scenario there is only one level of protection (i.e. the data-hiding process) making the transmission of sensitive data a higher security risk.

The capability of a client sending data to the server appended to the response allows implementations such as those described in [8] where other biometrics (i.e. such as faces) are sent hidden in the fingerprint image. They also present the case where a synthetic fingerprint acts as a carrier for the minutiae information of the real fingerprint image.

4 Experimental Results

The data-hiding algorithm was applied to databases 2 & 3 from the Fingerprint Verification Competition (FVC2000) [1]. These are databases of images obtained from capacitive and optical sensors in groups of 8 corresponding to the same

name	source	size (pixels)	samples	resolution
DB2	Low-cost Capacitive Sensor	256x364	100x8	500 ppi
DB3	Optical Sensor	448x478	100x8	500 ppi
NIST4	Scanned inked cards	512x512	250x2	500 ppi

Table 1. Data sets description.

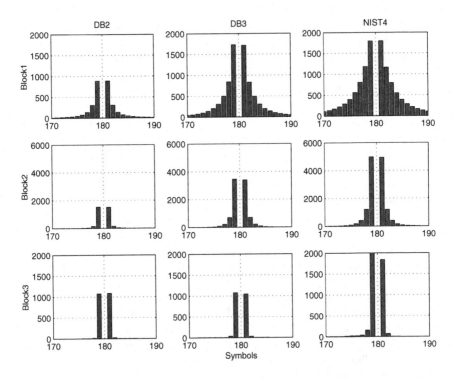

Fig. 5. Histograms of quantized indices per block for the three databases.

finger. Also, a set of NIST4 was used which is composed of images obtained from digitized FBI inked cards. These were obtained in groups of 2 corresponding to the same finger. Table 1 presents a description of these databases. Fig. 6 shows an example image from each database.

name	block 1	block 2	block 3
DB2	3094	3442	2190
DB3	8362	8948	2180
NIST4	12568	13816	4260

Table 2. Number of available replace sites per block at 0.75 bpp.

Fig. 5 shows the average histograms of symbols per block (e.g. block1 is subbands 0 to 18) for each of the databases when compressed at 0.75 bpp. Notice that as you converge into the higher frequencies (i.e. higher block) there is less variability among the values. Table 2 summarizes the data from Fig. 5. As can be seen, we can hide messages of considerable length in the images. Depending on the size of the messages that one expects we can choose to only hide data towards the tails of the histograms, reducing the amount of noise added to the image due to the message inserted. Fig. 6 (a), (c), and (e) are sample images from DB2, DB3, and NIST4 compressed at 0.75 bpp, while Fig. 6 (b), (d), and (f) are the corresponding images with all the replace sites in block 1 changed (i.e. the worst case scenario, since we would expect to have to change only half the bits). It is observed that there is no noticeable difference between the images, which implies that the hidden message does not cause a significant performance degradation on the authentication method.

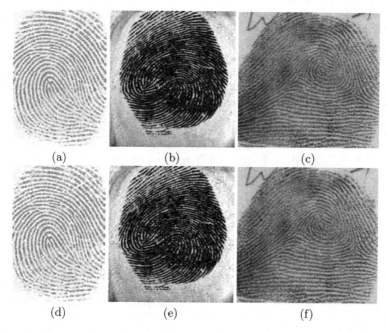

(a)	(b)	(c)
(d)	(e)	(f)

Fig. 6. A fingerprint image sample from (a) DB2, (c) DB3, and (e) NIST4 compressed at 0.75 bpp and their counterparts (b), (d), and (f) with the worst case hidden message.

5   Conclusions

In this paper, we have proposed secure extensions to our earlier data-hiding algorithm in the wavelet compressed domain for fingerprint images in order to make it very robust. The algorithm can easily be extended to other methods of compression such as JPEG 2000 and to other biometrics as well. We have demonstrated that the effect of the hidden message has no significant visual impact while providing a very secure environment for today's growing web-based market as well as the remote access business model. We have also shown that it can embed messages of significant length, which makes its applicability much broader. The proposed algorithm can easily be implemented in hardware and together with the FBI WSQ standard compression is an attractive feature to be bundled into a general purpose fingerprint sensor making it ideal for wide-spread use.

References

[1] *Fingerprint Verification Competition 2000.* http://bias.csr.unibo.it/fvc2000.

[2] W. Bender, D. Gruhl, N. Morimoto, and A. Lu. Techniques for data hiding. *IBM Systems Journal*, 35(3 & 4):313–335, 1996.

[3] M. Boliek, C. Christopoulos, and Majani E. (editors). JPEG2000 Part I Final Draft International Standard. Number ISO/IEC FDIS 15444-1. ISO/IEC JTC1/SC29/WG1 N1855, Aug. 2000.

[4] C. M. Brislawn, J. N. Bradley, R. J. Onyshezak, and T. Hopper. The FBI compression standard for digitized fingerprint images. In *Proc. SPIE*, volume 2847, pages 344–355, Denver, CO, Aug. 1996.

[5] C.M. Brislawn, J.N. Bradley, and T. Hopper. The FBI Wavelet/Scalar Quantization Standard for gray-scale fingerprint image compression.

[6] FBI. WSQ Gray-Scale Fingerprint Image Compression Specification. Document No. IAFIS-IC-0110 (v2), Feb. 1993. Drafted by T. Hopper, C. M. Brislawn and J. N. Bradley.

[7] C. T. Hsu and J. L. Wu. Hidden digital watermarks in images. *IEEE Trans. on Image Processing*, 8(1):58–68, Jan. 1999.

[8] A. K. Jain and U. Uludag. Hiding Biometric Data. *IEEE Trans. on Pattern Analysis and Machine Intelligence*, 25(11):1494–1498, Nov. 2003.

[9] M. Kobayashi M. D. Swanson and A. H. Tewfik. Multimedia Data Embedding and Watermarking Technologies. 86(6):1064–1087, June 1998.

[10] P. Moulin and M. K. Mihcak. A Framework for Evaluating the Data-Hiding Capacity of Image Sources. *IEEE Trans. on Image Processing*, 11(9):1029–1042, Sept. 2002.

[11] F. A. Petitcolas, R. J. Anderson, and M. G. Kuhn. Information Hiding - A Survey. 87(7):1062–1078, July 1999.

[12] M. Ramkumar and A. N. Akansu. Capacity Estimates for Data-Hiding in Compressed Images. *IEEE Trans. on Image Processing*, 10(8):1252–1263, Aug. 2001.

[13] N. K. Ratha, J. H. Connell, and R. M. Bolle. Secure Data Hiding in Wavelet Compressed Fingerprint Images. In *Proc. ACM Multimedia*, pages 127–130, Marina del Rey, CA, Oct. 2000.

Palmprint Authentication System for Civil Applications

David Zhang[1], Guangming Lu[2], Adams Wai-Kin Kong[1, 3], and Michael Wong[1]

[1] Biometrics Research Centre, Department of Computing
The Hong Kong Polytechnic University, Kowloon, Hong Kong
{csdzhang, csmkwong}@comp.polyu.edu.hk
http://www.comp.polyu.edu.hk/~biometrics
[2] Biocomputing Research Lab,
School of Computer Science and Engineering
Harbin Institute of Technology, Harbin, China
Luguangm@hit.edu.cn
[3] Department of Systems Design Engineering
University of Waterloo, Ontario, Canada N2L 3G1
adamskong@ieee.org

Abstract. In this paper, we present a novel biometric authentication system to identify a person's identity by his/her palmprint. In contrast to existing palmprint systems for criminal applications, the proposed system targets at the civil applications, which require identifying a person in a large database with high confidence in real-time. The system is constituted by four major components: User Interface Module, Acquisition Module, Recognition Module and External Module. More than 7,000 palmprint images have been collected to test the performance of the system. The system can identify 400 palms with a low false acceptance rate, 0.02%, and a high genuine acceptance rate, 98.83%. For verification, the system can operate at a false acceptance rate, 0.017% and a false rejection rate, 0.86%. The execution time for the whole process including image collection, preprocessing, feature extraction and matching is less than 1 second.

1 Introduction

There has been an ever-growing need to automatically authenticate individuals at various occasions in our modern and automated society, such as physical access control on building entrance and logical access control on computer logon. Traditional knowledge based or token based personal identification or verification is so tedious, time-consuming, inefficient or expensive, which is incapable to meet such a fast-pacing society. Knowledge-based approaches use "something that you know" to make a personal identification, such as password and personal identification number. Token-based approaches use "something that you have" to make a personal identification, such as passport or credit card. Since those approaches are not based on any inherent attributes of an individual to make the identification, it is unable to differentiate between an authorized person and an impostor who fraudulently acquires the "token" or "knowledge" of the authorized person. This is why biometrics identification or verification system started to be more focused in the recent years.

D. Maltoni and A.K. Jain (Eds.): BioAW 2004, LNCS 3087, pp. 217-228, 2004.
© Springer-Verlag Berlin Heidelberg 2004

Biometrics involves identifying an individual based on his/her physiological or behavioral characteristics. Many parts of our body and various behaviors are embedded such information for personal identification. In fact, using biometrics for person authentication is not new, which has been implemented over thousands years. Undoubtedly, face recognition is a direct and intuitive approach for human beings as the most common biometric. In addition, fingerprint and signature are two important biometrics technologies, which have been used to approbate the contents of a document or to authenticate a financial transaction. Furthermore, fingerprint can be used for criminal applications since latent prints can be remained on the object contacted by fingertips.

Because of the computerization of our society, automatic biometric solution is emerging for accurately identifying a person to solve diverse security problems. In the past decade, numerous research efforts have been put on this subject resulting in developing various techniques related to signal acquisition, feature extraction, matching and classification. Most importantly, various biometric systems including, fingerprint, iris, hand geometry, voice and face recognition systems have been deployed for various applications [1]. Among all biometric, hand-based biometric including, hand geometry and fingerprint is the most popular biometrics gaining 60% market share in 2003 [2].

The proposed palmprint system is also a hand-based biometric technology, exploiting the features in the inner surface of our palm for personal identification. Therefore, we expect that the palmprint system will receive a high user acceptance, like fingerprint, hand geometry and hand vein [3-6]. Because of the rich features including texture, principal lines and wrinkles on palmprints, we believe that they contain enough stable and distinctive information for separating an individual from a large population. We also expect that palmprints are robust to the noise influence because of the large surface area.

There have been some companies, including NEC and PRINTRAK, which have developed several palmprint systems for criminal applications [8-9]. On the basis of fingerprint technology, their systems exploit high resolution palmprint images to extract the detailed features like minutiae for matching the latent prints. Such approach is not suitable for developing a palmprint authentication system for civil applications. It requires a fast, accurate and reliable method for the personal identification. On the basis of our previous research work [10], we develop a novel palmprint authentication system to fulfill such requirements.

The rest of the paper is organized as follows. The system framework is shown in Section 2. The recognition module is described in Section 3. Experimental results of verification, identification, robustness, and computation time are provided in Section 4. Finally, conducting remarks are given in Section 5.

2   System Framework

The proposed palmprint authentication system has four major components: they are *User Interface Module*, *Acquisition Module*, *Recognition Module* and *External Module*. Fig. 1 shows the breakdown of each module of the palmprint authentication system. Fig. 2 shows the palmprint authentication system installed at Biometric Research Center, Department of Computing, The Hong Kong Polytechnic University.

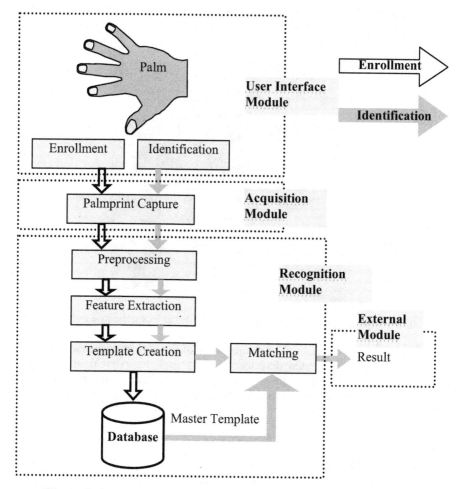

Fig. 1. The breakdown of each module of the palmprint authentication system.

The functions of each component are listed below:

A) *User Interface Module* provides an interface between the system and users for the smooth authentication operation. We designed a flat platen surface for the palm acquisition shown in Fig. 2. It is crucial to develop a good user interface such that users are happy to use the device.

B) *Acquisition Module* is the channel for the palm to be acquired for the further processing.

C) *Recognition Module* is the key part of our system, which will determine whether a user is authenticated. It consists of image pre-processing, feature extraction, template creation, database updating, and matching. Then it gives an identification/verification result.

D) *External Module* receives the signal come from the recognition module, to allow some operations to be performed, or denied the operations requested. This module actually is an interfacing component, which may be connected to another hardware components or software components. Our system presents an external interface for physical door access control or an employee attendance system.

Fig. 2. The palmprint authentication system installed at Biometric Research Center

Since the design philosophy and implementation of the user interface module and the acquisition module have been described in [10], and the external interface is an application dependent component. In this paper, we are not intended to discuss them further, and we will concentrate on the discussion about the recognition module in detail.

3   Recognition Module

After the palmprint images are captured by the Acquisition Module, they are fed into the recognition module for palmprint authentication. The recognition module is the key part of the palmprint authentication system, which consists of the stages of: image preprocessing, feature extraction, and matching.

3.1 Preprocessing

When capturing a palmprint, the position, direction and stretching degree may vary from time to time. As a result, even the palmprints from the same palm could have a little rotation and shift. Also the sizes of palms are different from one another. So, the preprocessing algorithm is used to align different palmprints and extract the corresponding central part for feature extraction [7]. In our palmprint system, both the rotation and translation are constrained to some extent by the capture device panel, which can locate the palms by several pegs. Then the preprocessing algorithm can locate the coordination system of the palmprints quickly by the following five steps:

Step 1: Use a threshold to convert the original grayscale image into a binary image, then using a low-pass filter to smooth the binary image.

Step 2: Trace the boundary of the holes *H1* and *H2* between those fingers.

Step 3: Compute the tangent of the holes *H1* and *H2*. *T1* and *T2* are the tangent points of *H1* and *H2*, respectively.

Step 4: Align *T1* and *T2* to determine the Y-axis of the palmprint coordination system and making a line passing through the midpoint of the two points *(T1* and *T2)*, which is perpendicular to this Y-axis to determine the origin of the system.

Step 5: Extract a sub-image of a fixed size based on the coordinate system (see Fig. 3). The sub-image is located at a certain area of the palmprint image for feature extraction.

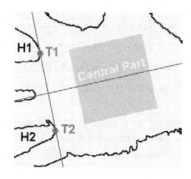

Fig. 3. The major steps on image preprocessing: *H1* and *H2* are boundary of the holes between the two fingers, where *T1* and *T2* are the tangent point of *H1* and *H2*, respectively. The central box is the sub-image of a palm.

3.2 Feature Extraction

The feature extraction technique implemented on the proposed palmprint system is modified from [10], where single circular zero DC Gabor filter is applied to the preprocessed palmprint images and the phase information is coded as feature vector called PalmCode. The modified technique exploited four circular zero DC Gabor filters with the following general formula

$$G_D = \frac{1}{2\pi\sigma^2}\exp\left\{-\frac{1}{2}\left[\frac{(x'-x_o)^2}{\sigma^2}+\frac{(y'-y_o)^2}{\sigma^2}\right]\right\}\left\{\exp(i2\pi\omega x')-\exp(-2\pi^2\omega^2\sigma^2)\right\} \quad (1)$$

where, $x' = x\cos\theta + y\sin\theta$ and $y' = -x\sin\theta + y\cos\theta$; (x_0, y_0) is the center of the function in the spatial domain of the function; ω is the frequency of the sinusoidal plane wave along the orientation, θ; σ is the standard deviations of the circular Gaussian function; θ is the direction of the filter. The four Gabor filters share the same parameters, σ and ω, only different in θ. The corresponding values of θ are 0, $\pi/4$, $\pi/2$ and $3\pi/4$.

In the previous approach, only the phase information is exploited but the magnitude information is totally neglected. The proposed method is to use the magnitude to be a fusion condition to combine different PalmCodes generated by the four Gabor filters. Mathematically, the implementation has the following steps.

The four Gabor filters are applied to the preprocessed palmprint image, I described as G_j*I, where G_j $(j=1, 2, 3, 4)$ is the circular zero DC Gabor filter and "*" represents an operator of convolution.

The square of the magnitudes of the sample point is obtained by $M_j(x,y) = G_j(x,y)*I \times \overline{G_j(x,y)*I}$, where "—" represents complex conjugate.

According to the fusion rule, $k = \arg\max_j(M_j(x,y))$, the phase information at point (x, y) is coded as the followings

$$h_r = 1 \quad if \quad Re[G_k * I] \geq 0, \tag{2}$$
$$h_r = 0 \quad if \quad Re[G_k * I] < 0, \tag{3}$$
$$h_i = 1 \quad if \quad Im[G_k * I] \geq 0, \tag{4}$$
$$h_i = 0 \quad if \quad Im[G_k * I] < 0. \tag{5}$$

This coding method is named as Fusion Code. More discussion and comparisons between Fusion Code and PalmCode are given in [11]. It can be proved that Fusion Code is independent of the local contrast and brightness of the palmprint images.

3.3 Matching

The feature matching determines the degree of similarity between two templates – the authentication template and the master template. Since the format of Fusion Code and PalmCode are exactly same, normalized hamming distance implemented in PalmCode is still useful for comparing two Fusion Codes. Fusion Code is represented by a set of bits. Mathematically, the normalized hamming distance is represented by

$$D_o = \frac{\sum_{i=1}^{N}\sum_{j=1}^{N} P_M(i,j) \cap Q_M(i,j) \cap \left((P_R(i,j) \otimes Q_R(i,j) + P_I(i,j) \otimes Q_I(i,j))\right)}{2\sum_{i=1}^{N}\sum_{j=1}^{N} P_M(i,j) \cap Q_M(i,j)}, \tag{6}$$

where P_R (Q_R), P_I (Q_I) and $P_M(Q_M)$ are the real part, imaginary part and mask of the Fusion Code $P(Q)$, respectively; $\otimes$ and $\cap$ are Boolean operators, XOR and AND, respectively. The ranges of normalized hamming distances are between zero and one. Zero represents perfect matching. Because of the imperfect preprocessing, one of the Fusion Code is vertically and horizontal translated to match the other again. The ranges of the vertical and the horizontal translations are defined from −2 to 2. The minimum D_0 value obtained from the translated matching is considered to be the final matching score.

4   Performance Evaluation

4.1 Testing Database

We collected palmprint images from 200 individuals using our palmprint capture device described in [10]. The subjects are mainly students and staff volunteers from The Hong Kong Polytechnic University. In this dataset, 134 people are male, and the age distribution of the subjects is: about 86% are younger than 30, about 3% are older than 50, and about 11% are aged between 30 and 50. In addition, we collected the palmprint images on two separate occasions. On each occasion, the subject was asked to provide about 10 images each of the left palm and the right palm. Therefore, each person provided around 40 images, resulting in a total number of 8,025 images from 400 different palms in our database. In addition, we changed the light source and adjusted the focus of the CCD camera so that the images collected on the first and second occasions could be regarded as being captured by two different palmprint devices. The average time interval between the first and second occasions was 70 days. The maximum and the minimum time intervals were 162 days and 1 day, respectively. Originally, the collected images had two kinds of sizes, 384×284 and 768×568. The larger image was resized to 384×284 so that the size of all the testing images used in the following experiments was 384×284 with 75dpi.

4.2 Experimental Results of Verification

Verification refers to the problem of confirming or denying a claim of individuals (Am I who I claim I am?). It is also considered as one-to-one matching. To obtain the verification result, two group experiments are carried out separately. In the first experiment, only one palmprint image of each palm is used for registration. In the first experiment, each palmprint image is matched with all other palmprint images in the database. A correct matching occurs if two palmprint images are from the same palm; incorrect matching otherwise. The total number of matching is 32,119,735. Number of genuine matching is 76,565 and the rest of them are incorrect matchings. Fig. 4(a) shows the probability of genuine and imposter distributions estimated by the correct and incorrect matchings. Some thresholds and corresponding false acceptance rates (FARs) and false rejection rates (FRRs) are listed in Table 1(a). According to Table 1(a), using one palmprint image for registration, the proposed system can be operated at a low false acceptance rate 0.096% and a reasonably low false rejection rate 1.05%.

In the second experiment, the testing database is divided into two databases, 1) registration database and 2) testing database. Three palmprint images of each palm collected in the first occasion are selected for the registration database. Totally, the registration database contains 1,200 palmprint images and the rest of them are for the testing database. In this verification test, each palmprint image is matched with all the palmprint images in the testing database. Therefore, each testing image produces three hamming distances for one registered palm. We take the minimum of them as the final hamming distance. For achieving statistically reliable results, this test is repeated for three times by selecting other palmprint images for the registration database. Total number of hamming distances from correct matchings and incorrect matchings are 20,475 and 8,169,525, respectively. Fig. 4(b) shows the probability of genuine and imposter distributions estimated by the correct and incorrect matchings, respectively. Some threshold values along with its corresponding false acceptance and false rejection rates are also listed in Table 1(a). According to Table 1(a) and Fig. 4, we can conclude that using three templates can provide better verification accuracy. In fact, using more palmprint images of the same palm during registration can provide more information to the system so that it can recognize the noise or deformed features. It is also the reason for commercial verification systems requiring more than one sample for registration.

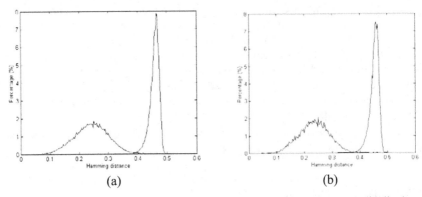

(a)   (b)

Fig. 4. Verification test results. (a) and (b) show the Genuine and imposter distributions for verification tests with one and three registered images per palm, respectively.

4.3 Experimental Results of Identification

Identification test is a one-against-many, N comparison process. In this experiment, N is set to 400, which is the total number of different palms in our database. Same as the previous verification experiment, the palmprint database is divided into two databases, 1) registration and 2) testing databases. The registration database contains 1200 palmprint images, three images per palm. The testing database has 6,825 palmprint images. Each palmprint image in the testing database is matched to all of the palmprint images in the registration database. Therefore, each testing image generates 3 correct and 1197 incorrect matchings. The minimum hamming distances of correct matchings and incorrect matchings are regarded as the identification hamming distances of genuine and impostor, respectively. This experiment is also called a one-trial test since the user only provides one palmprint image in the test to make one decision. In fact, a practical biometric system collects several biometric signals to make one decision. Therefore, in this experiment, we implement one-, two- and three-trial tests. In the two-trial test, a pair of palmprint images in the testing database belongs to the same palm is matched to all of the palmprint images in the registration database. Each pair of the palmprint images in the two-trial test generates 6 correct and 2,394 incorrect matchings. The minimum hamming distances of correct matchings and incorrect matchings are considered as the hamming distances of genuine and imposter, respectively. Similarly, in the three-trial test, the hamming distances of genuine and imposter are obtained from 9 correct and 3,591 incorrect matchings, respectively. Each test is repeated three times by selecting other palmprints from the registration database. In each test, the number of the hamming distances of genuine and imposter matchings both are 20,475. Fig. 5 shows ROC curves of the three tests and Table 1(b) lists the threshold values along with its corresponding FARs and FRRs of the tests. According to Fig. 5 and Table 1(b), more input palmprints can provide more accurate results.

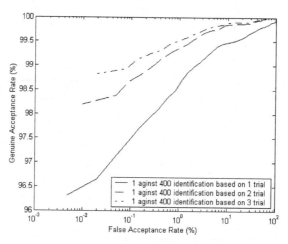

Fig. 5. The ROC curves are for a 1-against-400 identification testing with different number of trials.

4.4 Computation Time

Another key issue for a civilian personal authentication system is whether the system can run in real time. In other words, the system should be running as fast as possible. The proposed method is implemented using C language and Assemble language on a PC embedded Intel Pentium IV processor (1.4GHz) with 128M memories. The execution time for image collection, image preprocessing, feature extraction and matching are listed in Table 2. The total execution time for a 1-against-400 identification, each palm with 3 templates, is less than 1 second. Users will not feel any delay when using our system.

4.5 Robustness

As a practical biometric system, other than accuracy and speed, robustness of the system is another important issue. To verify the robustness of noise palmprints, Fig.

6(a) provides a clear palmprint image and Figs. 6(b)-(f) show five palmprint images, with different texts. Their hamming distances are given in Table 3; all of them are smaller than 0.29. Comparing the hamming distances of imposter in Tables 1 (a) and (b), it is ensured that all the hamming distances in Table 3 are relatively small. Fig. 6 and Table 3 illustrates that the proposed palmprint authentication system is very robust to the noise on the palmprint.

Table 1. False acceptance rates (FARs) and false rejection rates (FRRs) with different threshold values, (a) verification results and (b) 1-to-400 identification results.

(a)

Threshold	Registered image=1		Registered images=3	
	FAR (%)	FRR (%)	FAR (%)	FRR (%)
0.32	0.000027	8.15	0.000012	5.12
0.34	0.00094	4.02	0.0016	2.18
0.36	0.011	1.94	0.017	0.86
0.38	0.096	1.05	0.15	0.43
0.40	0.68	0.59	1.03	0.19

(b)

	Trial=1		Trial=2		Trial=3	
Threshold	FAR (%)	FRR (%)	FAR (%)	FRR (%)	FAR (%)	FRR (%)
0.320	0.0049	3.69	0.0098	1.80	0.020	1.17
0.325	0.0439	2.93	0.088	1.34	0.131	1.06
0.330	0.15	2.29	0.28	1.02	0.42	0.68
0.335	0.37	1.90	0.68	0.72	0.96	0.48
0.340	0.84	1.51	1.43	0.57	1.93	0.37
0.345	1.45	1.16	2.32	0.42	3.02	0.26

Table 2. Execution time of the palmprint authentication system.

Operations	Execution Time
Image collection	340ms
Preprocessing	250ms
Mask generation	9.8ms
Feature extraction	180ms
Matching	1.3μs

Table 3. The hamming distances of Fig. 6

Figs	6(b)	6(c)	6(d)	6(e)	6(f)
6(a)	0.19	0.21	0.27	0.29	0.28
6(b)		0.18	0.27	0.26	0.27
6(c)			0.27	0.28	0.28
6(d)				0.23	0.19
6(e)					0.19

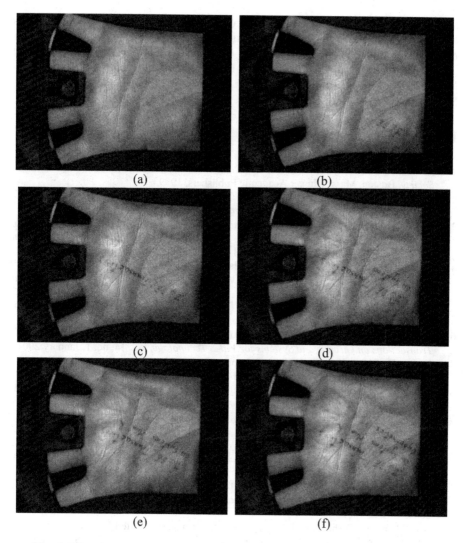

Fig. 6. Palmprint images with different texts for testing the robustness of the system.

5   Conclusion

In this paper, we have presented a novel biometric system based on the palmprint. The proposed system can accurately identify a person in real time, which is suitable for various civil applications such as access control. Experimental results show that the proposed system can identify 400 palms with a low false acceptance rate, 0.02%, and a high genuine acceptance rate, 98.83%. For verification, the system can operate at a false acceptance rate, 0.017% and a false rejection rate, 0.86%. The experimental results including accuracy, speed and robustness demonstrate that the palmprint authentication system is comparable with other hand-based biometrics systems, such as hand geometry and fingerprint verification system [12, 13, 14] and is practical for real-world applications. The system has been installed at the Biometric Research Center, Department of Computing, The Hong Kong Polytechnic University since March 2003 for access control (Fig. 2).

Reference

1. A. Jain, R. Bolle and S. Pankanti (eds.), *Biometrics: Personal Identification in Networked Society*, Boston, Mass: Kluwer Academic Publishers, 1999.
2. International Biometric Group's Biometric Market Report 2003-2007: http://www.biometricgroup.com/reports/public/market_report.html.
3. R. Sanchez-Reillo, C. Sanchez-Avilla and A. Gonzalez-Marcos, "Biometric identification through hand geometry measurements", *IEEE Transactions on Pattern Analysis and Machine Intelligence*, vol. 22, no. 10, pp. 1168-1171, 2000.
4. S.K. Im, H.M. Park, Y.W. Kim, S.C. Han, S.W. Kim and C.H. Kang, "An biometric identification system by extracting hand vein patterns", *Journal of the Korean Physical Society*, vol. 38, no. 3, pp. 268-272, 2001.
5. A. Jain, L. Hong and R. Bolle, "On-line fingerprint verification", *IEEE Transactions on Pattern Analysis and Machine Intelligence*, vol. 19, no. 4, pp. 302-314, 1997.
6. A.K. Jain, A. Ross and S. Prabhakar, "An introduction to biometric recognition", *IEEE Transactions on Circuits and Systems for Video Technology*, vol. 14, no. 1, January 2004.
7. G. Lu, D. Zhang, and K. Wang, "Palmprint Recognition Using Eigenpalms Features", *Pattern Recognition Letters*, vol. 24, pp. 1473-1477, 2003.
8. http://www.nectech.com/afis/download/PalmprintDtsht.q.pdf - NEC automatic palmprint identification system.
9. http://www.printrakinternational.com/omnitrak.htm - Prinkrak palmprint identification system.
10. D. Zhang, W.K. Kong, J. You and M. Wong, "On-line palmprint identification", *IEEE Transactions on Pattern Analysis and Machine Intelligence*, vol. 25, no. 9, pp. 1041-1050, 2003.
11. W.K. Kong and D. Zhang, "Feature-level fusion for effective palmprint identification", To appear in International Conference of Biometric Authentication, Hong Kong, 15-17, July, 2004.
12. A.K. Jain, S. Prabhakar, L. Hong and S. Pankanti, "Filterbank-based fingerprint matching", *IEEE Transactions on Image Processing*, vol. 9, no. 5, pp. 846-859, 2000.
13. A.K. Jain, L. Hong and R. Bolle, "On-line fingerprint verification", *IEEE Transactions on Pattern Analysis and Machine Intelligence*, vol. 19, no. 4, pp. 302-314, 1997.
14. R. Sanchez-Reillo, C. Sanchez-Avilla and A. Gonzalez-Marcos, "Biometric identification through hand geometry measurements", *IEEE Transactions on Pattern Analysis and Machine Intelligence*, vol. 22, no. 18, pp.1168-1171, 2000.

Writer Identification
Using Finger-Bend in Writing Signature

Seiichiro Hangai and Takeshi Higuchi

Tokyo University of Science, Department of Electrical Engineering
1-3 Kagurazaka, Shinjuku, Tokyo 162-8601, Japan

Abstract. In sign authentication, some feature parameters such as pen position, pen pressure and pen inclination are combined to get better performance. Considering that these features are results of individual contraction of muscles with different shape of skeletons, it is meaningful to measure time sequences of finger-bends for authenticating individuals. In this paper, we show the individuality in the bend of joints of fingers in signing, and we discuss the possibility of writer authentication.

1 Introduction

In order to secure the safe ubiquitous network system, biometrics information such as fingerprints, iris, retina and face are used for individual authentication. However, some people are protesting against it, because their privacies are threatened. Most familiar authentication method is to use the signature or the speech, which are not direct physical features but indirect behavioral features of the contraction of muscles or the movement of vocal organs. We think it is preferable to extract more essential features, i.e., characteristics and shape of muscles or tongue, control impulses to voluntary or involuntary muscles, and so on.

We have investigated and reported the online signature authentication method using time sequences of pen position, pen pressure and pen inclination [1-5]. Among those features, it was cleared that the pen pressure and inclination could be invaluable features to improve authentication rate and robustness to aging. Considering that the pen pressure and inclination are the result of contraction of muscles, there is a possibility of the improvement of writer authentication rate, if we can use the bend of joints of fingers in signing.

In this paper, we show the experimental method of collecting bends of various joints of fingers, and the evaluated results for writer authentication. We also discuss the possibility of the more reliable authentication.

D. Maltoni and A.K. Jain (Eds.): BioAW 2004, LNCS 3087, pp. 229-237, 2004.
© Springer-Verlag Berlin Heidelberg 2004

2 Measurement of Bend Angles of Joints in Signing

We have reported that the individuality is included in the variation of pen pressure and pen inclination in signing. This means that the clipping angle of fingers and the rotating angle of wrist could be used for authentication, if we can measure them.

Data glove, which is used for controlling objects in cyber space, has many sensors located on joints and wrist, and outputs information of bend angle and rotating angle. Fig.1 shows the data glove[6] and locations of sensors listed in Table 1. The resolution is 0.5 degree and the sampling frequency is 149 records/second.

Fig. 2 shows an example of signature and signals from a tablet[7], in which five writing information, i.e., x, y position $x(nT)$ and $y(nT)$, pen pressure $p(nT)$, pen azimuth $\theta(nT)$, and pen altitude $\phi(nT)$ are collected every T second, where T is the sampling period.

Fig. 3 also shows signals from the data glove of Fig.1.

After collecting signals, DP matching is performed to make the reference. Fig.4 (a) shows output signals from the sensor #2, when the same person signs three times. And, Fig.4 (b) shows the matched signals and the averaged signal, i.e., the reference pattern. The person p's reference pattern of the sensor j, $s_{rj}^{(p)}(nT)$, is calculated by the following equation,

$$s_{rj}^{(p)}(nT) = \frac{1}{N}\sum_{i=1}^{N} s_{rij}^{(p)}(nT) \tag{1}$$

,where $s_{rij}^{(p)}(nT)$ is the p's i-th signal of the sensor j after DP matching and N is the number of signature.

In the experiment using the data glove, we make the reference pattern set $R_p(nT)$ consisting of 18 reference patterns for the writer p as follows,

$$R_p(nT) = \left\{ s_{r0}^{(p)}(nT), s_{r1}^{(p)}(nT), s_{r2}^{(p)}(nT), \cdots, s_{r17}^{(p)}(nT) \right\} \tag{2}$$

The intra writer variance $V_{intra,j}$ and the inter writer variance $V_{inter,j}$ for the signals of the sensor j are calculated as follows,

$$V_{intra,j} = \sum_{i=1}^{N}\sum_{n} \left(s_{ij}^{(p)}(nT) - s_{rj}^{(p)}(nT) \right)^2 \tag{3}$$

$$V_{inter,j} = \sum_{p=1}^{P}\sum_{n} \left(s_{rj}^{(p)}(nT) - \overline{s_{rj}^{(p)}(nT)} \right)^2 \tag{4}$$

,where $\overline{s_{rj}^{(p)}(nT)}$ is the average of P persons' reference patterns of the sensor j.

The evaluation of 18 reference patterns from the data glove is done by the F value given as,

$$F_j = \frac{V_{inter,j}}{V_{intra,j}} \tag{5}$$

As the F value is higher, the pattern from the sensor j is more valuable for writer authentication.

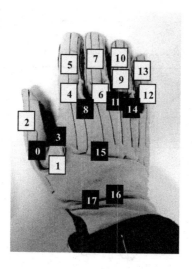

Fig. 1 Data Glove and locations of Sensors

Table 1 Name of Sensors on Data Glove in Fig.1

Sensor #	Location
0	Thumb rotation
1	Thumb inner joint
2	Thumb outer joint
3	Thumb-Index abduction
4	Index finger inner joint
5	Index finger middle joint
6	Middle finger inner joint
7	Middle finger middle joint
8	Index-Middle abduction
9	Ring finger inner joint
10	Ring finger middle joint
11	Middle-Ring abduction
12	Pinkie inner joint
13	Pinkie middle joint
14	Ring-Pinkie abduction
15	Palm arch
16	Wrist pitch (flexion/extension)
17	Wrist yaw(abduction/adduction)

(a) Signature

(b) Signals from Tablet

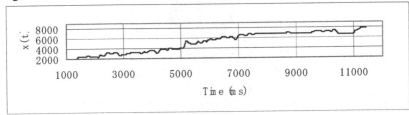

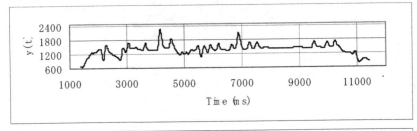

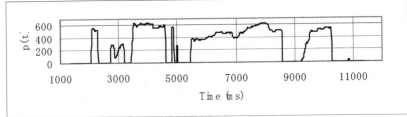

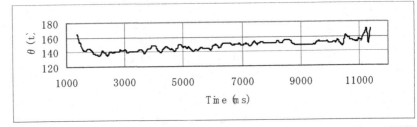

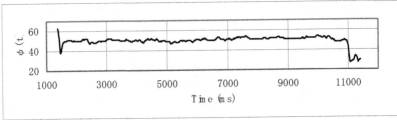

Fig. 2 An Example of Signature and Signals from the Tablet

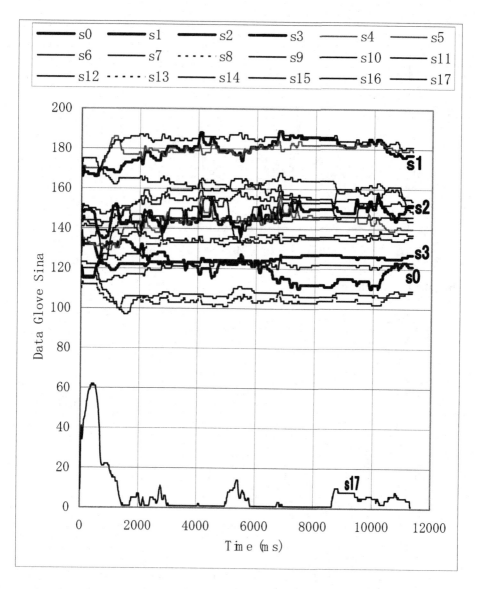

Fig.3 Signals from the Data Glove shown in Fig.1

3 Comparison of Signals from Data Glove

In order to compare the value of signals from 18 sensors of the data glove, we collect sign data by 25 writers. Each writer signs his name on the tablet with the data glove on right hand. The number of signs is eight.
(a) Before DP Matching

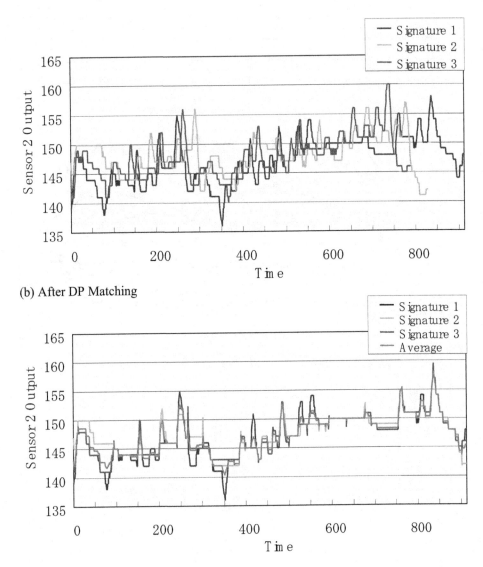

(b) After DP Matching

Fig.4 An Example of DP matching for #2 sensor output

The start and the stop of the measurement are determined by the pen pressure data obtained from the tablet a posteriori. After a writer signs eight times, DP matching is applied to the same sensor signals individually as shown in Fig.4 to create the reference pattern. The intra writer variance is calculated by this reference pattern and the time-companding signals from Eq(3). The inter writer variance is calculated by the 25 reference patterns and Eq(4).

Fig. 5 shows the relationship between F values derived from Eq.(5) and sensor number j. In the figure, the left bar is the value in case of signing in Japanese, and the right is the value in case of signing in English.

From the figure, the F value of Japanese shows higher than that of English. We think that this is caused by the experience of Japanese writers. In signing both Japanese and English, signals from sensor #1, #4, #6 and #9 show high F values. In signing Japanese, signal from sensor #12 also shows high F values. All of these sensors are located on inner joints, which are used to control pen pressure and pen inclination roughly. On the other hand, F values of signals from sensors on middle joints do not show high value. This is because the middle joints are used to control the pen accurately, and move without individuality. Joints of thumb, used for holding the pen, have some individuality.

Although we have expected that the information of wrist pitch and wrist yaw shows high individuality, no information is found in the signals from sensor #16 and #17.

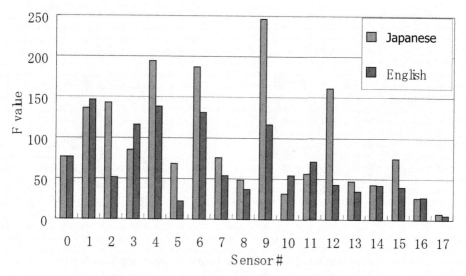

Fig. 5 The Relationship between F value and Sensor Number

4 Writer Authentication Performance

Fig. 6 shows the FAR and the FRR for the sunsors #1, #4, #6 and #9, when four samples are used to make a reference, and another four samples are used to evaluate the availability of each feature. The number of writers is 25.

From this figure, the sensor #1 corresponding to the bend-angle of thumb inner joint, shows the best result. It is expected that 90% or more identification rate is achieved only by the data from sensor #1. Also, other bend-angles of inner joints show individuality as same as F value shown in Fig.5.

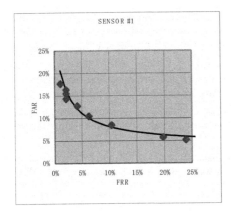

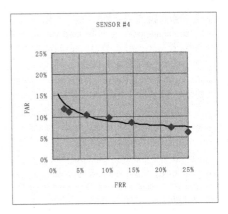

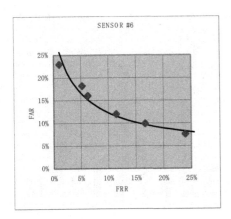

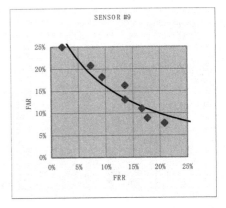

Fig. 6 FAR and FRR in Writer Identification using Data Glove

5 Discussion

From experimental results, it is cleared that the bend-angles of inner joints of fingers show high individuality in signing. Considering that the pen movement in signing is the result of individual contraction of muscles with different shape of skeletons, there is a possibility to derive more essential features suitable for writer authentication. The fact that the F values of $x(t), y(t), p(t), \theta(t), \phi(t)$ are 5.12, 1.34, 7.53, 18.73, 11.00 means the availability of the bend-angles of inner joints for writer authentication. Future studies include

    (1) Modeling the finger and its movement in signing,

    (2) Development of finger-bend measuring system,

and, we want to expand our study to the extraction of more essential features such as characteristics and shape of muscles or skeletons, control impulses to voluntary or involuntary muscles, and so on.

6 Conclusion

We have shown the individuality included in the angles of finger-bend experimentally. From signs of 25 writers, it is cleared that the angles of inner joints of thumb, index finger, middle finger and ring finger have individuality in signing. These angles affects pen inclination and pressure, which were proven to be invaluable parameters for writer authentication in the previous paper.

We hope to develop a more reliable authentication system for sign, which is preferable biometrics.

References

1. S.Hangai, S.Yamanaka and T.Hamamoto, 'On-Line Signature verification Based On Altitude and direction of Pen Movement', IEEE ICME2000, Aug. 2000.
2. S Yamanaka, T Hamamoto, S Hangai, 'Writer Verification using Altitude and Direction of Pen Movement', 15th ICPR2000, Sept. 2000.
3. Shinji Yamanaka, Masato Kawamoto, Takayuki Hamamoto, Seiichiro Hangai, 'Signature Verification Adapting to Intersession Variability', Proc. of IEEE ICME, pp.89-92, 2001
4. Masato Kawamoto, Takayuki Hamamoto, Seiichiro Hangai, 'Improvement of On-line Signature Verification System Robust to Intersession Variability', Biometric Authentication, LNCS2359, Springer, pp168-175, 2002
5. Yosuke Kato, Takayuki Hamamoto, Seiichiro Hangai ,'A Proposal of Writer Verification of Handwritten Objects', Proc. of IEEE ICME, 2002
6. http://www.immersion.com/3d/docs/cyberglove_datasheet.pdf
7. http://www.wacom.com/productinfo/9x12.cfm

3D Finger Biometrics

Damon L. Woodard and Patrick J. Flynn

Dept. of Computer Science and Engineering
University of Notre Dame, Notre Dame, IN 46556, USA
dwoodard@nd.edu, flynn@nd.edu

Abstract. This paper investigates the use of the back surface of the hand, specifically the fingers, as a biometric feature. We focus our efforts on the index, middle and ring fingers. We use segmented 3D range images of the back of the hand. At each pixel lying on one of the these fingers, the minimum and maximum curvature values are calculated and then used to compute the shape index, resulting in a shape index image of each of the three fingers. The shape index images are then compared to determine the similarity between two images. We use data sets obtained over time to analyze the stability of this feature, and examine the performance of each finger as a separate biometric feature along with the performance obtained by combining them. Our approach yields good results indicating this approach should be further researched.

1   Introduction

Much recent attention has been given to the problem of personal identification[6, 8, 9, 17]. Applications for personal identification can be found in many places in government and industry. An individual's identity is often established by a possession or knowledge of a piece of information[9]. These methods are subject to circumvention by misplacement or unauthorized sharing. This is not an issue with the use of biometrics as a means of personal identification. Biometric identifiers are based upon potentially distinctive physiological characteristics and therefore, cannot be misplaced or shared. Our research involves investigating the utility of 3D finger shape as a biometric identifier. The paper is organized as follows. The next section provides an overview of the prior related work. We follow with a description of data collection procedures and preprocessing tasks. Our experiments are then discussed. Lastly, we present our results and suggestions for future work.

2   Prior Work

Much of the related research for hand based biometrics can be categorized into two groups; hand geometry measurements and hand shape. It has been determined that the hand contains features that can be used to authenticate an individual's identity. The features include finger thickness and length, and palm thickness. These features are used in hand geometry based systems [10, 14, 16].

D. Maltoni and A.K. Jain (Eds.): BioAW 2004, LNCS 3087, pp. 238–247, 2004.
© Springer-Verlag Berlin Heidelberg 2004

Hand geometry is more widely used than hand shape. The Colombian Legislature uses a hand geometry system to confirm the identities of voting members prior to taking votes. The INS uses hand geometry based system to verify the identity of travelers at border crossings [4]. This technology is also used by many companies to keep track of employee time and attendance [9].

The wide use of hand geometry based systems can be attributed to the fact that they do not require large amounts of computational and storage resources to store feature information. Hand geometry systems seem to have the smallest template of all biometric identifiers. Additionally, the technique is simple, relatively simple to use, and inexpensive [6]. There are a number of hand geometry based commercial systems available today. Details of the algorithms used are hidden within patents [2, 5, 13, 15]. Despite this, some researchers have been successful in developing system capable of performance close to or matching that of commercial systems. One such system is the HaSIS system [16]. The system captured a total of 17 hand finger measurements from a subject. A total of 800 images, 8 images from 100 subjects were obtained for the experiment.The system achieved a false acceptance rate of 0.57% and false rejection rate of 0.86%. Another research effort involved the analysis of the various hand geometry measurements captured to determine which would have the most discriminating power [14]. The researchers also experimented with a number of comparison functions. The system was able to achieve and success rate of 97% and error rates much below 10% during verification.

The main disadvantage of the hand geometry based system is their low discriminative power. Most researchers believe that hand geometry alone is not sufficient to establish an individual's identity, making these system a bad choice for high security applications. The performance of these systems is very sensitive to the subject's hand placement. In an attempt to improve performance, rather than taking hand and finger measurements along fixed axes of the hand, researchers instead investigated using the hand's entire shape as a biometric feature.

Hand shape is not as popular as hand geometry measures but systems based on this technique have achieved comparable performance. Instead of using measurements of the hand for verification, Jain and Duta [7] used points on a hand silhouette contour as features. The authors addressed the problem of hand placement's effect on performance by first aligning the images before features are extracted. This technique eliminates the need for computation of the traditional set of features. The mean alignment error between two sets of silhouette points is used to quantify the match quality. The system was tested on a set of 353 images of 53 persons. The number of images from each person varied between 2 and 15. The system achieved a FAR of 2% and a FRR of 1.5%. The performance is comparable to commercially available hand geometry based systems. One consequence of using this approach is that the storage required to store the biometric feature is increased from the few bytes required by hand geometry measurements to an amount large enough to store a few hundred points on the hand contour.

The research performed in [12] takes a very different approach to hand shape based authentication. The image of the hand is acquired by first projecting a grating pattern over the back side of the subject's hand and capturing the image of the distorted pattern. The image is a 512×512 image which is sub-sampled into a 128×128 image. After the distorted grating image is captured, it is converted into a binarized image. Unlike hand geometry based authentication systems, this system does not use pegs to position the subject's hand for proper placement. Instead user of the system is responsible for proper hand placement during verification. The system generates a real-time view of the image to be captured and allows the user to make placement adjustments to achieve the best matching conditions. Once proper alignment is achieved, the image is converted to a binarized image. The system encodes the binarized image as a quad-tree. This approach results in a small storage requirement for the templates. The quad-tree is traversed to determine image similarity. The authors achieved a verification rate of 99.04% using 100 images. The FAR and FRR were each 0.48%.

Past research in hand biometrics does not examine the fine features of the hand's surface as a possible biometric identifier. We believe our research to be the first to do so. In the following sections, we describe the preprocessing steps involved in our experiments, provide details of experiment methods, present our results, and suggest future work.

3   Data Collection and Preprocessing

3.1   Data Collection

For data collection we used the Minolta 900/910 sensor. This scanner, produces both 640×480 range images as well as registered 640×480 color images. The scanner was positioned approximately 4 feet from a wall which was covered with a black piece of cloth. Black cloth was chosen to simplify the hand segmentation task to be performed later. The subject was instructed to place his/her hand flat against the wall with the fingers in a neutral position as the image was taken. After each image was obtained, the subject was instructed to remove his/her hand from the wall and then return it to approximately the same position. Data was collected over a period of two weeks with two images obtained the first week and three images obtained the second week this yielded five images per subject collected from 132 subjects over two weeks.

3.2   Preprocessing

Some preprocessing was required before we performed our experiments. The hand was segmented from the background of the each image. There was a pixel to pixel correspondence between intensity and range images, therefore a combination of edge and skin detection techniques was applied to the intensity image to reliably segment the hand. The RGB color space skin detection rules specified in [11] along with an implementation of a Canny edge detector made up the

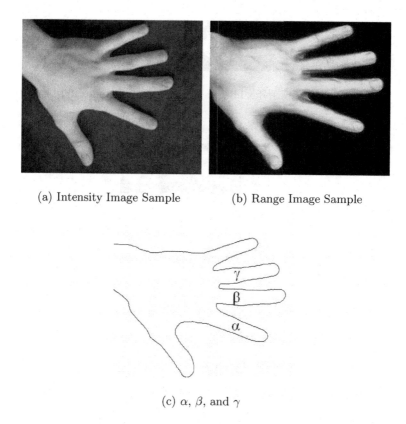

(a) Intensity Image Sample   (b) Range Image Sample

(c) α, β, and γ

Fig. 1. Sample Images and Silhouette

segmentation function. (Fig. 1(a)) shows a 640×480 color images of a hand; (fig. 1(b)) is a pseudo intensity image of the same hand rendered used the 640×480 range image.

Afterwards, the silhouette of the hand was computed. The index, middle, and ring fingers (denoted as α, β, and γ) and shown in (Fig. 1(c)), have fairly consistent placement among the subjects. The convex hull of the silhouette was then used to locate the valleys between the fingers. The valley positions were used as segment boundaries allowing for the α, β, and γ fingers to be extracted and processed individually.

A finger mask for each finger is then generated after extraction. To address finger pose variations, finger masks along with their corresponding range pixels are rotated so that the major axis of the finger mask is coincident with the horizontal axis in an output finger range image. Separate output images contain aligned data for these 3D fingers.

For each pixel of the finger mask, we calculate a surface curvature estimate at the corresponding range image pixel. The linear regression technique, summarized in Flynn and Jain [3], was employed. At each finger surface point of

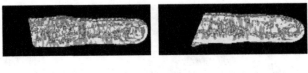

(a) α Shape Index Image   (b) β Shape Index Image

(c) γ Shape Index Image

Fig. 2. Shape Index Images

Surface Type	Interval	Color
Spherical Cup	[0, 0.125)	Gray
Trough	[0.125, 0.25)	Cyan
Rut	[0.25, 0.375)	Red
Saddle Rut	[0.375, 0.5)	Green
Saddle	[0.5, 0.625)	Blue
Saddle Ridge	[0.625, 0.75)	Orange
Ridge	[0.75, 0.875)	Yellow
Dome	[0.875, 1.0)	Violet
Spherical Cap	1.0	Magenta

Table 1. Shape Index Color Map

interest p, we obtained a set points S_p which "neighbor" it. We estimate the surface normal and two orthogonal vectors which span the tangent plane centered at p. A bi-cubic Monge Surface $z = f(x, y)$ is then fit to S_p using linear regression. From the result, we calculate the partial derivatives to obtain the principal curvature values κ_{min} and κ_{max}. These values are used to compute the *Shape Index SI* at each pixel, given by the formula:

$$SI = \frac{1}{2} - \frac{1}{\pi} \arctan \frac{(\kappa_{max} + \kappa_{min})}{(\kappa_{max} - \kappa_{min})}$$

SI is a scalar in [0,1] with values that allow shape classification. *SI* has been used successfully by Dorai and Jain [1] for free-form surface representation as well as global object recognition. We used this value to generate 80×240 pixel shape index images for each finger (Fig. 2). Table 1 presents the intervals corresponding to each surface class along with the color map used for shape index image generation. This representation is used for comparison in our experiments.

4   Experiments

A total of 660 images were collected over two weeks. During preprocessing, the three middle fingers were extracted from each image, resulting in a total of 1,980 shape index images. These images were grouped by finger type (α, β and γ) and time of collection. Images 1 and 2 of each subject were taken the first week and therefore used as galleries, whereas images 3-5 were obtained the following week and used as the probes during our experiments to analyze the effects of time on matching performance. In experiments analyzing matching performance on data collected the same day, images of each week served both as probe and gallery images. Overall, there were 14 different probe/gallery configurations; 8 same day and 6 different day.

For our first experiments, we compared a group of 132 probe shape images of the same finger type to a gallery consisting of the same type. In addition to these experiments, metric-level fusion was employed using a "max" rule (the highest finger match score is used) and "average" rule (the average match score is computed over all three fingers). The results of these experiments are discussed in the next section.

Presently, a very simple matching technique is used for the comparison of two shape index images. A correlation score is computed by the following formula:

$$SC(P,G) = \frac{1}{N} \sum_{(i,j)valid} I(P(i,j) - G(i,j))$$

where P and G are probe and gallery images with N valid mask pixels in common between them, and $I()$ is the indicator function that returns unity if its argument is zero and zero otherwise. Thus, the score is the fraction of valid shape pixels that agree in classification. During preprocessing, care was taken to align each finger image. To further ensure proper alignment, the probe images is shifted vertically by two pixels in each direction during comparison. A total of five correlation scores are actually calculated during a single comparison. The first is calculated with P and in its original position. The second and third scores calculated are calculated with with P shifted upward by one and two pixels respectively. Similarly, the fourth and fifth scores are computed with P shifted downward by one or two pixels. Horizontal shifting was also tried but did not improve results. The maximum of these five scores is returned as the match score.

5   Results

The β finger type seemed to perform slightly better on average than the α and γ finger types (Fig. 3). This can probably be explained by the fact that β images

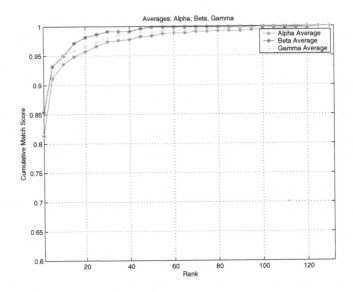

Fig. 3. α, β, γ Averages

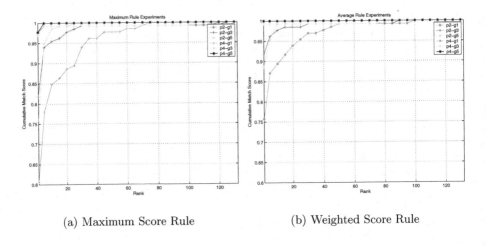

(a) Maximum Score Rule   (b) Weighted Score Rule

Fig. 4. Fusion Rule Experiments

typically have more pixel area within their finger masks than the α and γ finger types. The results is a more gradual decrease in match scores as the number of finger pixels in common between two images that are classified differently increases. (Fig. 4) depicts the result of applying our metric-level fusion rules during the experiments.

As with many other biometric features, the matching performance of experiments using data obtained on the same day is significantly higher than that

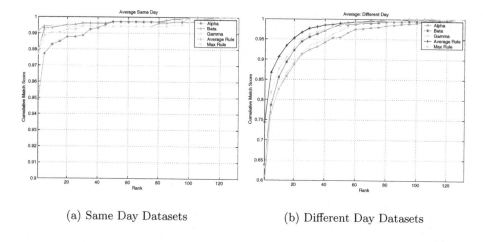

(a) Same Day Datasets   (b) Different Day Datasets

Fig. 5. Time Lapse Experiments

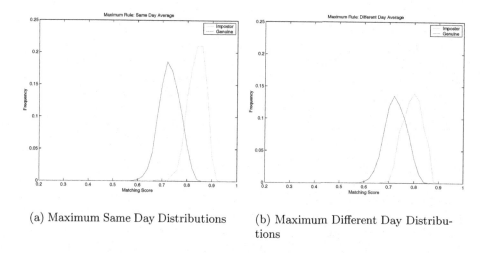

(a) Maximum Same Day Distributions   (b) Maximum Different Day Distributions

Fig. 6. Maximum Matching Score Distributions

of experiments using data obtained on different days, (Fig. 5). For the experiments using data obtained on the same day, matching probability was between 94.2% and 99.4% with the rank one score, whereas matching probability for different day experiments was between 60% and 74%. In both experiment scenarios, the weighted score technique achieved better matching performance than the maximum score rule or when using any single finger type. This performance improvement was more apparent in the different day data set experiments.

The distributions of the genuine and impostor matching scores were computed. The results were then grouped into experiments using data obtained on

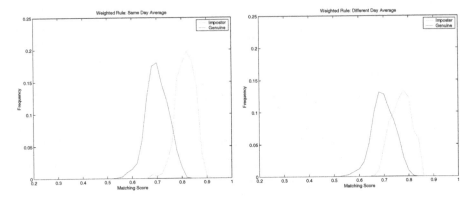

(a) Weighted Same Day Distributions   (b) Weighted Different Day Distributions

Fig. 7. Weighted Matching Score Distributions

the same day and experiments using data obtained on different days. The distributions for each group were then averaged (Fig. 6-7). For each experiment configuration, the genuine and impostor score distributions for the experiments using data obtained on the same day are better separated than those using data obtained on different days. This result was also obtained when viewing α, β, and γ separately. We believe that the separation between distributions will be much improved by using different matching rules to quantify image similarity.

6   Future Work

This paper proposes 3D hand shape (and more specifically finger shape) as a new personal identification biometric. Our results show that finger surface may be a viable biometric feature. We achieve a very high recognition rate when using data obtained on the same day. We plan to perform analysis on our current data as well as additional data in order to determine if the recognition rate can be significantly improved when using data collected over a longer time period. We also plan to experiment with additional classifiers, biometric fusion rules, and varying probe/gallery set sizes. We feel that these experiments may lead to better overall matching performance.

References

[1] Dorai, Chitra and Jain, Anil K. COSMOS-A Representation Scheme for Free-Form Surfaces. In *International Conference on Computer Vision*, pages 1024–1029, June 1995.
[2] Ernst, Richard H. Hand ID System. U.S. Patent No. 3576537, 1971.

[3] Flynn, Patrick J. and Jain, Anil K. On reliable curvature estimation. *Proc. IEEE Conf. Computer Vision and Pattern Recognition*, 89:110–116, 1989.

[4] Hays, Ronald J. INS Passenger Accelerated Service System(INSPASS). http://www.biometrics.org/REPORTS/INSPASS.html.

[5] Jacoby, Ian H, Giordano, Anthony J., and Fioretti, Warren H. Personal Identification Apparatus. U.S. Patent No. 3648240, 1972.

[6] Jain, Anil J., Hong, Lin and Pankanti, Sharath. Biometrics: Promising frontiers for emerging identification market. *Communications of the ACM*, pages 91–98, Feb. 2000.

[7] Jain, Anil K. and Duta, Nicolae. Deformable Matching Of Hand Shapes For Verification. In *Proceedings of International Conference on Image Processing*, Oct. 1999.

[8] Jain, Anil K. and Pankanti, Sharath. Anatomy of Performance. *The Institute of Electronics, Information, and Communication Engineers*, E00-A(1), Jan. 2001.

[9] Jain, Anil K., Bolle, Ruud, and Pankanti, Sharath. Introduction to Biometrics. In Jain, Anil K., Bolle, Ruud, and Pankanti, Sharath, editor, *BIOMETRICS Personal Identification in a Networked Society*, pages 1–41. Kluwer Academic Publishers, 1998.

[10] Jain, Anil K., Ross, Arun, and Pankanti, Sharath. A Prototype Hand Geometry-Based Verification System. In *Proc. of 2nd Int'l Conference on Audio- and Video-based Biometric Person Authentication(AVBPA)*, pages 166–171, Washington D.C., Mar. 1999.

[11] Kovač, Jure, Peer, Peter and Solina, Franc. Human Skin Colour Clustering for Face Detection. In Zajc, Baldomir, editor, *EUROCON 2003 - International Conference on Computer as a Tool*, Ljubljana, Slovenia, September 2003.

[12] Lay, Yun Long. Hand Shape Recognition. *Optics and Laser Technology*, 32(1):1–5, Feb 2000.

[13] Miller, Robert P. Finger Dimension Comparison Identification System. U.S. Patent No. 3576538, 1971.

[14] Sanchez-Reillo, Raul, Sanchez-Avila, Carmen, and Gonzalez-Marcos, Ana. Biometric Identification through Hand Geometry Measurements. *IEEE Transactions on Pattern Analysis and Machine Intelligence*, 22(10):1168–1171, Oct. 2000.

[15] Sidlauskas, David. 3D Hand Profile Identification Apparatus. U.S. Patent No. 4736203, 1988.

[16] University of Bologna. HaSIS: A Hand Shape Identification System. http://www.csr.unibo.it/research/biolab/hand.html.

[17] Woodward, John. Biometrics: Privacy's Foe or Friend. *Proc. of the IEEE*, 85(1), 1997.

Eye Movements in Biometrics

Paweł Kasprowski[1], Józef Ober[1,2]

[1]Institute of Computer Science, Silesian University of Technology, 44-100 Gliwice, Poland
kasprowski@polsl.pl
[2]Institute of Theoretical and Applied Informatics, Polish Academy of Science, Gliwice, Poland

Abstract. The paper presents a brand new technique of performing human identification which is based on eye movements characteristic. Using this method, the system measures human's eyes reaction for visual stimulation. The eyes of the person who is being identified follow the point on the computer screen and eye movement tracking system is used to collect information about eye movements during the experiment. The first experiments showed that it was possible to identify people by means of that method. The method scrutinized here has several significant advantages. It compiles behavioral and physiological aspects and therefore it is difficult to counterfeit and at the same time it is easy to perform. Moreover, it is possible to combine it with other camera-based techniques like iris or face recognition.

1   Introduction

Eyes are one of the most important human organs. There is a common saying that eyes are 'windows to our soul'. In fact eyes are the main 'interface' between environment and human brain. Therefore, it is not a surprise that the system which deals with human vision is physiologically and neurologically complicated.

Using eyes to perform human identification in biometric methods has a long tradition including well established iris pattern recognition algorithms [1] and retina scanning. However, as far as the authors of the paper know, there are not any researches concerning identification based on eye movement characteristic. It is a bit surprising because that method has several important advantages.

Firstly, it compiles physiological (muscles) and behavioral (brain) aspects. The most popular biometric methods like fingerprint verification or iris recognition are based mostly on physiological properties of human body. Therefore, what is needed for proper identification is only a "body" of a person who is to be identified. It makes it possible to identify an unconscious or - in some methods - even a dead person.

Moreover, physiological properties may be forged. Preparing models of a finger or even retina (using special holograms) is technically possible. As eye movement based identification uses information which is produced mostly by brain (so far impossible to be imitated), forging this kind of information seems to be much more difficult.

Although it has not been studied in the present paper, it seems possible to perform a covert identification, i.e. identification of a person unaware of that process (for instance using hidden cameras).

D. Maltoni and A.K. Jain (Eds.): BioAW 2004, LNCS 3087, pp. 248-258, 2004.

Last but not least, there are many easy to use eye tracking devices nowadays, so performing identification by means of that technique is not very expensive. For instance a very fast and accurate OBER2 [2] eye tracking system was used in the present work. It measures eye movements with a very high precision using infrared reflection and the production costs are comparable to fingerprint scanners.

2 Physiology of Eye Movements

When individual looks at an object, the image of the object is projected on to the retina, which is composed of light-sensitive cells that convert light into signals which in turn can be transmitted to brain via the optic nerve. The density (or distribution) of this light-sensitive cells on retina is uneven, with denser clustering at the centre of the retina rather than at the periphery. Such clustering causes the acuity of vision to vary, with the most detailed vision available when the object of interest falls on the centre of the retina. This area is called yellow dot or fovea and covers about two degrees of visual angle. Outside this region visual acuity rapidly decreases. Eye movements are made to reorient the eye so that the object of interest falls upon the fovea and the highest level of detail can be extracted [3].

That is why it is possible to define a 'gaze point' – an exact point a person is looking at in a given moment of time. When eyes are looking at something for a period of time this state of the eye is called a fixation. During that time the image which is projected on the fovea is analyzed by the brain. The standard fixation lasts for about 200-300 ms, but of course it depends on the complexity of an image which is observed. After the fixation, eyes move rapidly to another gaze point – another fixation. This rapid movement is termed a saccade. Saccades differ in longitude, yet always are very fast.

To enable brain to acquire image in real time, the system which controls eye movements (termed oculomotor system) has to be very fast and accurate. It is built of six extraocular muscles which act as three agonist/antagonist pairs. Eyes are controlled directly by the brain and its movements are the fastest reactions for changing environment.

3 Previous Researches Concerning Eye Movements

Eye movements are essential to visual perception [4], so it is not a surprise that there are a lot of researches on our vision. Most of them are concerned with neurobiological and psychological aspects of vision.

One of the first scientists who emphasized the importance of eye movements in vision and perception was Descartes (1596-1650). First known researches were made by French ophthalmologist, Emile Javal in 1879 [5]. He discovered that eyes move in a series of jumps (saccades) and pauses (fixations). His research was based only on his direct observation of eyes, so it could not be fully reliable. First eye-tracker was developed by Edmund Burke Huey in 1897. The way in which people read text was the first area of interest. It turned out – contrary to common point of view in those times – that people read more than one letter simultaneously. They read whole words or even whole phrases. The nature of reading ability was examined and the results were published in a comprehensive form in 1908 [6].

Other area of interest was how the brain processed images. It turned out that placements and order of fixations were strictly dependent on the kind of picture that was seen and on previous individual experience with that kind of pictures. The brain was believed to be attracted by the most important elements of the picture, and, after examining them, to focus on less important details. The acquired knowledge on the way the brain was processing information was used mostly in psychological research [7].

Another evolving field where eye trackers are used is research called *usability engineering* – the study of the way that users are interacting with products to improve those products' design. Among the most popular nowadays is the study of the usability of WWW pages [3][8][9].

Although there has not been any research of using eye movements to perform human identification, some authors noticed significant differences between people. Josephson and Holmes [8] tested the scanpath theory introduced by Stark and Norton [10] on three different WWW pages. They not only confirmed that individual learnt scanpaths (series of fixations) and repeated it when exposed on the same stimulation again, but they also noticed that each examined person learned a different scanpath.

Hornof and Halverson [11] tried to implement methods for automatic calibration of eye tracker. What is worth mentioning, they noticed that calibration errors were different for different persons and created the so-called 'error signatures' for each person being examined.

There are a lot of studies comparing the eye-movements of different categories of people, for instance males and females [9] or musicians and non-musicians [12].

4   Human Identification with Eye Movements' Information

4.1   How to Perform the Experiment

As was described in the previous section, eye movements may give a lot of information about an individual. The simplest way to obtain a probe seems to be just recording eye movements of a person for a predefined time. The method is very simple to conduct even without any cooperation from a person being identified. In fact the person may not even be aware of being identified, which gives opportunity for the so-called 'covert' identification. The main drawback of that method is the obvious fact that eye movements are strongly correlated with the image they are looking at. The movements would be quite different for a person looking at quickly changing environment (for instance a sport event or an action movie) than for a person looking simply at white solid wall. Of course one may say that human identification should be independent of visual stimulation. Indeed, theoretically it should be possible to extract identification patterns from every eye movement without knowledge of the character of stimulation. However, that kind of extraction seems to be very difficult and requires a lot of more comprehensive study and experiments.

On the basis of the described problems a simple upgrade of the system could add a module which registers the image which is the 'reason' of eyes' movements. In that kind of model we have a dynamic system for which we are registering input and the system's answer for that input.

Such improvement gives a lot more data to analyze, yet it also has several serious drawbacks. First of all, the hardware system is much more complicated. We need additional camera recorder which registers the image the examined person is looking at. Furthermore, we need to implement special algorithms to synchronize visual data with eye movement signal. A lot more capacity is also needed for data storing.

We must additionally be aware that camera 'sees' the world differently than a human eye, thus the image we register cannot be considered completely equivalent to eyes' input.

To be useful in biometric identification, a single experiment must be as short as possible. With no influence on stimulation we cannot be sure that in the short time of experiment we can register enough interesting information about a person being identified. Therefore, the natural consequence of that fact is introducing our own stimulation. That solution gives us opportunity for avoiding image registering, because when stimulation is known, registration is not necessary.

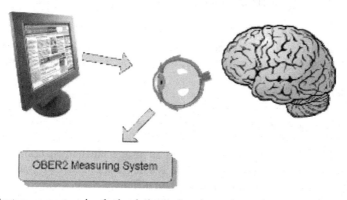

Fig. 1. System generates visual stimulation and registers the oculomotor system reaction.

The most convenient source of visual stimulation is a computer display. However, as in the previous methods, we should be aware of the fact that the monitor screen is only a part of the image that eyes see, so not the whole input is measured. Furthermore, the input may consist of non-visual signals. Sudden loud sounds may, for instance, cause rapid eye movements [13]. Nevertheless, that kind of experiment seems to be the simplest to realize.

4.2 Choosing Stimulation

The problem which emerges here is 'what should stimulation be?'
One may consider different types of stimulation for the experiment. The type of stimulation implies what aspect of eye movements is measured.

The simplest one could be just a static image. As has been already stated, eyes are moving constantly, even looking at the static image, to register every important element of image with fovea region fixation. According to Stark and Norton [n03] brain is creating a 'scanpath' of eye movements for each seen image.

The more sophisticated stimulation could be a dynamic one – like a movie or animation displayed on the screen. There may be different aspects of stimulation considered: color, intensity, speed, etc.

The problem with using eye movements in biometrics is that the same experiment will be performed on the same person a number of times. Firstly, there should be several experiments performed to enroll user characteristic. Then, the experiment is performed each time an individual wants to identify himself. It may be supposed that if the same stimulation is used each time, a person would be bored with it and eye movements would not be very interesting. The problem may be called a 'learning effect' as the brain learns the stimulation and acts differently after several repetitions of the same image.

The solution could be presenting different stimulation each time. The different types of stimulation should be as similar as possible to enable extraction of the same eye movements parameters for future analyses. On the other hand, they should be so different that a learning effect would be eliminated. The task is therefore not an easy one.

To be sure that an examined person cooperates with the system (e.g. they move their eyes) a special kind of stimulation called 'visual task' may be proposed. The visual task may be for instance finding a matching picture [11] or finding missing elements on a known picture [14],

A special kind of visual task could be a text reading task. In such an experiment a person just reads the text appearing on the screen. There are a lot of studies concerning eye movement tracking while reading a text and they give very interesting results [15][16]. Especially there are some theoretical models of human eyes movements like SWIFT [16]. After years of usage the human brain is very well prepared to control eye movements while reading a text and each human being has slightly different customs and habits based on different 'reading experience'.

Therefore, it may be assumed that by analyzing the way a person reads a specially prepared text a lot of interesting information may be extracted. And indeed there are a lot of researches concerning that subject [15][16][7].

Yet, when applying that to identification system, the problem of the learning effect appears once again. We may for instance notice that a person has a lot of problems with reading the word 'oculomotor'. However, presenting that word during each experiment causes that person's brain gets familiar with the word and that effect disappears.

Thus, the learning effect makes it impossible to repeat the same experiment and to get the same results. In other words, the experiment is not stationary for a number of trials. Each experiment performed on the same person is different, because previous experiments have changed the brain parameters. Of course that effect is clearly visible only when a lot of experiments are conducted on the same person .

It is a serious problem because, contrary to other eye movements experiments, the main attribute of identification system should be its repeatability for the same person. The experiment must be performed a lot of times giving the same results. A learning effect makes it very difficult.

A solution of that problem may be a stimulation which imposes on a person a spot the eyes should look at. The simplest form of that stimulation may be a 'wandering point' stimulation. It that kind of stimulation the screen is blank with only one point 'wandering' through it. The task of examined person is to follow the point with the eyes.

It is easier to analyze results of that kind of stimulation. That time we are not interested in examining *where* the person is looking but in examining *how* they look at the point. We may suppose that all results will be more or less similar to one another and our task is to extract the differences among people.

The main drawback of the method, however, is that it completely ignores the will of the person. The person cannot decide where to look at the moment and therefore we are loosing all information from brain's 'decision centre'. We may say that that kind of stimulation examines more the oculomotor system than the brain.

However, using it we can overcome the learning effect. Obviously it still exists, but in that experiment it may become our ally. A person who looks at the same stimulation a lot of times gets used to it and the results of the following experiments are converging to the same point.

Having that in mind we can suppose that, after a specific number of experiments, next probes will be very similar and therefore easier to identify. It is exactly the same effect as for the written signature:

A person is asked to write a word on the paper. It may be their surname for instance. The word on the paper looks typical for their handwriting style and it is possible for a specialist to identify them. Yet, when they are asked to write the same word over and over again, they get used to it and the brain produces the kind of automatic schema for performing that task. At this moment the handwritten word looks very similar every time and that is what we call a signature. Contrary to handwriting, the signature may be recognized even by an unqualified person – for instance a shop assistant.

We would like to use the same effect with the eye movements. First, we show a person the same stimulation several (as many as possible) times. After that process, the person's brain produces an automatic schema and results of the following experiments will start to converge. It, of course, makes the process of recognition (identification) easier – remember a handwriting specialist versus a shop assistant.

5   Experiment

The stimulation which has been eventually chosen was a 'jumping point' kind of stimulation. There are nine different point placements defined on the screen, one in the middle and eight on the edges, creating 3 x 3 matrix. The point flashes in one placement in a given moment. The stimulation begins and ends with a point in the middle of the screen. During the stimulation, point's placement changes in specified intervals.

That kind of stimulation has the advantage over others (especially 'wandering point') that it is very easy to perform even without a display. In fact, there are only nine sources of light needed (for instance just simple diodes).

The main problem in developing stimulation is to make it short and informative. Those properties are as if on two opposite poles, so a 'golden mean' must be found. We assumed that gathering one probe could not last longer than 10 seconds. To be informative it should consist of as many point position changes as possible. However, moving a point too quickly makes it impossible for eyes to follow it. Our experiments confirmed that the reaction time for change of stimulation is about 100-200 ms [14]. After that time eyes start a saccade which moves fovea to the new gaze point. The saccade is very fast and lasts not longer than 10-20 ms. After a saccade, the brain analyses a new position of the eyes and, if necessary, tries to correct it. So very often about 50 ms after the first saccade the next saccade happens. We can call it a 'calibration' saccade.

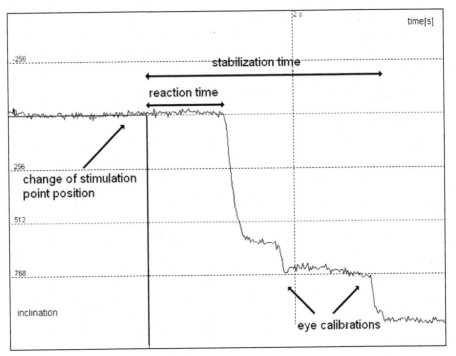

Fig. 2. Typical eye movement reaction for point jump in one axis. Reaction time is understood as the period of time between stimulation's change and eye reaction. Stabilization time is the time until fixation on a new gaze-point. Two calibration saccades may be observed.

5.1 Feature Extraction

After collecting data the main problem is how to extract information which is useful for human identification.

The dataset consists of probes. Each probe is the result of recording of one person's eye movements during about 8 seconds-lasting stimulation. As the experiments were made with frequency 250Hz the probe consists of 2048 single measurements. Each measurement consists of six integer values which are giving the position of a stimulation point on the screen (sx, sy), the position of the point the left eye is looking at (lx, ly) and the position of the point the right eye is looking at (rx, ry).

So in each experiment we are collecting a probe of 2048 x 6 = 12288 integer values.

The next step is to convert those values into a set of features. Each feature gives some information about a person who made that experiment. That information may be understandable – for instance "he is a male" or "his reaction time is less than 200 ms", but the meaning of the feature may be hidden also, giving only the value.

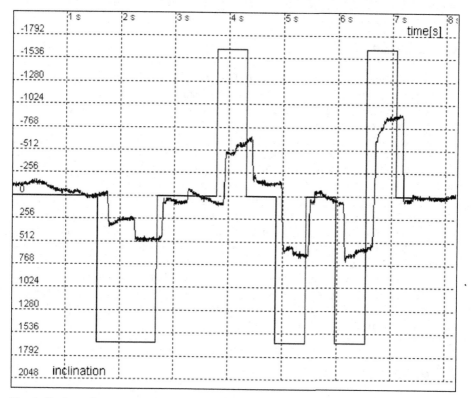

Fig. 3. Registered eye movements of left eye in horizontal axis as the answer to stimulation. Reaction times and drifts may be observed. One experiment gives four such waveforms.

The main problem is how to extract a set of features that have values for different probes of the same person as similar as possible and that have values for different person's probes as different as possible. The perfect solution would be finding features which have exactly the same values for the same person in every experiment.

As it was mentioned earlier, identification based on eye movement analysis is a brand new technique. The main disadvantage of that technique is that one cannot use recently published algorithms and just try to improve it with one's own ideas. Therefore, we could only try to use methods which have been successfully used with similar problems.

There are many different possibilities, for instance Karhunen-Loeve transform (popular PCA) [17], Fourier transform, cepstrum [21] or wavelets. Each of those techniques has been successfully used in different biometric applications like face, finger, voice or iris recognition. What may also be considered are features specific for the nature of the eye movement signal: average reaction time, average stabilization time, saccade velocity and acceleration etc..

It seems that each method may work as good as others. Therefore, a lot of work has to be done to compare those techniques. Cepstrum was used in the present work because of its success in voice recognition. The cepstrum is counted as the inverse Fourier transform of the logarithm of the power spectrum of a signal [21].

5.2 Classification

Having extracted features that are hopefully relevant to identification, the next step is to prepare a classification model. When we obtain the next unclassified probe, it would be possible, using that model, to estimate probability that the specific probe belongs to a specified person.

There are a lot of classification algorithms which can be used here. Their main property is creating a model based on information obtained from training data – a set of classified probes. Algorithms try to generalize rules that were found in the training set and to prepare a function which could be used to classify future probes.

Of course that generalization depends not only on the algorithm itself, but mostly on characteristic of a training data. Only if the training set is representative of the whole population and there are some (even hidden) rules in its features that could be helpful, classifying algorithm may work well. Therefore, proper feature extraction is the crucial element of that work.

There were four different classifying algorithms used in the present paper. Namely, k-Nearest Neighbor (for k=3 and k=7), Naïve Bayes [20], C4.5 Decision Tree [18] and Support Vector Machines [19]. Due to the lack of space for description of the algorithms, the reader directed to the referred materials.

6   Results

The experiment was performed on nine participants. Each participant was enrolled over 30 times and last 30 trials were used for classification, giving 270 probes for a training set.

First 15 cepstral coefficients were extracted from each of four waveforms. That gave 60 dimensional vectors for each probe. Then, nine training sets were generated – each for classifying one participant. One classifying model was generated from each set using different classification algorithms.

Each classification model was cross-validated using 10 fold stratified cross validation [20]. K-Nearest Neighbor algorithm with k=3 performed best with the average false acceptance rate 1.48 % with the best result 0.4 % and the worst result 2.5 % and false rejection rate in range of 6.7 % to 43.3 % with average 22.59 %.

Table 1. Results of data validation for different classification algorithms. Averages of false acceptance and false rejection rates (FAR and FRR) are counted from nine generated models

Algorithm	Average FAR	Average FRR
Naïve Bayes	17.49 %	12.59 %
C45 Decision Tree	3.33 %	35.56 %
SVM polynomial	1.60 %	28.89 %
KNN k=3	1.48 %	22.59 %
KNN k=7	1.36 %	28.89 %

7 Conclusion

The idea of personal identification using eye movement characteristic presented in the paper seems to be valuable addition to other well known biometric techniques. What makes it interesting is the easiness of combining it with, for instance, face or iris recognition. As all of those techniques need digital cameras to collect data, the system that uses the same recording devices to gather information about human face shape, eye iris pattern and – last but not least – eye movements characteristic may be developed. Of course there is a lot of work to be done to improve and test our methodology, but first experiments show the great potential of eye movements identification. That potential was acknowledged during 6th World Conference BIOMETRICS'2003 in London where a poster 'Eye movement tracking for human identification' [22] was awarded the title of 'Best Poster on Technological Advancement' and that encourages future effort.

References

1. Daugman, J.G.: High Confidence Visual Recognition of Persons by a Test of Statistical Independence, IEEE Transactions on Pattern Analysis and Machine Intelligence, vol. 15, no. 11 (1993) 1148-1160.
2. Ober, J., Hajda, J., Loska, J., Jamnicki, M.: Application of Eye Movement Measuring System OBER2 to Medicine and Technology. Proceedings of SPIE, Infrared Technology and applications, Orlando, USA, 3061(1) (1997)
3. Cowen, L., Ball, L.J., Delin, J.: An eye-movement analysis of web-page usability. Chapter in X. Faulkner, J. Finlay, & F. Détienne (Eds.): People and Computers XVI—Memorable Yet Invisible: Proceedings of HCI 2002. Springer-Verlag Ltd, London (2002)
4. Mast F.W. Kosslyn S.M. Eye movements during visual mental imagery. TRENDS in Cognitive Sciences Vol.6 No.7 (2002)
5. Javal, É.: Physiologie de la lecture et de l'écriture. Paris: Félix Alcan (1905)
6. Huey, E.B.: The Psychology and Pedagogy of Reading. With a Review of the History of Reading and Writing and of Methods, Texts, and Hygiene in Reading. New York: Macmillan (1908)
7. Duchowski, A. T.: A Breadth-First Survey of Eye Tracking Applications. Behavior Research Methods, Instruments & Computers (BRMIC), 34(4) (2002) 455-470

8. Josephson, S., Holmes, M. E.: Visual Attention to Repeated Internet Images: Testing the Scanpath Theory on the World Wide Web., Proceedings of the Eye Tracking Research & Application Symposium 2002.New Orleans, Louisiana (2002) 43-49

9. Schiessl, M., Duda, S., Thölke, A. & Fischer R.: Eye tracking and its application in usability and media research. MMI-Interaktiv, No.6, (2003) 41-50

10. Noton, D., Stark, L. W.: Scanpaths in eye movements during pattern perception. Science, 171 (1971) 308-311

11. Hornof, A. J., Halverson, T.: Cleaning up systematic error in eye tracking data by using required fixation locations. Behavior Research Methods, Instruments, and Computers, 34(4) (2002) 592-604

12. Kopiez, R., Galley, N.: The Musicians' Glance: A Pilot Study Comparing Eye Movement Parameters In Musicians And Non-Musicians. Proceedings of the 7th International Conference on Music Perception and Cognition, Sydney (2002)

13. Vatikiotis-Bateson, E., Eigsti, I.M., Yano, S., Munhall, K. Eye movement of perceivers during audiovisual speech perception. Perception and Psychophysics, 60(6), (1998) 926-940

14. Henderson, J. M., Hollingworth, A.: Eye Movements and Visual Memory: Detecting Changes to Saccade Targets in Scenes. Michigan State University, Visual Cognition Lab, Rye Lab Technical Report Tech Report No. 2001, 3 (2001)

15. Campbell, C. S., Maglio, P. P.: A robust algorithm for reading detection. Proceedings of the ACM Workshop on Perceptual User Interfaces (2002)

16. Engbert, R., Longtin, A., Kliegl, R. Complexity of eye movements in reading. International Journal of Bifurcation and Chaos (in press)

17. Loève M. M., Probability Theory, Princeton, NJ: Van Nostrand, (1955)

18. Quinlan, J. R.: C4.5: Programs for Machine Learning. San Mateo: Morgan Kaufmann (1993)

19. Cortes, C., Vapnik, V.: Support Vector Networks. Machine Learning, 20, (1995)

20. Witten, I. H., Frank, E.: Data Mining: Practical Machine Learning Tools and Techniques with Java Implementations. Morgan Kaufmann (1999)

21. Rabiner, L. R., Schafer, R. W.: Digital Processing of Speech Signals, Prentice Hall, Englewood Cliffs, NJ (1978)

22. Kasprowski, P., Ober, J. Eye movement tracking for human identification. 6th World Conference BIOMETRICS'2003, London (2003)

Integrating Faces, Fingerprints, and Soft Biometric Traits for User Recognition

Anil K. Jain, Karthik Nandakumar, Xiaoguang Lu, and Unsang Park

Department of Computer Science and Engineering
Michigan State University, MI - 48824, USA
{jain,nandakum,lvxiaogu,parkunsa}@cse.msu.edu

Abstract. Soft biometric traits like gender, age, height, weight, ethnicity, and eye color cannot provide reliable user recognition because they are not distinctive and permanent. However, such ancillary information can complement the identity information provided by the primary biometric traits (face, fingerprint, hand-geometry, iris, etc.). This paper describes a hybrid biometric system that uses face and fingerprint as the primary characteristics and gender, ethnicity, and height as the soft characteristics. We have studied the effect of the soft biometric traits on the recognition performance of unimodal face and fingerprint recognition systems and a multimodal system that uses both the primary traits. Experiments conducted on a database of 263 users show that the recognition performance of the primary biometric system can be improved significantly by making use of soft biometric information. The results also indicate that such a performance improvement can be achieved only if the soft biometric traits are complementary to the primary biometric traits.

1 Introduction

Biometric systems recognize users based on their physiological and behavioral characteristics [1]. Unimodal biometric systems make use of a single biometric trait for user recognition. It is difficult to achieve very high recognition rates using unimodal systems due to problems like noisy sensor data and non-universality and/or lack of distinctiveness of the chosen biometric trait. Multimodal biometric systems address some of these problems by combining evidence obtained from multiple sources [2]. A multimodal biometric system that utilizes a number of different biometric identifiers like face, fingerprint, hand-geometry, and iris can be more robust to noise and alleviate the problem of non-universality and lack of distinctiveness. Hence, such a system can achieve a higher recognition accuracy than unimodal systems. However, a multimodal system will require a longer verification time thereby causing inconvenience to the users.

It is possible to improve the recognition performance of a biometric system without compromising on user-friendliness by utilizing ancillary information about the user like height, weight, age, gender, ethnicity, and eye color. We refer to these traits as soft biometric traits because they provide some information about the individual, but lack the distinctiveness and permanence to sufficiently differentiate any two individuals (see Figure 1 for examples of soft biometric traits). The soft biometric traits can either be continuous or discrete. Traits such as gender, eye color, and ethnicity are discrete

D. Maltoni and A.K. Jain (Eds.): BioAW 2004, LNCS 3087, pp. 259–269, 2004.
© Springer-Verlag Berlin Heidelberg 2004

in nature. On the other hand, traits like height and weight are continuous variables. Heckathorn et al. [3] have shown that a combination of soft attributes like gender, race, eye color, height, and other visible marks like scars and tattoos can be used to identify an individual only with a limited accuracy. Hence, the ancillary information by itself is not sufficient to recognize a user. However, soft biometric traits can complement the traditional (primary) biometric identifiers like fingerprint and hand-geometry and hence improve the performance of the primary biometric system.

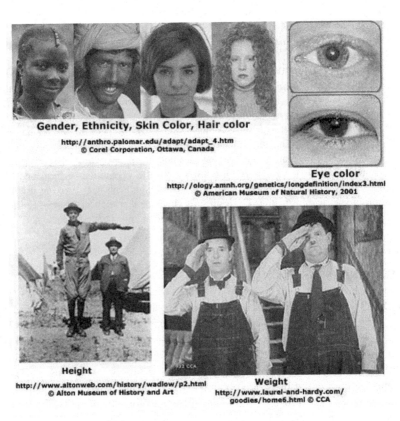

Fig. 1. Examples of soft biometric traits.

In order to utilize soft biometrics, there must be a mechanism to automatically extract these features from the user during the recognition phase. As the user interacts with the primary biometric system, the system should be able to automatically extract the soft biometric characteristics like height, weight, age, gender, and ethnicity in a non-obtrusive manner without any interaction with the user. In section 2 we present some of the methods that could be used for automatic extraction of the soft biometric information. Section 3 describes our framework for the integration of soft biometrics with the primary biometric system. The objective of this work is to analyze the impact of introducing soft biometric variables like gender, ethnicity, and height into the decision making process of a recognition system that uses faces and fingerprints as the primary biometric traits. The experimental results presented in section 4 give an insight on the effects of different soft biometric variables on the recognition performance.

2   Automatic Extraction of Soft Biometric Characteristics

Soft biometric characteristics like gender, ethnicity, and age could be derived from the facial image of the user. Several studies have attempted to identify the gender, ethnicity, and pose of the users from their facial images. Gutta et al. [4] proposed a mixture of experts consisting of ensembles of radial basis functions for the classification of gender, ethnic origin, and pose of human faces. They also used a SVM classifier with RBF kernel for gating the inputs. Their gender classifier classified users as either male or female with an average accuracy rate of 96%, while their ethnicity classifier classified users into Caucasian, South Asian, East Asian, and African with an accuracy of 92%. These results were reported on good quality face images from the FERET database that had very little expression or pose changes. Based on the same database, Moghaddam and Yang [5] showed that the error rate for gender classification can be reduced to 3.4% by using an appearance-based gender classifier that uses non-linear support vector machines. Shakhnarovich et al. [6] developed a demographic classification scheme that extracts faces from unconstrained video sequences and classifies them based on gender and ethnicity. Their demographic classifier was a Perceptron constructed from binary rectangle features. The learning and feature selection modules used a variant of the AdaBoost algorithm. Their ethnicity classifier classified users as either Asian or non-Asian. Even under unconstrained environments, they showed that a classification accuracy of more than 75% can be achieved for both gender and ethnicity classification. For this data, the SVM classifier of Moghaddam and Yang had an error rate of 24.5% and there was also a notable bias towards males in the classification (females had an error rate of 28%). Balci and Atalay [7] reported a classification accuracy of more than 86% for a gender classifier that uses PCA for feature extraction and Multi-Layer Perceptron for classification. Jain and Lu [8] proposed a Linear Discriminant Analysis (LDA) based scheme to address the problem of ethnicity identification from facial images. The users were identified as either Asian or non-Asian by applying multiscale analysis to the input facial images. An ensemble framework based on the product rule was used for integrating the LDA analysis at different scales. This scheme had an accuracy of 96.3% on a database of 263 users (with approximately equal number of users from the two classes).

Automatic age determination is a more difficult problem due to the very limited physiological or behavioral changes in the human body as the person grows from one age group to another. There are currently no reliable biometric indicators for age determination [9]. Buchanan et al. [10] have been studying the differences in the chemical composition of child and adult fingerprints that could be used to distinguish children from adults. Kwon and Lobo [11] present an algorithm for age classification from facial images based on cranio-facial changes in feature-position ratios and skin wrinkle analysis. They attempted to classify users as "babies", "young adults", or "senior adults". However, they do not provide any accuracy estimates for their classification scheme.

One can hope that age determination systems providing a reasonable estimate of the age of a person would be available in the near future.

The weight of a user can be measured by installing a weight sensor at the place where the users stand while providing the primary biometric. The height can be estimated from a sequence of real-time images obtained when the user moves into the view of the camera. Figure 2 describes a mechanism for simultaneous extraction of the height information and the facial image of a user. In this setup we assume that the position of the camera and the background scene are fixed. The background image (Figure 2(a)) is initially stored in the system. Two markers are placed in the background for calibration. The first marker is placed at a height H_{low} above the ground and the second marker is placed at a distance H_{ref} above the first marker. The vertical distance between the two markers in the background image is measured as D_{ref}. In our experiments, $H_{low} = 150\ cm$, $H_{ref} = 30\ cm$, and $D_{ref} = 67\ pixels$. The background image is subtracted from the current frame (Figure 2(b)) to obtain the difference image (Figure 2(c)). A threshold is applied to the difference image to detect only those pixels having large intensity changes. Median filtering is applied to remove the salt and pepper noise in the difference image. The background subtraction is usually performed in color domain [12]. However, for the sake of simplicity in deciding the threshold value and in the median filtering operation, we performed the subtraction in the gray-scale domain. The difference image is scanned from the top to detect the top of the head and the vertical distance between the top of the head and the lowermost marker is measured as D_{user} (in pixels). An estimate of the true height of the person (H_{user} in cm) is computed as:

$$H_{user} = H_{low} + \frac{D_{user}}{D_{ref}} H_{ref}. \tag{1}$$

After the estimation of the height, the face of the user is detected in the captured frame using the algorithm proposed by Hsu et al. [13]. After the detection of the facial region in the frame (Figure 2(d)), the face is cropped out of the frame and is used by the face recognition and gender/ethnicity extraction modules. Since, we have not collected sufficient data using this extraction process, we used an off-line face database in our experiments.

3   Framework for Integration of Soft Biometrics

We use the same framework proposed in [14] for integrating the soft biometric information with the primary biometric system. In this framework, the biometric recognition system is divided into two subsystems. One subsystem is called the primary biometric system and it is based on traditional biometric identifiers like fingerprint, face and hand-geometry. The primary biometric system could be either unimodal or multimodal. The second subsystem, referred to as the secondary biometric system, is based on soft biometric traits like age, gender, and height. Figure 3 shows the architecture of a personal identification system that makes use of fingerprint, face and soft biometric measurements. Let $\omega_1, \omega_2, \cdots, \omega_n$ represent the n users enrolled in the database. Let $\mathbf{x}$ be the feature vector corresponding to the primary biometric. Without loss of generality, let us assume that the output of the primary biometric system is of the form

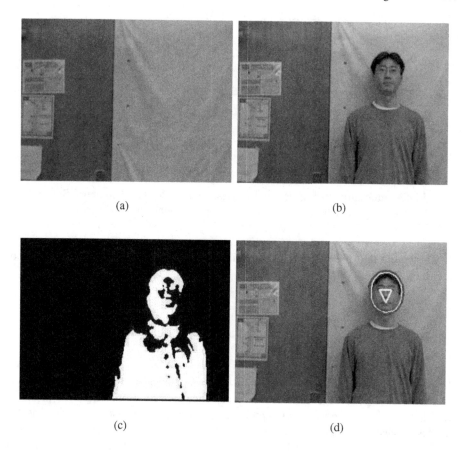

(a)   (b)

(c)   (d)

Fig. 2. Extraction of height and facial image from the user (a) background image (b) Current frame (c) Difference Image (d) Location of the face in the current frame.

$P(\omega_i \mid \mathbf{x})$, $i = 1, 2, \cdots, n$, where $P(\omega_i \mid \mathbf{x})$ is the probability that the test user is ω_i given the feature vector $\mathbf{x}$. If the output of the primary biometric system is a matching score, it is converted into posteriori probability using an appropriate transformation. For the secondary biometric system, we can consider $P(\omega_i \mid \mathbf{x})$ as the prior probability of the test user being user ω_i.

Let $\mathbf{y} = [y_1, y_2, \cdots, y_k, y_{k+1}, y_{k+2}, \cdots, y_m]$ be the soft biometric feature vector, where y_1 through y_k are continuous variables and y_{k+1} through y_m are discrete variables. The updated probability of user ω_i, given the primary biometric feature vector $\mathbf{x}$ and the soft biometric feature vector $\mathbf{y}$ i.e., $P(\omega_i \mid \mathbf{x}, \mathbf{y})$ can be calculated using the Bayes' rule.

$$P(\omega_i | \mathbf{x}, \mathbf{y}) = \frac{p(\mathbf{y}|\omega_i) \, P(\omega_i|\mathbf{x})}{\sum_{i=1}^{n} p(\mathbf{y}|\omega_i) \, P(\omega_i|\mathbf{x})} . \qquad (2)$$

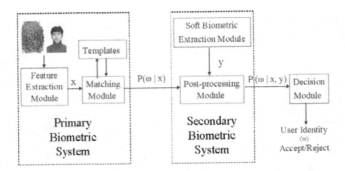

Fig. 3. Integration of Soft Biometric Traits with a Primary Biometric System
(x is the fingerprint feature vector, y is the soft biometric feature vector).

If we assume that the soft biometric variables are independent, equation (2) can be rewritten as

$$P(\omega_i|\mathbf{x}, \mathbf{y}) = \frac{p(y_1|\omega_i) \cdots p(y_k|\omega_i) P(y_{k+1}|\omega_i) \cdots P(y_m|\omega_i) P(\omega_i|\mathbf{x})}{\sum_{i=1}^{n} p(y_1|\omega_i) \cdots p(y_k|\omega_i) P(y_{k+1}|\omega_i) \cdots P(y_m|\omega_i) P(\omega_i|\mathbf{x})}.$$

(3)

In equation (3), $p(y_j|\omega_i)$, $j = 1, 2, \cdots, k$ is evaluated from the conditional density of the variable y_j for user ω_i. On the other hand, discrete probability $P(y_j|\omega_i), j = k + 1, k + 2, \cdots, m$ represents the probability that user ω_i is assigned to the class y_j. This is a measure of the accuracy of the classification module in assigning user ω_i to one of the distinct classes based on biometric indicator y_j. In order to simplify the problem, let us assume that the classification module performs equally well on all the users and therefore the accuracy of the module is independent of the user.
Let

$$p(\mathbf{y}) = \sum_{i=1}^{n} p(y_1|\omega_i) \cdots p(y_k|\omega_i) P(y_{k+1}|\omega_i) \cdots P(y_m|\omega_i) P(\omega_i|\mathbf{x}).$$

The logarithm of $P(\omega_i|\mathbf{x}, \mathbf{y})$ in equation (3) can be expressed as

$$\log P(\omega_i|\mathbf{x}, \mathbf{y}) = \log p(y_1|\omega_i) + \cdots + \log p(y_k|\omega_i) + \log P(y_{k+1}|\omega_i) + \cdots$$

$$+ \log P(y_m|\omega_i) + \log P(\omega_i|\mathbf{x}) - \log p(\mathbf{y}).$$

(4)

This formulation has two main drawbacks. The first problem is that all the m soft biometric variables have been weighed equally. In practice, some variables may contain more information than the others. For example, the gender of a person may give more information about a person than height. Therefore, we must introduce a weighting scheme for the soft biometric traits based on an index of distinctiveness and permanence; i.e., traits that have smaller variability and larger distinguishing capability will be given more weight in the computation of the final matching probabilities. Another potential pitfall is that any impostor can easily spoof the system because the soft characteristics have an equal say in the decision as the primary biometric trait. It is relatively easy to modify/hide one's soft biometric attributes by applying cosmetics and wearing other accessories (like mask, shoes with high heels, etc.). To avoid this problem, we assign smaller weights to the soft biometric traits compared to those assigned to the primary biometric traits. This differential weighting also has another implicit advantage. Even if a soft biometric trait of a user is measured incorrectly (e.g., a male user is identified as a female), there is only a small reduction in that user's posteriori probability and the user is not immediately rejected. In this case, if the primary biometric produces a good match, the user may still be accepted. Only if several soft biometric traits do not match, there is significant reduction in the posteriori probability and the user could be possibly rejected. If the devices that measure the soft biometric traits are reasonably accurate, such a situation has a low probability of occurrence. The introduction of the weighting scheme results in the following discriminant function for user ω_i:

$$g_i(\mathbf{x},\ \mathbf{y}) = a_0 \log P(\omega_i|\mathbf{x}) + a_1 \log p(y_1|\omega_i) + \cdots + a_k \log p(y_k|\omega_i) +$$

$$a_{k+1} \log P(y_{k+1}|\omega_i) + \cdots + a_m \log P(y_m|\omega_i), \tag{5}$$

where $\sum_{i=0}^{m} a_i = 1$ and $a_0 \gg a_i$, $i = 1, 2, \cdots, m$. Note that a_i's, $i = 1, 2, \cdots, m$ are the weights assigned to the soft biometric traits and a_0 is the weight assigned to the primary biometric identifier. It must be noted that the weights a_i, $i = 1, 2, \cdots, m$ must be made small to prevent the domination of the primary biometric by the soft biometric traits. On the other hand, they must large enough so that the information content of the soft biometric traits is not lost. Hence, an optimum weighting scheme is required to maximize the performance gain.

4   Experimental Results

Our experiments demonstrate the benefits of utilizing the gender, ethnicity, and height information of the user in addition to the face and fingerprint biometric identifiers. The face database described in [8] has been used in our experiments. This database has face images of 263 users, with 10 images per user. Our fingerprint database consisted of impressions of 160 users obtained using a Veridicom sensor. Each user provided four impressions of each of the four fingers, namely, the left index finger, the left middle finger, the right index finger, and the right middle finger. Of these 640 fingers, 263 were selected and assigned uniquely to the users in the face database. A Linear Discriminant Analysis (LDA) based scheme is used for face matching. Eight face images of each user were used during the training phase and the remaining two images were used as test images. The face matching score vector (of length 263) was computed for each test image as follows. The similarity of the test image to the 2104 (263 × 8) training images in the database was found and the largest of the 8 scores of a particular user was selected as the matching score for that user. Fingerprint matching was done using minutia features [15]. Two fingerprint impressions of each user were used as templates and the other two impressions were used for testing. The fingerprint matching score for a particular user was computed as the average of the scores obtained by matching the test impression against the two templates of that user. Thus, a fingerprint matching score vector for each test impression was computed. The separation of the face and fingerprint databases into training and test sets, was repeated 20 times and the results reported are the average for the 20 trials.

The ethnicity classifier proposed in [8] was used in our experiments. This classifier identifies the ethnicity of a test user as either Asian or non-Asian with an accuracy of 96.3%. If a "reject" option is introduced, the probability of making an incorrect classification is reduced to less than 1%, at the expense of rejecting 20% of the test images. A gender classifier was built following the same methodology used in [8] for ethnicity classification. The accuracy of the gender classifier without the "reject" option was 89.6% and the introduction of the "reject" option reduces the probability of making an incorrect classification to less than 2%. In cases where the ethnicity or the gender classifier cannot make a reliable decision, the corresponding information is not utilized for updating the matching score of the primary biometric system.

Since we did not have the height information about the users in the database, we randomly assigned a height 'H_i' to user ω_i, where the H_i's are drawn from a Gaussian distribution with mean 165 cm and a standard deviation of 15 cm. The height of a user measured during the recognition phase will not be equal to the true height of that user stored in the database due to the errors in measurement and the variation in the user's height over time. Therefore, it is reasonable to assume that the measured height H_i^* will follow a Gaussian distribution with a mean H_i cm and a standard deviation of 5 cm.

Let $P(\omega_i|s)$ be the posterior probability that the test user is user ω_i given the primary biometric score 's' of the test user. Let $y_i = (G_i,\ E_i,\ H_i)$ be the soft biometric feature vector corresponding to the user ω_i, where G_i, E_i, and H_i are the true values of gender, ethnicity, and height of ω_i. Let $y^* = (G^*,\ E^*,\ H^*)$ be the observed soft biometric feature vector of the test user, where G^* is the observed gender, E^* is the observed ethnicity, and H^* is the observed height. Now the final score after considering the observed soft biometric characteristics is computed as:

$$g_i(s,\ y^*) = a_0 \log P(\omega_i|s) + a_1 \log p(H^*|H_i) + a_2 \log P(G^*|G_i) + a_3 \log P(E^*|E_i)\,,$$

where $a_2 = 0$ if $G^* =$"reject", and $a_3 = 0$ if $E^* =$"reject".

Experiments were conducted on three primary biometric systems, namely, fingerprint, face, and a multimodal system using face and fingerprint as the individual modalities. Figure 4 shows the Cumulative Match Characteristic (CMC) of the fingerprint biometric system operating in the identification mode, and the improvement in performance achieved after the utilization of soft biometric information. The weights assigned to the primary and soft biometric traits were selected experimentally such that the performance gain is maximized. However, no formal procedure was used and an exhaustive search of all possible sets of weights was not attempted. The use of ethnicity and gender information along with the fingerprint leads to an improvement of 1% in the rank one performance as shown in Figures 4(a)and 4(b), respectively. From Figure 4(c), we can observe that the height information of the user is more discriminative than gender and ethnicity, and leads to a 2.5% improvement in the rank one performance. The combined use of all the three soft biometric traits results in an improvement of approximately 5% over the primary biometric system as shown in Figure 4(d).

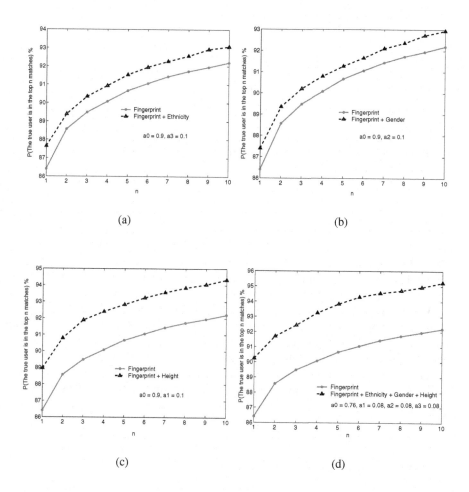

Fig. 4. Improvement in identification performance of fingerprint system after utilization of soft biometric traits.

The ethnicity and gender information did not provide any improvement in the performance of a face recognition system. This may be due to the fact that the gender and ethnicity classifiers, and the face recognition system use the same representation, namely, LDA for classification. The LDA algorithm for all the three classifiers operates on the same set of training images and hence it is highly likely that the features used for

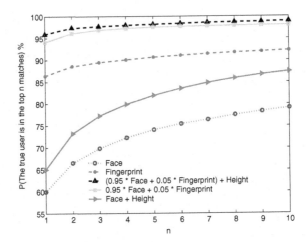

Fig. 5. Improvement in identification performance of (face + fingerprint) multimodal system after utilization of the height of the user.

these classification problems are strongly correlated. However, the height information is independent of the facial features and, hence, it leads to an improvement of 5% in the face recognition performance (see Figure 5). The failure of the ethnicity and gender information to improve the face recognition performance establishes that fact that soft biometric traits would help in recognition only if the identity information provided by them is complementary to that of the primary biometric identifier.

Figure 5 shows the CMC curves for a multimodal system using face and fingerprint as the individual modalities. In this system, the combined matching score of the primary biometric system is computed as a weighted average of the scores of the face and fingerprint modalities. We can observe that the rank one performance of this multimodal system is superior to that of the individual modalities by 8%. The addition of height as a soft biometric feature further improves the performance by 2%. This shows soft biometric traits can be useful even if the primary biometric system already has a high accuracy.

5   Summary and Future Directions

We have demonstrated that the utilization of ancillary user information like gender, height, and ethnicity can improve the performance of the traditional biometric systems. Although the soft biometric characteristics are not as permanent and reliable as the traditional biometric identifiers like fingerprint, they provide some information about the identity of the user that leads to higher accuracy in establishing the user identity. We have also shown that soft biometric characteristics would help only if they are complementary to the primary biometric traits. However, an optimum weighting scheme based the discriminative abilities of the primary and the soft biometric traits is needed to achieve an improvement in recognition performance.

Our future research work will involve establishing a more formal procedure to determine the optimal set of weights for the soft biometric characteristics based on their distinctiveness and permanence. Methods to incorporate time-varying soft biometric information such as age and weight into the soft biometric framework will be studied. The effectiveness of utilizing the soft biometric information for "indexing" and "filtering" of large biometric databases must be studied. Finally, more accurate mechanisms must be developed for automatic extraction of soft biometric traits.

References

[1] Jain, A.K., Bolle, R., Pankanti, S., eds.: Biometrics: Personal Identification in Networked Security. Kluwer Academic Publishers (1999)
[2] Hong, L., Jain, A.K., Pankanti, S.: Can Multibiometrics Improve Performance? In: Proceedings of IEEE Workshop on Automatic Identification Advanced Technologies, New Jersey, U.S.A. (1999) 59–64
[3] Heckathorn, D.D., Broadhead, R.S., Sergeyev, B.: A Methodology for Reducing Respondent Duplication and Impersonation in Samples of Hidden Populations. In: Annual Meeting of the American Sociological Association, Toronto, Canada (1997)
[4] Gutta, S., Huang, J.R.J., Jonathon, P., Wechsler, H.: Mixture of Experts for Classification of Gender, Ethnic Origin, and Pose of Human Faces. IEEE Transactions on Neural Networks **11** (2000) 948–960
[5] Moghaddam, B., Yang, M.H.: Learning Gender with Support Faces. IEEE Transactions on Pattern Analysis and Machine Intelligence **24** (2002) 707–711
[6] Shakhnarovich, G., Viola, P., Moghaddam, B.: A Unified Learning Framework for Real Time Face Detection and Classification. In: Proceedings of International Conference on Automatic Face and Gesture Recognition, Washington D.C., USA (2002)
[7] Balci, K., Atalay, V.: PCA for Gender Estimation: Which Eigenvectors Contribute? In: Proceedings of Sixteenth International Conference on Pattern Recognition. Volume 3., Quebec City, Canada (2002) 363–366
[8] Jain, A.K., Lu, X.: Ethnicity Identification from Face Images. In: Proceedings of SPIE International Symposium on Defense and Security : Biometric Technology for Human Identification (To appear). (2004)
[9] Woodward, J.D.: Testimony to the Commission on Online Child Protection on Age Verification Technologies. available at
http://www.copacommission.org/meetings/hearing1/woodward.test.pdf (2000)
[10] Buchanan, M.V., Asano, K., Bohanon, A.: Chemical Characterization of Fingerprints from Adults and Children. In: Proceedings of SPIE Photonics East Conference. Volume 2941. (1996) 89–95
[11] Kwon, Y.H., Lobo, N.V.: Age Classification from Facial Images. In: Proceedings of IEEE Conference on Computer Vision and Pattern Recognition. (1994) 762–767
[12] Hong, D., Woo, W.: A Background Subtraction for a Vision-based User Interface. In: Proceedings of Fourth International Conference on Information, Communications and Signal Processing, Pacific-Rim Conference On Multimedia, 1B3.3. (2003)
[13] Hsu, R.L., Mottaleb, M.A., Jain, A.K.: Face Detection in Color Images. IEEE Transactions on Pattern Analysis and Machine Intelligence **24** (2002) 696–706
[14] Jain, A.K., Dass, S.C., Nandakumar, K.: Can soft biometric traits assist user recognition? In: Proceedings of SPIE International Symposium on Defense and Security : Biometric Technology for Human Identification (To appear). (2004)
[15] Jain, A.K., Hong, L., Pankanti, S., Bolle, R.: An identity authentication system using fingerprints. Proceedings of the IEEE **85** (1997) 1365–1388

Robust Encoding of Local Ordinal Measures:
A General Framework of Iris Recognition

Zhenan Sun, Tieniu Tan, Yunhong Wang

Center for Biometrics Authentication and Testing
National Laboratory of Pattern Recognition, Institute of Automation,
Chinese Academy of Sciences, P.O. Box 2728, Beijing, 100080, P.R. China
{znsun, tnt, wangyh}@nlpr.ia.ac.cn

Abstract. The randomness of iris pattern makes it one of the most reliable biometric traits. On the other hand, the complex iris image structure and various sources of intra-class variations result in the difficulty of iris representation. Although diverse iris recognition methods have been proposed, the fundamentals of iris recognition have not a unified answer. As a breakthrough of this problem, we found that several accurate iris recognition algorithms share a same idea — local ordinal encoding, which is the representation well-suited for iris recognition. After further analysis and summarization, a general framework of iris recognition is formulated in this paper. This work discovered the secret of iris recognition. With the guidance of this framework, a novel iris recognition method based on robust estimating the direction of image gradient vector is developed. Extensive experimental results demonstrate our idea.

1 Introduction

With the increasing demands of security in our networked society, the technologies for personal identification work as the main solution to safeguard people's properties. Because the traditional human authentication methods based on what you possess or what you know are not reliable enough and inconvenient in practice, biometrics is emerging as an alternative approach [1,2]. Biometrics makes use of the physiological or behavioral characteristics of people such as fingerprint, iris, face, palmprint, gait, voice, etc. to identify a person [1]. After testing seven popular biometric systems, it is reported in [3] that iris recognition is the most reliable one. Iris pattern is a unique, stable and non-invasive biometric feature and well-suited for individual verification. Nowadays many iris recognition systems have been deployed in airports, border crossings, banks, buildings and so on [4].

But how to represent iris image contents effectively is a difficult problem. Like many other pattern recognition tasks, the challenge comes from grouping together all the different iris images arising from the same eye, which change dramatically with variations under various conditions of capture, such as illumination, human's attitude, openness of the eye and the model of the camera. Some important factors that may affect the performance of iris recognition system are discussed as follows:

D. Maltoni and A.K. Jain (Eds.): BioAW 2004, LNCS 3087, pp. 270-282, 2004.
© Springer-Verlag Berlin Heidelberg 2004

1) Iris normalization: Iris is an elastic membrane deformed by the pupil's dilation and constriction. So normalization is necessary to complement the deformation. Another goal of normalization is to establish a unified coordinate system to facilitate the further processing. A common practice in this step is to linearly unwrap the iris portion in image to the polar coordinates [5]. The scale and position invariance of all iris data are expected to be achieved by normalization. But the first order model ("rubber sheet") is not accurate enough to accommodate the non-linear distortion [6]. Although more complex normalization methods may be developed, the real time requirement can hardly be met because merely the linear mapping procedure is already time consuming.

2) Iris registration: Of course the rotation difference between two iris images can be solved by a brute force registration process, but the large computational cost makes it not preferred in real time application. A popular solution is to unwrap the reference iris ring at different initial angles (or transforms its feature to new versions that corresponds to different start angles). Then the input image is compared against all the rotated versions of the reference image respectively. At last the minimal matching distance is regarded as the dissimilarity between the two images. It is straightforward that more rotated versions are tried, higher possibility the two irises exhibit similarity, including inter-class irises. Therefore the number of rotations should be strictly controlled, resulting in the input and reference iris images can be only coarsely aligned. Additionally, the errors of iris localization and normalization make precise iris registration impossible.

3) Contrast variation: Because iris images are often captured non-invasively, the lighting setting can not be guaranteed constant. Under various illuminations, the intensity of iris image, even the absolute measure of contrast varies significantly.

4) Noise suppression: There are many kinds of noises need to be suppressed for reliable iris recognition, such as CCD camera noise, occlusion of eyelids and eyelashes, dust on eyeglasses and high light points caused by specular reflection, etc.

In conclusion, an effective iris recognition algorithm should be tolerant to the variations mentioned above while be capable of efficiently encoding the iris details. Since last decade, various algorithms for iris recognition have been presented [5-23]. But the basic mechanism of iris recognition, like the questions "What is the fundamental of iris recognition?" and "Which kind of iris feature is the most suitable for iris recognition?" have not been well answered. In this paper we want to interpret iris recognition from the view of local ordinal encoding and robust statistics, and establish a general framework of iris recognition so as to unify several most accurate algorithms in literature. The ultimate objective of our work is to derive new and improved iris recognition method with the guidance of this framework.

The remainder of this paper is organized as follows. Section 2 describes the basic principles of the general framework of iris recognition and three existing accurate iris recognition methods are unified in this framework. A novel iris recognition method based on this framework will be introduced in Section 3. Section 4 provides the experimental results prior to conclusions in Section 5.

2   Robust Encoding of Local Ordinal Measures

2.1   Motivation

The success of any object recognition system, whether biological or artificial, lies in using appropriate representation schemes [24]. The schemes should accommodate the intra-class variability without comprising the discriminative power in distinguishing the object [25]. Motivated primarily by psychophysical and physiological studies of the human visual system, Sinha [24] developed a candidate scheme that conceptual-izes the rapidly saturating contrast response functions of striate cortical neurons. The basic idea of his diagram is to encode objects based on the local relative relationships between a plurality of image patches. Although the absolute sensory stimuli values (including intensity, color and texture) of different regions change dramatically under varying conditions, their mutual ordinal relationships remain largely unaffected. This achievement is successfully applied for solving a wide spectrum of practical real-world problems, such as face detection (ratio template in Figure 1) [24], pedestrian detection (wavelet template) [25], stereo image pair correspondence [26], motion estimation and image-database search [27]. Furthermore, Sadr et al. [28] had demon-strated that the ordinal representation can faithfully encode signal structure and high-lighted the robustness and generalization ability of local ordinal encoding for the task of pattern recognition. Armed with the theory of local ordinal encoding, we attempt to explore the secret of iris recognition.

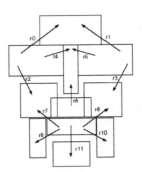

Fig. 1. Ratio template [24], this is a representation of the invariant ordinal structure of the image brightness on a human face under widely varying illumination conditions.

Another scientific fundamental useful for strengthening the robustness of iris fea-ture extraction is robust statistics. Robust statistics is a branch of statistics that studies the sensitivity of statistical procedures to departures from their underlying assump-tions [29]. Many robust techniques haven been successfully applied to computer vision [30,31]. In fact, Sadr et al. had pointed out that the scheme of local ordinal encoding shares the same spirit as loss functions used in robust statistics [28]. So a general framework for iris recognition based on local ordinal encoding and robust statistics is proposed with the following intentions:
1)   The science underlying the framework is appealed to be helpful to interpret, analyze and implement iris recognition;

2) Some seemingly unrelated iris recognition approaches can be unified in this framework;
3) New and improved iris recognition diagrams are expected to be derived based on this formulation.

2.2 A Unified Solution for Iris Recognition

Based on the above discussions and the insights into existing iris recognition algorithms [5-23], a general framework of iris recognition is summarized as follows with the ambition to against the intra-class iris variations:

1) Ordinal measures: Sinha's theory of qualitative representation [24] is versatile to object recognition, especially well suited for iris recognition. Because iris pattern is a random texture generated by many interlacing minute characteristics such as freckles, coronas, stripes and so on. The noise like chaos may disturb the precision of traditional segmentation based computer vision algorithms. But the richness of inter-region sharp intensity variations provides a good source of ordinal measures for class model construction. And only the qualitative contrast relationships across iris regions can be insensitive to various variations.

2) Local relationship: There are two reasons to choose local ordinal measures, not non-local relationships. First, the illumination variation between local regions is commonly less than that between non-local regions; Secondly, local comparison is easily implemented by filtering the normalized iris image with a differential operator, which is a common practice in image processing.

3) Holistic strategy: Due to the possibility that some iris region is smeared by noise, each ordinal relation by itself is not reliable enough and is too coarse to provide a good discriminant function to distinguish between members and non-members of an object class, it is necessary to consider many of the relations together (implicitly processing object structure holistically) to obtain the desired performance [24]. Therefore each component of the iris feature must correspond to an inequality relationship between a few different iris regions' average intensities. First the whole iris image is partitioned into regions, and then a relationship processor is performed on the regions. Features from all patches are concatenated to form the complete feature vector, which is a larger composite invariant.

4) Redundancy principle: To complement the alignment errors of iris images, the partitioned basic regions must overlap each other so that the features are same in neighborhood unless sharp variation occurs.

5) Robust encoding: Based on the sign of inequality relationship, a binary code is assigned to it, e.g. 1 denotes greater than and 0 represents smaller than. This compact iris code greatly facilitates the matching process.

6) Scale space principle: Not only because the distinctive spatial characteristics of the human iris are manifest at a variety of scales, but also the noise suppression requires a larger scale representation of the image structure. But on the other hand, the information of minute iris feature will lose and the difference between inter-class irises at coarser resolution will become less too, so the result of this tradeoff is that an intermediate scale should be carefully chosen or information at large scale and fine scale is integrated via a fusion scheme.

These principles establish a general framework of iris recognition, namely robust encoding of local ordinal measures (RELOM), rendering the representation of iris images insensitive to all sources of variations. The idea of RELOM is illustrated in Figure 2. In the framework, the differential filter acts as the ordinal information extractor. After robust encoding, the iris codes are combined to an iris template.

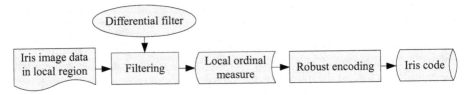

Fig. 2. Block diagram of robust encoding of local ordinal measures

2.3   Unification of Several Existing Iris Recognition Algorithms

In the field of iris recognition, there are various methods proposed [5-23]. Every algorithm has a different theory justifying its scientific reasonability. In this section, we want to unify three seemly different iris recognition algorithms [5,14,23] based on the novel framework—RELOM shown in Fig. 2. The only difference of these algorithms is the type of differential filter they choose, which is determinant to their recognition performance. Because these three iris recognition methods had explicitly or implicitly utilized the idea of RELOM, they all achieved good performance. Unification of these algorithms is helpful to understand the mechanism of iris recognition and enlighten new ideas.

Based on the research works on modeling the structure of simple cell receptive field profiles in the visual cortex [32,33], Daugman found that the 2D Gabor wavelet representation is suitable for image analysis and compression [34]. This theory was successfully applied to iris recognition [5-7]. Regarding the iris image as the modulation result based on multi-scale Gabor wavelets, Daugman [5] encoded the demodulated phase information as iris feature. The dissimilarity level between the input iris image and the registered template can be determined by the Hamming distance between their iris codes. The even and odd Gabor filters are shown in Figure 3a and 3b respectively, which are the differential operators used by Daugman. The linear filtering of an iris image with Gabor filter is equal to compare the intensity between the image regions covered the Gabor filter's excitatory lobes and the adjacent regions covered by inhibitory lobes. The operation result is encoded into 1 or 0 depending on its sign (positive or negative). Thus an inequality is constituted by the constant coefficients of the Gabor filters and the iris image intensity values varied with the position of the mask:

$$
IrisCode = \begin{cases} 1, & \sum_{i=1}^{K} p_i x_i \geq \sum_{j=1}^{K} n_j y_j \\ 0, & \sum_{i=1}^{K} p_i x_i < \sum_{j=1}^{K} n_j y_j \end{cases}
\qquad (1)
$$

where $p_i(i=1,2,...,K)$ denote the coefficients of the Gabor filter's excitatory lobes and $n_j(j=1,2,...,K)$ denote the absolute coefficients of the Gabor filter's inhibitory lobes, and $x_i(i=1,2,...,K)$ denote the intensity of iris image pixels covered by the Gabor filter's excitatory lobes and $y_j(j=1,2,...,K)$ denote the intensity of iris image pixels covered by the Gabor filter's inhibitory lobes. The coefficients satisfy $\sum_{i=1}^{K} p_i = \sum_{j=1}^{K} n_j$. Therefore each bit iris code's probability of being 1 or 0 is equal, i.e. 0.5. It is straightforward that the coefficients arrangement of Gabor filter is particularly suitable to complement the alignment error because the weights are assigned in inverse proportion to their distance to an image region's center. The 256 Bytes iris code corresponds to 2,048 invariant ordinal relationships between the weighted image regions. Only using the simple ratio template shown in Fig.1, Sinha achieved a correct face detection rate of about 80% with very few false positives [24]. We can image the great discriminating power of the 256 Bytes iris code.

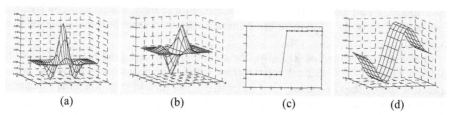

(a)   (b)   (c)   (d)

Fig. 3. Differential filters employed by different iris recognition algorithms; (a) Even Gabor filter; (b) Odd Gabor filter; (c) Discrete Haar wavelet; (d) Quadratic spline wavelet.

In [23], Noh et al. utilized the wavelet frame decomposition method for iris recognition. The result of one dimensional Haar wavelet transform (Fig. 3c) along column of an iris image in polar coordinates is quantized to 255s or 0s based on its sign. It is obviously a local ordinal measure, which is named as local feature [23]. Different from other methods, the geometric moment of the decomposition result was regarded as global feature and used for coarse-level classification so as to provide a set of candidates for further fine matching. Because the discriminating power of this method mainly depends on the local feature, we only discuss the local feature in this paper. Although 1D wavelet transform is faster than 2D filter processing, not only some information is loss but also the robustness of the local feature is weakened.

In our latest work [14], the dyadic wavelet transform is employed to detect the position of local sharp variation points. The whole procedure of feature extraction includes two steps:

1) A set of one-dimensional (1-D) intensity signals is constructed to effectively characterize the most important information of the original two-dimensional (2-D) image;

2) Using a particular class of wavelets, which is a quadratic spline with compact support, a position sequence of local sharp variation points in such signals is recorded as features.

Although the wavelet transform is performed on the 1D signal, the result is equal to 2D filtering because the 1D signal is the average of several adjacent lines of image signals. The real 2D differential operator is shown in Fig. 3d. Of course the filtered result $WTS(x)$ is also a kind of local ordinal measures. The robust encoding rule is defined as follows:

$$IrisCode = \begin{cases} 1, & WTS(x) > MinTh, WTS(x) < MaxTh, MaxTh - MinTh > MaxMinTh \\ 0, & \text{otherwise} \end{cases} \tag{2}$$

where the wavelet transform result between a local minimum and a local maximum is encoded as 1, $MinTh$ denotes the value of the local minimum, $MaxTh$ represents the value of the local maximum and $MaxMinTh$ denotes a predefine threshold whose purpose is to suppress the local extremum points that may correspond to faint characteristics in the iris image. Sinha had pointed out the ratios included in the invariant could, if desired, be augmented with approximate upper and low magnitude bounds [24].

No matter the spatial difference between these four kinds of filters, they all are capable of deriving the local ordinal information. And robust encoding strategy is also applied in all algorithms. So it is clear that these three iris recognition methods can be unified in the aforementioned framework. As a result, all the schemes have reported good recognition results.

Inspired by the idea of RELOM, the direction of image gradient vector also denotes a kind of local ordinal relationship, providing the information along which direction the intensity contrast is the most sharp. But how to strengthen the robustness of this representation is still a challenging problem.

3   Robust Estimating the Direction of Image Gradient Vector

In this section, a novel iris recognition diagram based on robust estimating the local dominant direction of gradient vector field (GVF) is presented, named as robust direction estimation (RDE).

RDE includes two parts: direction diffusion followed by direction filtering. The aim of direction diffusion is to enhance the main direction in a region and to suppress noises. Many published algorithms about direction or orientation diffusion can serve for this idea [35,36]. But the numerical implementation of these methods all involves many iterations, and what we care is not the process of diffusion or detail preserving, but the result of diffusion. So a simplification of their ideas is described as follows:

1) Gradient vector field computation. Sobel operator is utilized to generate the two components of image gradient vector, G_x and G_y.

2) Isotropic derivatives diffusion. Gaussian filter is the only kernel qualified for linear scale space generation. So the coarse representation of G_x or G_y is the result of convolution with a Gaussian window:

$$G'_x = G_x * g_\delta, \quad G'_y = G_y * g_\delta \tag{3}$$

where g_δ is a Gaussian filter with scale δ.

3) The phase angle A of the complex $G'_x + iG'_y$ is the diffusion result.

After direction diffusion, the enhanced gradient vector angle A across image plane can be regarded as a vector valued image. In the next step the iris feature— local dominant direction, should be robustly estimated from each region of A. Vector directional filters, a class of multi-channel image processing filters, are employed to select a typical one from the input angles in each window [37]. Following ideas from basic vector directional filter [37], directional filter (DF) is defined as follows:

Definition: The output of the DF, for input $\{\ A_i, i = 1, 2, \cdots, n\ \}$, is $A_{DF} = DF\{A_i, i = 1, 2, \cdots, n\}$, such that

$$A_{DF} \in \{A_i, i = 1, 2, \cdots, n\} \tag{4}$$

and

$$\sum_{i=1}^{n} Dis(A_{DF}, A_i) \le \sum_{i=1}^{n} Dis(A_j, A_i), \forall j = 1, 2, \cdots, n \tag{5}$$

where $Dis(A_i, A_j)$ denotes the difference between the angles A_i and A_j. It had been proved that the angle A_{DF} is the least error estimate of the angle location [37]. After coarse quantization, a more compact representation is obtained and the robustness of the whole statistical procedure is further strengthened. It should be pointed out the selection of quantization level is a tradeoff between the robustness, discriminability and other factors such as storage cost, computational costs. In this case, the angle scale of A_{DF}, from $-\pi$ to π, is quantized into six discrete values. The effect of robust direction encoding is illustrated in Figure 4.

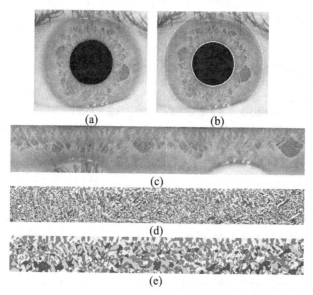

(a)   (b)

(c)

(d)

(e)

Fig. 4. Example of robust direction encoding; (a)Original image; (b)Result of iris localization; (c)Normalized iris image; (d)Direction encoding result of GVF from (c) without RDE; each color represents a direction quantization level; (e) Direction encoding result of GVF using RDE; its scale is obviously much coarser than that of (d).

After downsampling, the output of RDE is ordered to constitute a fixed length iris feature vector $(C_1, C_2, \cdots, C_N)$, where $C_i \in \{1, 2, 3, 4, 5, 6\}$ $(i = 1, 2, \cdots, N)$ and N is the dimension of the vector. To balance recognition accuracy and the complexity, N is chosen as 2560. Similar to Daugman's idea [5], the Hamming distance is adopted for measuring the dissimilarity between the acquired iris and the template iris. In order to complement the possible rotation difference between the two irises, template iris feature is converted to eleven versions corresponding to rotation angles $-10°, -8°, -6°, -4°, -2°, 0°, 2°, 4°, 6°, 8°, 10°$ respectively. And the minimum Hamming distance between the input and the eleven rotated versions of the template is the final matching result.

4   Experiments

4.1   Experimental Results

In order to evaluate the recognition performance of the ordinal measures (Gabor filters [5], discrete Haar wavelet (DHW) [23], quadratic spline wavelet (QSW) [14] and RDE), CASIA Iris Image Database is used as the test dataset, which has been worldwide shared for research purposes [38]. The database includes 2,255 iris image sequences from 306 different eyes (hence 306 different classes) of 213 subjects. To satisfy requirement of using images captured in different stages for training and testing respectively, 100 sequences taken at the early time are not used in the experiments. The images are separated to two sets: a training set of 918 template sequences (Three sequences per eye) and a testing set of 1,237 sequences of all people. For the images of the same eye, the time interval between the samples in the training set and the instances of testing set is more than one month and the longest interval is about six months. The format of the data is 8-bits gray level image with resolution 320×280. Ten images in each sequence are automatically selected by image quality assessment module [13], but there are still some poor quality iris images used. In order to test our scheme in a low Failure to Enrollment Rate (FTE) situation, we randomly select an image from the ten qualified images of each sequence to construct a challenging dataset.

All the algorithms are tested in two modes: identification and verification. In identification mode, each iris image in testing set is compared with the three templates of each class in training set and the least distance is regarded as the dissimilarity between the input and the class. At last the input is assigned to the class with minimal distance. If the assigned class is the input's class label, then a correct classification is reported or else a false classification is recorded. In the identification testing, all ordinal represents achieve 100% correct recognition rate. In verification mode, all possible comparisons are made between the data collected at the two different times. So there are a total of 918×1,237= 1,135,566 comparisons between the test images and the model data, including 3,711 intra-class comparisons and 1,131,855 inter-class comparisons. The ROC (Receiver Operating Characteristic) curve, a plot of FRR (false reject rate) against FAR (false accept rate) using different threshold values of Hamming distance, is illustrated in Figure 5. For the purpose of comparison, the verification performance of all the methods in the same dataset is shown in Fig. 5. To exclude the influence of various preprocessing and enhancement methods adopted by the four algorithms, all ordinal represents are extracted from the same normalized images like that in Fig.4c. The EER (equal error rate) curve is also drawn in Fig.5 for reference. It should be pointed out that both Daugman's and Noh's algorithms are coded following their publications [5,23]. Without strict image quality control or further filtering of poor quality images, the performance of their algorithms in our dataset is worse than that reported in their publications. And In our current implementations of all the methods, we did not carry out the schemes for eyelid and eyelash detection. However, this should not influence comparison experiments and the resulting conclusions in this paper.

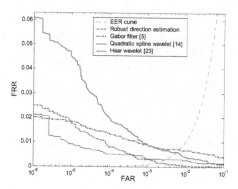

Fig. 5. Comparison of ROCs

The computer resource costs of these methods are shown in Table 1. All experiments are performed in Matlab on a personal computer.

Table 1. Comparison of computational cost and storage cost

Method / Cost	Gabor filter [5]	QSW [14]	DHW [23]	RDE
Computation	0.6 s	0.2 s	0.3 s	0.7 s
Storage	256 Bytes	320 Bytes	196 Bytes	960 Bytes

From the experimental results, we can see the Gabor filter [5], QSW [14] and RDE achieve comparable high recognition performance. The reason is straightforward. Based on the analysis in Section 2.3, these three algorithms all utilized 2-D ordinal measures. The DHW [23] used a kind of one dimensional ordinal measures. Of course it loses much information compared with 2-D ordinal representations, which directly lead its performance worse than other methods. Although the method of RDE costs more time and space, it achieves the lowest EER because both direction diffusion and direction filtering can strengthen the robustness of the ordinal measures. Considering the method of RDE's simplicity and the fact that the current implementation embodies no refinements (such as the angle distance based matching strategy), the RDE's performance is very encouraging.

4.2 Discussions and Future Work

Based on the above experimental results, we can draw a number of conclusions as well as find that some issues need to be further investigated.

1. After the testing on the real iris images, all the methods unified in the proposed framework are robust enough for iris recognition, which also demonstrates the success of the general framework. In our early comparative study [14], the methods that belong to this category, such as Daugman's algo.[5] and Tan's method [14] are more accurate than other methods. And Daugman's method [5-7] has been tested in many practical iris recognition systems. In addition to the visual neuroscience findings [24], all these evidences prove that local ordinal information is the best representation for iris recognition. Therefore in the future we should follow this direction.

2. In the experiments, we found that when the differential operator is more robust or variation insensitive, the whole method's recognition performance is better. Therefore for all methods in the proposed framework, the recognition difference comes mainly from the differential operators they chose, which is also the difference of the various ordinal relationships they selected. From the structure of the differential filter, we can analyze the recognition performance of this algorithm. This conclusion guides us to pay more attention to improve the differential operator's robustness.

3. After the local ordinal representation is determined, the encoding scheme is also very important for the recognition performance. The advance of robust statistics [29] and robust computer vision [30,31] provides many ideas to strengthen the robustness of iris code. In fact, the iris encoding can be regarded as a procedure of robust parameter estimation.

4. Sinha only encoded the salient discriminatory relationships in an image and the learned ratios may be assigned with different weights according to their significance [24], which enlightens us to characterize the most distinctive ordinal measures.

5. Although we commonly derive ordinal information from local comparisons, the latest research of Sinha Lab [39] reported that non-local encoding may be an effective scheme for representing image structure. Compared with local ordinal measures, the gray-level differences between long-distance lobes are more salient. We can try this idea for iris recognition.

5 Conclusions

A general framework of iris recognition——robust encoding of local ordinal measures is formulated in this paper. This work discovered the secret of iris recognition. Based on the idea of local ordinal invariant [24], several accurate iris recognition algorithms are unified in the simple framework. The ultimate objective of this work is to help people to develop new and improved iris recognition methods. As an example, local dominant direction of image's gradient vector is robustly estimated as an effective iris feature.

Acknowledgments

This work is funded by research grants from the Natural Science Foundation of China (Grant No. 60121302, 60275003, 60332010, 69825105) and the CAS.

References

1. A.K. Jain, R.M. Bolle and S. Pankanti (eds.): Biometrics: Personal Identification in Networked Society, Norwell, MA: Kluwer (1999)
2. D. Zhang (ed.): Automated Biometrics: Technologies and Systems, Norwell, MA: Kluwer (2000)
3. T. Mansfield, G. Kelly, D. Chandler and J. Kane: Biometric Product Testing Final Report, issue 1.0, National Physical Laboratory of UK (2001)
4. http://www.iridiantech.com
5. J. Daugman: High Confidence Visual Recognition of Persons by a Test of Statistical Independence, IEEE Trans. PAMI, Vol.15, No.11 (1993) 1148-1161
6. J. Daugman: Recognizing persons by their iris patterns, in: [1] 103-121
7. J. Daugman: Statistical Richness of Visual Phase Information: Update on Recognizing Persons by Iris Patterns, IJCV, Vol. 45, No.1 (2001) 25-38
8. R.P. Wildes, J.C. Asmuth, et al.: A Machine-vision System for Iris Recognition, Machine Vision and Applications, Vol.9 (1996) 1-8
9. W.W. Boles and B. Boashash: A Human Identification Technique Using Images of the Iris and Wavelet Transform, IEEE Trans. on Signal Processing, Vol.46, No.4 (1998) 1185-1188
10. Y. Zhu, T. Tan, Y. Wang: Biometric Personal Identification Based on Iris Patterns, ICPR (2000) 805-808
11. L. Ma, Y. Wang, T. Tan: Iris Recognition Based on Multichannel Gabor Filtering, ACCV (2002) 279-283
12. L. Ma, Y. Wang, T. Tan: Iris Recognition Using Circular Symmetric Filters, ICPR (2002) 414-417
13. L. Ma, T. Tan, Y. Wang and D. Zhang: Personal identification based on iris texture analysis, IEEE Trans. PAMI, Vol. 25, No.12 (2003) 1519-1533
14. L. Ma, T. Tan, Y. Wang and D. Zhang: Efficient Iris Recognition by Characterizing Key Local Variations, IEEE Trans. Image Processing (Accepted)
15. L. Ma, T. Tan, D. Zhang and Y. Wang: Local Intensity Variation Analysis for Iris Recognition, Pattern Recognition (Accepted)
16. S. Lim, K. Lee, et al.: Efficient Iris Recognition through Improvement of Feature Vector and Classifier, ETRI Journal, Vol. 23, No. 2 (2001) 61-70
17. R. Sanchez-Reillo and C. Sanchez-Avila: Iris Recognition With Low Template Size, AVBPA (2001) 324-329
18. C. Sanchez-Avila, R. Sanchez-Reillo, et al.: Iris-based Biometric Recognition using Dyadic Wavelet Transform, IEEE Aerospace and Electronic Systems Magazine (2002.8) 3-6

19. C. Tisse, L. Martin, L. Torres and M. Robert: Person Identification Technique Using Human Iris Recognition, Proc. of Vision Interface (2002) 294-299

20. C. Park, J. Lee, M. Smith and K. Park: Iris-Based Personal Authentication Using a Normalized Directional Energy Feature, AVBPA (2003) 224-232

21. B. Kumar, C. Xie and J. Thornton: Iris Verification Using Correlation Filters, AVBPA (2003) 697-705

22. K. Bae, S. Noh and J. Kim: Iris Feature Extraction Using Independent Component Analysis, AVBPA (2003) 838-844

23. S. Noh, K. Bae, J. Kim: A Novel Method to Extract Features for Iris Recognition System, AVBPA (2003) 862-868

24. P. Sinha: Qualitative representations for recognition. In: H.H. Bülthoff, S.-W. Lee, T.A. Poggio, C. Wallraven (Eds.): Biologically Motivated Computer Vision. Lecture Notes in Computer Science, Vol. 2525. Springer-Verlag, Heidelberg (2002) 249-262

25. C. Papageorgiou, M. Oren, and T. Poggio: A general framework for object detection, ICCV (1998) 555-562

26. D. Bhat and S. Nayar: Ordinal measures for image correspondence, IEEE Trans. on PAMI, Vol.20, No.4 (1998) 415-423

27. P. Lipson, E. Grimson, P. Sinha: Configuration based scene classification and image indexing CVPR (1997) 1007-1013

28. J. Sadr, S. Mukherjee, K. Thoresz and P. Sinha: The Fidelity of Local Ordinal Encoding. In: T. Dietterich, S. Becker & Z. Ghahramani (Eds.): Advances in Neural Information Processing Systems 14. MIT Press: Cambridge, MA (2002)

29. F. R. Hampel, E. M. Ronchetti, P. J. Rousseeuw and W. A. Stahel (eds.): Robust Statistics: The Approach Based on Influence Functions, Wiley, New York (1986)

30. P. Meer, D. Mintz, A. Rosenfeld and D. Y. Kim: Robust regression methods for computer vision-A review, IJCV, Vol.6, No.1 (1991) 59-70

31. C.V. Stewart: Robust parameter estimation in computer vision, SIAM Review, Vol. 41, No. 3 (1999) 513-537

32. J. Daugman: Two-dimensional spectral analysis of cortical receptive field profile, Vision Research, Vol. 20 (1980) 847-856

33. J. Daugman: Uncertainty relation for resolution in space, spatial frequency and orientation optimized by two-dimensional visual cortical filters, J. Opt. Soc. Am., Vol.2, No.7 (1985) 1160-1169

34. J. Daugman: Complete discrete 2D Gabor transforms by neural networks for image analysis and compression, IEEE Transactions on Acoustics, Speech and Signal Processing, Vol.36, No.7 (1997) 1169-1179

35. P. Perona: Orientation diffusion, IEEE Trans. Image Processing, Vol.7, No.3 (1998) 457-467

36. B. Tang, G. Sapiro, and V. Caselles: Diffusion of general data on non-flat manifolds via harmonic maps theory : The direction diffusion case, IJCV, Vol.36, No.2 (2000) 149-161

37. P. E. Trahanias and A.N. Venetsanopoueos: Vector Directional Filters—A New Class of Multichannel Image Processing Filters, IEEE Trans. Image Processing, Vol.2, No.4 (1993) 528-534

38. CASIA Iris Image Database, Chinese Academy of sciences, http://www.sinobiometrics.com/casiairis.htm

39. Balas, B.J. and P. Sinha: Dissociated Dipoles: Image Representation via Non-local Comparisons, CBCL Paper #229/AI Memo #2003-018, Massachusetts Institute of Technology, Cambridge, MA (2003)

A Novel Digitizing Pen for the Analysis of Pen Pressure and Inclination in Handwriting Biometrics

Christian Hook, Juergen Kempf, Georg Scharfenberg

University of Applied Sciences, Postbox 120327, 93025 Regensburg, Germany
christian.hook@mathematik.fh-regensburg.de
juergen.kempf@mikro.fh-regensburg.de
georg.scharfenberg@e-technik.fh-regensburg.de

Abstract. In this paper we introduce a novel multi-functional digitizing pen for the verification and identification of individuals by means of handwritten signatures, text or figures (biometric smart pen, BiSP). Different from most conventional graphics tablets the device measures the kinematics and the dynamics of hand movement during the writing process by recording the pressure (Px, Py, Pz) and inclination (α, β) of the pen. Characteristic behavioral patterns are numerically extracted from the signals and stored in a database. Biometric test samples are compared against reference templates using a rapid feature classification and matching algorithm. A first BiSP prototype based on pressure sensors is available for presentation. Preliminary results obtained from 3D pressure signals demonstrate a remarkable potential of the system for person verification and identification, and suggest further applications in the areas of neurology and psychiatry.

1 Introduction

Person authentication based on biometrical traits in handwriting is a compelling alternative for verification techniques using static biological features, e.g. iris scan, fingerprint or face recognition. Although, like any biometric pattern, the biometrics of handwriting is inherently prone to considerable statistical variability, there is a high potential for scientific and commercial applications due to the extensive information embedded in the kinematics and dynamics of handwritten signatures, figures or text. Up to date common systems of handwriting biometry use a digitizing tablet measuring only few physical variables with low sampling frequency and limited accuracy. In order to improve the handling of existing devices as well as their respective authentication performance and reliability, a multimodal biometrics system based on a digitizing ballpoint pen is being developed in our laboratory. This *biometrical smart pen* (*BiSP*) acquires and processes data resulting from handwriting on normal paper pads and from voiced speech. The pen comprises several different sensors measuring the statics, kinematics and dynamics of the hand movement. The ability to measure miscellaneous biometric patterns at the same time is the principal advantage and the main potential of our device [1]. In combination with a newly developed software for signal processing, feature extraction, data compression, database management and fast matching algorithms, our BiSP becomes an innovative

D. Maltoni and A.K. Jain (Eds.): BioAW 2004, LNCS 3087, pp. 283–294, 2004.
© Springer-Verlag Berlin Heidelberg 2004

system for widespread use in biometric person verification and identification applications. According to the specific software design and the implemented metrics and classification algorithms, the BiSP device is also well suited for the use in medical areas, e.g. for the classification and quantification of hand-motor dysfunctions and the analysis of fine motor movements of patients under drug treatment.

2 Hardware

A reliable biometric authentication system should be based on the combined analysis of multiple behavioral traits or physiological characteristics. In our group we are developing a unique multimodal biometric pen system which is in many respects superior to current pen or tablet based human computer input devices. The BiSP is equipped with a diversity of sensors monitoring (1) the static and dynamic pressure in three dimensions generated by handwriting, (2) the kinematics of inclination and of horizontal position of the pen and (3) the acoustics generated by handwriting on a paper pad or by voiced speech. The following prototypes of BiSP devices are developed:

OptoPen based on the optical computer mouse technique for measuring the horizontal positions x(t), y(t) of the pen tip moved across a paper pad during writing.

TiltPen detects the inclination angles $\alpha(t)$, $\beta(t)$ with respect to the vertical axis of the handheld pen by an electrolytic tilt sensor with a sampling rate of 100Hz and a sensitivity of 55mV per degree. This sensing technique mainly captures the fine neuro-motor function of the fingers holding the pen.

MicPen with an electret microphone placed inside the pen and shielded against background noise measures acoustical signals produced by writing on a paper pad. First results of this unique device are quite promising because the microphone signals provide valuable data for biometrics und handwriting recognition [2]. Optional the MicPen can record voiced speech signals. Therefore, the identification through handwriting and speech can be performed by the same device.

MechPen prototype as shown in Fig.1 equipped with different pressure sensors. The force or pressure resulting from handwriting on paper is transferred by the refill and monitored in horizontal directions x, y by strain gauges which are placed close to the front part of the refill. We use metal strain gauges integrated in a half-bridge circuit. Their output signals are conditioned by a low pass filter and a single supply instrumentation amplifier providing signals in a dynamic voltage range of 5V with a sensitivity of about 2V per Newton. In the z-direction i.e. the longitudinal axis of the pen the dynamics of force or pressure is detected by a piezoelectric sensor located at the end of the refill. The miniature piezoelectric sensor samples the change of force or pressure in the passive mode. The linear signals from the three pressure sensors are digitized with a 10 bit A/D converter at a sampling frequency of 500 Hz.

In this paper we focus on the handy MechPen device where the data transfer from pen to computer is done by wire (see Fig.1, *left*). An example of a 3D pressure signal generated by writing the character *Hello* is shown in Fig.1 (*right*). The characteristic features of the time series are essentially determined by the type of the written item and by the fine motor movements of the writing person.

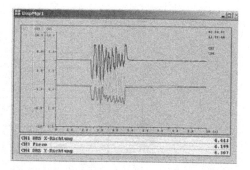

Fig. 1. *MechPen* prototype for biometric verification and identification (*left*). Example of pressure signals Px(t), Py(t) and Pz(t) acquired by writing the word *Hello* (*right*)

3 Software

Over the past twenty years many different techniques and advanced mathematical methods have been developed for biometrical person authentication. Depending on the category of measured patterns, i.e. physiological attributes or behavioral traits, and on the considered application, e.g. identification of terrorists, verification of employers etc. various algorithms for image processing, pattern recognition, speech recognition and signal processing are applied [3]. In general the task of a biometric authentication system is (1) the extraction and compression of biometric information and (2) the process of correlating, matching and validating a claimed or unknown identity with respect to a database of previously sampled templates. It is evident that one-to-one matching algorithms for the attestation of a person's identity have a different focus on system performance than one-to-many matching routines in real-time recognition devices. However, because the BiSP system offers a large variety of applications, the software developed in our mathematical department is designed to cover the full range of classification, verification and identification tasks. Obligatory for this broad functionality is the access to arbitrarily large databases of enrolled individuals, a high throughput rate, and an adequate recognition performance of the authentication algorithms.

Similar to the methods suggested in [4], [5] our software is based on the extraction of *global* statistical features manifest in $P_x(t)$, $P_y(t)$ and $P_z(t)$ pressure signals of handwritten items (i.e. characters, text or signatures). In this respect our approach is different from methods computing local and morphometric patterns of the collected samples (for a discussion of the feasibility of regional and global features cf. [6]). We extract a large set of features from a sample and use simple and rapid metrics for matching operations in feature space. The approach is systematic, general and remarkably flexible. It is not restricted to the analysis of pressure signals but applies equally well to kinematic data, i.e. the time course of tip position x(t), y(t) and pen tilt $\alpha(t)$, $\beta(t)$. Our software system comprises data pre-processing, feature extraction and neighbor classification, and maps the original signals to a strongly compressed binary representation in feature space. An overview of the program structure is given in Fig. 2.

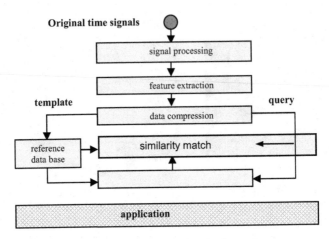

Fig. 2. Flow chart of authentication software

3.1   Feature Selection

The data used in our preliminary field tests consist of three pressure signals sampled simultaneously and digitized with 500 Hz A/D conversion rate (for an example of a typical pressure signal see Fig. 1.).

Our algorithm extracts altogether n = 110 features from the 3D pressure signals (e.g. length, mean value, standard deviation, skewness, number of peaks, number of radial loops, sweep of polar angle, line integrals, static moments of MAV signals, amplitude spectrum, nonlinear optimization parameters, etc.). These n stochastic variables represent a compressed image of the original time series, mapped to an n-dimensional feature vector. Taking a sufficiently large (sub)set from the recorded population of templates, we calculate the frequency distribution (histogram) of values for each of the n features with respect to the chosen (sub)set. Each histogram provides an empirical probability density of the particular feature. We compute the 1/3 and 2/3 quantils and split the observed range of the feature into three intervals. As a result, one third of the measured values fall into the left interval termed *small*, one third to the centered interval called *medium* and one third to the right interval termed *large* (cf. Fig. 3). In this manner the measured values are mapped to *qubits*, i.e. to the quantized states S = (10), M = (11) and L = (01). A fourth state can be used for the removal of outliers, F = (00) = *faulty*.

In summary, our scheme converts a sampled analog signal to an n-dimensional feature vector, and maps each real valued feature to three *fuzzy sets* with linguistic terms S, M, L, and step-like membership functions μ_S, μ_M, μ_L. Of course we have the option to bring in trapezoid shaped, or any other suitable membership function in a later stage of our analysis.

The frequency distribution obtained from the complete (sub)set is compared with the corresponding *individual* histograms, which are computed from repeated samples from one and the same person, respectively (Fig. 3). Features which show low repeatability, little overall or large individual variance, insufficient specificity and pro-

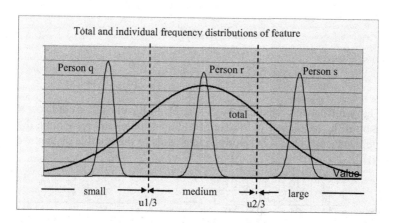

Fig. 3. Hypothetical probability density function (pdf) of total subset (not normalized) and three individual pdf of a particular feature (note: empirical pdf are generally non gaussian). Integral over total pdf is separated into three parts of equal area, fixing the 1/3 and 2/3 quantiles

nounced redundancy are discarded. The dimensionality of our feature space is thus reduced to the order of $n \approx 50$, and the final image of a given template (reference) or claim (query) is a very coarse-grained representation as qubit vector with elements (1,0), (1,1) or (0,1), respectively. This conversion is equivalent to the allocation of the collected sample to one out of $N \approx 10^{24}$ possible hypercubes in n-dimensional space, cf. Eqs. (1), (2).

$$M := \{ \ (10), (11), (01) \ \}^n \tag{1}$$

$$N := card(M) = |\ M\ | = 3^{50} \approx 10^{24} \ . \tag{2}$$

Given the balanced spread of feature values to the intervals *small, medium* and *large,* and assuming different features to be more or less mutually independent, the population of templates is expected to occupy the state space quite uniformly, with regional clusters belonging to samples from the same individual.

3.2 Metrics

We apply straightforward metrics in order to define measures for the *similarity* or *distance* between any given pair of given samples. Binary (qubit) feature vectors are compared against each other using XOR operations (cf. Eq. 3). For example, let us first evaluate the *distance* between a reference vector r (template) and a claimant vector q (query). According to the rules indicated in Fig. 4 the inference of r and q actually gives a vector h of singletons, with the linguistic terms *perfect match* (H), *average match* (M) or *zero match* (Z) assigned to each element. We choose $r = (r_1...r_n)$, $q = (q_1...q_n)$ and $h = (h_1...h_n)$, where r_i, q_i, $h_i \in \{(1,0), (1,1)\ (0,1)\}$, and defuzzify h according to Eq. 4. From this we obtain the distance D, which is simply the sum of all *ones* in the qubit vector h, otherwise known as the *Hamming* distance.

$$h := r \text{ XOR } q \qquad (3)$$

$$D := \sum_{j=1}^{n} \sum_{k=1}^{2} h_{j,k} \quad \Rightarrow \quad d = \frac{D}{2n}. \qquad (4)$$

We have introduced the index k, $k \in \{1, 2\}$, in $h_{j,k}$ in order to indicate the first and second bit of h_j, respectively. In case of n-dimensional feature vectors, the maximum absolute distance is $D_{max} = 2n$. Normalizing leads to the relative distance, $d = D/D_{max}$, ($d_{max} = 1$).

	10	11	01
10	00	01	11
11	01	00	10
01	11	10	00

$\longrightarrow$

	S	M	L
S	H	M	Z
M	M	H	M
L	Z	M	H

Fig. 4. Metrics for comparison of qubits from two samples using XOR operator ($\rightarrow$ *Hamming* distance of a particular element of a feature vector). Results of inference rule are the linguistic terms *perfect match* (H), *average match* (M) and *zero match* (Z)

For our further analysis it is appropriate to employ a quantity complementary to the distance, i.e. a measure for the *proximity* or *similarity* between two items r and q. For this we define the matching score, or briefly the *score* s of the two samples by the sum of zeroes in h,

$$S := \sum_{j=1}^{n} \sum_{k=1}^{2} \text{NOT } h_{j,k} \quad \Rightarrow \quad s = \frac{S}{2n} = 1 - d. \qquad (5)$$

Our metrics for the comparison of binary feature vectors can now be improved further by introducing a weighting vector $w = (w_1...w_n)$. Each element w_j, $j = 1...n$, is assigned a positive number according to the priority or significance of the corresponding feature. In order to scale the feature j with weight w_j, we transform the *Hamming* vector h as follows

$$h^* = \text{NOT } h. \qquad (6)$$

Using h^* we obtain an alternative measure for the proximity between r and q in terms of the relative *weighted score* s^*,

$$s^* = \frac{\sum_{j=1}^{n} \sum_{k=1}^{2} h_{j,k}^* \cdot w_j}{2 \cdot \sum_{j=1}^{n} w_j} \qquad (7)$$

Note that letting $w_j = 1$, $\forall j \in \{1,.. n\}$ leads to $s = s^*$. Conversely, choosing $w_j = 0$ for a particular $j \in \{1,.. n\}$ eliminates the contribution of the jth feature and, in effect, reduces the dimension of the feature space from n to n-1.

We put emphasis on the fact that we can optionally employ *individual weighting vectors* w_k for each person k, i.e. $w_k = (w_{k1}...w_{kn})$. These are calculated automatically, based on certain criteria related to mean values and standard deviations of each feature. Individual weighing improves authentication score rates significantly (compare Tab.1 with results given in [1]).

3.3 Classification and Matching

In order to reduce the computation time for online identification, our reference database with N entries (N feature vectors) is subjected to a classification procedure. A simple but most efficient heuristics limits the number of template comparisons to the order of N·logN, depending on the adjustable size of a decision threshold. Sub-threshold neighboring points are assigned to the same class (i.e. grouped). Classes are allowed to overlap in space, i.e. individual templates may be located within the boundaries of more than one class. On an intra-class level, template vectors belonging to the same person are averaged, thus defining an *individual prototype* vector of the person within the given class. Finally, each class is represented by a *class prototype* i.e. the qubit-representation of the algebraic mean of the individual prototype vectors.

Based on this hierarchical sequence of increasingly coarse data, the principal steps for the matching of a captured sample with the templates are (1) signal preprocessing of the query sample, (2) extraction and compression of feature values, (3) comparison against prototype vectors of classes, (4) comparison against prototype vectors of individuals within the *nearest neighbor classes* and, if necessary (5) application of more refined techniques for a final selection of the *best match*. Among such techniques are DTW, HMM, neural nets, AR/ARMA, covariance analysis, etc. (for an outline cf. [7]). The present work deals exclusively with the approach subsumed under steps (1) to (4). Various methods for the ultimate identification step (5) are presently being developed in collaboration with the universities of Frankfurt, Heidelberg, Passau and Pilsen.

4   Results

In order to critically evaluate the BiSP hardware and our authentication system, we performed two preliminary field trials A and B in our lab. We used the *MechPen* prototype measuring only the handwriting dynamics i.e. the time course of 3D pressure signals $P_x(t)$, $P_y(t)$, $P_z(t)$.

4.1 Reproducibility and Uniqueness

Field test A focused on the reproducibility and distinctiveness of written items collected repeatedly under optimal (i.e. identical) conditions. During a single session each item was written ten times in sequence by each person, respectively. The set of items consisted of eight primitives {*A, B, O, 4, 5, 8, +, Δ*}, five German words of similar length {*auch, oder, bitte, weit*}, a sequence of words {*Guten Morgen*} and the individual signature of the participant. Samples collected from a particular person were collected without intermediate displacement or rotation of the pen device. The corresponding reference database is therefore well suited to analyze whether (1) *equal items* written in several copies by the *same person* are matching well (reproducibility), (2) *different items* written by the *same person* are sufficiently dissimilar (uniqueness of pattern) and (3) *different or equal items* written by *different persons* map to distant points in feature space (biometric uniqueness). An example for obvious similarities and dissimilarities in repeated samples is depicted in Fig. 5.

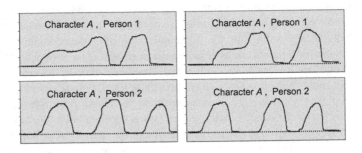

Fig. 5. Pressure signal $P_x(t)$ of handwritten letter *A*, collected twice from two different persons, respectively. Note similarity of time series obtained from same person (parallel figures), and dissimilarity of signals collected from different persons (vertical figures)

In order to quantify the *reproducibility* of objects, we matched pairs of binary feature vectors extracted from *equal items* written by the *same person*. Given ten samples per item and per candidate, we calculated the mean and standard deviation from 45 score values s (comparison of ½·10·9 pairs of same type according to Eq. 5, no weighting). These were again averaged over the total set of 15 enrolled persons (see Fig. 6).

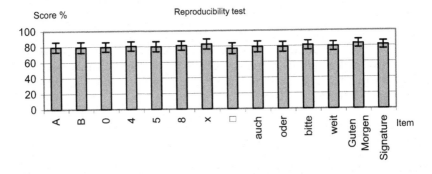

Fig. 6. Reproducibility test: Comparison of *equal items* written repetitively 10 times by *same individual*. Average score (%) and stdv calculated from 45 comparisons per item and per person. Figure shows the algebraic mean and stdv of individual averages, obtained from 15 enrolled persons, respectively

Expressing the relative score in percent (100% = identity), 80% of the feature vector qubits match on average. The reproducibility is very high, irrespective of the *type* of written item, let it be a character, word or the individual signature. Interestingly, the sequence *Guten Morgen* has maximum reproducibility, suggesting that certain meaningful combinations of words may be more suitable for authentication than signatures submitted in a more or less reflex like action.

An ultimate prerequisite for user authentication based on dynamic handwriting patterns is the *uniqueness* of the extracted information. Accordingly, an algorithm should be able to discriminate between two written objects, e.g. between *Miller* and *Smith*, *yes* and *no*, or even between two primitives like *A* and *B*. Accordingly, we compared combinations of different characters written by the *same* person and computed the similarity in terms of the score s. The results demonstrate an average score rate between 65% and 70%, independent of the particular individual (see Fig. 7).

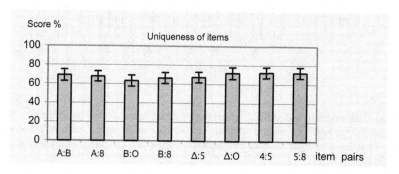

Fig. 7. Uniqueness of items: Matching of different characters written by same person (arbitrary examples). Average scores and stdv determined from 45 comparisons per character pair and per user. Table shows algebraic mean of average scores (%) and stdv, obtained from 15 users.

For a better interpretation of these findings it must be emphasized that two feature vectors with *randomly generated* element values (10), (11) or (01) have a theoretical average score of s = 0.55 (i.e. 55%). Therefore, two actual items must be termed *uncorrelated* or *dissimilar* if the score of their feature vectors is of the order of 55% or less. Because the metric proximity of different characters written by the same person is 65% (see Fig. 7) which is well above 55%, we conclude that specific *biometric information* must be embedded in even the shortest written objects. This finding suggests that a series of, say, four or six separately written characters might contain a similar amount of biometric information as an individual's signature. We therefore propose to utilize handwritten PINs or passwords, both for the conventional *authorization* as well as for biometric *authentication* of the claimant (BioPIN).

In order to discriminate between *persons*, the biometric authentication properties were tested by cross-checking the proximity of equal items written by different individuals. The resulting average scores were found to lie in a small range of 55% to 58%, with only little standard deviation (see Fig. 8). This low score rate proves that identical items written by different persons are much farther off in feature space than equal items written by the same person. Only the written + signs are fairly close in feature space (s = 68 %), forming a loose cluster. This finding is consistent with the fact that the writing of just two little strokes has indeed no potential for extensive biometric information.

We conclude that our software tool is adequate to discriminate between human individuals among the reference population, either by means of matching handwritten signatures, words or just a sequence of isolated characters.

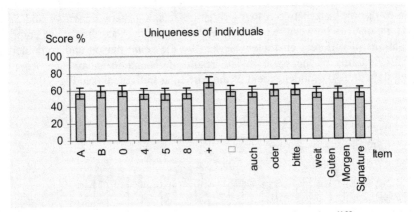

Fig. 8. Uniqueness of individuals: Matching of equal items written by different persons X,Y. Average scores and stdv computed from 10x10 pairs of items for each X,Y-combination of users. Figure shows algebraic mean of these average scores and stdv, obtained from 15 persons (105 X,Y-pairs)

4.2 Authentication Properties

In a second field trial B we tested the BiSP system (MechPen) with focus on its authentication properties under more realistic, i.e. non-identical conditions. Handwritten *signatures* were collected during 10 different sessions (5 days, morning and afternoon, respectively) from a set of N = 40 enrolled persons. A series of 10 successive signatures was written by each user during each session. Although many of the collected samples seemed to be outliers, no screening of the data was performed. However, samples from the first day were completely discarded because it took considerable time for the participants to accommodate to the somewhat unhandy and unergonomic pen design.

We removed three arbitrarily chosen signatures per person from the reference set and compared them against the remaining prototypes of the database in order to *verify* and *identify* the author of the signature. A score was termed *correct identification* if both the test sample and the computed best match belonged to the same person. Similarly, we speak of *correct verification* if the claimant is identical to at least one out of the three topmost matching candidates (rank 3 score). Corresponding results are shown in Tab.1. With respect to the data presented in [1], results have been considerably improved due to a modification of algorithms and the use of individual weighting vectors. The field trials A and B where conducted with an earlier prototype of the MechPen with insufficient handling properties. Therefore, most participants required some time (or a of number of trials) to accommodate to the handling of the pen, which might explain the tendency of identification scores to become stable after the second day. Taking into account that entries in the reference database are composed of samples from both accustomed and non-accustomed users, a further improvement of results could be expected if the population of reference data was collected solely from experienced persons.

Tab. 1. Authentication using test signatures from field trial A (15 persons enrolled; 7 templates and 3 test samples each), and field trial B (40 persons enrolled; 8 templates and 3 test samples per person, sampled at 3 different days). For definition of identification and verification score see text.

Field trial A	Identification score	Verification score
	98 %	100 %
Field trial B	Identification score	Verification score
2nd day	82 %	92 %
3rd day	89 %	92 %
4rd day	87 %	92 %
5th day	89 %	92 %

5 Summary

Statistical features computed from pressure signals of handwritten symbols or words contain important text-specific and user-specific information. Even a single character placed on a paper pad encodes an amazing amount of information with respect to the item itself, and to the individual fine motor function of hand and fingers.

The preliminary field trials reported in this paper were performed with pen prototypes of yet imperfect ergonomic design. Participants were not accustomed to handle the pen properly, and a considerable percentage of collected data was quite obviously affected through clenching or repositioning of the instrument. Besides, only traces of 3D pressure signals were sampled and analyzed while the kinematics of pen position and tilt angle was not considered. Despite of these adverse effects the results of our study are most convincing. We believe that the continuous progress in our pen design and our authentication software, as well as the inclusion of more degrees of freedom will improve the system performance significantly. In conclusion, the BiSP system has a remarkable potential for use in commercially employed biometric authentication machines. The results also suggest applications in the areas of neurology and psychology, because the developed hardware and software is most suitable for the classification of neuro-motor dysfunctions [8] or the monitoring of patients under drug treatment [9]. For further information about the project cf. [10].

Acknowledgments

The research and development was partly supported by a grant of the International Office the BMBF(AIF) and BMBF(IB), Germany, Projects FKZ/1708702 and CZE99/007 *Biometrical Smart Pen for Personal Identification.*

References

1. Hook, C., Kempf, J., Scharfenberg, G.: New Pen Device for Biometrical 3D Pressure Analysis of Handwritten Characters, Words and Signatures. Proceedings ACM Multimedia Berkeley, USA (2003) 38-44
2. Šoule, M., Kempf, J.: Handwritten Text Analysis through Sound. A New Device for Handwritting Analysis. In Proceedings IWSSIP, Prague, (2003) 254-257
3. Roy, A.H., Headrick, A.M.: Handwriting Identification. Facts and Fundamentals. 1st edn. CRC Press LLC, Boca Raton New York (1999)
4. Morita, H., Sakamoto, G., Ohishi, T., Komiya, Y., Matsumoto, T.: On-Line Signature Verifier Incorporating Pen Position, Pen Pressure, and Pen Inclination Trajectories. In: Bigun, J., Smeraldi, F. (eds.): Audio- and Video-Based Biometric Person Authentication. Lecture Notes in Computer Science, Vol. 2091. Springer-Verlag, Berlin Heidelberg New York (2001) 318-323
5. Lee, L., Berger, T., Aviczer, E. Cornell - Reliable On-Line Human Signature Verification Systems For Point-of-Sale Application. In IEEE Trans. Pattern Analysis and Machine Intelligence, 18 (6), (1996) 643-647
6. Pirlo, G.: Algorithms for Signature Verification. In: Fundamentals in Handwriting Recognition. Springer-Verlag, Berlin Heidelberg New York (1994) 435-454
7. Rohlík O., Mautner P., Matoušek V., Kempf J.: HMM Based Handwritten Text Recognition Using Biometrical Data Acquisition Pen. In: Proceedings of the 2003 IEEE International Symposium on Computational Intelligence in Robotics and Automation (CIRA 2003), Kobe (2003) 950-953
8. Mavrogiorgou, P et al: Kinematic Analysis of Handwriting Movements in Patients With Obsessive-Compulsive Disorder, J. Neurol.Psychiatry 70, (2001) 605-612
9. Lange, K.W., Tucha, O., Aschenbrenner, S., Gottwald, D., Eichhammer, P., Putzhammer, A., Sartor, H., Klein, H: The Effect of Antidepressant Medication on Handwriting of Patients With Depression. In: Proceedings of the 10th Biennial Conference of the International Graphonomics Society. University of Nijmegen, (2001) 52-57
10. www.bisp-regensburg.de

An Off-line Signature Verification System Based on Fusion of Local and Global Information

J. Fierrez-Aguilar, N. Alonso-Hermira, G. Moreno-Marquez, and
J. Ortega-Garcia

Biometrics Research Lab., ATVS
Universidad Politecnica de Madrid, Spain
{jfierrez,jortega}@diac.upm.es

Abstract. An off-line signature verification system based on fusion of two machine experts is presented. One of the experts is based on global image analysis and a statistical distance measure while the second one is based on local image analysis and Hidden Markov Models. Experimental results are given on a subcorpus of the large MCYT signature database for random and skilled forgeries. It is shown experimentally that the machine expert based on local information outperforms the system based on global analysis in all reported cases. The two proposed systems are also shown to give complementary recognition information which is exploited with a simple fusion strategy based on the sum rule.

1 Introduction

Automatic extraction of identity cues from personal traits (e.g., signature, fingerprint, speech, and face image) has given raise to a particular branch of pattern recognition, biometrics, where the goal is to infer identity of people from biometric data [1, 2]. The increasing interest on biometrics is related to the number of important applications where a correct assessment of identity is a crucial point.

This work is focused on off-line signature recognition (i.e., only signature image is given as input information for recognition) [3]. The importance of this biometric characteristic (because of its widespread use and legal and social acceptability) and the inherent variability of the signing process has motivated great research efforts in the last decade [4]. As a result, various pattern recognition strategies have been applied to this problem such as minimum distance classifiers [5], dynamic programming [6], neural networks [7], and Hidden Markov Models [8, 9].

One major research trend in biometric verification is the successful exploitation of the different information levels embodied in the biometric signal at hand. Examples can be found regarding fingerprint verification, where the combined utilization of global texture features and local minutiae-based descriptors has been shown to improve verification performance [10], or speaker verification, where the combination of prosodic descriptors and local acoustic features outperforms the state-of-the-art acoustic approach [11]. Regarding off-line signature

D. Maltoni and A.K. Jain (Eds.): BioAW 2004, LNCS 3087, pp. 295–306, 2004.
© Springer-Verlag Berlin Heidelberg 2004

recognition, some works on multi-expert approaches are [12] and [13]. For a theoretical framework on classifier combination and a comparative evaluation of common fusion strategies, we refer the reader to [14] and [15] respectively.

Two different machine experts have been built in this work. The first machine expert is described in Sect. 2. It is based on global image analysis and a minimum distance classifier as proposed in [5]. The second machine expert is described in Sect. 3. It is based on local image analysis and left-to-right Hidden Markov Models as used in [8] but with a novel local parameterization derived from the work in [5]. A simple fixed fusion strategy based on the sum rule [14] is used as the fusion algorithm as described in Sect. 4. Experimental procedure and results are given in Sect. 5. Some conclusions are finally extracted in Sect. 6.

2   Machine Expert Based on Global Information

2.1   Preprocessing

Input signature images are preprocessed in three consecutive stages as follows:

Binarization: Input images are first binarized by using the histogram-based global thresholding algorithm proposed in [16]. A morphological closing operation with a 3×3 squared structuring element [17] is applied then to the binarized image.

Segmentation: Signature is then segmented by using a bounding box which removes outer traces (this is because signature boundary normally corresponds to flourish with high intra-user variability). Left and right height-wide blocks having all columns with signature pixel count lower than threshold T_p, respectively top and bottom width-wide blocks having all rows with signature pixel count lower than T_p are discarded ($T_p = 15$ in the reported experiments).

Normalization: Database used for experiments have been acquired on a restricted size grid, so intra-user rotation variability is expected to be low and no rotation normalization is applied. Segmented signatures are resized in order to have a width of 512 pixels while maintaining the aspect ratio.

2.2   Feature Extraction

Slant directions of the signature strokes and those of the envelopes of the dilated signature images are used as features for recognition as proposed in [5]. These descriptors are extracted by using mathematical morphology operators [17].

Slant directions are analyzed as follows. The preprocessed signature image is eroded with the structuring elements shown in Fig. 1 thus generating 32 eroded binary images (the area of the structuring elements is 10 pixels and the angle between successive elements is approximately 11°). A slant direction feature subvector with 32 components is then generated, where each component is computed as the signature pixel count in each eroded image.

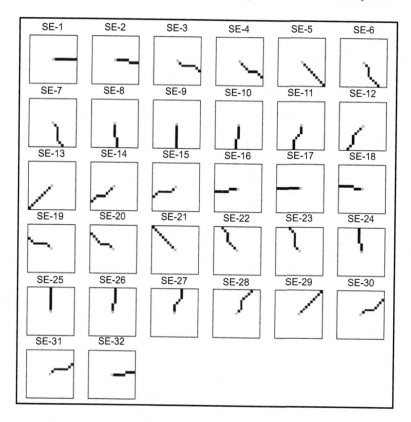

Fig. 1. Structuring elements used for slant direction feature extraction. Origin of the structuring element is indicated in light gray.

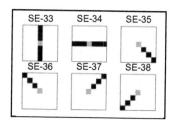

Fig. 2. Structuring elements used for envelope feature extraction. Origin of the structuring element is indicated in light gray.

Envelope is analyzed as follows. Preprocessed signature image is successively dilated 5 times with each one of the 6 structuring elements in Fig. 2 (areas of SE-33/34 and SE-35/36/37/38 are 7 and 4 pixels respectively). An envelop feature sub-vector with 5×6 components is finally generated, where each component is computed as the signature pixel count in the difference image between successive dilations.

Preprocessed signature is finally parameterized as a column vector **o** with 62 coordinates by concatenating slant and envelop feature sub-vectors.

2.3   Similarity Computation

Each client of the system or target T is represented by a statistical model $\lambda_T = \{\mu_T, \sigma_T\}$, where μ_T and σ_T denote mean and deviation vectors respectively. These are estimated by using an enrollment set of K parameterized signatures $\{\mathbf{o}_T^{(1)}, \ldots, \mathbf{o}_T^{(K)}\}$ as follows:

$$\mu_T = \frac{1}{K} \sum_{k=1}^{K} \mathbf{o}_T^{(k)} \tag{1}$$

$$\sigma_{Tj} = \sqrt{\frac{1}{K} \sum_{k=1}^{K} \left(o_{Tj}^{(k)} - \mu_{Tj} \right)^2} \quad j = 1, \ldots, 62 \tag{2}$$

where o_{Tj}, μ_{Tj} and σ_{Tj} are the jth coordinates of $\mathbf{o}_T$, μ_T and σ_T respectively.

Similarity score between a parameterized test signature **o** and a claimed model $\lambda_T = \{\mu_T, \sigma_T\}$ is computed as the inverse of the Mahalanobis distance [18]:

$$s_{global}(\mathbf{o}, \lambda_T) = \frac{1}{\sqrt{\sum_{j=1}^{62} \frac{1}{\sigma_{Tj}^2} (o_j - \mu_{Tj})^2}} \tag{3}$$

3   Machine Expert Based on Local Information

3.1   Preprocessing

Input signature images are preprocessed in two consecutive steps as follows:

Binarization: Input images are binarized as in Sect. 2.1.
Segmentation: Signature is segmented by using the bounding box procedure as described in Sect. 2.1 but with a lower signature pixel count threshold ($T_p = 5$ in the experiments).

3.2   Feature Extraction

Slant directions and envelopes are locally analyzed by using an approach similar to the one summarized in Sect. 2.2 but applied to blocks.

Preprocessed signature images are divided into height-wide blocks of 64 pixels width with an overlapping between adjacent blocks of 75%. Rightmost block is discarded. Feature extraction is carried out as in Sect. 2.2 within each block. In this way, each signature is represented by a matrix **O** whose T columns are 62-tuples each one corresponding to one block.

3.3   Similarity Computation

In this case a Hidden Markov Model (HMM) is used to represent each client or target $\mathcal{T}$ of the system. Basically, a HMM models a doubly stochastic process governed by a finite state Markov Chain and a set of random functions. At discrete time instant t an observation symbol $\mathbf{o}_t$ is generated according to the random function associated to the current state [19]. The model is hidden in the sense that the underlying state which generated each symbol cannot be deduced from simple symbol observation.

Formally, a HMM is described as follows:

N: which is the number of hidden states $\{S_1, \ldots, S_N\}$. The state at discrete time t is denoted as q_t. For the experiments reported in this work, $N = 4$ is used.

A: which is the state transition matrix $A = \{a_{ij}\}$ where

$$a_{ij} = \Pr\left(q_{t+1} = S_j \mid q_t = S_i\right) \qquad 1 \le i, j \le N \qquad (4)$$

B: which are the parameters of the observation symbol density functions. In this work, the observation density function in state j is modelled as a mixture of M multi-variate Gaussian densities

$$b_j\left(\mathbf{o}\right) = \sum_{m=1}^{M} c_{jm} N\left(\mathbf{o}, \boldsymbol{\mu}_{jm}, \boldsymbol{\Sigma}_{jm}\right) \qquad 1 \le j \le N \qquad (5)$$

Thus $B = \{c_{jm}, \boldsymbol{\mu}_{jm}, \boldsymbol{\Sigma}_{jm}\}$, $1 \le j \le N$, $1 \le m \le M$. For the experiments reported in this work, $M = 8$ is used.

π: which is the initial state distribution $\boldsymbol{\pi} = \{\pi_j\}$ where

$$\pi_j = \Pr\left(q_1 = S_j\right) \qquad 1 \le j \le N \qquad (6)$$

A left-to-right topology with no transition skips between states is used in this work. In order to estimate the model $\lambda_{\mathcal{T}} = \{\boldsymbol{\pi}_{\mathcal{T}}, A_{\mathcal{T}}, B_{\mathcal{T}}\}$ for client $\mathcal{T}$, an enrollment set of K parameterized signatures $\{\mathbf{O}_{\mathcal{T}}^{(1)}, \ldots, \mathbf{O}_{\mathcal{T}}^{(K)}\}$ is used. Estimation is carried out maximizing

$$\prod_{k=1}^{K} \Pr\left(\mathbf{O}_{\mathcal{T}}^{(k)} \middle| \lambda_{\mathcal{T}}\right) \qquad (7)$$

by using the iterative Baum-Welch procedure [19]. Initial estimations of the model parameters needed for the iterative training algorithm are computed using homogenous length duration state splitting and vector quantization as described in [20].

The similarity score of an input signature parameterized as $\mathbf{O} = \{\mathbf{o}_1, \ldots, \mathbf{o}_T\}$ claiming the model $\lambda_{\mathcal{T}}$ is computed as

$$s_{local}\left(\mathbf{O}, \lambda_{\mathcal{T}}\right) = \frac{1}{T} \log \Pr\left(\mathbf{O} \middle| \lambda_{\mathcal{T}}\right) \qquad (8)$$

by using the Viterbi algorithm [19].

4   Fusion of Global and Local Information

Two sound theoretical frameworks for combining classifiers with application to biometric verification are described in [21] and [14], the former from a risk analysis point of view [22] and the later according to the statistical pattern recognition theory [23]. Both of them concluded that the weighted average is a good way of combining the similarity scores provided by the different experts or information levels. Machine learning approaches have also been applied for combining biometric classifiers [24]. The weights, or the parameters of the learning machines, can be estimated off-line using development data, thus leading to *fixed* fusion schemes, or can be estimated by using training data, thus leading to *trained* fusion schemes. Both approaches have their advantages and disadvantages as discussed in [25].

In this work, a fixed fusion strategy based on the sum rule is used. Similarity scores of the global and local experts are averaged after being linearly mapped into the range $[0, 1]$. For estimating the mapping function, a development corpus comprising 25 signers and their associated forgers is used. Development corpus is not used in subsequent experiments.

5   Experiments

5.1   Database and Experimental Protocol

A subcorpus of the larger MCYT bimodal database [26] is used for the experiments. MCYT database encompasses fingerprint (optical and capacitive acquisition) and on-line signature data (x, y, pressure, azimuth and altitude trajectories of the pen) of 330 contributors from 4 different Spanish sites. In case of signature, high skilled forgeries are also available (forgers are provided the signature images of the clients to be forged and, after training with them several times, they are asked to imitate the shape with natural dynamics, i.e., without breaks or slowdowns)

Signature information were acquired in MCYT project by using an inking pen and paper templates over a pen tablet (each signature is written within a 1.75×3.75 cm^2 frame), so signature images were available on paper. Paper templates of 75 signers (and their associated skilled forgeries) have been randomly selected and digitized with an scanner at 600 dpi (dots per inch). Resulting subcorpus comprises 2250 signature images, with 15 genuine signatures and 15 forgeries per user (contributed by 3 different user-specific forgers). Some examples of genuine signatures (left and central columns) and forgeries (right column) are given in Fig. 3 for the four types of signatures encountered in MCYT corpus, namely: simple flourish, complex flourish, name with simple flourish and name with complex flourish.

Signature subcorpus is further divided into training and test sets in order to give holdout system performance error figures [27]. In case of considering skilled forgeries, training set comprises either 5 or 10 genuine signatures (it depends

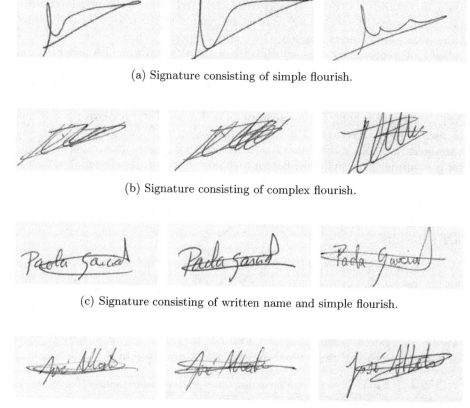

(a) Signature consisting of simple flourish.

(b) Signature consisting of complex flourish.

(c) Signature consisting of written name and simple flourish.

(d) Signature consisting of written name and complex flourish.

Fig. 3. Signature examples from MCYT corpus. Genuine signatures (left and central columns) and skilled forgeries (right column) are depicted for the four types of signatures encountered in MCYT corpus (from (a) to (d)).

on the experiment) and test set consist of the remaining samples (i.e., 10 or 5 genuine signatures and 15 forgeries per user). As a result, either $75 \times 5 = 375$ or $75 \times 10 = 750$ client similarity scores and $75 \times 15 = 1125$ impostor similarity scores are used for reporting results. In case of considering random forgeries (i.e., impostors are claiming others' identities but are using their own signatures), client similarity scores are as above and the number of impostor similarity scores is $75 \times 74 \times 5 = 27750$.

In verification or authentication (the problem addressed here) a claim is made concerning the identity of a person and the biometric system has to take the binary decision of accepting or rejecting it based on the information extracted from the considered biometric trait regarding a predetermined threshold. In a verification context, two situations of error are possible: an impostor is accepted (false acceptance, FA) or the correct user is rejected (false rejection, FR). Performance measures of verification systems are related to the frequency with which these situations of error happen. One common performance measure is the so-called EER (equal error rate) which is the point attained when FA and FR rates coincide [2].

In this work, the overall system performance when *a posteriori* user-independent decision thresholds are used is reported by means of DET plots [28], which are graphical representations of FA vs. FR rates with a particular axis scaling. Average EER tables when using *a posteriori* user-dependent thresholds are also given following the operational procedure proposed in [29] for computing the individual EER for each user. For more details on *a priori* and *a posteriori* decision thresholding techniques and their application to signature verification, we refer the reader to [30].

5.2 Results

Verification performance of the proposed global, local and combined off-line signature machine experts are given for *a posteriori* user-dependent decision thresholding in Table 1 (skilled forgeries) and Table 2 (random forgeries).

Table 1. System performance on **skilled forgeries** for *a posteriori* user-dependent decision thresholding. Average EERs are given in %

	5 training samples	10 training samples
Global Expert	21.84	18.93
Local Expert	14.51	12.22
Combined Expert	11.00	9.28

Table 2. Verification performance on **random forgeries** for *a posteriori* user-dependent decision thresholding. Average EERs are given in %

	5 training samples	10 training samples
Global Expert	8.64	5.12
Local Expert	4.35	1.59
Combined Expert	2.69	1.14

Worth noting, the system based on local analysis and HMMs outperforms the system based on global analysis and Mahalanobis distance in all cases, even when the enrollment set size is small (5 signatures). The two systems are also shown to provide complementary information for the verification task, as the combined

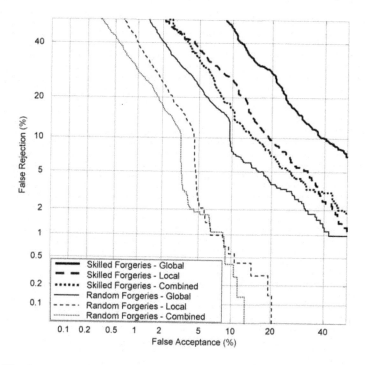

Fig. 4. Verification performance for *a posteriori* user-independent decision thresholding (5 training samples)

system always outperforms the best performing individual expert. In particular, when considering skilled forgeries and 10 training samples, the system based on global analysis leads to 18.93% EER while the proposed combined system leads to 9.28% EER, so a relative improvement of 51% is obtained as compared to published works in this area (the global expert follows closely the system proposed in [5]). In case of random forgeries and 10 training samples, 5.12% EER and 1.14% EER are obtained for global and combined experts respectively. In this case, a relative improvement of 78% is obtained.

Verification performances of individual and combined systems for *a posteriori* user-independent decision thresholds are plotted in Fig. 4 for 5 training signatures, respectively in Fig. 5 for 10 training signatures. The above pointed out comments also hold in this case, i.e., the expert based on local analysis outperforms the other one based on global description and both of them provide complementary information for the verification task.

Another effect which can be observed is the fact that error figures with user-dependent decision thresholding (see Tables 1 and 2) are lower than error figures when user-independent decision thresholds are used (see Figs. 4 and 5). This effect has also been noticed in other signature verification works [31], [30].

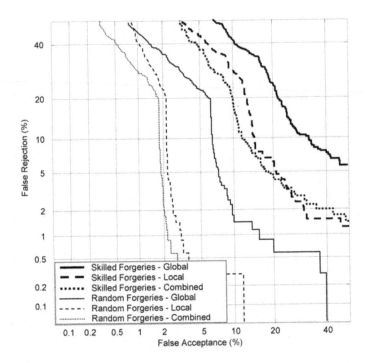

Fig. 5. Verification performance for *a posteriori* user-independent decision thresholding (10 training samples)

6   Conclusions

An off-line signature recognition system based on fusion of local and global analysis of input images has been described.

Slant directions of the signature strokes and those of the envelopes of the dilated signature images are used as features for recognition. Global analysis is based on extracting features for the whole preprocessed signature image and a statistical distance measure. Local analysis is based on extracting features per height-wide blocks and left-to-right Hidden Markov Models.

Experimental results are given on a subcorpus of the large MCYT signature database comprising 2250 different signature images from 75 contributors. Verification performance on random and skilled forgeries is given for user-dependent and user-independent decision thresholds. The machine expert based on local information is shown to outperform the system based on global analysis in all reported cases. The two proposed systems are also shown to give complementary recognition information which is exploited with a simple fixed fusion strategy based on the sum rule. Relative improvements in the verification performance as high as 51% (skilled forgeries) and 78% (random forgeries) are obtained as compared to published works.

Future work includes the evaluation of the proposed system on the full MCYT database [26] and the exploitation of the revealed user-dependencies either by using a trained fusion strategy [32], [33] or by using target-dependent score normalization techniques [30].

7 Acknowledgements

This work has been supported by the Spanish Ministry for Science and Technology under project TIC2003-08382-C05-01. J. F.-A. also thanks Consejeria de Educacion de la Comunidad de Madrid and Fondo Social Europeo for supporting his doctoral research.

References

[1] Jain, A.K., Bolle, R., Pankanti, S.: Biometrics - Personal Identification in a Networked Society. Kluwer (1999)

[2] Jain, A.K., Ross, A., Prabhakar, S.: An introduction to biometric recognition. IEEE Trans. on Circuits and Systems for Video Technology **14** (2004) 4–20

[3] Plamondon, R., Lorette, G.: Automatic signature verification and writer identification: The state of the art. Pattern Recognition **22** (1989) 107–131

[4] Plamondon, R., Srihari, S.N.: On-line and off-line handwriting recognition: A comprehensive survey. IEEE Trans. on PAMI **22** (2000) 63–84

[5] Lee, L.L., Lizarraga, M.G.: An off-line method for human signature verification. In: Proc. of the Intl. Conf. on Pattern Recognition, ICPR. (1996) 195–198

[6] Guo, J.K., Doermann, D., Rosenfeld, A.: Local correspondence for detecting random forgeries. In: Proc. of ICDAR. (1997) 319–323

[7] Huang, K., Yan, H.: Off-line signature verification based on geometric feature extraction and neural network classification. Pattern Recognition **30** (1997) 9–19

[8] Justino, E., Bortolozzi, F., Sabourin, R.: Off-line signature verification using HMM for random, simple and skilled forgeries. In: Proc. of ICDAR. (2001) 1031–1034

[9] Muramatsu, D., Matsumoto, T.: An HMM signature verifier incorporating signature trajectories. In: Proc. of ICDAR. (2003) 438–442

[10] Ross, A., Jain, A.K., Reisman, J.: A hybrid fingerprint matcher. Pattern Recognition **36** (2003) 1661–1673

[11] Campbell, J.P., Reynolds, D.A., Dunn, R.B.: Fusing high- and low-level features for speaker recognition. In: Proc. of EuroSpeech. (2003) 2665–2668

[12] Bajaj, R., Chaudhury, S.: Signature verification using multiple neural classifiers. Pattern Recognition **30** (1997) 1–7

[13] Cordella, C.P., Foggia, P., Sansone, C., Vento, M.: Document validation by signatures: A serial multi-expert approach. In: Proc. of ICDAR. (1999) 601–604

[14] Kittler, J., Hatef, M., Duin, R., Matas, J.: On combining classifiers. IEEE Trans. on Pattern Anal. and Machine Intell. **20** (1998) 226–239

[15] Fierrez-Aguilar, J., Ortega-Garcia, J., Garcia-Romero, D., Gonzalez-Rodriguez, J.: A comparative evaluation of fusion strategies for multimodal biometric verification. In: Proc. of AVBPA, LNCS-2688, Springer (2003) 830–837

[16] Otsu, N.: A threshold selection method from gray-level histograms. IEEE Trans. on Systems, Man and Cybernetics **9** (1979) 62–66

[17] Gonzalez, R.C., Woods, R.E.: Digital Image Processing. Addison-Wesley (2002)

[18] Theodoridis, S., Koutroumbas, K.: Pattern Recognition. Academic Press (2003)

[19] Rabiner, L.R.: A tutorial on hidden markov models and selected applications in speech recognition. Proceedings of the IEEE **77** (1989) 257–286

[20] Fierrez-Aguilar, J., Ortega-Garcia, J., Gonzalez-Rodriguez, J.: A function-based on-line signature verification system exploiting statistical signal modeling. Intl. Journal of Image and Graphics (2004) (accepted).

[21] Bigun, E.S., Bigun, J., Duc, B., Fischer, S.: Expert conciliation for multimodal person authentication systems by Bayesian statistics. In: Proc. of IAPR Intl. Conf. on Audio- and Video-based Person Authentication, AVBPA. (1997) 291–300

[22] Bigun, E.S.: Risk analysis of catastrophes using experts' judgments: An empirical study on risk analysis of major civil aircraft accidents in europe. European J. Operational Research **87** (1995) 599–612

[23] Duda, R.O., Hart, P.E., Stork, D.G.: Pattern classification. Wiley (2001)

[24] Verlinde, P., Chollet, G., Acheroy, M.: Multi-modal identity verification using expert fusion. Information Fusion **1** (2000) 17–33

[25] Duin, R.P.W.: The combining classifier: to train or not to train? In: Proc. of the IAPR Intl. Conf. on Pattern Recognition, ICPR, IEEE CS Press (2002) 765–770

[26] Ortega-Garcia, J., Fierrez-Aguilar, J., Simon, D., et al.: MCYT baseline corpus: A bimodal biometric database. IEE Proceedings Vision, Image and Signal Processing **150** (2003) 395–401

[27] Jain, A.K., Duin, R., Mao, J.: Statistical pattern recognition: A review. IEEE Trans. on Pattern Anal. and Machine Intell. **22** (2000) 4–37

[28] Martin, A., Doddington, G., Kamm, T., Ordowski, M., Przybocki, M.: The DET curve in assessment of decision task performance. In: Proc. of ESCA Eur. Conf. on Speech Comm. and Tech., EuroSpeech. (1997) 1895–1898

[29] Maio, D., Maltoni, D., Cappelli, R., Wayman, J.L., , Jain, A.K.: FVC2000: Fingerprint Verification Competition. IEEE Trans. on PAMI **24** (2002) 402–412

[30] Fierrez-Aguilar, J., Ortega-Garcia, J., Gonzalez-Rodriguez, J.: Target dependent score normalization techniques and their application to signature verification. In: Proc. of ICBA, LNCS, Springer (2004) (to appear).

[31] Jain, A.K., Griess, F., Connell, S.: On-line signature verification. Pattern Recognition **35** (2002) 2963–2972

[32] Jain, A.K., Ross, A.: Learning user-specific parameters in a multibiometric system. In: Proc. of ICIP. Volume 1. (2002) 57–60

[33] Fierrez-Aguilar, J., Garcia-Romero, D., Ortega-Garcia, J., Gonzalez-Rodriguez, J.: Exploiting general knowledge in user-dependent fusion strategies for multimodal biometric verification. In: Proc. of ICASSP, IEEE (2004) (to appear).

Fingerprint Verification by Decision-Level Fusion of Optical and Capacitive Sensors

Gian Luca Marcialis and Fabio Roli

Department of Electrical and Electronic Engineering – University of Cagliari
Piazza d'Armi – 09123 Cagliari (Italy)
{marcialis, roli}@diee.unica.it

Abstract. Although some papers argued that multi-sensor fusion could improve performances and robustness of fingerprint verification systems, no previous work explicitly dealt with such topic, and no experimental evidence has been reported. In this paper, we show by experiments that a significant performance improvement can be obtained by decision-level fusion of two well-known fingerprint capture devices. As, to the best of our knowledge, this is the first work on multi-sensor fingerprint fusion, we believe that it can contribute to stimulate further researches on this promising topic.

1 Introduction

Fingerprints [1] are one of the most widely used biometrics for personal verification, mainly due to their difficult reproducibility, and the impossibility to forget them. Personal verification is aimed to grant or deny the access to certain critical resources (e.g., computer, ATM, or a restricted area in a building). The person that would access to a certain resource submits to the automatic verification system her/his identity and fingerprint. The system matches the given fingerprint with the one stored in its database and associated to the claimed identity. A degree of similarity, named "score", is computed. If such score is higher than a certain acceptance threshold, then the person is classified as a "genuine" (i.e., the claimed identity is accepted). Otherwise the person is classified as an "impostor", and the access to the required resource is denied.

Although many algorithms to match two fingerprints have been proposed so far, it is very difficult to obtain verification performances which satisfy the stringent requirements of many real fingerprint verification applications. In order to improve performances and robustness of fingerprint verification systems, various data fusion approaches have been proposed: fusion of multiple matching algorithms, multiple fingerprints, and multiple impressions of the same fingerprint [2-6].

In some works [6-7], it has been argued that fusion of different imaging sensors could improve performances and robustness of fingerprint verification systems. However, to the best of our knowledge, no previous work explicitly dealt with such topic, and no experimental evidence has been reported.

In our opinion, the investigation of multi-sensor fingerprint fusion has been discouraged by the required increase of system's cost and user co-operation. These

D. Maltoni and A.K. Jain (Eds.): BioAW 2004, LNCS 3087, pp. 307-317, 2004.

issues, which also hold for the case of multi-modal systems [7], point out that a multi-sensor fingerprint verification system should realize a good trade-off between the performances improvement and the system's cost increase. In other words, the acceptability of a multi-sensor fingerprint verification system strictly depends on the increase of verification accuracy achievable with respect to that of a single-sensor system. With regard to this issue, it is worth noting that information fusion theory and results achieved in other application fields support the hypothesis that combining information coming from different physical sensors can substantially improve fingerprint verification performances [8].

Moreover, other reasons can be raised to justify multi-sensor fingerprint fusion: to allow a higher coverage of the user population (a certain fingerprint sensor can be suitable only for certain types of fingerprints), and to discourage fraudulent attempts to deceive the system (submission of fake fingers could require different kinds of fake fingers for each sensor).

In this paper, we started to investigate the fusion of two well-known fingerprint sensors by adopting a simple fusion strategy. The selected capture devices are an optical and a capacitive sensor. The fusion strategy is performed at the so-called "decision-level" [8], that is, the matching scores separately provided by the two sensors are combined by score transformation (fusion rules) [3-4]. We show by experiments that the performance improvement theoretically and practically achievable by optical and capacitive sensor fusion can justify the system's cost and user co-operation increases. Results also show that such improvement can be obtained by simple fusion rules.

The paper organisation is as follows. Section 2 describes the proposed fusion architecture. Section 3 reports experimental results. Section 4 concludes the paper.

2 The Proposed Fusion Architecture

Figure 1 shows the architecture of the proposed multi-sensor fingerprint verification system. Firstly, the image of the user finger is acquired by the optical and the capacitive sensors. Then, the images are processed and two sets of features per image are extracted, in terms of minutiae-points. A minutiae-based matching algorithm is separately applied to the optical and capacitive minutiae sets, so providing two matching scores. Such scores are fused by score transformation.

2.1 The Selected Fingerprint Sensors

In this first stage of our research, we selected an optical and a capacitive sensor because they are the most widely used, and their cost is low with respect to other fingerprint sensors [1, 9]. Moreover, their technology is considered "mature". Finally, as it has been shown that fusion is effective when the information provided by different acquisition sources is used [8], their integration can be expected to work well.

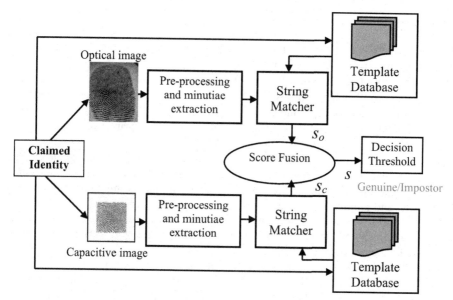

Fig. 1. Architecture of the proposed multi-sensor fingerprint verification system.

The optical sensors are characterised by a LED light source and a CCD placed on the side of a glass platen constituting a glass prism, on which the fingerprint to acquire is placed. The LED illuminates the fingerprint and the CCD captures the light reflected from the glass. According to the Snell law, the light is totally reflected in correspondence of the ridges, while it is totally absorbed in correspondence of the valleys. So, the CCD captures the light with high degree of luminance where a ridge is localised. The luminance degree decreases from the ridges to the valleys. Although the high image quality, the optical scanners cannot be easily integrated in PC or other electronic devices, because of their dimensions due to the prism inside such devices. Xia and O'Gorman [9] report various technological innovations to improve the optical sensors, especially in order to reduce their dimension. As an example, a "sheet prism" is introduced, so reducing the dimension of the sensor.

The core of the capacitive sensors is the sensing surface, which is made up of a two-dimensional array of silicon capacitor plates. The second plates are considered to be the finger skin. The capacitance is dependent on the distance between the finger skin, i.e. ridges and valleys, and the plates. The captured image is derived from the capacitance measures from each array element. The main limitation of the capacitive sensors is that the sensing area dimension depends on the number of capacitive plates. The sensors cost strongly increases with such number. Consequently, such sensors have a small sensing area, with the strong limitation that they often cannot guarantee a sufficient number of details to reliably match two fingerprints.

The different acquisition physical principles of such sensors are expected to be promising for a fusion algorithm [8]. Moreover, novel technological innovations [9] could allow to simplify the integration of such sensors in a unique acquisition module, in order to limit the overall system's cost and the user co-operation increase.

2.2 Fingerprint Image Processing

Our pre-processing of fingerprint images provided by the optical and capacitive sensors is characterised by the following steps (Figure 2):
- fingerprint enhancement by FFT and rank transformation;
- fingerprint image binarisation and separation from the background (we considered as background the image regions too sharp or poorly contrasted);
- thinning and skeletonisation of the obtained fingerprint image in order to reduce each ridge line to 1 pixel of width;
- post-processing of the obtained fingerprint image in order to delete the spurious ridges and to merge the interrupted ridge lines.

Finally, the minutiae-points are extracted. The minutiae-points [1] are defined as bifurcation and termination of each ridge line. The orientation of each minutia is also computed according to the dominating orientation of the ridge line which the minutia belongs to. Such features are widely used for fingerprint verification. They have shown to be the most appropriate features to this end [1-6].

The algorithm we selected to match the minutiae sets of two fingerprint is the so-called "String" algorithm [10]. The String algorithm can be summarised as follows. Let X be the template minutiae set. Let Y be the input minutiae set. For each minutia $x \in X$, the following algorithm is performed. For each $y \in Y$, x is aligned to y. After this alignment, x and y match perfectly. Let $A(x, y) = \{(x_i, y_i), x_i \in X, y_i \in Y : aligned(x_i, y_i) = true\}$ be the set of other couples of aligned minutiae. x_i and y_i are considered as aligned on the basis of a pre-defined "minutiae distance" not exceeding a certain fixed threshold. At the end of such loops, the value $\max_{x,y}\{|A(x, y)|\}$ is converted in a matching score by the formula:

$$score = \frac{\left(\max\{|A(x, y)|\}\right)^2}{|X| \cdot |Y|} \tag{1}$$

As usual, the obtained matching score is a real value between 0.0 and 1.0. It represents the degree of similarity between the compared fingerprint. The higher such value, the higher the degree of similarity.

It is worth remarking that, in our system, the String algorithm is applied separately to the input-template minutiae extracted from the images provided by the optical and the capacitive sensors (Figure 1).

2.3 Decision-Level Fusion of Optical and Capacitive Sensors

Let s_o and s_c be the matching scores provided by the matching algorithm applied to the images acquired from the optical and the capacitive sensors, respectively (Figure 1):
- Apply the following transformation to the above scores s_o and s_c to implement the fusion:

$$s = f(s_o, s_c) \tag{2}$$

Compare the obtained score value s with a threshold. The claimed identity is classified as "genuine user" if:

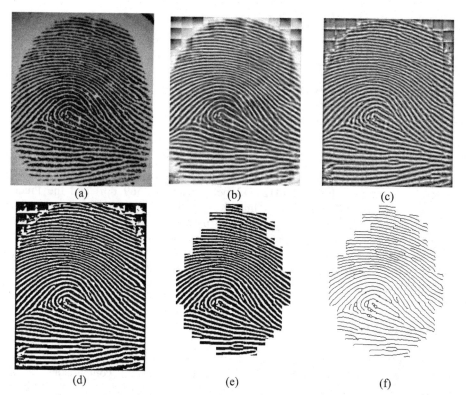

(a)   (b)   (c)

(d)   (e)   (f)

Fig. 2. Pre-processing of the fingerprint image. (a) Original fingerprint image acquired with an optical sensor. (b) Image processed by FFT. (c) Rank transformation. (d) Threshold-based binarisation. (e) Fingerprint/background segmentation. (f) Thinning, skeletonisation, and post processing: spurious ridges deletion, and interrupted ridges merge.

$$s > threshold \qquad (3)$$

otherwise it is classified as "impostor".

It is easy to see that the above methodology can be also used for the case of more than two matchers based on multiple sensors.

We investigated two kinds of score transformations according to eq. (2) to implement the fusion rule. The first fusion rule belongs to the so-called "fixed" fusion rules, because they require no parameter estimation. In particular, we investigated the mean of the scores (Mean):

$$s = \frac{s_o + s_c}{2} \qquad (4)$$

The second fusion rule belongs to the so-called "trained" fusion rules, because they require a training phase in order to set a certain number of parameters. In particular, we investigated the logistic transformation (Logistic):

$$s = \frac{1}{1 + \exp\left[-\left(w_0 + w_1 s_o + w_2 s_c\right)\right]} \qquad (5)$$

The parameters of the logistic transformation (w_0, w_1, w_2) were computed by a gradient descent algorithm with a cross-entropy loss function [11].

3 Experimental Results

3.1 The Data Set

According to the FVC protocol [12], we created a data set containing 1,200 multisensor fingerprint images captured from 20 volunteers (Figures 3 and 4). We used the Biometrika FX2000 (312x372 pels images at 569 dpi) and the Precise Biometrics MC100 (250x250 pels images at 500 dpi) as optical and capacitive sensors. The forefingers, the ringfingers and the middle-fingers of both hands were acquired (six classes per person). According to the FVC protocol [12], the total number of classes (different fingerprints) is 6*20 = 120. Ten impressions of each finger were acquired, so creating the data base containing 1,200 multi-sensor fingerprint images.

3.2 Experimental Protocol

For each verification algorithm we computed two sets of scores. The first one is the so called "genuine-matching scores" set G, made up of all comparisons among fingerprints of the same identity. A score from the set G belongs to the "genuine user" class. The second one is the "impostor matching scores" set I, made up of all comparisons among fingerprints of different identities. A score from the set I belongs to the "impostor" class. The total number of genuine and impostor comparisons was 5,400 and 1,398,000, respectively.

We randomly subdivided the above sets in two parts of the same size, so that: $G=G1 \cup G2$, $I=I1 \cup I2$. Sets $G1$ and $G2$, as well as $I1$ and $I2$, are disjoint. The training set $Tr=\{G1, I1\}$ was used to compute the weights of the logistic fusion rules. The test set $Tx=\{G2, I2\}$ was used to evaluate and compare the performances of algorithms.

Performances were assessed and compared in terms of:
- Equal Error Rate (EER) on the training set, correspondent to the error rate computed at the threshold value for which the percentage of genuine users wrongly rejected by the system (FRR) is equal to the percentage of impostors wrongly accepted by the system (FAR);
- Generalisation errors, i.e., we computed FAR and FRR on the test set using the EER threshold previously estimated.
- Total Error Rate (TER) [13], which is the overall generalisation error rate of the system computed at the EER threshold.

We also investigated the "complementarity" among results provided by optical and capacitive sensors, in order to analyse at which extent their fusion can allow recovering those fingerprints wrongly recognized by one sensor. Such analysis pointed out the potentialities of optical and capacitive sensor fusion.

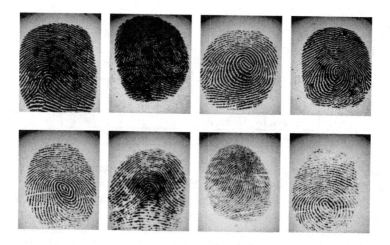

Fig. 3. Examples of fingerprint images acquired from the optical sensor.

Fig. 4. Examples of fingerprint images acquired from the capacitive sensor.

3.3 Results

Table 1 summarises our results in terms of EER on the training set (second column) and FAR and FRR on the test set computed with the EER threshold previously estimated (third and fourth columns).

As expected, the capacitive sensor performs notably worse than the optical one. This is mainly due to the reduced sensing surface (it is evident from Figures 3-4), which also reduces the number of extracted minutiae. This also causes that multiple impressions of the same fingerprints correspond to different parts of them, so the extracted minutiae do not match each others.

Table 1. Errors of the single and multi-sensor fingerprint verification systems. The EER is computed on the training set. FAR and FRR are computed on the test set using the EER threshold estimated from the training set.

	EER	FAR	FRR
Optical	3.4%	3.2%	3.6%
Capacitive	18.5%	18.2%	18.8%
Fusion by Mean	2.9%	3.1%	2.8%
Fusion by Logistic	2.3%	2.4%	2.3%

Results about fusion point out the performance improvement in terms of EER. In particular, fusion by logistic allows to reduce the EER from 3.4% to 2.3%. Results in terms of test set errors also point out that fusion allows improving the robustness of the system: in fact, the deviation between the expected (training set) performance (Table 1, second column) and test set performance (Table 1, third and fourth columns) is reduced by fusion, especially when the logistic fusion rule is used (Table 1, fifth row).

3.4 Analysis of Sensor Complementarity

With regard to results reported in section 3.3, it is worth noting that the performance difference between optical and capacitive sensors could limit the effectiveness of the fusion rules we used [8]. However, fusion provides performances better than the ones of the optical sensor (Table 1). This result suggests that optical and capacitive sensors are strongly complementary. The term "complementarity" refers to the overlapping degree among the sets of misclassified fingerprints of the optical and capacitive matchers [8]. The less such overlapping degree, the more the number of patterns theoretically "recoverable" (i.e., which can be correctly recognized) by a fusion rule. The maximum number of such patterns is theoretically recovered by the so-called "oracle" fusion rule [8]. The oracle is the ideal fusion rule able to select the matcher, if any, that correctly recognizes the input fingerprint. Accordingly, the oracle provides the minimum verification error achievable by fusion of optical and capacitive matchers. In other words, the oracle points out the maximum performance achievable by the investigated multi-sensor fusion.

In order to investigate such performance, we computed the Total Error Rate (TER) achieved by the individual matchers at the EER threshold, and the correspondent TER provided by the oracle. The TER value is given by the following formula:

$$TER(s^*) = \frac{N_i \cdot FAR(s^*) + N_g \cdot FRR(s^*)}{N_i + N_g} \qquad (6)$$

In eq. (6), s^* is the acceptance threshold on which the TER is computed, N_i and N_g are the number of impostor and genuine matching scores in the data set. Results are reported in Table 2.

Table 2. Results of the individual matchers and the oracle fuser in terms of Total Error Rate (TER) computed on the test set at the EER threshold estimated on the training set.

	Optical	Capacitive	Oracle
TER	3.2%	18.5%	0.7%

Reported results show that fusion is theoretically able to reduce the verification error rate close to zero. Obviously, this is just a theoretical lower bound for any fusion rules, as the oracle performance can be only approximated by fusion algorithms [14]. Nevertheless, this result points out that optical and capacitive matchers exhibit a very high degree of complementarity.

In order to show at which extent the investigated fusion rules allow recovering those fingerprints wrongly recognized by one sensor, we report in Table 3 the percentage of patterns recovered by fusion and wrongly classified by one sensor. Reported results refer to the percentages of fingerprints misclassified by one of the considered sensor and recovered, i.e., correctly classified, by the different fusion rules.

Table 3. Percentages of genuine and impostor fingerprints misclassified by one of the considered sensor and recovered, i.e., correctly classified, by the different fusion rules (the term "recover" rate is used for indicating these percentages). For each sensor, recover rates are computed with respect to the maximum number of wrongly classified genuine (second and fourth columns) and impostor patterns (third and fifth columns) in the test set.

	Recover Rate Optical Sensor		Recover Rate Capacitive Sensor	
	Genuine	Impostor	Genuine	Impostor
Fusion by Mean	87.1%	91.7%	93.6%	86.7%
Fusion by Logistic	75.8%	70.7%	97.9%	94.3%

Reported results are particularly relevant for the capacitive sensor. Although such sensor exhibits a performance considerably worse than that of the optical one, the information provided by the capacitive sensor is sufficient to recover many patterns wrongly classified by the optical sensor. For example, fusion by simple mean allows recovering 91.7% of impostor fingerprints which were wrongly classified by the optical sensor. This result contributes to increase the interest about the potentialities of multi-sensor fusion.

4 Conclusions

In this paper, a multi-sensor fingerprint verification system, based on the fusion of optical and capacitive sensors, has been presented. To the best of our knowledge, no work about such kind of fusion has been proposed so far, although it presents some substantial advantages, as discussed in section 1.

Reported results showed that the proposed multi-sensor system can improve performances of the best individual sensor (the optical sensor). Moreover, the analysis of the complementarity between optical and capacitive matchers pointed out the potentialities of multi-sensor fusion, which can theoretically achieve very low verification errors, so justifying the increase of the system's cost and user co-operation. The capability of recovering many patterns misclassified by one sensor contributes to increase the interest in such kind of fusion.

It is worth remarking that the same feature extraction process has been applied separately to the images produced by each capture device, and a simple fusion rule has been applied. Hence, the proposed system is very simple to implement.

Reported results are preliminary. Further work will concern the investigation of other fingerprint sensors, and the application of different matching algorithms and fusion rules.

Acknowledgments

This work was partially supported by the Italian Ministry of University and Scientific Research (MIUR) in the framework of the research project on distributed systems for multisensor recognition with augmented perception for ambient security and customisation.

References

[1] D. Maltoni, D. Maio, A.K Jain, and S. Prabhakar, Handbook of Fingerprint Recognition, Springer Verlag, 2003.

[2] A.K. Jain, S. Prabhakar, and S. Chen, Combining Multiple Matchers for a High Security Fingerprint Verification System. Pattern Recognition Letters, 20 (11-13) 1371-1379, 1999.

[3] G.L. Marcialis and F. Roli, Experimental results on Fusion of Multiple Fingerprint Matchers. Proc. 4th Int. Conf. on Audio and Video-Based Person Authentication AVBPA03, J. Kittler and M.S. Nixon Eds., Springer LNCS2688, pp. 814-820, 2003.

[4] G.L. Marcialis and F. Roli, Perceptron-based Fusion of Multiple Fingerprint Matchers. Proc. First Int. Work. on Artificial Neural Networks in Pattern Recognition ANNPR03, M. Gori and S. Marinai Eds., pp. 92-97, 2003.

[5] A. Ross, A.K. Jain, and J. Reisman, A Hybrid Fingerprint Matcher. Pattern Recognition, 36 (7) 1661-1673, 2003.

[6] S. Prabhakar and A.K. Jain, Decision-level Fusion in Fingerprint Verification. Pattern Recognition 35 (4) 861-874, 2002.

[7] A.K. Jain, R. Bolle, and S. Pankanti (Eds.), BIOMETRIC – Personal Identification in Networked Society. Kluwer Academic Publishers, Boston/Dordrecht/London, 1999.

[8] T. Windeatt and F. Roli (Eds.), Multiple Classifier Systems, Springer Verlag, Lecture Notes in Computer Science, Vol. 2709.

[9] X. Xia and L. O'Gorman, Innovations in fingerprint capture devices. Pattern Recognition, 36 (2) 361-369, 2003.

[10] A.K. Jain, L. Hong, and R. Bolle, On-line Fingerprint Verification. IEEE Transactions on Pattern Analysis and Machine Intelligence 19 (4) 302-314, 1999.

[11] C.M. Bishop, Neural Networks for Pattern Recognition. Oxford University Press, 1995.

[12] D. Maio, D. Maltoni, R.Cappelli, J.L. Wayman, and A.K. Jain, FVC-2000: Fingerprint Verification Competition. IEEE Transactions on Pattern Analysis and Machine Intelligence 24 (3) 402-412, 2002.

[13] P. Verlinde, P. Druyts, G. Chollet, and M. Acheroy, A multi-level data fusion approach for gradually upgrading the performances of identity verification systems, in B.Dasarathy Ed., Sensor Fusion: Architectures, Algorithms and Application III, vol.3719, pp.14-25, Orlando, FL, USA, SPIE Press, 1999.

[14] G. Giacinto and F. Roli, Dynamic Classifier Selection Based on Multiple Classifier Behaviour. Pattern Recognition 34 (9) 179-181, 2001.

Fusion of HMM's Likelihood and Viterbi Path for On-line Signature Verification

B. Ly Van, S. Garcia-Salicetti, B. Dorizzi

GET/INT (Institut National des Télécommunications), Dépt. EPH, INTERMEDIA,
9 rue Charles Fourier, 91011 EVRY France
{Bao.Ly_van, Sonia.Salicetti, Bernadette.dorizzi}@int-evry.fr

Abstract. We describe a method fusing two complementary scores descended from a Hidden Markov Model (HMM) for on-line signature verification. The signatures are acquired using a digitizer that captures pen-position, pen-pressure, and pen-inclination. A writer is considered as being authentic when the arithmetic mean of two similarity scores obtained on an input signature is higher than a threshold. The first score is related to the likelihood given by a HMM modeling the signatures of the claimed identity; the second score is related to the most likely path given by such HMM (Viterbi algorithm) on the input signature. Our approach was evaluated on the BIOMET database (1266 genuine signatures from 87 individuals), as well as on the Philips on-line signature database (1530 signatures from 51 individuals). On the Philips database, we study the influence of the amount of training data, and on the BIOMET database, that of time variability. Several Cross-Validation trials are performed to report robust results. We first compare our system on the Philips database to Dolfing's system, on one of his protocols (15 signatures to train the HMM). We reach in these conditions an Equal Error Rate (EER) of 0.95%, compared to an EER of 2.2% previously obtained by Dolfing. When considering only 5 signatures to train the HMM, the best results relying only on the likelihood yield an EER of 6.45% on the BIOMET database, and of 4.18% on the Philips database. The error rates drop to 2.84% on the BIOMET database, and to 3.54% on the Philips database, when fusing both scores by a simple arithmetic mean.

Keywords: Score Fusion, Hidden Markov Models, Viterbi path, Hamming distance, on-line signature verification

1 Introduction

The market of biometrics, nowadays, is composed of a great number of different modalities. The more performant ones, such as iris or fingerprint, suffer of a lack of acceptability by the population because of their intrusiveness. Besides, behavioral modalities, such as voice and face scan, are more natural but suffer from a lack of accuracy.

Signature is a behavioral modality used since a long time in everyday life, and therefore nowadays considered as non-intrusive by the general public. Also, it requires unexpensive hardware to be captured, and is easily sampled by the user in

D. Maltoni and A.K. Jain (Eds.): BioAW 2004, LNCS 3087, pp. 318-331, 2004.
© Springer-Verlag Berlin Heidelberg 2004

common portable electronic devices like Personal Digital Assistants (PDAs) and smartphones. Its main drawback however concerns variability: signature has strong intra-class and time variability, and in some cases a user may have more than one signature. Another fact is the facility of producing forgeries: signatures are visible, and no special device is needed to generate imitations, the impostor only has to do the gesture of signing. Moreover, the traditional use of signatures in civilian applications has strongly motivated imposture (imposture scenari will probably evolve in other modalities, with their common use in a civilian framework). Contrary to what occurs with other biometric modalities (voice, fingerprints, speech etc…), the evaluation of a signature verification system is done on a database containing not only random forgeries (the signatures of other writers) but also skilled forgeries. This renders the problem more difficult because the distributions of true versus impostor signatures, for a given writer, may have a large intersection.

Most works in On-line Signature Verification use Dynamic Time Warping techniques (DTW [1]), [2], [3] or Hidden Markov Models (HMM [1]) [4], [5], [6], [7], [8], [9], [10]. DTW is exploited in this framework to compare the input sequence to a stored template (there may be several templates too), since their lengths are different. HMMs are used to model the client's signature intrinsic variability; commonly, the decision of acceptance or rejection is taken by comparing the HMM's log-likelihood to a threshold. In this work, we use an HMM modeling of signatures, and produce first results using only

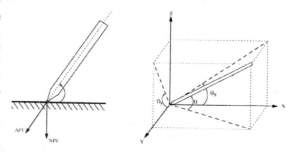

Fig. 1. Inclination angles of the Philips Signature Database

the log-likelihood information. We then show that the Viterbi path given by the HMM is complementary to the likelihood information. We thus propose to combine two similarity scores, derived from those informations, by a simple arithmetic mean. We evaluate this new approach on two different databases: the BIOMET database, collected in the framework of the French GET (Groupe des Ecoles des Télécommunications) research project called BIOMET ("Biometric Multimodal Identity Verification"), in which a multimodal database was acquired, containing the signature modality [11]. The other is the Philips on-line signature database [4].

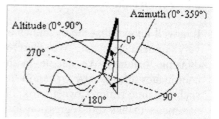

Fig. 2. The azimuth and altitude angles of the BIOMET database

This paper is organized as follows: we first describe in detail the verification system; we then explain the experimental conditions, that is the description of the two databases used in this work and of three experimental protocols. Finally, results are given and analyzed.

2 System Design

2.1 Preprocessing

As described in [4] and in [11], the digitizer captures from each signature several items of information: the coordinates of each point

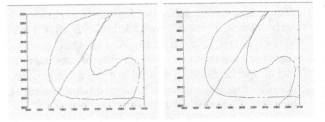

Fig. 3. The effect of coordinate filtering (*right*) on the initial signature (*left*)

sampled on the trajectory (*x(t), y(t)*), the pressure *p(t)* in such a point, and the pen-inclination information, e.g. the position of the pen in space, that is differently represented in both databases used: in the Philips database, what is encoded is the "pen-tilt" of the pen in *x* and *y* directions, that is two angles resulting from the projection of the pen in each of the coordinate planes *xOz* and *yOz* (see Fig. 1). In the BIOMET database, the standard *azimuth* and *altitude* angles in the literature are used (see Fig. 2).

We observed some noise in the data, due to both quantification and to the high sampling rate of the digitizer. Different filtering strategies were thus chosen according to each parameter. An analysis of the spectrum of each coordinate on several signatures showed that more than 95% of the signal's power is represented by frequencies below 10 Hz. This confirms that low frequencies are the most informative ones in signatures, whereas high frequencies represent involuntary oscillations of the pen during the signing process. The filtering is done with a 3rd order FIR (Finite Impulse Response) low-pass filter with cut-off frequency of 10 Hz. Figure 3 shows how the shape of the signature is kept while the oscillations due to the capture by the digitizer are removed.

Also, the pen-inclination has few sharp variations during the signing process. Our goal was to keep this information while removing oscillations. A median filter of window size 5 was judged as the best compromise [12]: the window shifts along the pen-tilt signal one point at a time, and the median value of the signal in the window is attributed to all the points in the window.

2.2 Feature Extraction

It is well known that the dynamics of a signing process is very signer-dependent. We therefore extracted several dynamic features. We denote in the following the pen coordinates at time *t* by *x(t)* and *y(t)*. In order to estimate such dynamic features, we approximate the derivative of a parameter thanks to a regression formula [13] of order *N* given below, instead of using differences between consecutive samples. The expression giving the order *N* regression on a parameter *x(t)* at time *t* is the following:

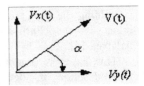

Fig. 4. The alpha angle

$$reg(x(t), N) = \frac{\sum_{k=1}^{N} k(x(t+k) - x(t-k))}{2\sum_{k=1}^{N} k^2} . \tag{1}$$

We consider a regression of order $N=2$. This permits to obtain derivative curves that present softened waveforms, since small noisy variations are removed. 25 dynamic features are considered. Some are extracted at each point of the signature, computed according to equation (1):

- the speed in x and y directions:

$$v_x(t) = reg(x(t),2) . \tag{2}$$

$$v_y(t) = reg(y(t),2) . \tag{3}$$

- the absolute speed:

$$v(t) = \sqrt{v_x^2 + v_y^2} . \tag{4}$$

- the acceleration in x and y directions:

$$a_x(t) = reg(v_x(t),2) . \tag{5}$$

$$a_y(t) = reg(v_y(t),2) . \tag{6}$$

- the absolute acceleration:

$$a(t) = \sqrt{a_x^2 + a_y^2} . \tag{7}$$

- the tangential acceleration:

$$a_t(t) = reg(\|v(t)\|,2) . \tag{8}$$

- the angle α and its cosine and sine:

$$\cos\alpha(t) = \frac{v_x(t)}{\|v(t)\|} . \tag{9}$$

$$\sin\alpha(t) = \frac{v_y(t)}{\|v(t)\|} . \tag{10}$$

- the angle

$$\phi(t) = reg(\alpha(t),2) . \tag{11}$$

as well as its cosine and sine.

- the pressure p
- the pressure variation

$$\Delta(p(t)) = reg(p(t),2) . \tag{12}$$

- the pen-inclination measured by two angles β, γ
- the order one variation of the two pen-inclination angles β, γ

$$\Delta\beta(t) = reg(\beta(t),2) . \tag{13}$$

$$\Delta\gamma(t) = reg(\gamma(t),2) . \tag{14}$$

- the curvature radius:

$$r(t) = \frac{a_t(t)}{reg(\phi(t),2)} \ . \tag{15}$$

- the normalized coordinates $(x(t)-x_g, y(t)-y_g)$ relatively to the gravity center (x_g, y_g) of the signature.

Some features are devoted to compute the information in a neighborhood of each point:
- the length to width ratio on windows of size 5 and 7 sampled points, centered on the current point.
- the ratio of the minimum over the maximum speed on a window of 5 points, centered on the current point.

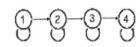

Fig. 5. Hmm topology

2.3 The Signature HMM

A continuous left-to-right HMM was chosen to model each signer's characteristics: this means that each person's signature is modeled through a double stochastic process, characterized by a given number of states with an associated set of transition probabilities among them, and, in each of such states, a continuous density multivariate Gaussian mixture. A complete HMM description can be found in [1].

The topology of our signature HMM only authorizes transitions from each state to itself and to its immediate right-hand neighbors. Also, the covariance matrix of each multivariate Gaussian in each state is considered diagonal.

Optimal Number of State s. The number of states in the HMM modeling the signatures of a given person is determined according to the total number T_{total} of all the sampled points available when putting together the signatures that are used to train the HMM. We found necessary to have in average at least 30 sampled points per Gaussian for a good reestimation process, and we fixed the number of Gaussians per state to 4. Then, the number of states N is computed as:

$$N = \left\lfloor \frac{T_{total}}{4*30} \right\rfloor \ . \tag{16}$$

Let's notice that this number depends not only on the length of signatures, but also on the amount of signatures available for training. Indeed, when there are more signatures in the training database, we consider that it is better to train the HMM with the same number of sampled points per state and to use more states, than increasing the number of sampled points per state. Since in a HMM each state is devoted to

++ odd states
⁓ even states

Fig. 6. The segmentation of a training signature modeled by a 10 states HMM

model a stationary part of the signature, when increasing to a certain extent the number of states, we obtain a better modeling of the signature.

Figure 6 shows on a given training signature, the range of points modeled by each state, when using 5 signatures to train a HMM.

Personalized Feature Normalization.
To improve the quality of the modeling, we also normalized per person each of the 25 features described in section 2.2, in order to give the same standard deviation to each of them. This guarantees that each parameter contributes with the same importance to the emission probability computation performed by each state on a given feature vector. On the other hand,

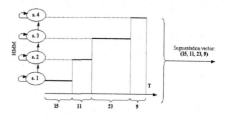

Fig. 7. Computation of the Segmentation Vector

this permits a better training of the HMM, since each Gaussian marginal density is neither too flat nor too sharp. Indeed, if it is too sharp, it will not tolerate too much variations of a given parameter in genuine signatures or, in other words, the probability value will be quite different on different genuine signatures.

This normalization factor depends on the standard deviation of each parameter on the training database of the given person, and on a multiplicative factor σ_{opt} that we optimized on all the population. Indeed, the normalization of feature x is done as follows:

$$x' = \frac{\sigma_{opt} * x}{\sigma_x}.$$ (17)

where $\overline{\sigma_x}$ is the mean standard deviation of feature x considering the signatures of the training database. During the test phase, the signature will be normalized by the normalization factor of the corresponding HMM.

Why is fusion interesting? The Baum-Welch algorithm [1] is used for parameter reestimation. In the verification phase, the Viterbi algorithm [1] permits to compute an approximation of the log-likelihood of the input signature given the model, as well as the sequence of visited states (called "most likely path" or "Viterbi path"). Given a signature's most likely path, we consider a N-components *segmentation vector*, N being the number of states in the claimed identity's HMM.

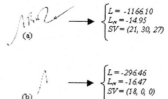

Fig. 8. A genuine signature (*a*) and a forgery (*b*) with their likelihoods (*raw: L, normalized: L_N*) and segmentation vectors (*SV*)

This vector has in the ith position, the number of feature vectors that were associated to state i by the Viterbi path (see Fig.7).

As the length of a signature influences considerably the value of the log-likelihood, the latter is normalized by the number of sampled points in the signature, as in other works [4], [8], [10]. We may indeed use the *normalized* log-likelihood to verify the claimed identity. But in this case shown in Figure 8, if a forger imitates only some part of the signature (usually the easiest part), the *normalized* log-likelihood of this forgery will be close to that obtained on a genuine signature (despite the fact that the original log-likelihoods are very different (see Fig. 8)). This happens because the forged part of the signature is "emitted" with high probability by few states of the HMM, namely those modeling that part of the genuine signature. Thus, only those states will be visited by the Viterbi path. Therefore, the segmentation vectors of the genuine and the forged signatures are very different (see Fig. 8). The example of figure 8 shows indeed that using only likelihood information renders difficult to discriminate such signatures contrary to what happen with segmentation vectors.

In this paper, we study the use of the Viterbi path in addition to the likelihood information. Figure 9 represents the log-likelihood-based score (*Likelihood score*) and the Viterbi path-based score (*Viterbi score*) jointly, on data from the BIOMET database. We notice that those scores are quite complementary: indeed, the exclusive use of the *Likelihood score* yields a very important overlap of genuine and impostor distributions. Moreover, Figure 9 shows that the *Viterbi score* combined to the *Likelihood score* reduces this overlap. It is thus sufficient to simply average both scores. We explain in the following how to compute the *Likelihood score*, the *Viterbi score* and how to fuse those two scores.

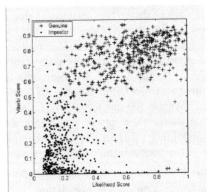

Fig. 9. Likelihood score vs Viterbi score

2.4 Scores Computation

Likelihood Score. On a test signature, we compute the distance d_l (Likelihood distance) between its log-likelihood and the average log-likelihood on the training database. This distance is then shifted to a similarity value s_l (Likelihood score) between 0 and 1, by the use of an exponential function

$$s_l = \exp(\frac{-d_l}{25}) \ . \tag{18}$$

where 25 is the number of features; indeed, dividing d_l by the number of features permits to guarantee that only the "almost linear" part of the exponential function is exploited.

Viterbi Score. We characterize each of the training signatures by a *segmentation vector*. For a test signature, we compute the Hamming distance d_h between its associated *segmentation vector* and all the *segmentation vectors* of the training database, and we average such distances. This average distance is then shifted to a similarity measure s_v (Viterbi score) by an exponential function:

$$s_v = \exp(\frac{-d_h}{30*N}) \ . \tag{19}$$

The normalization factor 30 in the denominator corresponds to the minimum number of sampled points per Gaussian, as previously explained in equation (16), and N is the number of components of *segmentation vector*. Those factors are used to map the scores s_v into the [0, 1] interval in an efficient way. Indeed, this way, the "almost linear" part of the exponential function is exploited.

The extra computational cost to obtain the Viterbi score is very low compared to that of the traditional likelihood approach. Indeed, the Viterbi path is already available when using the Viterbi algorithm for verification, as we do. Then, to compare the segmentation vectors of two signatures having lengths T_1 and T_2, the complexity is $O(T_1+T_2)$.

Fusion Score. The HMM framework permits thus to obtain, on a given test signature, two similarity measures (s_l and s_v), as described previously. We fuse these two informations by a simple arithmetic mean:

$$s = \frac{s_l + s_v}{2} \ . \tag{20}$$

3 Experimental Setup

As all scores belong to the [0, 1] interval, we let the decision threshold vary in this interval to obtain a ROC [14] or DET curve [15]. For each value of the decision threshold, we compute the Total Error Rate (TE) on the test database (all the genuine signatures that are not used to train the HMM of the clients, as well as forgeries). We also compute as usually the False Acceptance Rate (FA) and False Rejection Rate (FR). Both the Equal Error Rate (EER) and Minimum Total Error Rate (TE min) points will be reported in results.

3.1 Databases

Philips On-line Signature Database. Signatures in the Philips database [4] were captured on a digitizer at a sampling rate of up to 200 Hz. At each sampled point, the digitizer captures the coordinates $(x(t),y(t))$, the axial pen pressure $p(t)$ (Fig. 1), and the "pen-tilt" of the pen in x and y directions, that is two angles resulting from the projection of the pen in each of the coordinate planes xOz and yOz.

This database contains data from 51 individuals: 30 genuine signatures of each individual, and different kind of forgeries of each signature. Three types of forgeries were considered: "over the shoulder" (O.S.), "home improved" (H.I.) and "professional" (P.R.). The first kind of forgeries (O.S.) was captured by the forger after seeing the genuine signature being written, that is after learning the dynamic properties of the signature by observation of the signing process. Of course, in this case, the forger also learns the spatial image of the signature. The second type of forgeries (H.I.) is made in other conditions: the forger only imitates the static image of the genuine signature, and has the possibility of practicing the signature at home. Finally, the last kind of forgeries (P.R.) is produced by individuals who have professional expertise in handwriting analysis. They use their experience in discriminating genuine from forged signatures to produce high quality spatial forgeries.

This database contains 1530 genuine signatures, 1470 "over the shoulder" forgeries (30 per individual except two), 1530 "home improved" forgeries (30 per individual), and 200 "professional" forgeries (10 per individual for 20 individuals).

BIOMET On-line Signature Database. Signatures in the BIOMET database were acquired on a digitizer WACOM Intuos2 A6, with an ink pen, at the sampling rate of 100Hz. At each sampled point of the signature, the digitizer captures the (x, y) coordinates, the pressure p and two angles (*azimuth* and *altitude*), encoding the position of the pen in space (Fig. 2).

The signatures were captured in two sessions with five months spacing between them. In the first session, 5 genuine signatures and 6 forgeries were captured per person. In the second session, 10 genuine signatures and 6 forgeries were captured per person. The 12 forgeries of each person's signature were made by 4 different impostors (3 per impostor in each session). Impostors try to imitate the image of the genuine signature.

As for certain persons in the database some genuine signatures or some forgeries are missing, we selected 87 individuals for our experiments. In these conditions, we have at disposal 1266 genuine signatures and 960 forgeries.

3.2   Verification Protocols

Protocol on the Philips Database (Protocol 1). We chose the same protocol as the one described in [4] in order to compare our results to those in [4]. In this framework, a lot of genuine signatures are available to train the HMM of a person, that is 15 signatures. The remaining 15 genuine signatures and the forgeries are used for testing purposes. Training and tests were made 10 times, as the HMM is sensitive to the initialization (done by K-means). The ROC curve is plotted considering the scores given by the 10 HMMs configurations on the testing signatures. We compute the number of False Acceptances and False Rejections as a summation of the latter over the set of HMM configurations.

Protocol on the Philips Database with few training data (Protocol 2). In this framework, we have only 5 genuine signatures available to train the HMM of a person. We sample randomly 5 signatures out of the 30 genuine signatures available in the Philips database, to train a HMM; the remaining 25 genuine signatures and the forgeries are used for testing purposes. We repeat this process 50 times. The DET curve is plotted considering the scores given by the 50 HMM configurations on the testing signatures.

This protocol is used to compare our new approach based on the fusion of two different informations given by the HMM, to the standard HMM-based verification framework.

Protocol on the BIOMET Database with few training data (Protocol 3). We have only 5 genuine signatures available to train the HMM of a person. We sample randomly 5 signatures out of the 10 genuine signatures available in the second session of the BIOMET database, to train a HMM. We repeat this process 50 times. The DET curve is plotted considering the scores given by the 50 HMM configurations on the testing signatures. There are two test configurations: in both, all the forgeries available (from both sessions) are used, leading to a single FA rate for each value of threshold. There are in this case two values of the FR rate: one corresponds to training and testing on genuine data captured in the same session (5 genuine for training, and 5 genuine for testing from the second session), and the other corresponds to training and testing on data captured in two different sessions (5 genuine for training from the second session, and 5 genuine for testing from the first session).

This protocol is also used to compare our new approach based on the fusion of two different informations given by the HMM, to the standard HMM-based verification framework.

Using the BIOMET database permits to study the influence of time variability, since the spacing between the two sessions is quite important (5 months).

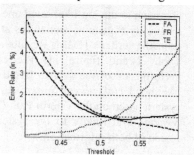

Fig. 10. ROC curve for protocol 1 with $\sigma_{opt}=1.6$

4 Results

4.1 Protocol 1

We give below the results in function of different values of the multiplicative factor σ_{opt} (see equation 17) that we optimized on all the population:

Table 1. Results of the signature verification system based only on the likelihood information, given by HMM trained on 15 genuine signatures. Different normalization factors σ_{opt} have been tested. NN stands for No Normalization

σ_{opt}	NN	0.7	1	1.3	1.6	2	2.5	3.2	6	10
TE min (%)	1.32	1.59	0.97	0.92	0.88	0.97	1.10	1.23	1.98	1.98
EER (%)	1.35	2.04	1.02	0.96	0.95	1.03	1.13	1.24	1.99	2.02

Table 1 shows the important influence of the normalization factor: for instance, when $\sigma_{opt}=10$, the EER value is twice the value attained in the best case ($\sigma_{opt}=1.6$). The best result is obtained with $\sigma_{opt}=1.6$, leading to an EER of 0.95% (Fig. 10). This result is very good compared to those reported in [4] an EER of 2.2% is obtained on the same database and experimental conditions. We also noticed that there is an interval ($\sigma_{opt} \in [1,4]$) in which the performance are quite stable. After this study, the value of $\sigma_{opt}=2$ is used for protocols 2 and 3.

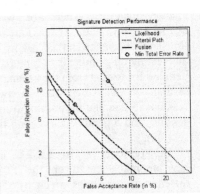

4.2 Protocol 2

This protocol permits to compare our new approach to the log-likelihood one. Indeed, we have only 5 genuine signatures at disposal to train the writer's HMM. Results are given in Table 2 and figure 11. We compare the performance of the system based on the log-likelihood (*Likelihood System*) to that of the system based on the Viterbi Path (*Viterbi Path System*), and finally to the system based on fusion of both informations.

Fig. 11. DET curve for protocol 2

Table 2. Results of signature verification based on likelihood information, Viterbi path and fusion of both informations, tested on the Philips Database

	Likelihood	Viterbi Path	Fusion
TE min (%)	3.73	7.66	3.26
EER (%)	4.18	8.12	3.54

At the EER point, we notice that results are improved from 4.18% to 3.54% (15% of improvement).

4.3 Protocol 3

We see that the influence of time variability is very important on all systems compared in Table 3. Globally, error rates get degraded of about 50% when testing on the 1st session compared to tests made on the 2nd session.

Also, it is worth noticing that the *Viterbi Path System* gives on this database a better performance than the *Likelihood System* alone. This can be explained by the fact that in the BIOMET database, there is a strong

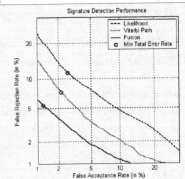

Fig. 12. DET curve for protocol 3 on genuine test data from the 2nd session

intra-class variability, even in a same session (of course, time variability increases this problem). In these conditions, the use of the likelihood system is not sufficient to reach an acceptable level of performance, and fusion appears as a good strategy. The *Likelihood System* reaches an EER of 6.45% and fusion lowers such rate to 2.84% (56% of improvement) when testing on the 2nd session (Fig. 12).

Let's also recall that 50 trials (for protocols 2 and 3) or 10 trials (for protocol 1) were made to train and test the verification system to strengthen the confidence level of such results. Figure 13 shows the average DET curve and the 50 DET curves corresponding to 50 trials of the fusion system on the BIOMET database (protocol 3). Considering a single trial, the EER varies from 2.1% to 3.7% when testing on the 2nd session, while on data from the 1st session it varies from 7% to 10%.

Table 3. Results of signature verification based on likelihood information, Viterbi path and fusion of the both informations, tested on the BIOMET Database

genuine test data		Likelihood	Viterbi Path	Fusion
2nd session	TE min (%)	5.27	3.71	2.47
	EER (%)	6.45	4.07	2.84
1st session	TE min (%)	14.30	7.44	6.95
	EER (%)	16.70	9.21	8.57

5 Conclusion and Perspectives

We have presented in this work a continuous HMM-based approach to model signatures of a writer. We compared this model to the HMM-based approach presented by Dolfing, using his protocol, decribed in [4]. We have shown that our model permits to improve the results presented by Dolfing in [4], from an EER of 2.2% to one of 0.95%. We have also improved our previous results [7] [8], thanks to a better choice of the features extracted on the signature, and to a personalized normalization of such features that enhances the quality of the writer's model.

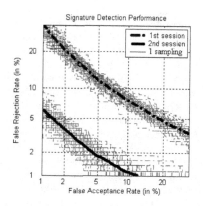

Fig. 13. Average and single DET curves of 50 trials

We have exploited in this paper, the complementarity of informations provided by both the likelihood and the *segmentation vector* (Viterbi path) of the HMM modeling a given writer. This fusion strategy has never been used before in the literature. It is also worth noticing that the *segmentation vector* alone may be more efficient for verification using databases presenting a strong intra-class variability.

We have shown that the combination of such two informations permits to improve significantly writer verification. A simple but commonly used score fusion strategy (arithmetic mean) was justified in our experimental framework. Indeed, the fusion score permits to better separate the genuine and impostor distributions. In the best case, 56% of errors made by the system using only the *Likelihood Score*, are removed when fusing such score with the *Viterbi Score*: the EER drops from 6.45% to 2.84%. Our results are very robust thanks to a Cross-Validation strategy.

Also, as discussed in the paper, the fusion of these two informations renders the system resistant to specific forgery scenario. In the future, we will evaluate the efficiency of our approach on databases enriched by different forgery scenario.

6 Acknowledgements

The authors would like to thanks Philips for having put at disposal its database. This work is part of the GET research project BIOMET.

7 References

1. L. Rabiner, B.H. Juang, "Fundamentals of Speech Recognition", Prentice Hall Signal Processing Series, 1993.
2. Y. Komiya, T. Matsumoto, "On-line Pen Input Signature Verification PPI (Pen-Position / Pen-Pressure / Pen-Inclination)," IEEE, 1999.
3. A.K. Jain, Friederike D. Griess and Scott D. Connell, "On-line Signature Verification", Pattern Recognition, vol. 35, no. 12, pp. 2963--2972, Dec 2002.
4. J.G.A. Dolfing, "Handwriting recognition and verification, a Hidden Markov approach", Ph.D. thesis, Philips Electronics N.V., 1998.
5. R. Kashi, J. Hu, W.L. Nelson, W. Turin, "A Hidden Markov Model approach to online handwritten signature verification", International Journal on Document Analysis and Recognition, Vol. 1, pp. 102-109, 1998.
6. G. Rigoll, A. Kosmala, "A systematic comparison of on-line and off-line methods for signature verification with Hidden Markov Models", Proc. of 14th International Conference on Pattern Recognition, pp. 1755-1757, Brisbane, Autralia, 1998.
7. M. Fuentes, S. Garcia-Salicetti, B. Dorizzi "On-line Signature Verification: Fusion of a Hidden Markov Model and a Neural Network via a Support Vector Machine", Proc. of International Workshop on Frontiers of Handwriten Recognition-8, pp. 253-258, Niagara on the Lake, Canada, August 2002.
8. M. Fuentes, D. Mostefa, J. Kharroubi, S. Garcia-Salicetti, B. Dorizzi, G. Chollet, "Identity Verification by fusion of biometric data: on-line signature and speech", Proc. of the COST-275 Workshop, Rome, 2002.
9. J. Ortega-Garcia, J. Gonzalez-Rodriguez, D. Simon-Zorita, S. Cruz-Llanas, "From Biometrics Technology to Applications regarding face, voice, signature and fingerprint Recognition Systems", in Biometrics Solutions for Authentication in an E-World, (D. Zhang, ed.), pp. 289-337, Kluwer Academic Publishers, July 2002.
10. J. G. A. Dolfing, E. H. L. Aarts, and J. J. G. M. Van Oosterhout, "On-line signature verification with hidden Markov models", Proc. of the International Conference on Pattern Recognition, pp. 1309-1312, Brisbane Autralia, 1998.

11. S. Garcia-Salicetti, C. Beumier, G. Chollet, B. Dorizzi, J. Leroux-Les Jardins, J. Lanter, Y. Ni, D. Petrovska-Delacretaz, "BIOMET: a Multimodal Person Authentication Database Including Face, Voice, Fingerprint, Hand and Signature Modalities", Proc. of 4th International Conference on Audio and Vidio-Based Biometric Person Authentication, pp. 845-853,Guildford, UK, 2003.
12. K.R. Castleman, "Digital Image Processing", Prentice Hall, 1996.
13. F. K Soong, A.E. Rosenberg, "On the Use of Instantaneous and Transitional Spectral Information in Speaker Recognition", IEEE Trans. on Acoust., Speech and Signal Proc., vol. ASSP-36, no. 6, pages 871-879, 1988.
14. J.P. Egan, "Signal Detection Theory and ROC analysis", Academic Press, New York, 1975.
15. A. Martin, G. Doddington, T. Kamm, M. Ordowski, M. Przybocki, "The DET Curve in Assessment of Detection Task Performance", Proc. EUROSPEECH'97, Vol. 4, pp. 1895-1898, Rhodes Greece, 1997.

A New Approach on Multimodal Biometrics Based on Combining Neural Networks Using AdaBoost

K. Maghooli[1] and M.S. Moin[1, 2]

[1] Biomedical Engineering Dept., Science and Research Campus, Islamic Azad University,
Tehran, Iran
{maghooli, moin}@itrc.ac.ir
[2] Biometrics Research Lab., Iran Telecommunication Research Center (ITRC),
Tehran, Iran

Abstract. In this paper, we propose a new approach in the field of multimodal biometrics, based on AdaBoost. AdaBoost has been used to overcome the problem of limited number of training data in unimodal systems, by combining neural networks as weak learners. The simplest possible neural network, i.e. only one neuron, plays the role of a weak learner in our system. We have conducted different experiments with different number of AdaBoost iterations (experts) and input features. We compared the results of our AdaBoost based multimodal system, using features of three different unimodal systems, with the results obtained separately from these unimodal systems, i.e. a GMM based speaker verification, an HMM based face verification and a SVM based face verification. It has been shown that even the average FAR of the multimodal system (%0.058) is much less than the lowest FARs of each of the unimodal systems (%0.32 for SV, %4 for HMM based face verification and %1 for SVM based face verification systems), while the average FRR of the multimodal system is acceptable (%2.1).

1 Introduction

Biometric verification systems have evolved from using unimodal data to multimodal data, since multimodal systems exhibit higher performances in different aspects.

Biometric systems using a single biometric trait have to contend with problems like noisy data, restricted degrees of freedom, failure-to-enroll, spoof attacks, and unacceptable error rates. Multimodal biometric systems that use multiple traits of an individual for authentication alleviate some of these problems while improving the verification performance.

In general, information fusion can be performed in three different levels: (1) input (2) features and (3) decision. Due to the large dimension of input space, input fusion is not used in multimodal biometrics. On the other hand, works on feature fusion yields to better results comparing to unimodal biometric systems. In [1], a number of feature fusion and decision fusion techniques were implemented and compared for combining the DCT[1] visual features with traditional acoustic features.

---

[1] Discrete Cosine Transform

D. Maltoni and A.K. Jain (Eds.): BioAW 2004, LNCS 3087, pp. 332-341, 2004.
© Springer-Verlag Berlin Heidelberg 2004

Hierarchical discriminant feature fusion and asynchronous decision fusion by means of the multi-stream Hidden Markov Model consistently improved ASR[2] for both clean and noisy speech.

In current decision fusion multi-modal verification systems, different modalities are processed by specially designed modality experts, where each expert gives an opinion score for the claimed identity. A high score indicates that the person is a true claimant, while a low score suggests that he/she is an impostor. In order to make the final decision to either accept or reject the claim, the scores from different modality experts are combined in a decision level.

Several works on decision fusion are done including: Impostor distribution function on face and fingerprint [2], SVM[3] on face and voice [3,4,5], modified cost Bayesian on voice and face/lip movement[3,6,7,8,9,10], adaptive modified cost Bayesian on face and voice [7], C4.5 decision tree and MLP on face and voice[3], DS[4] theory on voice and lip movement [6], and probabilistic theory on face, voice and lip movement [6,11,1,12], K-Means [13,14,15], AND ‹OR , BEST ‹ FKM[5] ‹ FVQ[6]‹ FDKM[7]‹ FDVQ[8]‹ MRBF[9] [13] on voice and face/lip movement, PDBNN[10] on face and hand geometry [16], linear combination on face and voice [17,18,19], majority vote on face, voice and lip movement [20,21], PCA[11] [22], Supervised soft decision fusion on face, voice and fingerprint [23].

Fusion level, fusion method, input biometrics, input database and test conditions are different in the above mentioned methods, thus, it's difficult to compare these methods and to determine the best amongst all. However, in a general point of view, methods based on intelligent approaches such as fuzzy methods and neural networks, which have the best fusion performances, are suggested as the best candidates for implementing multimodal biometric systems.

In this paper, we propose a new approach for multimodal biometrics, based on AdaBoost[12]. Adaboost is basically a method for improving classifier accuracy, by first performing iterative search to locate the regions/ examples that are more difficult to predict, then, thorough each iteration, by rewarding accurate predictions on those regions and finally, by combining the rules from each iteration [24-25].

AdaBoost has been used to overcome the problem of limited number of training data in unimodal systems, by combining neural networks as weak learners.

We compared the results of our AdaBoost based multimodal system, using features of three different unimodal systems, with the results obtained separately from these unimodal systems, i.e. a GMM based speaker verification, an HMM based face verification and a SVM based face verification.

---

[2] Audio-Visual automatic Speech Recognition
[3] Support Vector Machine
[4] Dempster shafer
[5] Fuzzy K-Means
[6] Fuzzy Vector Quantization
[7] Fuzzy Data K-Means
[8] Fuzzy Data Vector Quantization
[9] Median Radial Basis Function
[10] Probabilistic Decision Based Neural Network
[11] Principle Component Analysis
[12] Adaptive Boosting

Input: sequence of N examples $(x_1, y_1), \ldots, (x_N, y_N)$
with labels $y_i \in Y = \{1, \ldots, k\}$

Init: $D_1(i) = 1/N$ for all i	**Init:** let $B = \{(i,y) : i \in \{1, \ldots, N\}, y \neq y_i\}$ $D_1(i,y) = 1/\|B\|$ for all $(i,y) \in B$

Repeat:
1. Train neural network with respect to distribution D_t and obtain hypothesis $h_t : X \to Y$

2. calculate the weighted error of h_t:
$$\epsilon_t = \sum_{i:h_t(x_i) \neq y_i} D_t(i)$$
abort loop if $\epsilon_t > \frac{1}{2}$

3. set $\beta_t = \epsilon_t/(1 - \epsilon_t)$

4. update distribution D_t
$$D_{t+1}(i) = \frac{D_t(i)}{Z_t}\beta_t^{\delta_i}$$
with $\delta_i = (h_t(x_i) = y_i)$
and Z_t a normalization constant

Output: final hypothesis:
$$f(x) = \arg\max_{y \in Y} \sum_{t:h_t(x)=y} \log\frac{1}{\beta_t}$$

Repeat:
1. Train neural network with respect to distribution D_t and obtain hypothesis $h_t : X \times Y \to [0,1]$

2. calculate the pseudo-loss of h_t:
$$\epsilon_t = \frac{1}{2}\sum_{(i,y) \in B} D_t(i,y)(1 - h_t(x_i, y_i) + h_t(x_i, y))$$

3. set $\beta_t = \epsilon_t/(1 - \epsilon_t)$

4. update distribution D_t
$$D_{t+1}(i) = \frac{D_t(i)}{Z_t}\beta_t^{\frac{1}{2}((1+h_t(x_i,y_i)-h_t(x_i,y))}$$
where Z_t is a normalization constant

Output: final hypothesis:
$$f(x) = \arg\max_{y \in Y}\sum_t \left(\log\frac{1}{\beta_t}\right)h_t(x,y)$$

Fig. 1. Basic β-type AdaBoost algorithm (left), multi-class extension using confidence scores (right).

The reminder of this paper is organized as follows. Section 2 is dedicated to a brief description of AdaBoost algorithm. Section 3 presents our system specifications. Section 4 contains the details of experiments and results. Section 5 includes a comparison between the results obtained from unimodal and multimodal systems. Discussion and concluding remarks are presented in Section 6.

2 AdaBoost

AdaBoost is a boosting algorithm, running a given weak learner several times on slightly altered training data, and combining the hypotheses to one final hypothesis, in order to achieve higher accuracy than the weak learner's hypothesis would have.

The main idea of AdaBoost is to assign each example of the given training set a weight. At the beginning all weights are equal, but in every round the weak learner returns a hypothesis, and the weights of all examples classified wrong by that hypothesis are increased. That way, the weak learner is forced to focus on the difficult examples of the training set. The final hypothesis is a combination of the hypotheses of all rounds, namely a weighted majority vote, where hypotheses with lower classification error have higher weight.

In this section, the two versions of AdaBoost, called β-type and α-type, are described. We present pseudo-code for the two versions of β-type AdaBoost algorithm in Fig. 1. These two versions are identical for binary classification problems and differ only in their handling of problems with more than two classes [26].
α-type AdaBoost algorithm can be presented as follow:

- Initialize distribution over the training set $D_1(i) = 1/m$.
- For t=1, ..., T:

    - Train *Weak Learner* using distribution D_t.

    - Choose a weight (or confidence value) $\alpha_t \in R$.

    - Update the distribution over the training set:

$$D_{t+1}(i) = \frac{D_t(i)e^{-\alpha_t y_i h_t(x_i)}}{Z_t} \qquad (1)$$

We should choose α_t to minimize Z_t (normalization factor). It has been shown that α can be found analytically as follows:

$$\alpha = \frac{1}{2}\ln\left(\frac{1+r}{1-r}\right) \qquad (2)$$

where:

$$r = \sum_i D_i u_i, \qquad r \in [-1,+1] \qquad (3)$$

$$u_i = y_i h(x_i) \quad ,z=z_t, \quad D=D_t, \quad h=h_t, \quad \alpha=\alpha_t \qquad (4)$$

and y_i is the target output, u_i is positive if hypothesis $h(x_i)$ is correct, and negative if it is incorrect.

3 System Specifications

Three types of features were used as neural networks inputs:
1- ΔMFCC[13] coefficients extracted from person's speech signal (28 coefficients),
2- DCT[14] coefficients extracted from person's face image (25 coefficients),
3- Eigen-face coefficients extracted from person's face image (30 coefficients).
The sequence of these features produces a combined feature vector with 83 elements. However, we have conducted different experiments with different number of features, less than and equal 83.
In our system, neural networks have been used as weak learners in AdaBoost. In order to meet the requirement of a weak learner, we selected the simplest structure of a typical neural network, i.e. a simple neuron. Consequently, each weak learner had one

---

[13] Mel-Frequency Cepsteral Coefficient
[14] Discrete Cosine Transform

output whose the value determined the weak learner's vote concerning the identity of an individual. Since the hyperbolic tangent was used as the neurons activation function, a positive output indicated a positive verification result and a negative output indicated a negative verification result.

Nguyen-Widrow weights initialization, Levenberg-Marquardt back-propagation learning algorithm and MSE[15] criteria were used in neural networks training phases.

4 Experiments and Results

We have conducted our experiments on a data set formed from 190 samples, i.e. ten samples from 19 persons. We used leave-one-out technique to obtain statistically validated results from neural networks and AdaBoost, during training and test phases. We measured the global performance of the systems using the three following indices: FAR[16], FRR[17] and Error (total percent of miss classifications).

We first designed a system with all of the inputs (83 inputs) presented to each of the weak learners, and then examined the effect of the number of inputs on the system performance by modifying the number of each weak learner's inputs.

For the full input weak learner case, we have tested a system implemented using α-Type AdaBoost with different number of iterations, T (Fig. 2). As described in Section 2, this number corresponds to the number of experts in AdaBoost. We mention again that each of the curve points in Fig. 2 were obtained by averaging the results of several leave-one-outs experiments.

Fig.2 shows that the error rates converge, after only six iterations, to the following values:

- FAR = %0.05,
- FRR = %2.1 and
- ERROR = %0.17.

We have also examined the effect of the number of inputs on the system performance by modifying the number of each weak learner's inputs during our experiments, i.e. using less than 83 inputs for each neuron. In each experiment, the number of inputs for different experts (neurons) was identical, but, for different experts, inputs were taken from different parts of the 83 elements feature vectors.

Fig. 3 shows the results of the experimentations using different numbers of input features presented to each weak learner.

It is shown in Fig. 3 that the minimum value of FAR+FRR corresponds to 9 iterations (experts) and the following values:

- FAR = %0.17,
- FRR = %7.89 and
- ERROR = %0.58.

Also, the minimum value of FAR corresponds to only 5 iterations (experts) and the following values:

---

[15] Mean Square Error
[16] False Acceptance Rate
[17] False Rejection Rate

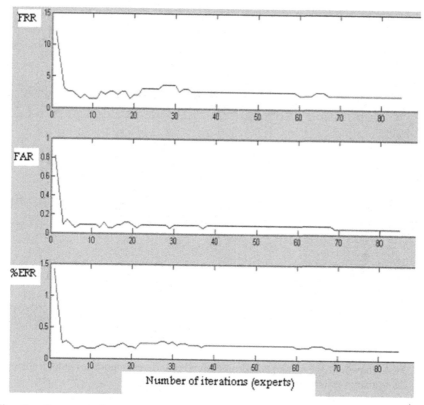

Fig. 2. System performance indices obtained with different number of iterations. FRR (above), FAR (middle) and Error (below) converges after about six iterations.

- FAR = %0.058,
- FRR = %15.27 and
- ERROR = %0.86.

Comparing these results with the results obtained   from full input connection weak learners, presented earlier in this section, we can conclude that the best results belong to the system with full input connection.

5 Comparison with Unimodal Systems

We compared the results of our AdaBoost based multimodal system, using features of three different unimodal   systems, with   the   results obtained separately from these unimodal systems, which are:

- A GMM based speaker verification system using ΔMFCC coefficients (28 coefficients),
- An HMM based face verification system using DCT coefficients (25 coefficients) [26] and

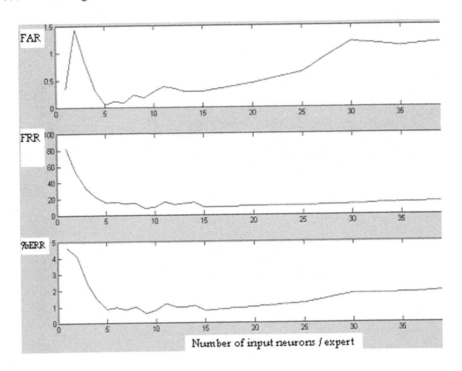

Fig. 3. FRR (above), FAR (middle) and Error (below) of different number of input features for each weak learner in AdaBoost

- A SVM based face verification system using Eigen-face coefficients (30 coefficients) [27].

Table 1 shows the FAR and FRR of these unimodal and multimodal systems. Obviously, even the average FAR of our multimodal system is much less than the lowest FARs of each of the unimodal systems, while the average FRR of the multimodal system is still acceptable.

Table 1. The results obtained from different unimodal and multimodal systems.

	Speaker Verification Using GMM	Face Verification Using HMM	Face Verification Using SVM	Multimodal Biometric System Using AdaBoost
FRR	%0.32	%15	%1	%2.1
FAR	%0.32	%4	%1	%0.058

6 Discussion and Conclusions

In order to propose an new and efficient multimodal biometric system, we have conducted several experiments using AdaBoost as an efficient way to combine unimodal features extracted from face and speech signals of individuals. Obviously, the main goal was to optimize the system design with respect to the verification error and computational cost.

In order to minimize the computational cost, according to the AdaBoost condition for weak learners, we selected a very simple expert as weak learner, i.e. a single neuron. Also, based on our experiments, we showed that using an α-type AdaBoost structure with full input weak learner's connections (83 inputs for each expert), we obtained a FAR as low as %0.058 with only six experts.

We have also presented the results of comparison of our best AdaBoost based multimodal system with three different unimodal systems. Focusing our attention on FAR, which plays a very important role in secure environments, we showed that even the average FAR of the multimodal system is much less than the lowest FARs of each of the unimodal systems, while the average FRR of the multimodal system is acceptable. The future work consists of a detailed analysis of the results including error analysis and testing our system on datasets containing an important number of biometrics simples.

References

1. Neti, CH., Potamianos, G., Luettin, J., Matthews, I., Glotin, H., and Vergyri, D., "Large vocabulary audio-visual speech recognition: a summary of the johns Hopkins summer 2000 workshop", *Proc. IEEE Work. Multimedia Signal Process*, Cannes, 2001, pp. 619-624.
2. Hong, L., and Jain, A., "Integrating faces and fingerprints for personal identification", *IEEE transactions on pattern analysis and machine intelligence*, Vol.20, No.12, December 1998, pp.1295-1307.
3. Yacoub, S.B., Abdeljaoued, Y., and Mayoraz, E., "Fusion of face and speech data for person identity verification", *IEEE transactions on neural networks*, Vol.10, No.5, September 1999, pp. 1065-1074.
4. Ben-Yacoub, S., Luttin, J., Jonsson, K., Matas, J., and Kittler, J., "Audio-Visual person verification", *IEEE computer society conference on computer vision and pattern recognition*, Vol.1, 1999, pp.580-585.
5. Fierrez-Aguilar, J., Ortega-Garcia, J., Gonzalez-Rodriguez, J., "Fusion strategies in multimodal biometric verification", *International Conference Proceedings on Multimedia and Expo (ICME '03)*, Vol. 3, 6-9 July 2003, pp. 5 -8.
6. Chibelushi, C.C., Deravi, F., and Mason, J.S., "Audio-Visual person recognition: an evaluation of data fusion strategies", *European conference on Security and detection*, 1997, pp. 26-30.
7. Sanderson, C., and Paliwal, K.K., "Noise compensation in a multi-modal verification system", *IEEE International Conference Proceedings (ICASSP '01) on Acoustics, Speech, and Signal Processing*, Vol.1, 7-11 May 2001, pp. 157 – 160.
8. Richard G., et.al., "Multimodal verification for teleservices and security application (M2VTS)", *IEEE International conference on multimedia computing and systems*, Vol. 2 ,1999 , pp.1061-1064.

9. Osadciw, L., Varshney, P., Veeramachaneni, K., "Improving personal identification accuracy using multisensor fusion for building access control applications", *Proceedings of the Fifth International Conference on Information Fusion*, Vol. 2, 8-11 July 2002, pp. 1176 - 1183.

10. Cattin, P.C., Zlatnik, D., Borer, R., "Sensor fusion for a biometric system using gait", *International Conference on Multisensor Fusion and Integration for Intelligent Systems (MFI 2001)*, 20-22 Aug. 2001, pp. 233 -238.

11. Froba, B.,Rothe, C., Kublbeck, C., "Evaluation of sensor calibration in a biometric person recognition framework based on sensor fusion', *Fourth IEEE international conference on automatic face and gesture recognition proceedings*, 2000, pp. 512-517.

12. Meyer, G., and Mulligan, J., "Continuous audio-visual digit recognition using decision fusion", *IEEE International Conference Proceedings (ICASSP '02) on Acoustics, Speech, and Signal Processing*, Vol.1, 13-17 May 2002, pp. I-305 - I-308.

13. Chatzis, V., Bors, A.G., and Pitas, I., "Multimodal decision-level fusion for person authentication", *IEEE transactions on systems, man, and cybernetics-part a: systems and humans*, Vol. 29, No. 6, November 1999, pp.674-680.

14. Wanger, T., Dieckmann, U., "Multi-Sensorial inputs for the identification of persons with synergetic computers", *Proceedings of the IEEE International conference on image processing (ICIP-94)*, Vol.2, 1994, pp. 287-291.

15. Wanger, T., Dieckmann, U., "Sensor-Fusion for robust identification of persons: a field test", *Proceedings of IEEE International conference on image processing*, Vol.3, 1995, pp. 516-519.

16. Lin, S.H., and Kung, S.Y., "Probabilistic DBNN via expectation-maximization with multi-sensor classification applications", *International conference on image proceedings*, Vol. 3, 1995, pp. 236-239.

17. Jain, A.K., and Ross, A., "Learning user-specific parameters in a multibiometric system", *Proceeding of International Conference on image processing (ICIP)*, Rochester, New York, September 22-25, 2002.

18. Mezcua, B.R., Garcia-Plaza, D., Fernandez, C., Domingo-Garcia, P., and Fernandez, F., "Biometrcs verification in a real environment", *Proceedings of IEEE 33rd Annual International carnahan conference on security technology*, 1999, pp. 243-246.

19. Sanderson, C., and Paliwal, K.K.,"Multi-Modal person verification system based on face profiles and speech", *Fifth international symposium on signal processing and its applications ISSPA '99*, Brisbane , Australia ,22-25 August 1999, pp.947-950.

20. Alim, O.A., Elboughdadly, N., Morchedi C.E., Safwat E., Abouelseoud G., El Badry N., Mohsen N., "Identity verification using audio-visual features", *Seventeenth national radio science conference*, Minufiya University, Egypt, Feb.22-24, 2000, pp. 1-8.

21. Kittler, J., Messer, K., "Fusion of multiple experts in multimodal biometric personal identity verification systems", *Proceedings of the 12th IEEE Workshop on Neural Networks for Signal Processing*, 4-6 Sept. 2002 , pp. 3 -12.

22. Chen, T., Hsu, Y.J., Liu, X., Zhang, W., "Principle component analysis and its variants for biometrics", *Proceedings of International Conference on Image Processing*, Vol. 1, 22-25 Sept. 2002, pp. I-61 -I-64.

23. Bigun, J., Fierrez-Aguilar, J., Ortega-Garcia, J., Gonzalez-Rodriguez, J., "Multimodal biometric authentication using quality signals in mobile communications", *Proceedings of 12th International Conference on Image Analysis and Processing*, Sept. 17-19, 2003, pp. 2 -11.

24. Freund, Y. and Schapire, R.E., "Experiments with a New Boosting Algorithm", *Machine Learning: Proceedings of the Thirteenth International Conference*, 1996, pp. 148-156.

25. Schapire, R.E. and Singer, Y. "Improved Boosting Algorithms Using Confidence-rated Predictions", *Proceedings of the Eleventh Annual Conference on Computational Learning Theory*, 1998.

26. Cartmell, C., "AdaBoost, Artificial Neural Nets and RBF Nets", Department of computer science, University of Sheffield, 2002.
27. M. S. Moin, N. Moghaddam Charkari and S. Naderi, "1D-HMM for Face Verification: Optimizing the Model by Improving the Algorithm and Intelligent Selection of Training Set", *Proceedings of the 8thAnnual International CSI Computer Conference (CSICC'2003)*, Mashhad, Iran, Feb. 25-27, 2003, pp. 365-369.
28. M. S. Moin and E. Roozegar, "Optimizing SVM for Face Verification", *Proceedings of the 8thAnnual International CSI Computer Conference (CSICC'2003)*, Mashhad, Iran, Feb. 25-27, 2003, pp. 370-375.

Author Index

Abhyankar, A., 100
Alonso-Hermira, N., 295
Atkinson, T.J., 184

Baltatu, M., 171
Bolle, R.M., 205

Cabello, E., 70
Cappelli, R., 57
Chen, J.S., 146
Chen, T.P., 89
Choi, J., 1
Conde, C., 70
Connell, J.H., 205

D'Alessandro, R., 171
D'Amico, R., 171
Dorizzi, B., 318
Drygajlo, A., 124

Entrena, L., 195

Fierrez-Aguilar, J., 295
Figueroa-Villanueva, M.A., 205
Flynn, P.J., 238
Fong, K.F., 146
Franco, A., 57

Garcia-Salicetti, S., 318
Goseling, J., 158

Hangai, S., 229
Higuchi, T., 229
Hook, C., 283
Huang, X., 45

Jain, A.K., 134, 259

Kasprowski, P., 248
Kempf, J., 283
Kim, J., 1
Kong, A.W.-K., 217
Kryszczuk, K.M., 124

Li, S.Z., 32, 45
Liu, W., 32
Liu-Jimenez, J., 195
Lorch, H., 111
Lu, G., 217

Lu, X., 259
Ly Van, B., 318

Maghooli, K., 332
Marcel, S., 24
Marcialis, G.L., 307
Moin, M.S., 332
Montes Diez, R., 70
Moon, Y.S., 146
Moreno-Marquez, G., 295
Morguet, P., 89, 111
Morier, P., 124

Nandakumar, K., 259
Nanni, L., 57
Novikov, S., 80

Ober, J., 248
Ortega-Garcia, J., 295

Park, U., 259

Ratha, N.K., 205
Rodriguez, Y., 24
Roli, F., 307
Ross, A., 134

Samaras, D., 10
Sanchez-Reillo, R., 195
Scharfenberg, G., 283
Schröder, H., 111
Schuckers, M.E., 184
Schuckers, S., 100
Sun, Z., 270

Tan, T., 32, 270
Tuyls, P., 158

Ushmaev, O., 80

Wang, Y., 32, 45, 270
Wong, M., 217
Woodard, D.L., 238

Yau, W.Y., 89
Yi, J., 1

Zhang, D., 217
Zhang, L., 10

Lecture Notes in Computer Science

For information about Vols. 1–3034

please contact your bookseller or Springer-Verlag

Vol. 3139: F. Iida, R. Pfeifer, L. Steels, Y. Kuniyoshi (Eds.), Embodied Artificial Intelligence. IX, 331 pages. 2004. (Subseries LNAI).

Vol. 3133: A.D. Pimentel, S. Vassiliadis (Eds.), Computer Systems, Architectures, Modeling, and Simulation. XIII, 562 pages. 2004.

Vol. 3129: Q. Li, G. Wang, L. Feng (Eds.), Advances in Web-Age Information Management. XVII, 753 pages. 2004.

Vol. 3128: D. Asonov (Ed.), Querying Databases Privately. IX, 115 pages. 2004.

Vol. 3127: K.E. Wolff, H.D. Pfeiffer, H.S. Delugach (Eds.), Conceptual Structures at Work. XI, 403 pages. 2004. (Subseries LNAI).

Vol. 3125: D. Kozen (Ed.), Mathematics of Program Construction. X, 401 pages. 2004.

Vol. 3123: A. Belz, R. Evans, P. Piwek (Eds.), Natural Language Generation. X, 219 pages. 2004. (Subseries LNAI).

Vol. 3121: S. Nikoletseas, J.D.P. Rolim (Eds.), Algorithmic Aspects of Wireless Sensor Networks. X, 201 pages. 2004.

Vol. 3120: J. Shawe-Taylor, Y. Singer (Eds.), Learning Theory. X, 648 pages. 2004. (Subseries LNAI).

Vol. 3118: K. Miesenberger, J. Klaus, W. Zagler, D. Burger (Eds.), Computer Helping People with Special Needs. XXIII, 1191 pages. 2004.

Vol. 3116: C. Rattray, S. Maharaj, C. Shankland (Eds.), Algebraic Methodology and Software Technology. XI, 569 pages. 2004.

Vol. 3115: P. Enser, Y. Kompatsiaris, N.E. O'Connor, A.F. Smeaton, A.W.M. Smeulders (Eds.), Image and Video Retrieval. XVII, 679 pages. 2004.

Vol. 3114: R. Alur, D.A. Peled (Eds.), Computer Aided Verification. XII, 536 pages. 2004.

Vol. 3113: J. Karhumäki, H. Maurer, G. Paun, G. Rozenberg (Eds.), Theory Is Forever. X, 283 pages. 2004.

Vol. 3112: H. Williams, L. MacKinnon (Eds.), Key Technologies for Data Management. XII, 265 pages. 2004.

Vol. 3111: T. Hagerup, J. Katajainen (Eds.), Algorithm Theory - SWAT 2004. XI, 506 pages. 2004.

Vol. 3110: A. Juels (Ed.), Financial Cryptography. XI, 281 pages. 2004.

Vol. 3109: S.C. Sahinalp, S. Muthukrishnan, U. Dogrusoz (Eds.), Combinatorial Pattern Matching. XII, 486 pages. 2004.

Vol. 3108: H. Wang, J. Pieprzyk, V. Varadharajan (Eds.), Information Security and Privacy. XII, 494 pages. 2004.

Vol. 3107: J. Bosch, C. Krueger (Eds.), Software Reuse: Methods, Techniques and Tools. XI, 339 pages. 2004.

Vol. 3105: S. Göbel, U. Spierling, A. Hoffmann, I. Iurgel, O. Schneider, J. Dechau, A. Feix (Eds.), Technologies for Interactive Digital Storytelling and Entertainment. XVI, 304 pages. 2004.

Vol. 3104: R. Kralovic, O. Sykora (Eds.), Structural Information and Communication Complexity. X, 303 pages. 2004.

Vol. 3103: K. Deb, e. al. (Eds.), Genetic and Evolutionary Computation – GECCO 2004. XLIX, 1439 pages. 2004.

Vol. 3102: K. Deb, e. al. (Eds.), Genetic and Evolutionary Computation – GECCO 2004. L, 1445 pages. 2004.

Vol. 3101: M. Masoodian, S. Jones, B. Rogers (Eds.), Computer Human Interaction. XIV, 694 pages. 2004.

Vol. 3100: J.F. Peters, A. Skowron, J.W. Grzymala-Busse, B. Kostek, R.W. Świniarski, M.S. Szczuka (Eds.), Transactions on Rough Sets I. X, 405 pages. 2004.

Vol. 3099: J. Cortadella, W. Reisig (Eds.), Applications and Theory of Petri Nets 2004. XI, 505 pages. 2004.

Vol. 3098: J. Desel, W. Reisig, G. Rozenberg (Eds.), Lectures on Concurrency and Petri Nets. VIII, 849 pages. 2004.

Vol. 3097: D. Basin, M. Rusinowitch (Eds.), Automated Reasoning. XII, 493 pages. 2004. (Subseries LNAI).

Vol. 3096: G. Melnik, H. Holz (Eds.), Advances in Learning Software Organizations. X, 173 pages. 2004.

Vol. 3094: A. Nürnberger, M. Detyniecki (Eds.), Adaptive Multimedia Retrieval. VIII, 229 pages. 2004.

Vol. 3093: S.K. Katsikas, S. Gritzalis, J. Lopez (Eds.), Public Key Infrastructure. XIII, 380 pages. 2004.

Vol. 3092: J. Eckstein, H. Baumeister (Eds.), Extreme Programming and Agile Processes in Software Engineering. XVI, 358 pages. 2004.

Vol. 3091: V. van Oostrom (Ed.), Rewriting Techniques and Applications. X, 313 pages. 2004.

Vol. 3089: M. Jakobsson, M. Yung, J. Zhou (Eds.), Applied Cryptography and Network Security. XIV, 510 pages. 2004.

Vol. 3087: D. Maltoni, A.K. Jain (Eds.), Biometric Authentication. XIII, 343 pages. 2004.

Vol. 3086: M. Odersky (Ed.), ECOOP 2004 – Object-Oriented Programming. XIII, 611 pages. 2004.

Vol. 3085: S. Berardi, M. Coppo, F. Damiani (Eds.), Types for Proofs and Programs. X, 409 pages. 2004.

Vol. 3084: A. Persson, J. Stirna (Eds.), Advanced Information Systems Engineering. XIV, 596 pages. 2004.

Vol. 3083: W. Emmerich, A.L. Wolf (Eds.), Component Deployment. X, 249 pages. 2004.

Vol. 3080: J. Desel, B. Pernici, M. Weske (Eds.), Business Process Management. X, 307 pages. 2004.

Vol. 3079: Z. Mammeri, P. Lorenz (Eds.), High Speed Networks and Multimedia Communications. XVIII, 1103 pages. 2004.

Vol. 3078: S. Cotin, D.N. Metaxas (Eds.), Medical Simulation. XVI, 296 pages. 2004.

Vol. 3077: F. Roli, J. Kittler, T. Windeatt (Eds.), Multiple Classifier Systems. XII, 386 pages. 2004.

Vol. 3076: D. Buell (Ed.), Algorithmic Number Theory. XI, 451 pages. 2004.

Vol. 3074: B. Kuijpers, P. Revesz (Eds.), Constraint Databases and Applications. XII, 181 pages. 2004.

Vol. 3073: H. Chen, R. Moore, D.D. Zeng, J. Leavitt (Eds.), Intelligence and Security Informatics. XV, 536 pages. 2004.

Vol. 3072: D. Zhang, A.K. Jain (Eds.), Biometric Authentication. XVII, 800 pages. 2004.

Vol. 3071: A. Omicini, P. Petta, J. Pitt (Eds.), Engineering Societies in the Agents World. XIII, 409 pages. 2004. (Subseries LNAI).

Vol. 3070: L. Rutkowski, J. Siekmann, R. Tadeusiewicz, L.A. Zadeh (Eds.), Artificial Intelligence and Soft Computing - ICAISC 2004. XXV, 1208 pages. 2004. (Subseries LNAI).

Vol. 3068: E. André, L. Dybkjær, W. Minker, P. Heisterkamp (Eds.), Affective Dialogue Systems. XII, 324 pages. 2004. (Subseries LNAI).

Vol. 3067: M. Dastani, J. Dix, A. El Fallah-Seghrouchni (Eds.), Programming Multi-Agent Systems. X, 221 pages. 2004. (Subseries LNAI).

Vol. 3066: S. Tsumoto, R. Słowiński, J. Komorowski, J.W. Grzymala-Busse (Eds.), Rough Sets and Current Trends in Computing. XX, 853 pages. 2004. (Subseries LNAI).

Vol. 3065: A. Lomuscio, D. Nute (Eds.), Deontic Logic in Computer Science. X, 275 pages. 2004. (Subseries LNAI).

Vol. 3064: D. Bienstock, G. Nemhauser (Eds.), Integer Programming and Combinatorial Optimization. XI, 445 pages. 2004.

Vol. 3063: A. Llamosí, A. Strohmeier (Eds.), Reliable Software Technologies - Ada-Europe 2004. XIII, 333 pages. 2004.

Vol. 3062: J.L. Pfaltz, M. Nagl, B. Böhlen (Eds.), Applications of Graph Transformations with Industrial Relevance. XV, 500 pages. 2004.

Vol. 3061: F.F. Ramos, H. Unger, V. Larios (Eds.), Advanced Distributed Systems. VIII, 285 pages. 2004.

Vol. 3060: A.Y. Tawfik, S.D. Goodwin (Eds.), Advances in Artificial Intelligence. XIII, 582 pages. 2004. (Subseries LNAI).

Vol. 3059: C.C. Ribeiro, S.L. Martins (Eds.), Experimental and Efficient Algorithms. X, 586 pages. 2004.

Vol. 3058: N. Sebe, M.S. Lew, T.S. Huang (Eds.), Computer Vision in Human-Computer Interaction. X, 233 pages. 2004.

Vol. 3057: B. Jayaraman (Ed.), Practical Aspects of Declarative Languages. VIII, 255 pages. 2004.

Vol. 3056: H. Dai, R. Srikant, C. Zhang (Eds.), Advances in Knowledge Discovery and Data Mining. XIX, 713 pages. 2004. (Subseries LNAI).

Vol. 3055: H. Christiansen, M.-S. Hacid, T. Andreasen, H.L. Larsen (Eds.), Flexible Query Answering Systems. X, 500 pages. 2004. (Subseries LNAI).

Vol. 3054: I. Crnkovic, J.A. Stafford, H.W. Schmidt, K. Wallnau (Eds.), Component-Based Software Engineering. XI, 311 pages. 2004.

Vol. 3053: C. Bussler, J. Davies, D. Fensel, R. Studer (Eds.), The Semantic Web: Research and Applications. XIII, 490 pages. 2004.

Vol. 3052: W. Zimmermann, B. Thalheim (Eds.), Abstract State Machines 2004. Advances in Theory and Practice. XII, 235 pages. 2004.

Vol. 3051: R. Berghammer, B. Möller, G. Struth (Eds.), Relational and Kleene-Algebraic Methods in Computer Science. X, 279 pages. 2004.

Vol. 3050: J. Domingo-Ferrer, V. Torra (Eds.), Privacy in Statistical Databases. IX, 367 pages. 2004.

Vol. 3049: M. Bruynooghe, K.-K. Lau (Eds.), Program Development in Computational Logic. VIII, 539 pages. 2004.

Vol. 3047: F. Oquendo, B. Warboys, R. Morrison (Eds.), Software Architecture. X, 279 pages. 2004.

Vol. 3046: A. Laganà, M.L. Gavrilova, V. Kumar, Y. Mun, C.J.K. Tan, O. Gervasi (Eds.), Computational Science and Its Applications – ICCSA 2004. LIII, 1016 pages. 2004.

Vol. 3045: A. Laganà, M.L. Gavrilova, V. Kumar, Y. Mun, C.J.K. Tan, O. Gervasi (Eds.), Computational Science and Its Applications – ICCSA 2004. LIII, 1040 pages. 2004.

Vol. 3044: A. Laganà, M.L. Gavrilova, V. Kumar, Y. Mun, C.J.K. Tan, O. Gervasi (Eds.), Computational Science and Its Applications – ICCSA 2004. LIII, 1140 pages. 2004.

Vol. 3043: A. Laganà, M.L. Gavrilova, V. Kumar, Y. Mun, C.J.K. Tan, O. Gervasi (Eds.), Computational Science and Its Applications – ICCSA 2004. LIII, 1180 pages. 2004.

Vol. 3042: N. Mitrou, K. Kontovasilis, G.N. Rouskas, I. Iliadis, L. Merakos (Eds.), NETWORKING 2004, Networking Technologies, Services, and Protocols; Performance of Computer and Communication Networks; Mobile and Wireless Communications. XXXIII, 1519 pages. 2004.

Vol. 3040: R. Conejo, M. Urretavizcaya, J.-L. Pérez-de-la-Cruz (Eds.), Current Topics in Artificial Intelligence. XIV, 689 pages. 2004. (Subseries LNAI).

Vol. 3039: M. Bubak, G.D.v. Albada, P.M.A. Sloot, J.J. Dongarra (Eds.), Computational Science - ICCS 2004. LXVI, 1271 pages. 2004.

Vol. 3038: M. Bubak, G.D.v. Albada, P.M.A. Sloot, J.J. Dongarra (Eds.), Computational Science - ICCS 2004. LXVI, 1311 pages. 2004.

Vol. 3037: M. Bubak, G.D.v. Albada, P.M.A. Sloot, J.J. Dongarra (Eds.), Computational Science - ICCS 2004. LXVI, 745 pages. 2004.

Vol. 3036: M. Bubak, G.D.v. Albada, P.M.A. Sloot, J.J. Dongarra (Eds.), Computational Science - ICCS 2004. LXVI, 713 pages. 2004.

Vol. 3035: M.A. Wimmer (Ed.), Knowledge Management in Electronic Government. XII, 326 pages. 2004. (Subseries LNAI).